A BRIEF HISTORY OF
ANCIENT CHINA

A BRIEF HISTORY OF ANCIENT CHINA

Edward L. Shaughnessy

BLOOMSBURY ACADEMIC
LONDON • NEW YORK • OXFORD • NEW DELHI • SYDNEY

BLOOMSBURY ACADEMIC
Bloomsbury Publishing Plc
50 Bedford Square, London, WC1B 3DP, UK
1385 Broadway, New York, NY 10018, USA
29 Earlsfort Terrace, Dublin 2, Ireland

BLOOMSBURY, BLOOMSBURY ACADEMIC and the Diana logo are
trademarks of Bloomsbury Publishing Plc

First published in Great Britain, 2023

Cover image © Chinese terracotta army figures.
wusuowei/Adobe Stock.

A catalogue record for this book is available from the British Library.

A catalog record for this book is available from the Library of Congress.

ISBN: HB: 978-1-3501-7041-4
PB: 978-1-3501-7037-7
ePDF: 978-1-3501-7039-1
eBook: 978-1-3501-7038-4

Typeset by RefineCatch Limited, Bungay, Suffolk

To find out more about our authors and books visit www.bloomsbury.com
and sign up for our newsletters.

CONTENTS

Contents

Essays

Hereditary Houses

Biographies

FIGURES

MAPS

TABLES

PREFACE

For the content that one would normally expect to see in a Preface, please turn to Chapter 60: "Author's Postface."

Since this book is intended to be a brief introduction to early China, I have strived to keep extraneous detail to a minimum. For this reason, it will suffice here to explain a few conventions used throughout the book.

- Chinese characters appear only in cases where they are essential for illustrating features of the argumentation.

- Titles of early Chinese writings are given in English translation; more detail about these writings is given in Chapter 23: "Essay on Literature."

- The standard traditional source for the period is *Records of the Historian* of Sima Qian (*c.* 145–89), which I will refer to frequently throughout the book.

- Important terms are occasionally given in *pinyin* Romanization, but these too have been kept to a minimum.

- Except in one case, where it is noted, all translations included in this book are original; citations are given in endnotes.

- Since most readers who wish to consult the original of traditional texts will doubtless do so online, in which case there are no page numbers, with the exceptions of the *Analects* of Confucius and *Mencius*, for which I give the traditional book and chapter numbers, I cite all other texts just by title and chapter title. However, for unearthed documents, which are not so readily available or easily searchable, I provide a full reference to the publication of record.

- Since the period under discussion, roughly 2000–200 BCE, is entirely Before the Common Era, I have generally refrained from adding BCE to each and every date.

- Dates of reign of rulers generally follow those of *The Cambridge History of Ancient China*, with only a very few differences.

BASIC ANNALS

CHAPTER 1
BASIC ANNALS OF YAO AND SHUN

According to relatively late traditions, Chinese civilization began with a series of culture heroes, the Three August Ones: Suiren, the inventor of fire; Fuxi, the tamer of beasts; and Shennong, the creator of agriculture, and the Five Thearchs: the Yellow Thearch, who first suppressed various competitors for power, and then having brought peace to the realm established norms of government for it; Zhuanxu, the grandson of the Yellow Thearch who, after emerging victorious from a succession struggle with one Gong Gong, formed a government assisted by three primary ministers: Goumang, in charge of the forests, Zhurong, in charge of fire; and Julong, in charge of the soil; Thearch Ku, a great grandson of the Yellow Thearch, a "benevolent and august, gracious and sincere" ruler, but especially notable for having had four principal wives, with each of whom he is said to have sired a son who would eventually become the high ancestor of one of China's early realms: Hou Ji, the Lord of Millet, the high ancestor of the Zhou people; Xie, the progenitor of the Shang people; Thearch Zhi, who succeeded Thearch Ku, but then proved to be unworthy; and Fangxun, better known as Yao, who succeeded Thearch Zhi and would become one of the Five Thearchs. With this one, admittedly quite lengthy sentence, we have passed through the first millennium or so of China's traditional history, or perhaps more properly of China's traditional mythology. The names in this first sentence have been known to all Chinese since no later than the Han dynasty, but they properly belong to the stuff of legend and mythology, not history. Therefore, this being a historical record of ancient China, we need say no more about them.

Yao too belongs more to mythology than to history. Nevertheless, since many of the earliest histories of Chinese civilization begin with him, and college surveys of Chinese civilization were once routinely referred to as "Yao to Mao" courses, it seems appropriate for us to do so as well. For instance, the first chapter of the *Exalted Scriptures*, one of the five Chinese classics, is called the "Canon of Yao." It describes how Yao deputed four brothers of the Xi and He families to use the stars to determine the astronomical equinoxes and solstices and to establish a 366-day year. With the calendar established, Yao then ruled, apparently effortlessly, for the next seventy years, the common people and even the birds and the beasts thereby being able to live in accordance with the seasons, planting in spring, growing through the summer, harvesting in autumn, and storing things for the winter.

After these seventy years of reign and having become in his turn aged, Yao began to search for a successor. Various sycophants proposed different people, including first Yao's own son Dan Zhu; Yao rejected them all. Finally, the chiefs of the sacred mountains recommended to him a man named Shun, an aging bachelor who had achieved a reputation as a virtuous son and brother despite living with a father who was blind, both physically and morally, a deceitful step-mother, and a younger half-brother who was the favorite of his parents. Yao tested him by marrying his two daughters to Shun. When Shun proved to be an equally virtuous husband, Yao determined to turn the government over to him little by little. Shun took on ever greater responsibilities, winning universal acclaim for his abilities. After three years, Yao attempted to yield power to Shun. Although Shun presided over the rituals appropriate to the ruler, he declined to accept the title. Thus, Yao continued to rule, at least nominally for another twenty-five years. In the ninetieth year of his reign, Yao retired to Tao, the place he had first been deputed to rule. Ten years later, in his hundredth year, Yao died.

After observing three years of mourning for the deceased ruler, Shun attempted to pass authority on to Danzhu, Yao's son. However, the people would not hear of this and so Shun finally came to rule in his own right. His first efforts in this endeavor were to seek out capable administrators to assist him. Chief among these was Yu, who was put in charge of the rivers and streams. Others were put in charge of what we would today call agriculture, health and human services, the judiciary, labor, the environment, and culture and the arts. Like Yao before him, once having entrusted authority to these assistants, Shun did not interfere in their work, and yet almost all operated smoothly. Of course, in recognition that sometimes things did go wrong, Shun is credited with standardizing the first legal code, though he is also supposed to have tempered the most severe of the punishments. Similarly, while there were those, referred to as the "Four Criminals" (Gong Gong, Huan Dou, San Miao, and Gun), who resisted his rule, Shun merely banished them to the ends of the known earth. Once that was done, all under Heaven (*tianxia*) submitted.

Almost like Yao, who is said to have died in the hundredth year of his reign, Shun died at the age of one hundred, having ruled in his own right for exactly fifty years. But just like Yao, before dying Shun declined to pass power to his own son, offering it instead to Yu, the hydraulic engineer. Much of this is recounted in the "Canon of Shun," the second chapter in the canonical *Exalted Scriptures.*

It would be easy to dismiss these stories of Yao and Shun as nothing more than myths and legends, which they surely are. There is no reason to believe that at the time they were said to have lived, from roughly 2200 to just before 2000 BCE, any local societies in what is today China had reached such a level of government, much less extending control over the entirety of the Chinese landmass. Nevertheless, well over a thousand years after this time, during the time that will be the main focus of this book, Yao and Shun were continually held up as paradigms of proper rule, the Golden Age of highest antiquity. This is to be seen not only in the *Exalted Scriptures*, which, as noted above, begins with the "canons" of these rulers, but also in many of the classical philosophical writings, including especially those concerning Confucius and his followers. Some rulers of this later period would even try to imitate their example, at least by deputing executive authority to a rising ministerial class. However, in the late fourth century when the ruler of the state of Yan, the capital of which was more or less where Beijing is now located, attempted to go so far as to abdicate in favor of his prime minister, the rulers of other states viewed this as an existential threat to their own royal prerogatives. In 314, the neighboring state of Qi invaded Yan, deposing the prime minister, Zi Zhi. This incident is often viewed as one of the pivotal moments in the disintegration of the ancient Chinese state system, and its significance was already widely recognized by statesmen and philosophers—what we might call political scientists—of the time.

One of the political scientists who was very much implicated in this incident, Mencius (*c.* 385–303), who was serving as an advisor to the king of Qi at the time, framed his entire political philosophy around Yao and Shun. One chapter of the book that bears his name, the "Wan Zhang" chapter, is almost entirely devoted to stories about Yao and Shun. In another chapter, that focuses on the question of human nature, whether humans are inherently good or evil (or perhaps a little of both), when asked whether humans can all become a Yao or a Shun, Mencius responded in the affirmative: "If you wear Yao's clothes, chant Yao's words, and enact Yao's acts, this is Yao and nothing else." On the other hand, "If you wear Jie's clothes, chant Jie's words, and enact Jie's acts, this is Jie and nothing else,"[1] Jie being the last ruler of the Xia dynasty, the period that is said to have followed the rule of Yao and Shun. Elsewhere Mencius said, "After the deaths of Yao and Shun, the Way of the sages declined and violent rulers arose one after another."[2] This was only a slight exaggeration.

CHAPTER 2
BASIC ANNALS OF XIA

Tradition has it that during his own reign, Shun appointed Yu, the person in charge of the waterways, to take over as de facto ruler. When Shun then died, Yu attempted to yield power to Shun's son, Shang Jun, returning to his home in a land called Xia. However, expressing their dissatisfaction with Shang Jun, the various local lords from throughout the realm are said to have followed Yu and prevailed upon him to take his place in command. He would be known as the Lord of Xia.

Records of the Historian of Sima Qian contains a genealogy for Yu indicating that he was a great-great grandson of the Yellow Thearch, a grandson of Zhuanxu, and a son of Gun. Gun attained notoriety at the time of Yao for failing to control flood waters that are supposed to have covered all of what is today central China. Gun attempted to hold back the waters by building dams and levees. After what we are told was nine years this plan proved to be unsuccessful and the floodwaters overwhelmed the defenses, Yao's successor Shun appointed Yu to try in his turn. Unlike Gun, Yu's method was the dredge the rivers, so that the water would flow out to the sea.

Yu, usually referred to with the single adjective "great" before his name (usually rendered in English as "Yu the Great"), is mainly renowned in Chinese legend for having brought this flood under control. This probably reflects a social memory of a time when north China was warmer and much moister than it became it later times, and the flood basin of the Yellow River extended over much of the north China plain. In recent times, there have been attempts to identify this work with a single great flood, most recently focusing on a flood that a team of geologists claim to have occurred in 1920 BCE when an earthquake caused a landslide creating a dam on the upper reaches of the Yellow River. According to this theory, when the dam burst, it released a massive wave of water downstream. This suggestion has been met with suspicion.

The earliest record associating Yu with controlling the waters comes in a bronze inscription of the first half of the ninth century BCE, which begins:

Heaven commanded Yu to spread out the land; pulling down the mountains and deepening the rivers, he then differentiated the regions and established government, sending down a reflective virtue on the people.[3]

With the water under control, Yu is said to have divided the territory of China into nine different regions, establishing as well a transportation network among them. He then made a grand tour of the entire realm, differentiating the regions on the basis of their natural environments and establishing taxes—termed tribute—according to the produce appropriate to each. These regions are still used to identify macro-regions of China, seen for instance in the names of regional cuisines. Yu is supposed to have started in the north, in what is today Shanxi province, and then proceeded in a more or less clockwise direction. The names, approximate locations in modern-day China, and the some of the principal tribute goods are as follows:

Jizhou (Shanxi): leather clothing

Yanzhou (northern Henan, northwestern Shandong): lacquer and silk

Qingzhou (eastern Shandong): salt and sea products

Xuzhou (southern Shandong, Anhui and Jiangsu): paulownia wood, pearls

Yangzhou (Zhejiang, Fujian and Jiangxi): metal and jade

Jingzhou (Hubei and Hunan): feathers, ivory and hides

Yuzhou (Henan): lacquer and silk

Liangzhou (Sichuan and southern Shaanxi): chime-stones, metal, bearskins

Yongzhou (central and northern Shaanxi, Gansu and Ningxia): jade

A newly discovered manuscript entitled *Rongcheng shi* (the name of one of the putative rulers prior to the time of Yao and Shun) from the Warring States period, says of Yu's rule:

He then made use of what was near at hand to know of that which was distant, he rejected disputation and practiced simplicity, making use of what the people wanted to bring together the benefits of heaven and earth. This is why those nearby rejoiced in his rule, while those far away came of their own accord. Everyone both within and beyond the four seas all requested to submit themselves to him.[4]

It is no wonder that Yu came to be seen in all texts of this period as the progenitor of dynastic rule in China.

While serving as de facto ruler during the last years of Shun's rule, Yu had been assisted by two men whose virtues would also be praised by the *Exalted Scriptures*: Gao Yao and Yi. After the death of Shun, Yu sought to emulate Shun's example by naming Gao Yao as de facto ruler. Unfortunately, Gao Yao died before he could do so. When Yu himself was about to die just a few years later, he recommended that Yi succeed him as ruler. There are different accounts of what happened upon the death of Yu the Great. The orthodox historical tradition, represented for instance by *Records of the Historian*, states that Yi, like Yu before him, voluntarily went into exile so that Yu's own son, Qi, could succeed him. However, an alternative scenario was recorded in a text known as the *Bamboo Annals*, which was discovered in a tomb of the early third century BCE that was robbed in 279 CE. According to this *Bamboo Annals*, the death of Yu the Great precipitated a civil war between Qi and Yi. In a great battle at a place called Gan, Qi's forces killed Yi, ensuring that Qi succeed his father as ruler. Also known as the Lord of Xia, Qi then succeeded his father, his reign thereafter seen as marking the beginning of dynastic rule in China.

When Qi died, he was succeeded in turn by his son Tai Kang, and then after just four years of misrule, by Tai Kang's younger brother Zhong Kang. Zhong Kang's reign includes what seems to be the earliest dated record in Chinese history. According to the "Punishment of Yin" chapter of the *Exalted Scriptures*, the brothers Xi and He, who had been appointed by Yao to maintain the timing of the seasons by observing the stars, had come to neglect their duties. This text says that sometime during the reign of Zhong Kang, on the first day of the last month of autumn, a solar eclipse took the people by surprise because Xi and He were lost in drunkenness. The *Bamboo Annals* provides a precise date for this eclipse: the day *gengxu*, the forty-seventh day of the sixty-day cycle used for dates in ancient China, of the ninth month of the fifth year of Zhong Kang's reign, which in the chronology determined by the early editors of the *Bamboo Annals* corresponds with 1948 BCE. There was a nearly complete solar eclipse on October 16, 1876, that would have been visible from the area the Xia is said to have ruled and which is consistent with at least the month of both records, if not of the day of the record in the *Bamboo Annals*.

After the reign of Zhong Kang, succession reverted to a father-son pattern, with only a pair of more or less insignificant exceptions, through eleven more generations (of thirteen further rulers in all), coming finally to a ruler named Jie. He would go down in Chinese history as the first of the paradigmatic last rulers of dynasties, so evil that both Heaven and the people turned against them. In the case of Jie, during the second half of his reign, a new ruler of Xia's eastern neighbors, the Shang, came to power; this was Tang. Not only was he himself renowned for being virtuous, but he was also advised by a particularly able minister, named Yi Yin. Through a series of interactions between the Xia and Shang, the Shang finally attacked and drove Jie into exile bringing the Xia dynasty to an ignominious end, sometime in the middle of the sixteenth century.

The historicity of the Xia dynasty is one of the most vexed questions in the study of ancient Chinese history. For scholars in China, not only is the Xia the first dynasty in the traditional account of Chinese civilization, but archaeologists have also uncovered a relatively sophisticated culture located about where the Xia is supposed to have been located and about the time that the Xia is supposed to have been there, roughly 1900–1500. This is the Erlitou Culture centered on the site Yanshi Erlitou, just east of Luoyang in northwestern Henan province. The Erlitou Culture is sandwiched between two other cultures: the earlier Longshan Culture, a long-lived Neolithic culture that extended across the north China plain, and the later Erligang Culture, the type-site and core area of which was to the east, around the modern city of Zhengzhou in northeastern Henan province.

The Erlitou site shows sophisticated building remains, usually referred to as palaces, and also the earliest bronze ritual vessels ever discovered in China. While the culture takes its name from this principal site, it also extends north and south of the great bend of the Yellow River with hundreds of lesser sites sharing the same culture. These sites encompass much of present-day Henan and southwestern Shanxi provinces, largely coinciding with the areas that Chinese tradition ascribes to the Xia dynasty. Archaeologists divide the Erlitou site into four strata indicative of four different developmental periods, the site reaching its height of development in the third stratum, only to show signs of being eclipsed and destroyed in the fourth stratum. With the final destruction of the Erlitou Culture about 1600 or 1500, the culture of the area was replaced by that of the Erligang culture from areas further to the east. Chinese historians see this as a sign of the Xia struggle with the rising Shang state, traditionally supposed to have originated in what is today northeastern Henan province.

All of this material culture is certainly suggestive of the Xia state. However, some historians, principal among whom are Western historians of China, note that no writing of any kind has been found among the Erlitou remains and thus there is no proof tying this to Xia. Moreover, they argue that the level of cultural development is not suggestive of the sort of governmental apparatus that one would associate with a dynastic state, even the first of the Three Dynasties of China. In many ways, the debate over the historicity of the Xia is a matter of definition. However, throughout traditional Chinese history, including during most of the ancient period that is the focus of this book, the Xia was held up as an example of how governments could rule effectively, and also how they could come to a crashing end. Therefore, whether and in what way the Xia actually existed is probably ultimately less important than how later people imagined it to have existed.

CHAPTER 3
BASIC ANNALS OF SHANG

The "Basic Annals of Xia" chapter above already alluded to the defeat of Jie, the last ruler of Xia, by Tang, the ruler of Shang, and also to the incursion of the Erligang Culture into the sphere of the earlier Erlitou Culture. Both of these developments, thought to have taken place in the middle of the sixteenth century, are seen to herald the beginning of the Shang dynasty. Whereas, the historicity of the Xia dynasty is still much debated, with the Shang dynasty—at least the last portion of the dynasty—we fully enter into the historical period, by which we mean that there are contemporary written records attesting to its existence. These records, in the form of inscriptions on ritual bronze vessels and especially records of divination inscribed into the shells of turtles and the scapula bones of oxen, are the earliest examples of writing in China. Although specialized study is required to be able to read these inscriptions, they are recognizably ancestral to Chinese writing still in use today, making it the world's longest lasting script still in continuous use.

Legendary histories of the Shang begin well before the time of Tang. According to the poem "Dusky Bird" in the *Hymns of Shang* section of the *Classic of Poetry*, Heaven commanded a dusky bird, often identified as a raven or a swallow, to descend and give birth to the Shang people. More developed myths say that a woman named Jiandi swallowed the bird's egg and became pregnant. Jiandi is supposed to have been a secondary wife of Thearch Ku, a great grandson of the Yellow Thearch. The child born to her was a son: Xie. When Xie was grown, he gained merit by assisting Yu the Great in controlling the flood waters, and so was appointed by Shun to rule over the area of Shang, located in the eastern part of present-day Henan province. Thus began a long-time totem association between the Shang people and birds.

Records of the Historian continues the Shang genealogy through thirteen generations, before coming finally to Tang, known also as Cheng Tang (the Completing Tang) or by his temple name Tian Yi or Tai Yi. The "Yi" of this Tian Yi or Tai Yi is the second of the ten "Heavenly Stems," names associated with ten suns that produced the ten days of the Shang week. Thereafter, all

Shang kings would be known posthumously by one of these ten names, usually prefaced by an adjective to differentiate them from others with the same name, and would receive sacrificial offerings on that particular day of the week. By the end of the dynasty, it would require thirty-six weeks to complete a cycle of five different sacrifices to all of the deceased kings and also their primary consorts; since this sacrificial cycle approximated one solar year, the word for "sacrifice" came to be used to designate the "year" as well.

Tang lived at the same time as Jie, the paradigmatically evil last ruler of the Xia dynasty. Like Yao and Shun in the period before the Xia dynasty had been established, Tang was assisted by a particularly virtuous minister, Yi Yin, who served as an intermediary between the Shang and Xia. However, when Jie proved to be recalcitrant, Tang and the Shang attacked him and forced him into exile. According to the orthodox Chinese historical tradition, there could only be one legitimate ruler at a time, but there had to be a ruler. Jie's defeat constituted the end of the Xia and the beginning of the Shang dynasty.

Tang was succeeded in turn by twenty-nine rulers. Unlike many later dynasties, especially the Zhou, which practiced father-son succession, royal succession in the Shang often passed from elder brother to younger brother before eventually moving on to the next generation. This was true of the generation following that of Tang, rule moving from Wai Bing to Zhong Ren. With the death of Zhong Ren, Yi Yin, still alive and now very much the power behind the throne (though it is worth noting that there were no thrones in ancient China; chairs came to China from India along with Buddhism some fifteen hundred years after this time), intervened to ensure succession to Tang's eldest grandson, Tai Jia. Unfortunately, according to later legends, at first Tai Jia proved unfit to rule, so Yi Yin intervened again and exiled him (or, rather, imprisoned him) to the Paulownia Palace for three years. According to the legends, after these three years, Tai Jia reformed his behavior and, after being reinstated by Yi Yin, went on to be one of the great Shang rulers. This three-year exile at the beginning of his reign is probably an early manifestation of the later custom of observing a three-year mourning period when the ruler, or one's own father, passed away, and may also be tied to ministers acting on behalf of the king-in-waiting during this period. Whatever the validity of this observation, it is certainly the case that by the Warring States period Yi Yin would take his place at the head of the pantheon of virtuous ministers that was held up as a counterweight to royal power.

According to traditional sources, after the time of Tai Jia, another nine generations passed, with brothers often contending for power. During this time, rulers frequently moved their capitals across the flood plain of the Yellow River, sometimes settling to the north of the river and sometimes to its south. The tenth generation was ruled successively by four separate brothers: Yang Jia, Pan Geng, Xiao Xin, and Xiao Yi. A tradition canonized by inclusion in the *Exalted Scriptures* holds that Pan Geng moved the capital yet again, giving a speech to urge the people to relocate to the south of the Yellow River; this speech is recorded as the "Pan Geng" chapter, regarded by many as the earliest reliable text in the *Exalted Scriptures*. Since by the time of Pan Geng, there has yet to be found any contemporary evidence of writing, this view of the date of the "Pan Geng" chapter is questionable. What is more, there is good evidence that the Shang capital at about this time was located well to the north of the Yellow River, and not to its south, though there is some uncertainty as to the location of the Yellow River at this time; when it empties into the North China Plain, it has frequently changed course, there being records of some twenty-six course changes just since 595 BCE, with the river sometimes flowing into the sea to the north of the mountainous Shandong peninsula and sometimes to its south. However, evidence suggests that in the thirteenth century BCE, the Yellow River flowed to the south of Anyang, as it does also today.

Recent archaeological excavations seem to show that toward the middle of the thirteenth century, there existed a major palace site just to the north of the Huan River near present-day Anyang, Henan. It is likely that this site, referred to as Huanbei Shang Cheng (the Shang City to the North of the Huan River), was the capital of Pan Geng. This site fills an important interval between two other archaeological cultures associated with the Shang dynasty: the Erligang Culture, centered on the present-day city of Zhengzhou, Henan, and the Yinxu or Anyang Culture, centered on the present-day city of Anyang. Heretofore, although there were manifest similarities between these two cultures, there also seemed to be a gap between the end of the Erligang Culture and the beginning of the Yinxu Culture. It is now clear that the Huanbei site was inhabited after the end of the Erligang period and immediately preceded the move to the Yinxu site, which contemporary written records show to have been the final capital of the last nine Shang kings. Since the Huanbei site prominently featured a palace structure, it seems reasonable that it should have been the home of Pan Geng or one or more of his three brothers who reigned as Shang kings.

With the generation following that of the four brothers, Yang Jia, Pan Geng, Xiao Xin, and Xiao Yi, we move finally into China's historical period proper. This is the reign of Wu Ding (r. *c.* 1225–1189), the son of Xiao Yi. Later historical sources credit it with being very lengthy, fifty-nine years, and with marking a resurgence in Shang power. There is reason to believe that his reign was quite long-lasting, even if not the fifty-nine years it is credited with in traditional histories, stretching for a decade or more both prior to and after 1200. There is also good reason to see it as marking a dramatic growth in Shang power. Habitation of the Yinxu site, which is all but synonymous with late Shang culture, began with this reign, or possibly just before it. The first phase of the Yinxu Culture shows a modest continuation of Erligang Culture. But in what is known as Phase Two of this culture, coinciding with the late period of Wu Ding's reign and perhaps that of his first reigning son Zu Geng (*c.* 1188–1178), the material remains show explosive growth, both in terms of quantity and quality. This is also the period of the first oracle-bone inscriptions, prayers incised into the shells of turtles or the scapula bones of oxen that serve as China's earliest written records.

As many as two hundred thousand pieces of oracle bone have now been unearthed from the vicinity of the Yinxu site, which means literally "Waste of Yin" ("Yin" being another name for the Shang). The site sits in a bend of the Huan River just northwest of the modern city of Anyang, the northernmost city of Henan province. It is strategically located toward the north end of the north China plain, just to the east of the southern tip of the Taihang Mountains, a mountain range that runs north-south from the west of modern-day Beijing south almost to the Yellow River; it traditionally served to divide China into two zones: Shandong (literally "to the east of the mountains," not to be equated with the province of the same name) and Shanxi (literally "to the west of the mountains," also not necessarily to be equated with the province of the same name.

It was the discovery of oracle bones at the very end of the nineteenth century CE that attracted attention to Yinxu, ushering modern archaeology into China. Excavations have been ongoing there, almost without interruption, for almost a hundred years now, and have revealed a sophisticated bronze using culture. The oracle bones begin with Phase Two of the Yinxu Culture and continue until the last of the Shang kings, Di Xin (r. 1086–1045). However, far and away the greatest number of pieces, making up more than half of the total, come from the reign of Wu Ding. Divinations from his time concerned virtually every topic that might concern a king, from the weather to the harvest, from military affairs to the birth-giving of his numerous wives, and extending even to his own toothaches. A simple example of harvest divinations reads:

> Crack-making on *bingchen* (day 53 of the 60-day cycle), (the diviner) Que affirmed: We will receive millet harvest.
>
> Crack-making on *bingchen* (day 53), (the diviner) Que affirmed: We will not expect to receive millet harvest. Fourth month.[5]

As can be seen here, at this early period divinations were regularly presented as positive-negative alternatives, although the Shang seem to have indicated their preference by inserting the word "to expect" in the side that they did not wish to happen.

Other prayers were for more specific actions, among which military campaigns are a frequent topic. The following divination took place in the first half of the part of Wu Ding's reign for which there are oracle-bone inscriptions.

> Crack-making on *xinyou* (day 58), (the diviner) Que affirmed: In this period, the king will ally with Wang Cheng to attack Xiawei, (for if he does) he will receive aid in it.
>
> Crack-making on *xinyou* (day 58), (the diviner) Que affirmed: In this period, the king ought not ally with Wang Cheng to attack Xiawei, (for if he does) he will not expect to receive aid in it.[6]

This divination came in the context of a major Shang expansion to the west of the Taihang Mountains. It is likely that this expansion put the Shang in contact with other advanced cultures to the north and further west of the mountains, contact that may explain the dramatic innovations seen in the Shang material culture of this time. These innovations include most notably horse-drawn chariots and a new tradition of jade sculpting. Even bronze casting, which the Shang had mastered from the beginning of the dynasty, underwent explosive development.

These developments were on full display in the tomb of Consort Hao (Fu Hao), one of the main consorts of Wu Ding. The excavation of the tomb in 1976 was one of the most sensational discoveries of that decade, often regarded as the Golden Age of Chinese archaeology. Located in the very middle of the Yinxu site, it is the only tomb associated with the royal family that has been found intact, the tombs of the kings on the other side of the Huan River all having been looted in early antiquity. Already before the discovery her tomb, Consort Hao was well known from the oracle-bone inscriptions of Wu Ding's reign, with divinations about her leading troops into battle, as well as several births. Buried with her in her tomb were over 200 ritual bronze vessels as well as 130 weapons, 23 bells, and the four earliest bronze mirrors ever found in China; 755 jade objects, including some that were probably a thousand years old or more already at the time of her burial; 564 bone objects; 6,900 cowrie shells (a form of wealth in ancient China); a number of stone, pottery, and ivory pieces; as well as sixteen human offerings buried in the fill above the tomb chamber. The statue of her erected outside of the Yinxu Museum portraying her as an Amazonia warrior is certainly fanciful, but the bronzes in the museum that were cast for her are unquestionably masterpieces of design and casting technology.

The resurgence of Shang power under Wu Ding doubtless manifested itself in ways other than just material culture. It is likely that an alliance of local groups located across a broad swath of central China, what is now southwestern Shanxi, all of northern Henan, much of western Shandong, and at least southern Hebei provinces, acknowledged the Shang king as one of, if not the most important powers of the time. By the time Wu Ding died, about 1190, his eldest son, known posthumously as Xiao Ji (Filial Ji) or Zu Ji, had already predeceased him. Therefore, the succession passed first to one younger brother, Zu Geng, and then to another: Zu Jia (r. c. 1177–1158). Under Zu Geng, life seems to have continued very much as it had under Wu Ding. Among the oracle-bone inscriptions of his reign there are records of sacrifices to Ding or Father Ding, but there is little else to differentiate them from the sorts of divinations performed for Wu Ding. However, the succession of Zu Jia brought with it major structural changes in the ways that divination was performed, so much so that Dong Zuobin (1895–1963), one of the most important early scholars of oracle-bone inscriptions, termed it the advent of a New School. The most obvious change was in the initiation of systematic sacrifices to the royal ancestors, but it is likely that there were other changes as well. For instance, the range of topics subject to divination became greatly narrowed, often to just the single positive prayer that "In the next ten-day week there will be no misfortune." This led another important scholar of oracle-bone inscriptions, David N. Keightley (1932–2017), to suggest that this was evidence of a paradoxical theological reversal: whereas the wide-ranging divinations under Wu Ding and Zu Geng routinely resulted in the king predicting trouble for the Shang state, under the New

School divination became radically optimistic, the prognostications of the king being invariably "Auspicious." Although Dong Zuobin thought that these reforms of the New School were more or less short-lived, with it alternating back and forth with the Old School, in fact more recent studies of Shang history show that divination continued according to the New School procedures until the very end of the dynasty, perhaps 125 years later.

In addition to the narrowing of topics to be divined, it would seem that there was also some narrowing of the areas in which the Shang could project their power. Groups located to the west of the Taihang Mountains that had been allied with Wu Ding now came to be referred to with the suffix "land" (*fang*), which in Shang usage indicated enemies. This seems to suggest that the Shang realm withdrew back to the east of the Taihang Mountains, a retrenchment that may have cut them off from the source of many of the innovations that had marked Wu Ding's reign. The next four or five reigns following Zu Geng's are unremarkable. The oracle-bone inscriptions confirm that they continued the Shang tradition of passing power from elder brother to younger brother, and later sources suggest that they were all quite short. However, neither of these features characterize the last king of the Shang; named Zhòu and known posthumously as Di Xin ("Di" being the word "thearch"), he has gone down in Chinese tradition as the second of the paradigmatically evil last rulers.

Di Xin succeeded his father Di Yi (r. 1105–1087) probably in 1086, and would go on to have a very lengthy reign, before finally being overthrown in 1045. Both contemporary oracle-bone inscriptions and later traditions suggest that he ruled vigorously, at least at first. In 1077–1076, he personally led what seems to have been a nine-month long military campaign eastwards into the Huai River valley of what is today southern Shandong and northern Anhui provinces. The progress of this campaign can be followed by the divinations that he regularly performed praying for its success. The following are just a few of more than one hundred inscriptions that pertain to this campaign.

Jiawu (day thirty-one of the sixty-day cycle), the king made cracks and affirmed: "Making for me wine and my grain, I will march in alliance with Xi of You to campaign against People Land, and the ancestral altars above and below will give me aid in it, and will not inflict defeat or trouble. Reporting at the Great City Shang, there will be no harm in the bones." The king prognosticated and said: "Auspicious." In the ninth month, meeting the *hui*-ritual to Shang Jia; it is the tenth ritual cycle.[7]

Jiayin (day fifty-one), the king made cracks at Bo and affirmed: "Today I will march to Hong, and there will be no disaster."

Yimao (day fifty-two), the king made cracks at Hong and affirmed: "Today I will march to Li, and there will be no disaster."[8]

Crack-making on *guisi* (day thirty), Huang affirmed: "In the next ten-day week the king will have no trouble." In the twelfth month, it was when the king was campaigning against the People Land. At Zang.

Crack-making on *guimao* (day forty), Huang affirmed: "In the next ten-day week the king will have no trouble." In the first month, it was when the king was coming from campaigning against the People Land, at Yong, the hamlet of Lord Xi of You.[9]

Granted, the topics of the divinations are not particularly revealing, but they show at least when the campaign began, and how the inscriptions can be arranged one after the other. Importantly, the simple change in the last two inscriptions indicating that "the king was campaigning against the People Land" and "the king was coming from campaigning against the People Land" indicates a turning point in the campaign. Other evidence suggests that the Shang forces had just won a decisive victory, capturing and then executing the leader of the People Land.

While Di Xin was campaigning in the east, there were renewed developments to the west of the Shang domain. Even further west than the area that Wu Ding had brought under control at the beginning of the preceding century, a rival power called the Zhou was beginning to form alliances of its own. Later sources portray Di Xin as haughtily neglecting the Zhou threat, ruthlessly persecuting the people, and dismissing remonstrations by his own kinsmen. Whatever the truth of these traditions, it is certain that Zhou eventually did mount a successful campaign against Shang, defeating the Shang army and killing Di Xin, thus bringing an end to the Shang dynasty. This is often regarded as the single most decisive event in ancient Chinese history, ushering in the 800 years of the Zhou dynasty, the third of ancient China's fabled Three Dynasties.

CHAPTER 4
BASIC ANNALS OF ZHOU

The Zhou people, like the Shang, traced their ancestry back to a miraculous conception. According to their traditions, the woman Jiang Yuan, whose name means "Origin of the Jiang," a family with whom the Zhou intermarried, became pregnant after having stepped in the footprint of Di or the God on High. Regarding the child as inauspicious, she several times attempted to abandon him and even named him Qi ("Abandoned"), but each time he survived through the intervention of nature, with horses and oxen refusing to trample him when he was placed in a road and birds using their wings to warm him when he was placed on ice. According to the myth, as the child grew he learned to cultivate grains and beans to feed himself. At the time of the ruler Shun, because the common people were starving, Shun put Qi in charge of agriculture. He then taught his skills to others, coming to be known as Hou Ji, the "Lord of Millet."

After Qi or Hou Ji, the Zhou genealogy passes through twelve generations, during which time the Zhou people are said to have lived among the wild peoples of the north and west. By the time of the Shang king Wu Ding, it is possible that Zhou enters the historical record proper, there being oracle-bone inscriptions about Shang first attacking a people called Zhou, and then, somewhat later, having peaceful relations with them. Where this Zhou was located is a point of contention among modern Chinese historians. Some historians locate it along the Fen River, a major tributary of the Yellow River flowing through present-day Shanxi province between the Taihang Mountain range to the east and the north-south stretch of the Yellow River to the west, an area in frequent contact with Shang about the time of Wu Ding. Many other historians argue that Zhou was located west of the Yellow River, in the high plateau area to the north of the Wei River, another major tributary of the Yellow River. It seems that there is still insufficient archaeological evidence to resolve this debate. Nevertheless, it is clear that shortly after this time, that is by the mid to late twelfth century, the Zhou people moved still further west, establishing themselves at an upland plain called Zhouyuan, the "Plain of Zhou." This is the area that they would thereafter always regard as their homeland. From this time on for almost three hundred years, there is plentiful archaeological evidence testifying to their life there.

The Zhou's own history of themselves begins with a sagely figure named Chang, better known as King Wen, who is said to have ruled for fifty years (1099/1056–1050). During the latter part of this half century of rule, Zhou began to extend its power back toward the east, eventually coming into contact again with Shang. Both Zhou and Shang traditions hold that Chang was captured and imprisoned by Di Xin, the last ruler of Shang, but that he was eventually released and given a mandate to exercise authority over the Shang western region. This would seem to have been de facto recognition of the developing situation in that area, over which Shang had effectively lost control several generations earlier.

Chang died before the Zhou competition with Shang came to its ultimate conclusion. Nevertheless, he was credited ever after as the first king of the Zhou, posthumously referred to as Wen Wang, the "Cultured King." He was succeeded by his son Fa, who would come to be known as Wu Wang, the "Martial King" (r. 1049/1045–1043), since it was he who led the Zhou army in the battle that would defeat Di Xin and bring the Shang dynasty to its close. All Zhou kings thereafter, and indeed most emperors throughout later Chinese history, would be known by some similar adjective understood to characterize their reign.

Numerous Zhou texts, both traditional and archaeologically excavated, refer to Kings Wen and Wu as the two founders of the dynasty, the father representing its civil virtues and the son its military power. According to later traditions, that King Wen died before the conquest absolved him of the crime of regicide, his son, King Wu, taking on the responsibility for killing the reigning Shang king. One recently discovered text written on bamboo strips describes a dream that King Wen's wife, Tai Si, had with a clear premonition of Zhou's victory.

> Tai Si dreamed of seeing that in the Shang court were brambles, and then that the young son Fa took the Zhou court's catalpa and planted it in their midst, transforming into pine and cypress, white oak and sawtooth oak. She awakened alarmed, and reported it to the king.[10]

Plants and animals, as well as all sorts of celestial and terrestrial phenomena were thought to be imbued with unique powers to predict the future. "Brambles," a sort of thorn-bush the most pronounced characteristic of which is its needle-sharp barbs, was a particularly ominous plant. On the other hand, the catalpa is a beautiful, stately deciduous tree, which later came to be called "the king of trees." Pine and cypress, white oak and sawtooth oak, in their turn, were thought to represent constancy and assistance. That Fa, i.e., King Wu, planted a catalpa tree in the midst of the brambles growing in the Shang court is an obvious image of the Zhou conquest, whereas the brambles transforming into the various lesser trees signified the change of the Shang from armed opponents into loyal subjects. Since the dream was so obviously auspicious, modern interpreters of the text have struggled to understand why Tai Si should have "awakened alarmed"; could she not see that it portended the Zhou victory? The answer seems obvious: that the victory would be achieved by Fa, the son, meant that King Wen, Tai Si's husband, would die before it could happen.

The conquest was not long in coming after King Wen's death. Within just a few years, King Wu led the Zhou army on campaign to the east, crossing the Tongguan Pass through the mountains that separate the modern provinces of Shaanxi to the west and Henan to the east, coming out into the north China plain very near to Erlitou, which many historians say was the capital of the Xia dynasty, and then turning north to cross the Yellow River at a place called Mengjin Ford. Having crossed the Yellow River, the Zhou army was within just a few days march of the Shang capital region. The two armies met at a place called Muye, Shepherd's Wild, just southwest of modern Anyang. The Zhou won a decisive victory, though there are conflicting accounts as to how bloody the battle was. The earliest account, probably dating not too much later than the event itself, describes horrendous Shang casualties, later described as the field being drenched in blood. On the other hand, the later Confucian philosopher Mencius (c. 385–303) rejected any suggestion of bloodshed, saying that when the most virtuous of rulers met the most despicable, the latter's soldiers would lay down their arms and gladly accept defeat.

It is probably irrelevant just how bloody the battle may have been. It has always been viewed as one of the great turning points in Chinese history, when in a single day one dynasty was decisively brought to an end and another began. Modern historians in China have shed a great deal of ink trying to determine when that day was. According to the chronology used in this book, it was January 15, 1045 BCE. It is important to note that that date is by no means universally accepted, but it can't be too far wrong, if at all.

While we might be able to pinpoint the exact date of the battle at Shepherd's Wild, it would be mistaken to think that the Shang army just laid down its weapons and that the state ceased to exist. This is not to say that Zhou did not win a great victory. However, after King Wu returned with his army to the Zhou homeland, some seven hundred kilometers to the west, there remained a powerful Shang presence throughout the area "east of the mountains" (i.e., the Taihang Mountains). King Wu is said to have deputed three of his younger brothers to oversee population centers within this area, in the case of the Shang capital region doing so in partnership with Di Xin's surviving son Wu Geng. When King Wu died, more or less suddenly, just two years later, and yet another brother, Dan, the Duke of Zhou, assumed power in the Zhou capital, Zhou rule, not yet very stable, was thrown into turmoil; the brothers in the east, deeply suspicious of the Duke of Zhou, joined in rebellion with their Shang subjects. This precipitated a civil war that is said to have lasted three years, but which did have the salutary effect of decisively consolidating Zhou rule of the entire eastern region, stretching to the sea in present-day Shandong province, and north as far as present-day Beijing, the northern entrance to the North China Plain.

King Wu is also said to have had a dream, though perhaps more figuratively than the literal dream that Tai Si, King Wen's wife, is reported as having had: King Wu dreamed of establishing a new capital alongside the Luo River in the northwestern corner of present-day Henan province. This was very near where he had crossed the Yellow River with the Zhou army on the way to their fateful battle with Di Xin and the Shang army, and also just a few dozen kilometers from Erlitou, said to have been the capital of the Xia dynasty (though it is doubtful that anyone alive at that time was aware of that site, which had been destroyed already some five hundred years earlier). Perhaps the most important thing about this proposed new capital—at Luoyang—was that it was at the center of the territory that the Zhou now controlled. Indeed, one bronze vessel, called the *He zun* (bronze vessels are conventionally referred to by the name of the patron for whom they were cast and by the type of vessel; here "He" is the patron's name and *zun* is the type of vessel, a wine serving vessel), cast just a few years later bears an inscription in which King Wu's son, King Cheng (the "Completed King"; r. 1042/1035–1006), addressed a group of young Zhou leaders assembled there and referred to the area as the "central region" (*zhong yu* or *zhong guo*), the latter of these two pronunciations regarded as the first reference to the name by which China is typically known: Zhongguo, the "Middle Kingdom."

It was when the king first moved (his) residence to Chengzhou and again received King Wu's abundant blessing from heaven. In the fourth month, *bingxu* (day 23), the king addressed the ancestral young princes in the Capital Chamber, saying:

In the past, your deceased-fathers and elders were capable of assisting King Wen. And so King Wen received this great mandate. It was after King Wu had conquered the great city Shang, then (he) respectfully reported to Heaven, saying:

I shall reside (in) this central region (and) from it govern the people.

Wuhu! Although you are but young princes without experience, look upon the elders' merit with respect to Heaven, and carry out the commands and reverently make offerings! Help the king make firm his virtue so that Heaven may look favorably upon our weakness.

The king completed the address. He was awarded cowries, thirty strands, and herewith makes for Lord Yan this treasured offertory vessel. It is the king's fifth ritual cycle.[11]

As just mentioned, King Wu was succeeded by his eldest son, Song, who would be known as King Cheng, the "Completed King." It was during his reign that the eastern capital at Luoyang was established, and the city there was known throughout Zhou times as Chengzhou, the "Completed Zhou," whether in reference to this king's efforts or not. According to tradition, the first years of King Cheng's reign were dominated by the Duke of Zhou, ruling in his stead as regent. To whatever extent this was actually the case, or simply reflected different parties contending for power, it seems clear that King Cheng did eventually assume complete control of the Zhou governing apparatus. Among other effects of King Cheng's rule, which continued for thirty-seven years, was firm establishment of the principle of primogeniture: succession by the king's eldest son. It was probably at this time that the Zhou kings came to be called *Tianzi*, the "Son of Heaven," and also at this time that the Zhou claimed that their rule was mandated by Heaven. This was the inception of the "Mandate of Heaven," which would be used by all subsequent dynasties to justify their right to rule.

Son of Heaven or not, King Cheng was able to rule the extensive eastern territories the Zhou had conquered through a sort of colonization, deputing his uncles and brothers and old allies of the Zhou to move with their kinsmen east and establish their own city-states at militarily strategic locations. Thus, Lord Feng of Kang, one of the king's uncles, was installed in the former Shang capital region; this would become the state of Wèi. Dan, the Duke of Zhou, was given an area further east, just at the base of the imposing Mount Tai in present-day Shandong province; this was the state of Lu. The Grand Duke Wang, not a blood relative of the Zhou house but the commander of the Zhou army at the battle of Muye, was sent to an area further north; this was the state of Qi. Still further north, near the site of present-day Beijing, guarding the northern entrance to the north China plain, Duke Shi of Shao, another son of King Wen (though by a secondary consort), established the city-state of Yan; the Duke of Shao would join the Duke of Zhou as King Cheng's most important advisers. Two of King Cheng's younger brothers were sent to colonize areas to the north and south of the eastern capital at Chengzhou: Shu Yu was sent to the valley of the Fen River in Shanxi province, establishing the state of Jin, while another brother, whose name is unknown, was sent into the mountainous area of central Henan province, where he established the state of Ying. Other relatives and allies established scores of other city-states. During the Western Zhou dynasty, these colonies would be at least nominally under the control of the Zhou king. They would later develop into the independent states of the Eastern Zhou dynasty, about which we will speak later.

King Cheng was succeeded in turn by his eldest son, Zhao, who would be known as King Kang, the "Peaceful King" (r. 1005–978). Inscribed bronze vessels from these two reigns attest that they were not particularly peaceful, as Zhou armies consolidated their control throughout north China. According to these inscriptions, all of the Zhou efforts were successful, as they probably were. However, it is also worth remembering that bronze vessels were cast to commemorate successes, and not failures. The lack of any inscriptional testimony to Zhou failures ought not to be understood to mean that there were no Zhou failures. Indeed, in the fourth or fifth reign of the dynasty (depending on whether King Wen or King Wu is considered as the first reigning king), Jia, the eldest son of King Kang succeeded to rule, known as King Zhao, the "Radiant King" (r. 977/975–957). While numerous bronze vessels from his time bear inscriptions about one or perhaps two military campaigns that he led south into present-day Hubei province, it is only from veiled allusions in later texts that we learn that one of these campaigns resulted in a great Zhou defeat, in the course of which the Western Six Armies were decimated and the king himself was drowned in the Han River. This campaign would mark the high-water mark of Zhou rule. Thereafter, direct Zhou control would be limited to the two capital areas, the original capital along the Wei River in present-day Shaanxi province and the new capital along the Luo River in present-day Henan province, though they would continue to maintain indirect control over their colonies established at strategic locations throughout north and central China for almost another two centuries.

A second result of King Zhao's disastrous southern campaign would have even greater and even longer lasting implications for Zhou rule. King Zhao was succeeded by his eldest son, Man, known as King Mu, the "Ripened King" (r. 956–918). We can imagine that King Mu, presumably still quite young when rule was suddenly thrust upon him, faced an existential threat, with much of the Zhou army destroyed and many of the elders of the state dead. In traditional histories of Zhou rule, the only things that we learn about King Mu's lengthy reign are that he traveled extensively into what is now known as Central Asia, apparently engaging there in some sort of a romance with the Western Queen Mother, and that he established a law code for the state. We can probably disregard the first of these as nothing more than the stuff of legend. The second point may also be more legend than real, but there is substantial evidence, even if all circumstantial, in the numerous vessels bronze vessels cast during his reign, that King Mu did oversee a radical reorganization of Zhou rule.

A group of vessels cast on behalf of a man named Li, the scion of an old Zhou family named Shan, may be the first indication of this reorganization of Zhou rule. This family was not well known when these vessels were discovered in 1955 in Meixian, a county on the south side of the Wei River about a hundred kilometers to the west of the capital region at present-day Xi'an and just across from the Zhou homeland known as the Zhouyuan. However, over the next several decades, many more bronze vessels with long inscriptions cast on behalf of Li's descendants would be found there, showing that the family was an important support to the Zhou kings throughout the entirety of the Western Zhou dynasty. One of the vessels cast for Li, known as the *Li fangyi*, commemorates Li's appointment to take control of both the Six Armies, which seem to have been a sort of royal bodyguard stationed in the vicinity of the western capital, and also the Yin Eight Armies, armies made up of non-Zhou soldiers stationed near the eastern capital Chengzhou. The inscription on the vessel records Li's investiture. From this time until the end of the Western Zhou, investitures of this sort would be the most frequent occasion for the casting of the most important inscribed bronze vessels. The *Li fangyi* inscription is an excellent example of this sort of investiture inscription, differing from the great majority of other such inscriptions only in that in addition to recording the king's speech, it also features Li's spoken response to the king. This might reflect the power being vested in him, and perhaps also his senior status vis-à-vis the young King Mu.

It was the eighth month, first auspiciousness; the king entered into the Zhou Temple. Duke Mu at the right of Li stood in the center of the courtyard, facing north. The king in writing commanded Yin to award Li red knee-pads, a black girdle-pendant, and bit and bridle, saying:

> Herewith supervise the royally enacted Three Supervisors of the Six Armies: the Supervisor of Lands, Supervisor of the Horse and Supervisor of Work.

The king commanded Li, saying:

> Concurrently supervise the Six Armies' and the Eight Armies' seals.

Li bowed and touched his head to the ground, daring in response to extol the king's beneficence, herewith making for my cultured grandfather Lord Yi this treasured offertory vessel. Li said: "The Son of Heaven is very blessed and very well-founded, for ten thousand years protecting our ten thousand states." Li dares to bow and touch his head to the ground, saying: "Array my person to continue my predecessors' treasured service."[12]

Many other inscriptions from King Mu's time and thereafter suggest that Li's appointment to take command of the Zhou armies would mark an important transition in the way the Zhou state was governed. Up to this time, the Zhou kings seem to have called upon their close relatives to perform whatever service was required at any given time, seemingly a good example of what Max Weber referred to as "patrimonial rule." However, from this time on bronze inscriptions show that the Zhou government came to be staffed by people appointed to designated offices, presumably more on the basis of their qualifications than on their blood relationship with the king; this seems to be the beginning of "bureaucratic rule," which would characterize most governments in China ever after.

King Mu's rule, or perhaps that of his son, Yihu, known as King Gong, the "Supported King" (r. 917–900), also marked the beginning of other changes in Zhou lives. Probably the most important of these were changes in the ritual system upon which Zhou society was based. This is now generally referred to in studies of Western Zhou history as the "Ritual Reform" or even "Ritual Revolution." This may sound like a religious reformation, and in some ways it was. But unlike the Protestant Reformation in Europe, the Western Zhou Ritual Reform was not a matter of belief, but was almost wholly concerned with practice. Prior to this time, rituals surrounding burials and the ongoing cult to the ancestors were celebrated by (male) members of a family; even if these families were not just the nuclear family with which we are now familiar, it probably did not include more members than those living together. However, after the Ritual Reform, ritual celebrations came to be multi-media spectacles, with large audiences observing musicians playing drums and bells and chime-stones suspended from racks and ritual specialists celebrating offerings at altars on which were arrayed sets of bronze vessels, graduated in size and differing in function. It goes without saying that the musicians required expert knowledge to play their instruments, the bells of which featured two separate tones an octave apart, depending on where on the bell they were struck. The priests at the altar presumably also required specialized knowledge of how to perform their ceremonies. These changes in the performance of rituals paralleled the bureaucratization of the Zhou government. They too would last throughout the Zhou dynasty, and indeed long thereafter.

While events in the reign of King Mu are reasonably well reported in the traditional historical record, that record is all but silent concerning his son, King Gong. In fact, for the next three kings as well, King Yih, the "Steady King" (r. 899–873), the son of King Gong; King Xiao, the "Filial King" (r. 882–866), who anomalously among all Western Zhou kings was not his predecessor's son but rather his uncle; and King Yi, the "Even King" (r. 865–858), King Yih's son, *Records of the Historian* says nothing more than the following:

> When King Gong died, his son Jian, King Yih, came to power. In King Yih's time, the royal court declined and the poets composed satires. When King Yih died, King Gong's younger brother Bifang came to power; this was King Xiao. When King Xiao died, the many lords installed Xie, the son of King Yih. This was King Yi. When King Yi died, his son Hu, King Li, came to power.[13]

If it were not for inscribed bronze vessels from the time, which have been unearthed in considerable number over the last four or five decades, there would be almost nothing to add to this. As it is, the bronze inscriptions provide more information about general tendencies than they do about specific events. The trend toward bureaucratization of the government noted above for the reign of King Mu certainly grew ever stronger. On the other hand, there are signs of a general breakdown of social order. A new type of bronze inscription makes its first appearance at this time: commemorations of victories in law suits, especially those involving land disputes. Although these bronze inscriptions are not at all as plentiful as the investiture inscriptions mentioned above, they seem to suggest that an increase in population brought competition for natural resources, especially land, in the capital regions, and especially that of the Wei River valley. The inscription on the *Qiu Wei ding* is representative of these court cases.

> It was the first month, first auspiciousness, *gengxu* (day 47), Wei took the States-lord Li to court before the Elder of Jing, Elder Yifu, the Elder of Ding, the Elder of Liang, and Elder Sufu, saying: "I am in charge of King Gong's irrigation works to the east of the Great Chamber of Shao going northward to the two rivers of Rong. Li had said: 'I will give you five fields.'"
>
> The officials then interrogated Li, saying: "Did you sell the fields or not?" Li conceded saying: "I sold all five fields." The Elder of Jing, Elder Yifu, the Elder of Ding, the Elder of Liang, and Elder Sufu then reached a verdict, making Li swear an oath. Then they commanded the three supervisors: Supervisor of Lands Yiren Fu, Supervisor of the Horse Shanren Bang, Supervisor of Works Fu Ju, and the Interior Scribe's associate Si Zou to survey Qiu Wei's four fields of Li, and to give him his home at his city: the northern boundary as far as the Li fields; the eastern boundary as far as the San fields; the southern boundary as far as the San fields and Zhengfu fields; and the western boundary as far as the Li fields.
>
> States-lord Li gave all of these fields to Qiu Wei. Li's youngest son Su, Li's supervisors Shen Ji, Qing Gui, Bin Biao, Gan of Xing, Changyi of Jing, and Wei's young son Zhu Qi feasted me.
>
> Wei herewith makes for my cultured deceased-father this treasured caldron. May Wei for ten thousand years eternally treasure and use it. It is the king's fifth year.[14]

It is unclear who the "States-lord Li" of this inscription was, but that he bore the title of "States-lord" suggests that he was a man of some prominence, and the inscription certainly indicates that he had extensive land holdings, at least prior to this trial.

Of course, inscriptions such as that on the *Qiu Wei ding* provide only anecdotal evidence. There are no statistics from this early period, nor does archaeology provide any real information about economic developments. However, it seems clear that some old established families fell into decline, their lands being carved up among other families. There is also some evidence that some of the people who worked those lands absconded. Although it is not clear where they may have gone, it is perhaps a reasonable guess that they migrated eastward, where the former colonies were growing increasingly estranged from the capital region, all but declaring their independence from the greater Zhou state.

There are even more subtle hints of turmoil in the middle of this period. A great many bronze vessels that surely date to the first decades of the ninth century contain "full dates," which is to say the year of reign, month, phase of the moon (one of four discrete notations that seem to refer to the new moon, the full moon, and the waxing and waning half-moons), and the day in the cycle of sixty days used in ancient China. While there are questions about all four of the elements within these date notations, it should be possible to use them to reconstruct the calendar of the period, and especially the regnal calendars of the kings. However, the dates are too numerous and too contradictory to fit within the three or four decades when they must have been cast, unless one posits some overlap between them. This led David S. Nivison (1923–2014), one of the most creative scholars of the chronology of the period, to suggest that the anomalous succession from King Yih to his uncle King Xiao was brought about by a crisis at court, and that King Yih was forced to flee to a place known in the received literature as Feiqiu, the "Waste Mound" while his uncle, King Xiao, declared himself king in the capital. King Yih continued to live in exile for another decade. Adherents of both "kings" cast bronze vessels using two different regnal calendars such that there could be two different dates for the same year. While this suggestion is entirely hypothetical, not only does it resolve the problem of the contradictory date notations in the contemporary bronze inscriptions, but it is also consistent with the greater social and political trends of the time.

Although the legitimate succession was restored with the reign of King Yi, this did not stop the deterioration of royal power. Other traditional histories than just that of *Records of the Historian* report mainly that King Yi was sickly and that his reign did not last long (in fact, it almost certainly lasted only eight years). Although *Records of the Historian*, quoted above, indicates that it was the "many lords" who installed him in power, apparently in an attempt to restore the regular succession, their support was not reciprocated by the new king. A record in the *Bamboo Annals* states that just two years after his installation, the king executed the Lord of Qi, boiling him in a bronze caldron. Of course, we can only guess at the context of this event, if it is even true at all, but it certainly seems consistent with the increasing deterioration in relations between the royal court in the west and the eastern states.

Social unrest certainly reached a boil during the reign of King Yi's son Hu, known as King Li, the "Terrible King" (r. 857/853–842/828). Given King Yi's short reign, it is likely that King Li came to power when still very young, and indeed there is some evidence in the *Bamboo Annals* and also in fully dated bronze inscriptions that he restarted his regnal calendar a few years after originally succeeding his father, perhaps indicative of his coming of age. In any event, his regnal calendar confused Sima Qian, the author of *Records of the Historian*, and with that also threw into doubt the chronology of all preceding kings. This confusion has persisted to the present time.

According to *Records of the Historian*, other historical texts, and even contemporary poetry, the problems of King Li's reign began with his preference for one minister named the Duke of Rong over another: Rui Liangfu. There is a criticism attributed to Rui Liangfu suggesting that the disagreement between these two ministers stemmed from one of the perennial debates of economic policy: over taxation and the redistribution of wealth. Rui Liangfu is quoted as saying:

> Will the royal court debase itself? The Duke of Rong loves to monopolize profits but is not aware of their great difficulty. Profits are produced by the hundred things and supported by heaven and earth. For one to monopolize them, the harm will be great indeed. Heaven and earth and the hundred things are for all to take; how can it be acceptable to monopolize them! Those angered will be extremely many, but he is not prepared for the great difficulty. To advise the king in this way, how will the king endure for long! One who is king of the people is one who directs profits and distributes them to high and low.... Now if the king learns to monopolize profits, will it be acceptable! If a common person were to monopolize profits, he would be called a bandit. If the king were to do it, his followers would be few indeed. If you make use of the Duke of Rong, Zhou will surely be ruined.[15]

As the story goes, the king paid no attention to Rui Liangfu's argument, and instead employed the Duke of Rong, increasing taxes and treating the people cruelly. Others, including the Duke of Shao, the descendant of one of the founding fathers of the dynasty, also remonstrated against the king to no avail.

This was not the only problem besieging the Zhou court. Contemporary bronze inscriptions record that the royal army was dispatched to defend against incursions from the south that reached almost to the eastern capital at Luoyang. However, in something extremely rare, at least one of these bronze inscriptions, that on the *Yu ding*, states that this royal army was defeated, and was only rescued when one Duke Wu, the "Martial Duke," apparently the ruler of one of the eastern states, now all but independent of the royal house, sent his own army to stop the invasion. The inscription reflects the crisis facing the Zhou state at this time.

Yu said, "Illustrious and great august ancestor Duke Mu was capable of standing beside and assisting the prior kings and settling the four quarters. And so, Duke Wu also did not put at a distance or forget my sagely grandfather and deceased-father Youdashu and Yishu, commanding Yu to continue my grandfather and deceased-father's governance in the country of Jing. And so, Yu also does not dare be disordered and myopic in supporting my ruler's command.

Wuhu, oh woe! Because heaven has sent down great destruction on the region below, and also since the Lord of E, the Border Protector, has led the Southern Huai Peoples and the Eastern Peoples broadly to attack our southern regions and eastern regions as far as Lihan, the king then commanded the Western Six Armies and the Yin Eight Armies, saying, "Tear apart and attack the Lord of E, the Border Protector; do not leave old or young."

And so, the armies were ever more fearful and trembling, and did not succeed in attacking E. And so, Duke Wu then dispatched Yu to lead one hundred of the duke's war chariots, two hundred charioteers, and one thousand infantry, saying, "In rescuing my resolute plan, assist the Western Six Armies and the Yin Eight Armies to attack the Lord of E, the Border Protector. Do not leave old or young."

When Yu took Duke Wu's infantry and chariotry and advanced as far as E, ramming and attacking E, he was victorious, capturing their leader, the Border Protector. And so, Yu, having had success, dares in response to extol Duke Wu's illustrious dazzling glory, herewith making this great treasured caldron. May Yu for ten thousand years have sons' sons and grandsons' grandsons to treasure and use it.[16]

Meanwhile, the *Bamboo Annals* says that the western capital region was also coming under attack by warriors from further to the north and west. This attack was successfully repelled, as might be attested by yet another bronze inscription that many historians think dates to this time, but it would not be the end of the threat.

Eventually, in 842, the earliest commonly accepted date in Chinese history, the people and the great families rose up against King Li, driving him into exile well away from the royal capital. While the king was in exile, control of the state fell to one He, the Elder of Gong, another great family, though one that had come to prominence much more recently than that of the Duke of Shao. This interregnum, which lasted for fourteen years, brought the great families enough time to re-establish the royal court, if only temporarily. When King Li died, still in exile, He, the Elder of Gong, restored King Li's son, Jing, known posthumously as King Xuan, the "Announced King" (r. 827–782). King Xuan would rule for forty-six years, longer than any other Zhou king. His reign would begin with great promise that the former glories of the state could be restored, but by the end of his reign the forces pulling the state apart would prove to be inexorable.

Although King Xuan, like his father King Li, must have come to power as a very young man, he seems to have navigated the early years of his reign more successfully than did his father. Virtually the only thing that *Records of the Historian* says about this time is that he modeled himself on the founding kings of the dynasty, Kings Wen, Wu, Cheng and Kang, and that the "many lords," meaning the rulers of the now all but independent states in the east, presented themselves at court once again. Again, the *Bamboo Annals* is more informative, noting military campaigns against the western enemies, now given the name Xianyun, almost surely a transcription of one enemy's name in a non-Sinitic language, in the third and fifth year of his reign. At least the note for the fifth year has been confirmed by a contemporary bronze inscription. In the sixth year, the royal army turned its attention to the threat on the southeastern front. These campaigns seem to bespeak a young king taking the initiative to reclaim the extensive territories first conquered by those founding kings of the dynasty. However, in the twelfth year of his reign, two different events occurred that probably suggest that this restoration would not be a simple matter. The events point to two threats affecting the royal court: one external and one internal. Although these two events themselves can be dated to the twelfth year, the threats to the Zhou royal house were not momentary, but rather would continue to develop throughout the remainder of the dynasty, which would end decisively less than fifty years later.

First, a series of bronze vessels with lengthy inscriptions indicate that there were further hostilities with the Xianyun, but this time certainly initiated by the Xianyun. One of the inscriptions, on the *Duo You ding*, makes it clear that the Zhou forces reacted only after a Xianyun attack once again reached almost to the gates of the western capital. Once again, Duke Wu had to dispatch his own army to the rescue, under the leadership of Duo You, who may have been a younger brother of King Xuan. The second problem to beset King Xuan in the twelfth year of his reign was the death of yet another Duke Wu: this one the ruler of the state of Lu (the name meaning "Martial Duke" was popular for rulers of many states). Lu, located in the southwestern part of present-day Shandong province, at the foot of Mount Tai, the holiest of Chinese mountains, had been founded by Dan, the Duke of Zhou, at the very beginning of the dynasty, in the immediate aftermath of the civil war following King Wu's death. Ruled by the direct descendants of the Duke of Zhou, Lu enjoyed prestige far beyond what its modest size might otherwise deserve. There are records suggesting that King Xuan attempted to influence which of Duke Wu's two sons should succeed him to rule in the state: the elder son Kuo, who would ordinarily be the default choice, or the younger Xi, who was favored by King Xuan. The prime minister Fanzhong Shanfu advised the king against intruding in this succession. Fanzhong Shanfu's advice is a classic example of both the political philosophy of the time and also the style of argumentation.

> To discard the elder and install the younger is improper; being improper, it will surely overturn the king's mandate, and overturning the king's mandate will surely result in killing him. Therefore, in issuing commands you cannot be improper. When commands are not put into effect the government will not stand, and when put into effect improperly the people will reject their superiors. For inferiors to serve superiors and for the younger to serve the older is what is proper. Now if the Son of Heaven determines the lord, installing the younger, this will teach the people to be contrary. If Lu does not submit to him, the other lords will imitate them and the king's mandate will be obstructed. If they do not submit to him and kill him, this would be you yourself killing the king's mandate. Killing him you lose, and not killing him you lose. My Lord should consider it.[17]

The king did not pay any attention to his minister's advice, installing the younger brother Xi. Ten years later the people of Lu rebelled against Xi, assassinated him, and installed Boyu, the son of the elder brother Kuo, as the legitimate ruler of Lu. After another ten years, King Xuan personally led an army east into present-day Shandong to attack Lu, killing Boyu, and installing the surviving son of Duke Wu to be the new lord. According to *Records of the*

Historian, the result of all of this interference in the affairs of a de facto independent state was that the rulers of most of the other states turned against the royal commands, just as Fanzhong Shanfu had predicted twenty years before.

In China, there is an old saying that "the earth does not cherish its treasures," originally used to justify the mining of precious metals and stones, but now more commonly used with respect to archaeological discoveries being unearthed. In 1993, tomb robbers in Houma, Shanxi opened a tomb in the cemetery of early rulers of the state of Jin, one of the old Zhou colonies founded at the beginning of the dynasty and one that would go on to become the strongest state of the Springs and Autumns period from the seventh century through the early fifth century. The tomb robbers stole from the tomb fourteen bronze bells inscribed with a very lengthy inscription showing that they were made for Su, Lord of Jin. Although the inscription, the *Jin Hou Su bianzhong,* does not mention Lu specifically, the place names mentioned in it are all in Lu, and the dates mentioned in it correspond to when King Xuan led his campaign there to oust Boyu as the ruler of Lu.

It was the king's thirty-third year. The king personally toured and inspected the eastern states and the southern states. In the first month, after the growing brightness, *wuwu* (day 55), the king walked from Zongzhou. In the second month, after the full moon, *guimao* (day 40, *sic*), the king entered into Chengzhou. In the second month, after the dying brightness, *renyin* (day 39), the king continued going to the east. In the third month, at the dying brightness, the king commanded Su, Lord of Jin:

Lead your armies leftward crossing Huo and to the north crossing ... to attack the Su barbarians.

Su, Lord of Jin cut off 120 heads and captured 23 prisoners. The king arrived at Xun Citadel. The king personally inspected the armies from a distance. The king arrived at the Lord of Jin's camp. The king descended from his chariot and, standing facing south, personally commanded Su, Lord of Jin: "From the northwest corner, ram and attack Xun Citadel." Su, Lord of Jin led his secondary legion, young princes, and spearmen to advance and descend entering into it, cutting off 100 heads and capturing 11 prisoners. The king arrived at Naolie. The barbarians of Naolie went out fleeing. The king commanded Su, Lord of Jin: "Lead the Grand Chamber's junior vassals and charioteers to follow, and catch and pursue them." The Lord of Jin cut off 110 heads and captured 20 prisoners. The Grand Chamber's junior vassals and charioteers cut off 150 heads and captured 60 prisoners.

It was when the king turned back, returning to Chengzhou. The lord's legions arranged the Army Palace. In the sixth month, first auspiciousness, *wuyin* (day 15), at dawn the king entered the Grand Chamber and assumed position. The king called out to the Provisioner Hu, saying: "Summon Su, Lord of Jin." (Lord Jin) entered the gate and stood in the middle of the court. The king personally awarded him four colts. Su bowed and touched his head to the ground, and accepting the horses then exited. Turning around he entered, bowing and touching his head to the ground. On *dinghai* (day 24), at dawn the king was in charge at the city's Attack Palace. On *gengyin* (day 27), at dawn the king entered the Grand Chamber. Supervisor of Works Yangfu entered at the right of Su, Lord of Jin. The king personally presented Su, Lord of Jin with one bucket of black-millet sweet-wine, a bow and one hundred arrows, and four horses.

Su dares to extol the Son of Heaven's illustrious and fine beneficence, herewith making these prime concordant *yang* bronze bells, with which to summon to approach the prior cultured men. May the prior cultured men be strict on high and respected below, abundantly sending down on me much good fortune. May Su for ten thousand years without bound have sons' sons and grandsons' grandsons eternally to treasure these bells.[18]

Jin, the state closest to the Zhou royal capitals Zongzhou (the western capital near present-day Xi'an) and Chengzhou, was just developing into a power in its own right, and positioned itself as a fervent supporter of the Zhou royal house. However, even with the military support of Jin, the Zhou royal army was defeated in a series of battles over the course of the next ten years. As the fortunes of his rule declined, King Xuan grew paranoid. In 785, he ordered that the ruler of the small state of Du, known as the Elder of Du, be executed, apparently because of a dream the king had had. Just before he was killed, the Elder of Du issued a prediction that others later throughout Chinese history would also repeat:

Milord wishes to kill me though I am innocent. If the dead have no consciousness, then it will end with that. But if the dead have consciousness, then within three years I will certainly cause milord to know of it.[19]

Three years later, in 782, King Xuan was out hunting when the Elder of Du appeared, and shot him in the chest with an arrow. While later Chinese literature treats this as a ghost story, it is more likely that this "Elder of Du" was the previous lord's son, who would also have been known as the Elder of Du and who had fled into exile in Jin when his father was executed. Regardless of the actual cause, King Xuan did die in this year, bringing his long reign to a close.

He was succeeded by his son, King You, the Somber King (r. 781–771), who would be the last king of the dynasty. His short reign has also provided plentiful grist for the mill of later Chinese fiction. The most famous of the stories concerns his concubine Bao Si, with whom the king became enamored. She is supposed to have been hard to please, rarely smiling. However, one day the beacon fires were lit indicating that the country was under attack; allies came rushing to defend the capital, only to find that it was a false alarm. Bao Si found this very funny, not only smiling but even laughing. The king then had the beacon fires lit repeatedly, though soon the allies grew tired of the game. When eventually the country really was under attack, none of them came, the capital was sacked and the king was killed. Of course, this is all a fairy tale, designed to blame a woman for the fall of the dynasty. Still, there appears to have been at least a kernel of truth in the story. There does seem to have been a concubine named Bao Si, for whom King You deposed his original queen, the daughter of the ruler of the state of Shen, theretofore an important ally of the Zhou kings. What is more, he also replaced the son of the queen from Shen, Yi Jiu, with the son of Bao Si, Bo Pan, as crown prince. Needless to say, this angered the ruler of Shen, who then joined with others, including the western enemies of Zhou, to overthrow King You. A recently unearthed manuscript written in the fourth century BCE, given the name *Annals* (*Xinian*) by its modern editors, narrates these events, providing some new information but also raising new questions.

> King You of Zhou took as wife a woman from Western Shen, who gave birth to King Ping (the Calm King). The king then took a girl of the Bao people; this was Bao Si, who gave birth to Bo Pan. Bao Si was beloved of the king, and the king and Bo Pan drove off King Ping, who fled to Western Shen. King You raised the army and surrounded King Ping at Western Shen, but the people of Shen would not give him up. The people of Zeng then surrendered to the Western Rong, and with them attacked King You; King You and Bo Pan were then destroyed, and Zhou came to an end. The states-lords and many governors then

installed King You's younger brother Yu Chen at Guo; this was King Hui (the Kind King) of Xie, who reigned for twenty-one years. Qiu, Lord Wen (the Cultured Lord) of Jin, then killed King Hui at Guo. For nine years Zhou was without a king, and the states-lords and many governors thereupon began not to come to court at Zhou. The Lord of Jin then met King Ping at Shao'e, and installed him in the Capital Encampment. In the third year, he then moved east, settling at Chengzhou.[20]

It is clear from this account that there was both a period of time during which there were two different kings of Zhou, King Hui, the "Kind King" (r. 770–750), the younger brother of King You, and King Ping, the "Even King" (r. 770–720), the son of the queen from Shen, and also a period of nine years during which there was no king, at least no king in the capital. The account is ambiguous about this latter point, and modern scholars have proposed different interpretations, none of which is wholly convincing. Nevertheless, it is certain that the court of King You was riven by at least two different factions, with the state of Guo supporting the king, while the state of Jin joined Shen and other states to support Yi Jiu, the son of the queen from Shen. This was perhaps the first manifestation of the wars between the states that would characterize the next five hundred years of the Zhou dynasty, traditionally termed the Eastern Zhou period, since the king had moved to the eastern capital at Chengzhou—modern Luoyang in Henan.

The Zhou dynasty persisted through another twenty-one kings after King Ping, but the period brought a progressive weakening of the Zhou king's power, to the point that he was eventually a mere figurehead. There were several more cases of intra-family fighting, as for instance between the sons of King Xi (the "Awarded King"; r. 681–677), Lang and Tui, who battled back and forth for five years, each claiming to be king, before Lang was finally conclusively installed as King Hui (the "Kind King"; r. 676–652; not to be confused with King Hui of Xie), or between the two sons of King Hui himself, Zheng and Shu Dai, who similarly each claimed to be king, calling on different allies, including in Shu Dai's case the non-Chinese mountain people living to the north of the capital region. Zheng eventually called on the state of Jin, which by this time had become the real power in north China, for support; Duke Wen (the Cultured Duke; r. 636–628) of Jin reinstated Zheng as King Xiang (the "Uplifted King"; r. 651–620) as king and killed Shu Dai. Duke Wen then subjected King Xiang to the indignity of summoning him to an audience at the Jin city Heyang. Although the official annals of the time referred to this euphemistically as "The king took an inspection tour to Heyang," everyone understood that the power now lay with the lords of the states, especially those recognized as "premier" (*ba*), as was Duke Wen of Jin. The last king to rule, King Nan (the "Blushing King"; r. 314–256), saw the capital itself divided into two separate cities, West Zhou and East Zhou (not to be confused with the Western Zhou and Eastern Zhou periods). Caught between the major powers to the north and east of him, which were the successor states to the former state of Jin, and the rising power of the west, the state of Qin, King Nan, ensconced in the city of West Zhou, tried to pit all sides against each other, to no avail. When he died in 256 BCE, the term used to describe his death was no longer the term reserved for kings, but rather the simple verb "to die," indicating that he was no longer recognized as a king; indeed, the name by which he is known to history, King Nan, is not one of the traditional posthumous names used for Zhou kings. Seven years after his death, in 249, Qin took over the city of East Zhou as well, bringing a quiet end to what would prove to be China's longest dynasty, stretching just over or under eight hundred years, depending on how one defines its beginning.

CHAPTER 5
THE BASIC ANNALS OF QIN

Although the Qin dynasty (221–207) was far and away the shortest of China's major dynasties, officially lasting only fourteen years, not only was it one of the oldest states of ancient China, but its legacy has proved to be as long lasting as that of the Zhou dynasty, which preceded it. Indeed, even the name by which China is known throughout most of the world—"China"—derives from Qin (pronounced like "chin"). Qin is supposed to have ruled with a harsh hand, one that caused the recently conquered peoples to resent it. Whatever the truth of this, it is certainly the case that the dynasty that succeeded it, the Han (202 BCE–220 CE), adopted most of the Qin administrative innovations, even while reviling the Qin as barbaric. This Han prejudice against Qin has influenced most subsequent appraisals of the dynasty. It has only been in recent years, with new archaeological discoveries revealing much about the early history of the state, long before it became the predominant power of the Warring States period, and also about the government administration after its conquest of those other states, that historians have begun to revise their views of Qin. While it is true that Qin did introduce many innovations, some of them most certainly harsh, it is also the case that Qin was deeply conservative in its cultural practices, preserving much of the Zhou dynasty legacy.

The origins of the Qin people, a people bearing the surname Ying, was one of the major debates of twentieth-century historiography, with some employing some archaeological evidence to argue that Qin came from the western Warriors (often translated as "barbarians") while others employed other archaeological evidence to argue that they came from the eastern Peoples (yet another term also often translated as "barbarians"). The common denominator of these two arguments, of course, was that Qin was somehow barbarian. *Records of the Historian*, which after all, is supposed to have been based—at least in this part—on the annals of the Qin court itself, claimed that an early Qin ancestor named Feilian was an ally of the last Shang kings, thus placing Qin in the east. This tradition recently received strong corroboration from the newly unearthed Tsinghua University manuscript *Xinian* or *Annals*, which says that Feilian joined with Luzi Sheng, the ostensible "son" of King Zhòu, also known as Di Xin (r. 1086–1046), the last king of the Shang dynasty, in his brief rebellion against the Zhou conquerors. According to the *Annals*, Feilian attempted to flee eastward into what is today the province of Shandong, probably at or near the place where the Duke of Zhou would later establish the Zhou colony of Lu; Feilian was killed there by the pursuing Zhou. The *Annals* goes on to record that the remaining Qin people were then forced to migrate to Zhuyu, identified as a mountain in present-day Gansu province, to the west of even Zhou itself. There they were supposed to provide a barrier between Zhou and its western enemies. This would seem to explain the conflicting archaeological evidence concerning Qin cultural practices: it originated in the east but long lived in the west, and so adopted practices of both areas.

More recent archaeological excavations provide material support for the *Annals* account. For instance, an early Qin settlement site has been excavated at Majiaping, Gansu, very near to Zhuyu Mountain, where the Qin people were supposed to have been transferred. Tomb-robbing at another nearby mountain, Dabuzishan in Lixian county, Gansu, alerted local archaeologists to yet another settlement site—indeed, very probably an early capital of Qin—near which there was a cemetery with tombs of two different Qin lords; these tombs contained bronze vessels bearing inscriptions indicating that they were made for "Dukes of Qin." This too has prompted a debate among historians as to which dukes of Qin they may have been, and also explained the provenance of numerous other bronze vessels with similar inscriptions that had come onto the antique market in the 1990s; they must have come from other tombs at Dabuzishan that had been robbed before the archaeologists arrived on the scene.

The most likely identifications for the two tombs excavated at Dabuzishan are Duke Zhuang (r. 821–778) and Duke Xiang (r. 777–766), whose reigns coincided with a period of increasing relations between Qin and the kings of Zhou. This was a time when the Zhou capital area was coming under attack by the western power Xianyun. The *Bamboo Annals* records that Qin Zhong, the immediate predecessor of Duke Zhuang, was commanded by King Xuan of Zhou (r. 827–782) to attack the Xianyun; however, the attack was unsuccessful, and Qin Zhong was killed. It was Duke Zhuang who took revenge for this, and consolidated Qin control over the Jing River valley of eastern Gansu and western Shaanxi. During the reign of Duke Xiang, Qin again came to the aid of the Zhou kings, though the Zhou capital itself was overrun by the Xianyun and the last king of Western Zhou, King You (r. 781–771) was killed. Qin allied for the first time with the powerful state of Jin, located northeast of the Zhou capital along the north-south stretch of the Yellow River, to protect the Zhou move to their eastern capital at Luoyang in present-day Henan.

Step by step, Qin began moving eastward, first to the area of modern Baoji, Shaanxi, and then later, in 677, to still closer to the old Zhou homeland area of the Zhouyuan, where they established a new capital called Yong. This would remain the Qin capital for more than three hundred years. It was there that another important early Qin archaeological discovery was made. In 1978, eight bells were discovered at Taigongmiao—the Temple of the Great Duke—Shaanxi, near this new capital. All eight bells bore the same inscription, the content showing that they had been cast for Duke Wu of Qin (r. 697–678), and reveals too that his wife, Wang Ji, was a daughter of the Zhou king himself. More important, the inscription suggests that the rulers of Qin were already beginning to think of themselves as the proper rulers of all China. It is worth quoting in full.

The Duke of Qin said: "Our ancestors received the Mandate of Heaven, and were awarded residence and received the territory. Valiant and radiant were Duke Wen, Duke Jing and Duke Xian, grandly advancing on high and radiantly joining august Heaven to bring under control the barbarian lands." The duke said to his consort Wang Ji: "I the small child morning and night assiduously respect my sacrifices in order to receive many blessings, to be able to enlighten my heart and harmonize the administrators and sires, and to nurture all those to my left and right. Being abundantly and truly proper I have received bright virtue to use peace and stability to bring together my territory and have begun to bring about the submission of all the barbarian peoples. I make these harmonic bells, their perfect pitch being *duan-duan* and *yong-yong*, in order to entertain the august lords and to receive great blessings, pure favor, many gifts, and a long-life of ten thousand years. May the dukes of Qin reign in position and receive the great mandate and extend it throughout the four quarters. May they be treasured in peace.[21]

In the decades after the reign of Duke Wu, Qin grew to be the predominant power in the Wei River valley of western China, the former capital region of the Zhou kings. Its growing influence brought it into contact with—and occasional conflict with—the state of Jin to its east, which was then also growing in power. Jin was based in present-day Shanxi province along the

Fen River, which like the Wei River of Shaanxi province, where Qin was now based, was one of the two major tributaries of the Yellow River. These two river valleys form one continuous geological formation, separated only by the north-south stretch of the Yellow River. The two states periodically fought for control of the fertile strip of land on the west bank of the Yellow River.

The early peak of Qin power came during the lengthy reign of Duke Mu (r. 659–621), a reign that coincided with several important developments in the eastern states, and especially in the state of Jin. First, in 642, Duke Huan of Qi, long recognized as the "premier" among the rulers of all of the states, died, setting off a succession struggle within his own state that weakened it for generations to follow. Jin was poised to assume the predominant position among the states, but it too was riven by domestic turmoil and fraternal battles. Jin lords alternately sought support from Duke Mu, and double-crossed him. In the end, Duke Mu lent his support to Chong'er, one of the Jin princes who had long been in exile. In 636, with the active support of Duke Mu of Qin, Chong'er reentered Jin, and claimed his position as ruler; he would be known posthumously as Duke Wen of Jin (r. 636–628). As long as he was alive, relations between Qin and Jin were peaceful. However, after his death in 628, the alliance between Jin and Qin dissolved, and the two states again began to attack each other. In 624, Duke Mu personally led an army into Jin territory, but in the end he was unsuccessful. This would bring to an end for more than three centuries any hopes that Qin might have had to expand toward the east. Instead, it returned its attention to the west and the south.

Duke Mu's death in 621 was commemorated by one of the most memorable poems of the *Classic of Poetry*: "The Yellow Bird." Three noblemen of the Ziju lineage of the ducal clan had promised to accompany the duke to his grave. The poem consists of three stanzas, each describing one of the three noblemen. The first stanza is representative of all three.

> *Kriâu-kriâu* calls the yellow bird, Stopping on that bush of thorns.
> Who will follow the Ripened Duke? Sudden Rester of the Ziju.
> Let it be this Sudden Rester, A special one of a hundred.
> Looking down upon his pit, Trembling, trembling is his shaking.
> That azure heaven up above, How it cuts off our finest men.
> Oh, if we could but ransom him, A hundred men would give their lives.[22]

Another tomb of another Qin duke reveals something of the wealth that the state was able to accumulate in the aftermath of Duke Mu's death. The tomb of Duke Jing (r. 577–537), in Fengxiang county, Shaanxi, just outside of the Qin capital Yong, was so large that its excavation took ten years, from 1976 until 1986. It is far and away the largest tomb anywhere in China (or all of Asia, for that matter, including the more famous tomb of the First Emperor), over 300 meters long and covering an area of 5334 square meters. Although the tomb chamber itself had long since been emptied by tomb robbers (archaeologists counted 247 different shafts dug by tomb-robbers over the centuries), a ledge just above the tomb chamber revealed the remains of 166 people who were killed to accompany the duke in death, and the tomb fill contained remains of another twenty persons, an eerie reminder of the three noblemen who accompanied Duke Mu to his grave just about one hundred years earlier.

During these three centuries, Qin seems to have been content in what was now its homeland of the Wei River valley, a fertile agricultural zone protected on all side by mountain barriers. In the fifth and early fourth centuries BCE, especially during the reign of Duke Xian (r. 385–362), Qin began to expand again, but this time to the south. In 387, it defeated the southwestern state of Shu for control of the Qinling Mountains and the headwaters of the Han River. The Qinling Mountains were a natural barrier between the Wei River valley that was the center of Qin and the vast Chengdu plain to the west in present-day Sichuan, which Shu had long controlled, and the Han River Valley to the east, which led to the heartland of the major southern state of Chu. By the middle of the century, Qin's expansion down the Han River brought it into frequent contact—and frequent conflict with Chu. From this time on, Chu would be one of two great adversaries of Qin.

In the middle of the fourth century, Qin also moved its capital from near present-day Baoji, Shaanxi further east to Xianyang, near present-day Xi'an. This move of the capital brought about an important demographic shift among the Qin people: whereas most tombs from about 700 until this time have been excavated in the western part of present-day Shaanxi province, beginning in the middle of the fourth century almost all tombs are found in the vicinity of the new capital. This eastward shift of the capital also announced Qin's renewed urge to expand toward the east and to confront the other states there. This was an initiative spearheaded by Gongsun Yang, better known as Wei Yang or Shang Yang (d. 338). Shang Yang was a foreigner, who traveled to Qin from his native Wei, eventually becoming chancellor of state under Duke Xiao (r. 361–338). He is generally credited with instituting a series of administrative reforms that strengthened the Qin government. These reforms took agriculture and warfare as the foundation of the Qin state. They were codified in a series of laws that were ruthlessly enforced. Among these laws was the provision that the law would extend equally to all members of society, regardless of their social status, doing away with the age-old dispensation from punishment for members of the nobility. This included even the crown-prince, the future Lord Huiwen (r. 337/324–311). On the other hand, in order to encourage people to join the army Shang Yang also devised a system of ranks that could be won through military accomplishments. Based on the ranks that they won, soldiers were given fields of a specific size to farm. Sons were to inherit lower ranks than their fathers, giving them an incentive to join the army as well and to win their own ranks. There was another important advantage to these ranks: people convicted of crimes could exchange their ranks for reduced sentences, including avoiding mutilating punishments.

The need to reward soldiers with fields led Qin to redistribute the land of the entire realm. To deal with this need, Qin developed a sophisticated administrative structure to keep track of its people, who were the most important assets to the state. The state kept detailed records for each household, listing the name, age, and rank of each member. They also organized the households into five-family units that were responsible for each other's obligations. Male members of the household had to register for state service at the age of eighteen, and one man from each household was required to work for the state for one month each year on such state projects as digging ditches, canals, and irrigation works, and building roads, dikes, and walls. With this labor, the state embarked on a massive infrastructure project, creating thirty-one counties, linked by a consolidated road system. The state also standardized the size of fields, which were marked off into long rectangles by wider and narrower footpaths, making it easy to calculate the taxes owed for each field. It is interesting that the results of these infrastructure projects, and especially the land distribution markers, are still visible in satellite images of the area today.

As successful as Shang Yang's reforms were, they also created many enemies for him, especially among the nobility. When his patron Duke Xiao died in 338, Duke Huiwen accused Shang Yang of conspiring to rebel against him, and ordered that he and his entire family be executed. Shang Yang's execution was by the particularly grisly "dismemberment by chariot," in which his limbs and neck were tied to five separate chariots, all pulling in different directions. Shang Yang is credited with having written the book *The Book of the Lord Shang*, which provides a philosophical rationale for his administrative reforms and especially for his notion of government by laws.

This book is generally regarded as the first expression of the system of thought that would come to be known as Legalism. Although Legalism was later reviled by Confucians, it was adapted by most governments throughout Chinese history.

Lord Huiwen's succession was celebrated by the states of Chu and Shu, among others, as well as by the Zhou king. Taking advantage of the wealth and stability that Shang Yang's administrative reforms had brought about, Lord Huiwen initiated a series of military campaigns directed against the state of Wei, one of the states into which the former great state of Jin had divided. In 329, Qin finally retook the areas along the Yellow River that Qin and Jin had fought over more than three hundred years earlier. Then, in 324, following a fashion that rulers of the other states had adopted in the preceding decades, Huiwen declared himself king of Qin. In the following decade, Qin won a series of decisive battles, against all three of the successor states of the Jin, as well as against the far northern states of Yan and Qi. More important, in 316, Qin would decisively defeat Shu for control of the Chengdu Plain. This would prove to be the granary that would feed the armies that carried the Qin campaigns over the course of the following century, campaigns that eventually culminated in the unified empire. Four years later, in 312, Qin attacked down the Han River, winning a large amount of land there, which they turned into yet another new Qin administrative district: the Central Han County.

King Huiwen's son King Wu of Qin (r. 310–307) reigned for only four years. He was succeeded in turn by the young King Zhaoxiang (r. 306–251). Although his succession was contested by others, and the early years of his reign saw several notable military setbacks, by the 290s he appointed the general Bai Qi (d. 257), originally a nobleman from Chu, to lead the Qin armies. In the more than thirty years that Bai Qi led the army, he is said to have captured more than seventy cities and to have killed more than a million enemy soldiers, without ever suffering a single defeat. Among his more notable victories was the defeat and occupation of the great state of Chu in 278. Added to its earlier defeat and occupation of Shu, this brought almost the entire Yangzi River valley, including its largest tributary the Han River, under the control of Qin. His final victory came in 260. After months of fierce fighting with the state of Zhao, during which the Qin army was on the brink of starvation, King Zhaoxiang finally ordered the aged Bai Qi to take personal control of the army. Bai Qi feigned a retreat, withdrawing his army to a strongly fortified position and drawing the Zhao army into a trap. He sent his cavalry around the Zhao army cutting it off from its supply train.

The Zhao army dug in at a place called Changping, in the southern part of present-day Shanxi province. The Qin army, reinforced by the local inhabitants who were promised by King Zhaoxiang that they would all be rewarded by one degree of rank, surrounded them. After forty-six days, the Zhao army numbering 200,000 men finally surrendered. Bai Qi ordered all but 246 young boys to be buried alive. Sparing the boys was not a humanitarian gesture, but rather was intended for them to return to the Zhao capital and spread the word of how ferocious the Qin army was. In 1995, local archaeologists in Changping county, Shanxi, uncovered a trench in which they found numerous skeletons, perhaps some of the Zhao soldiers who had been buried alive.

Two years later, Bai Qi was sent again to attack the Zhao capital. However, in the meantime Zhao had rebuilt its army and repaired its relations with other states, who decided to resist the Qin advance. When Bai Qi objected to King Zhaoxiang that the Zhao capital was impregnable, Zhaoxiang sent his premier, Fan Ju (d. 255), to order him to attack nonetheless. Bai Qi feigned illness and refused to do so. With this, the king replaced him, demoted him to the rank of a common soldier, and ordered him to man the defense lines on Qin's western border. When the renewed Qin attack on the Zhao capital failed, the king sent Bai Qi a sword and ordered him to commit suicide. Bai Qi is said to have exclaimed that his only crime was to have killed the defenseless Zhao soldiers at the battle of Changping; with that he slit his own throat and died.

After the lengthy reign of King Zhaoxiang, the reigns of the next two Qin kings, King Xiaowen (r. 250) and King Zhuangxiang (r. 249–247), were especially short. Prior to his succession, King Zhuangxiang, whose personal name was Ying Yiren, had been held as a hostage in the state of Zhao, a result of Qin's defeat by Zhao ten years earlier. There he came to know a wealthy merchant named Lü Buwei (291–235), who used bribes to have him selected as the heir apparent. When Zhuangxiang became king, he appointed Lü Buwei as his chancellor, in charge of the government. When the king then died in the fourth year of his reign, he was succeeded by his teenage son, Ying Zheng (b. 259; r. 246–221 as king of Qin, then 221–210 as Qin Shi Huangdi, the First Emperor). Lü Buwei continued as chancellor, and even as regent for the young boy. Throughout Chinese history there have been insinuations that Lü Buwei was actually Ying Zheng's biological father, since his mother had been a consort of Lü Buwei before marrying King Zhuangxiang; this was probably a rumor started in the following Han dynasty to disparage both of these kings.

In 238, while Lü Buwei was still chancellor, he became involved in the first threat against King Zheng. Fearful that King Zheng would learn that his mother, Queen Dowager Zhao, had been his consort prior to being married to King Zhuangxiang, Lü Buwei plotted through a series of complicated disguises to have her replaced by a man. This man, Lao Ai, subsequently became her lover, and the two had two sons of their own. In 238, they attempted to overthrow King Zheng in an attempt to name one of their own sons to be king. King Zheng foiled the plot and had Lao Ai torn apart by the chariots, the same method of execution that had been carried out one hundred years earlier against Shang Yang. Lü Buwei was granted the honor of committing suicide by drinking poison, which he did in 235, thus ending one of the more curious chapters in China's long history of court intrigue.

Lü Buwei was replaced as chancellor by Li Si (*c.* 280–208). Li Si had been a student of the great Confucian philosopher Xunzi (*c.* 316–217), but turned his back on Confucian moralism and espoused the Legalist doctrines of Shang Yang, which were still popular in Qin. He would remain chancellor for twenty-seven years, throughout the remainder of Ying Zheng's reign both as king of Qin and as First Emperor, and even into the reign of the Second Emperor (r. 209–207). He would play a major role in creating the Qin empire. The campaigns that led to the creation of that empire began in 230. The first of the six remaining states to fall was the neighboring state of Han, followed two years later by its nemesis of thirty years earlier—and the state where Ying Zheng had been born—Zhao. Over the next seven years, the remaining states would fall one by one: first Yan, then Wei, then Chu, and finally, in 221 the northeastern state of Qi. For the first time since the end of the Western Zhou dynasty in 771—and really for the first time ever—almost all of China was united under a single ruler. Ying Zheng proclaimed a new title for himself: Shi Huangdi, the First Emperor, and had an ancient jade carved with a text written by Li Si: "Received the Mandate from Heaven, May He Be Long-lived and Eternally Flourishing." This seal of authority would be passed from ruler to ruler and from dynasty to dynasty for over a thousand years before finally being lost in the tenth century CE.

Having conquered their enemies in the east, Qin now needed to devise a means to govern them. Some advisors argued that Qin should follow the model of the earlier Zhou dynasty, appointing relatives of the royal family to rule them as quasi-colonies. But the First Emperor rejected this model, extending instead the administrative structure that Qin had used in its own state since the time of Shang Yang, organizing the empire into thirty-six "commanderies," more or less the equivalent of modern provinces. Under these, there were counties, townships and neighborhoods. Each of these was responsible for reporting to the level above it, with the commanderies reporting directly to the capital. Recent archaeological discoveries at the small village of Liye in western Hunan province show that even the periphery of the Qin empire was in constant communication with levels above it, and those levels transmitted to it orders from the capital. This communication was facilitated by the infrastructure projects Qin had undertaken in the preceding century, the pace of construction accelerating still further with the unification. Other reforms were also intended to unite the country. These included standardizing the axle-widths of carts (akin to standardizing the gauge of railroad tracks in more recent history), standardizing units of weights and measure, and standardizing as well the currency. Another standardization may have been the most important: the standardization of the script. Prior to the Qin unification, each of the independent states had developed its own way of writing. With unification, and with the centralized administration of the government, all reports were required to be written in the same script, that which had been in use in Qin. While many of the Qin reforms were very forward looking, the reform of the script was actually quite conservative: the script used in Qin evolved directly from that of the Zhou royal house some five hundred years before.

These reforms were all constructive, and would be looked back upon favorably by later Chinese historians. Two other reforms, however, would provoke unending criticism. In 213, acting upon a memorial written by Li Si designed to unify thought as well, the First Emperor decreed that most books were to be burned. Excluded from this prohibition were "practical books"—those concerning such topics as the annals of the state of Qin, as well as astrology, agriculture, divination, and medicine. The classical literature, especially the *Poetry* and *Scriptures*, by then associated with Confucian teaching, were especially prohibited. In the following year, 460 of the officials at court, all of them having attained their position on the basis of their traditional education, are said to have been buried alive. Li Si certainly wrote the memorial recommending the abolition of books, but it is now much debated just how effective it really was. It is also doubtful that the scholars at court were buried alive, it being likely that this charge was invented during the subsequent Han dynasty as a way of justifying the overthrowal of the Qin.

In 210, the First Emperor, by then almost sixty years old, undertook his fifth tour of the eastern portions of his empire. In September of that year, he became ill and died in Pingyuan county in the northwestern part of

Shandong province. Li Si, who was traveling with the emperor, determined to keep the death secret from all but a handful of people including Ying Huhai, a young son of the First Emperor, and Zhao Gao (d. 207), allegedly the tutor of Huhai. While returning the corpse to the capital at Xianyang, a two-month wagon journey to the west, Li Si is said to have forged an order from the First Emperor naming the young son Huhai to be his successor, apparently because he would be easy to control. Fearful that the plot would be discovered, the forged order also commanded the First Emperor's eldest son and presumptive heir, Fusu, to commit suicide. Also ordered to commit suicide was Meng Tian, who, as commander-in-chief of the Qin army, was a rival power. Fusu and Meng Tian did as they were ordered, and Huhai became the Second Emperor. Before long Zhao Gao moved against Li Si, accusing him of plotting against the Second Emperor. In 208, Li Si was sentenced to die by the "Five Punishments," not to be confused with death by Five Chariots; this form of execution entailed each of the usual forms of mutilation: first cutting off the nose, then a hand, then a foot, then castration, and finally being cut in half at the waist. In the next year, Zhao Gao turned on the Second Emperor himself, assassinating him and installing a young boy, Ying Ziying, ostensibly Huhai's son, as emperor. On the day that Ziying was to be installed as the third emperor of Qin, Ziying ordered that Zhao Gao be executed as well. Ziying did become emperor, and reigned for forty-six days, before surrendering the city of Xianyang in January of 206 BCE to Liu Bang (256–195), the eventual founding emperor of the Han dynasty (r. 202–195). Later that year, when Xiang Yu (c. 232–202), then an ally but soon to become an adversary of Liu Bang, arrived at Xianyang, he ordered that Ziying be executed along with all male members of the imperial family. This brought an ignominious end to the short-lived Qin dynasty.

The Qin dynasty and especially the First Emperor have been criticized throughout most of Chinese history for their harsh policies. Their policies were harsh, to be sure, but they were not particularly extraordinary for their day, and from their own perspective were designed to bring about peace and security for the state and its people. In retrospect, much of the criticism, coming from the succeeding Han dynasty, was self-interested, intended to justify its own rule. Virtually unacknowledged at the time was to just what extent Han administration was indebted to the Qin reforms. A telling anecdote illustrates the debt: when the Qin capital Xianyang was being pillaged at the end of the Qin dynasty, most of the pillagers sought the many treasures there. However, one of the advisers to Liu Bang took Qin's administrative documents, census records, and maps, knowing that these were the real treasures of government. To the extent that the administration of the Qin government became the model for not just the Han dynasty, but for most succeeding dynasties and governments down to the present day, it is understandable that the name for China throughout most of the world derives from Qin.

MAPS AND TABLES

.

CHAPTER 6
TOPOGRAPHICAL MAP OF CHINA

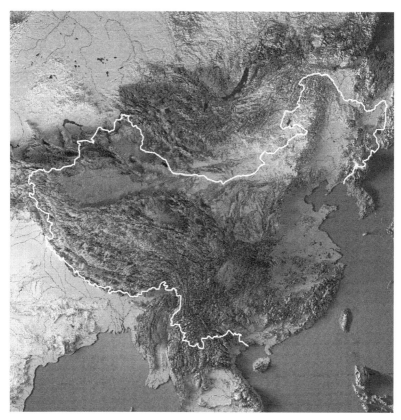

Map 6.1 Topographical map of China.

CHAPTER 7
THE NINE REGIONS OF YU THE GREAT

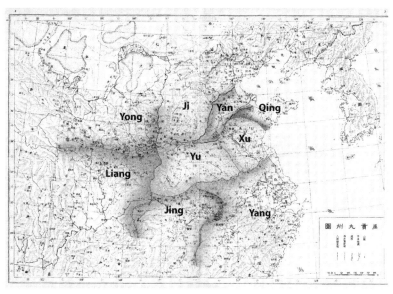

Map 7.1 The nine regions of Yu the Great.

辛
未

CHAPTER 8
SHANG POLITICAL MAPS OF ANCIENT CHINA

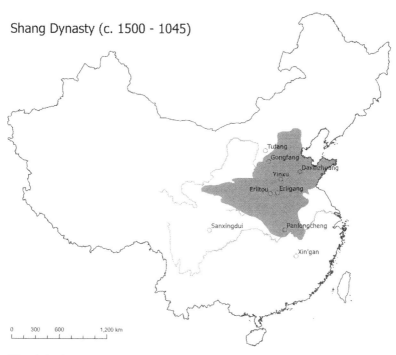

Map 8.1 Shang political map.

Western Zhou Dynasty (1045 - 771)

Map 8.2 Western Zhou political map.

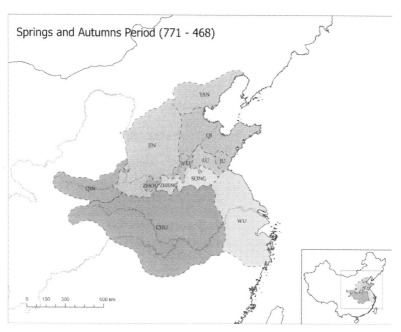

Map 8.3 Springs and Autumns period political map.

Maps and Tables

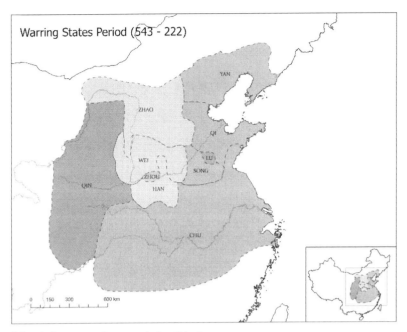

Map 8.4 Warring States period political map.

CHAPTER 9
ARCHAEOLOGICAL SITES OF
ANCIENT CHINA

Map 9.1 Map of archaeological sites of ancient China.

癸
酉

CHAPTER 10
GENEALOGIES AND CHRONOLOGIES OF RULERS OF XIA, SHANG, AND ZHOU

Xia	Shang	Zhou
Yu	Tang	Western Zhou
Qi	Wai Bing	Wen (1099/1056–1050)
Tai Kang	Zhong Ren	Wu (1049/1045–1043)
Zhong Kang	Tai Jia	Cheng (1042/1035–1006)
Xiang	Wo Ding	Kang (1005–978)
Shao Kang	Tai Geng	Zhao (977/975–957)
Zhu	Xiao Jia	Mu (956–918)
Huai	Yong Ji	Gong (917–900)
Mang	Tai Wu	Yih (899–873)
Xie	Zhong Ding	Xiao (c. 872–866)
Bu Jiang	Wai Ren	Yi (865–858)
Jiong	Hedan Jia	Li 857/853–842/828
Jin	Zu Yi	Gonghe (841–828)
Kong Jia	Zu Xin	Xuan (827–782)
Gao	Wo Jia	You (781–771)
Fa	Zu Ding	Eastern Zhou
Jie	Nan Geng	Ping (770–720)
	Yang Jia	Huan (719–697)
	Pan Geng	Zhuang (696–682)

Maps and Tables

Xia	Shang	Zhou
	Xiao Xin	Xi (681–677)
	Xiao Yi	Hui (676–652)
	Wu Ding (c. 1225–1189)	Xiang (651–619)
	Zu Geng (c. 1188–1178)	Qing (618–613)
	Zu Jia (c. 1177–1158)	Kuang (612–607)
	Lin Xin (c. 1157–1149)	Ding (606–586)
	Kang Ding (c. 1148–1132)	Jian (585–572)
	Wu Yi (c. 1131–1117)	Ling (571–545)
	Wen Ding (c. 1116–1106)	Jing (544–520)
	Di Yi (1105–1087)	Jing (519–476)
	Di Xin (1086–1045)	Yuan (475–469)
		Zhending (468–441)
		Kao (440–426)
		Weilie (425–402)
		An (401–376)
		Lie (375–369)
		Xian (368–321)
		Shenjing (320–315)
		Nan (314–256)
		Lord of East Zhou (255–249)

CHAPTER 11
CHRONOLOGIES OF RULERS OF MAJOR STATES OF THE SPRINGS AND AUTUMNS PERIOD

(L.= Lord [*Hou*]; D.=Duke [*Gong*]; K.=King [*Wang*])

Lu	Qi	Jin	Qin	Chu	Zheng	Yan	Wu
D. Xiao	D. Zhuang	L. Wen	D. Xiang	Ruo Ao	D. Huan	L. Qing	
796–769	794–791	780–746	777–766	790–764	806–771	790–767	
D. Hui	D. Xi	L. Zhao	D. Wen	Xiao Ao	D. Wu	L. Ai	
768–723	790–698	745–740	765–716	763–758	770–744	766–765	
D. Yin	D. Xiang	L. Xiao	D. Ning	Fen Mao	D. Zhuang	L. Zheng	
722–712	697–686	739–724	715–704	757–741	743–701	764–729	
D. Huan	D. Huan	L. E	D. Chu	K. Wu	D. Li	L. Mu	
711–694	685–643	723–718	703–698	740–690	700–697	728–711	
D. Zhuang	D. Xiao	L. Ai	D. Wu	K. Wen	D. Zhao	L. Xuan	
693–662	642–633	717–710	697–678	689–677	696–695	710–698	
D. Min	D. Zhao	Xiaozi	D. De	Du Ao	Zi Wei	L. Huan	
661–660	632–613	709–707	677–676	676–672	694	697–691	
D. Xi	D. Yi	L. Min	D. Xuan	K. Cheng	Zi Yi	D. Zhuang	
659–627	612–609	706–679	675–664	671–626	693–680	690–658	
D. Wen	D. Hui	D. Wu	D. Cheng	K. Mu	D. Li	D. Xiang	
626–609	608–599	678–677	663–660	625–614	679–673	657–618	
D. Xuan	D. Qing	D. Xian	D. Mu	K. Zhuang	D. Wen	D. Huan	Shou Meng
608–591	598–582	676–651	659–621	613–591	672–628	617–602	585–561

Maps and Tables

Lu	Qi	Jin	Qin	Chu	Zheng	Yan	Wu
D. Cheng 590–573	D. Ling 581–554	D. Hui 650–637	D. Kang 620–609	K. Gong 590–560	D. Mu 627–606	D. Xuan 601–587	Zhu Fan 560–548
D. Xiang 572–542	D. Zhuang 553–548	D. Wen 636–628	D. Gong 608–604	K. Kang 559–545	D. Ling 605	D. Zhao 586–574	Yu Ji 547–544
D. Zhao 541–510	D. Jing 547–490	D. Xiang 627–621	D. Huan 603–577	Jia Ao 544–541	D. Xiang 604–587	D. Wu 573–555	Yu Mei 543–527
D. Ding 509–495	Yan Ruzi 489	D. Ling 620–607	D. Jing 576–537	K. Ling 540–529	D. Dao 586–585	D. Wen 544–549	Liao 526–515
D. Ai 494–477	D. Dao 488–485	D. Cheng 606–600	D. Ai 536–501	K. Ping 528–516	D. Cheng 584–571	D. Yi 548–545	He Lü 514–496
	D. Jian 484–481	D. Jing 599–581	D. Hui 500–491	K. Zhao 515–489	D. Xi 570–565	D. Dao 535–529	Fu Chai 495–477
	D. Ping 480–456	D. Li 580–573	D. Dao 490–477	K. Hui 488–432	D. Jian 654–530	D. Gong 528–524	
		D. Dao 572–558			D. Ding 529–514	D. Ping 523–505	
		D. Ping 557–532			D. Xian 513–501	D. Jian 504–493	
		D. Zhao 531–526			D. Sheng 500–477	D. Xian 492–465	
		D. Qing 525–512					
		D. Ding 511–475					

CHAPTER 12
CHRONOLOGIES OF RULERS OF MAJOR STATES OF THE WARRING STATES PERIOD

(L.= Lord [*Hou*]; D.=Duke [*Gong*]; K.=King [*Wang*])

Qin	Jin	Wei	Han	Zhao	Chu	Jiang Qi	Yan
D. Dao	D. Ding			Xiangzi	K. Hui	D. Ping	D. Xiao
490–477	511–475			475–425	488–432	481–456	497–455
D. Ligong	D. Chu			Huanzi	K. Jian	D. Xuan	D. Cheng
476–443	474–458/52	L. Wen	L. Wu	424	431–408	455–405	454–439
D. Zao	D. Jing	445–396	424–409	L. Xian	K. Sheng	D. Kang	D. Min
442–429	451–434	L. Wu	L. Jing	423–409	407–402	404–379	438–415
D. Huai	D. You	395–370	408–400	L. Lie	K. Dao	_____	D. Jian
428–425	433–416	L. Hui	L. Lie	408–387	401–381	Tian Qi	414–370
D. Ling	D. Lie	369/335	389–387	L. Jing	K. Su	Daozi	D. Huan
424–415	415–389	K. Hui	L. Wen	386–375	380–370	410–405	369–362
D. Jian	D. Huan	334–319	386–377	L. Cheng	K. Xuan	L. He	D. Wen
414–400	388–369	K. Xiang	L. Ai	374–350	369–340	404–384	361–337
D. Hui		318–296	376–374	L. Su	K. Wei	L. Yan	K. Yi
399–387		K. Zhao	L. Yi	349–326	339–329	383–375	336–321
Chuzi		295–277	374–363	K. Wuling	K. Huai	D. Huan	K. Kuai
386–385		K. Anxi	L. Zhao	325–299	329–299	374–357	320–312
D. Xian		276–243	362–333	K. Huiwen	K. Qingxiang	L. Wei	K. Zhao
384–362				298–266	298–263	356–335	311–279

Maps and Tables

Qin	Jin	Wei	Han	Zhao	Chu	Jiang Qi	Yan
D. Xiao		K. Jingmin	K. Xuanhui	K. Xiaocheng	K. Xiaolie	K. Wei	K. Hui
361–338		242–228	332–312	265–245	262–238	334–320	278–272
K. Huiwen		Wang Jia	K. Xiang	K. Daoxiang	K. You	K. Xuan	K. Wuxiao
337/324–311		227–225	311–296	244–236	237–228	319–301	271–258
K. Wu			K. Xi	Wang Qian	Wang Fuchu	K. Min	K. Xiao
310–307			291–273	235–228	227–223	300–284	257–255
K. Zhao			K. Huanhui	Daiwang Jia		K. Xiang	Wang Xi
306–251			272–239	227–222		283–265	254–222
K. Zhuangxiang			Wang An			Wang Jian	
249–247			238–230			264–221	
K. Zheng							
246/221–210							

CHAPTER 13
HISTORICALLY IMPORTANT NON-RULERS IN ANCIENT CHINA

2000–1500	Gao Yao (2)	Yi Yin (2, **36**)					
1500–1100	Consort Hao (3, 17, **37**)	Fu Yue (**36**)					
1100–1000	Feilian (5)	Luzi Sheng (5, 24, **38**)	Duke of Zhou (4, 15, 19, 24, 34, 38)	Grand Duke Wang (4, 26)	Grand Protector (24, 25, 38)	Feng (19)	Jizi (34, **38**)
1000–900	Nangong Kuo (32)	Yu (18, 35)	Duke of Zhai (**39**)	Lu, Elder of Jing (4, 19, **40**)	Qiu Wei (4, 19, 40)	Rui Liangfu (4)	
900–800	Duo You (4, 17)	Yin Jifu (**41**)					
800–700	Bao Si (4, **42**)						
700–600	Guan Zhong (18, 26, 31)	Li Ji (27, **43**)	Zhao Dun (18, 29, 30)				
600–550	Zi Chan (14, 18, 19, 24, **46**, 47	Shu Xiang (18, 19, 46)	Ding Jiang (**44**)	Maestro Kuang (**45**)	Mu Jiang (**43**)	Shusun Qiaoru (43)	

Maps and Tables

550–500	Laozi (**51**)	Confucius (14, 16, 20, 24, 36, **48**, 49, 50, 51)	Wu Zixu (31, 33, 47)	Sun Wu (17, 18, 28, 47, **52**)	Yan Hui (**49**)	Zi Lu (**49**)		
500–450	Fan Shi (33)	Xi Shi (33)	Zhibo (27, 29)	Zi Gong (**49**)	Zi Xia (28, **49**)	Zengzi (**49**)	Wu Qi (28, 53)	
450–400	Li Kui (18, 19, 28, 30)							
400–350	Shang Yang (5, 18, 19, 28, **53**, 58)	Shen Buhai (18, 30, 58)						
350–300	Mencius (15, 20, 26, 28, 36, **50**, 51)	Zhang Yi (31)	Zhuangzi (**51**)	Bian Que (**55**)	Sun Bin (**52**)	Zi Zhi (25, 26, 29, 36)	Shao Tuo (**54**)	Qu Yuan (**56**)
300–250	Xunzi (16, 20, **50**, 58)	Bai Qi (5, 29)	Song Yu (**56**)					
250–200	Lü Buwei (5, 29)	Han Feizi (30, 50, **58**)	Li Si (5, 18, 30, 50, 57, **58**, 59)	Xi (Happy) (19, **57**)	Jing Ke (**25**)	Chen She (**59**)	Zhao Gao (58, 59)	

(Chapters in which they are mentioned are given in parentheses, biographies in bold. Some placements are only chronologically approximate. This listing is restricted just to figures mentioned in this book, for which it can serve as a sort of index.)

ESSAYS

CHAPTER 14
ESSAY ON THE HEAVENS

The stars shined brighter in antiquity. Even if this were not actually the case, it was certainly true perceptually. Once the sun went down, without ambient light to compete with their brightness or pollution in the skies to filter it, the stars were the entertainment for the night. Just as modern movie stars fill their fans with awe, even more so—as far as we call tell—the nightly shows of the heavenly stars inspired awe in their ancient observers. Those observers saw patterns in the stars, which from an early period gave the Chinese term for "astronomy": *tianwen* "heavenly patterns."

Archaeologists in China suggest that they have uncovered artifactual evidence of one of the most important of these patterns from a tomb of the fourth millennium BCE. Tomb M45, excavated in 1987 at Puyang, Henan, appears to show the deceased flanked by cowrie shells arranged in the shapes of a dragon and a tiger.[1] In later Chinese astronomy, these two forms were seen high in the sky, to the east and west respectively. The dragon in particular is understood to be a representation of a group of stars stretching from the two stars Spica α and ζ, through eight stars the curling shape of which suggested to observers in the West a scorpion (and thus the constellation Scorpio). Observers in ancient China saw all of these stars as a single constellation, which they named "Dragon" (*Long*), Spica α and ζ being identified as its two "Horns" (*Jiao*) and the eight stars of Scorpio being its "Tail" (*Wei*), with intervening stars making up the "Neck" (*Gang*) and the "Heart" (*Xin*): ⟨glyph⟩, which the oracle-bone form of the character for dragon, ⟨glyph⟩, matches very well.

The ancient observers of the heavenly patterns saw too that the apparent motion of the stars was not at all random, but rather recurred predictably night in and night out, year in and year out. When correlated with events on the ground, these appearances gave rise to the calendar—and to the expectation even in the depths of winter that life would continue along with the constancy of the sky. Although in winter the Dragon would not be visible at all in the night sky, star gazers knew that at the beginning of February its Horns would appear again in the eastern sky at dusk; that by mid-summer the entirety of that constellation would be arrayed across the southern sky; and that in the autumn it would again sink, head first, below the western horizon. On earth, plants, trees and even many animals would correspond with the movements of the Dragon: coming out in spring, coming to full flower in summer, being ready for harvest in autumn, and hibernating in the winter.

What purports to be the oldest statement concerning astronomy in the Chinese literary tradition is found in the "Canon of Yao" chapter of the *Exalted Scriptures*. In it, the legendary ruler Yao commanded two brothers, or perhaps two clans, the Xi and He, to "calculate and depict the sun and the moon, the stars and planets, and respectfully allot to the people the seasons." After this, according to this chapter, Yao appointed members of the two clans to reside in the east, south, west, and north, and to determine the correct times of the solstices and equinoxes. It goes on that once the spring solstice is determined, "the folk divide up and the birds and beasts mate and breed," while at the autumn solstice "the folk are calm and the birds and the beasts grow new feathers and fur." This correlation between the stars and the seasons would continue ever after to be a defining feature of Chinese astronomy.

The correlation between the stars and the seasons would give rise to a genre of literature known in the West as "stars and seasons" texts; these attest to an early environmental consciousness. One of the earliest such manuals is in a chapter entitled "The Four Seasons" in the *Guanzi*, one of the most important early works of political philosophy. It recounts the specific activities appropriate to each season. The text begins by noting: "Commands have their seasons; if there were no seasons, then it would be necessary to observe and follow whence the heavens come, but with the five vastnesses and six murkinesses, who could know it?" However, thanks to the sages of the past, the seasonal commands had already been catalogued and been made available in this text. The commands for spring are as follows.

> The eastern quadrant is designated to the stars; its season is spring; its breath is the wind. The wind generates wood and bone. Its virtues are joy and growth which are emitted in moderation. Make seasonal its activities and commands: repair and clean the places of the spirits, and respectfully pray that decay be blocked; venerate the upright yang, put in order the dikes, hoe and plant the fields, erect bridges, repair canals,

roof the houses and fix the plumbing; resolve grievances and pardon the guilty, bringing the four quarters into communication. Then the soft breezes and sweet rains will come, the hundred families will be long-lived, and the hundred insects will be abundant. This is called the virtue of the stars. The stars control the emission of the winds.

This is why if in spring you enact the governances of winter then there will be exhaustion; if you enact the governances of autumn, then there will be frost; if you enact the governances of summer, then there will be desires. This is why in the third month of spring, on the *jia* and *yi* days, you issue the five governances, the first of which is caring for youths and orphans and releasing the guilty; the second of which is bestowing ranks and rewards; the third of which is repairing canals when the ice has thawed and returning men who have absconded; the fourth of which is called levelling the precipices, repairing the boundary markers, and erecting the field rows; and the fifth of which is called not killing the young animals and not plucking flowers and cutting stems. If these five governances are timely, then the spring rains will come.[2]

This correlation between the stars and seasons, between astronomy and the calendar, was perhaps the most important practical aspect of ancient Chinese star-gazing. There was also a systematic logic in the early Chinese understanding of the night sky. Ancient Chinese texts divided the heavenly bodies into four general categories: the sun; moon; asterisms, which included what we now call "stars" (i.e., fixed asterisms) and "planets" ("moving stars"), as well as such occasional manifestations as comets; and constellations, i.e., groupings of stars. As seen from the earth, the sun appears to move vis-à-vis the stars along a fixed path, the ecliptic. This apparent motion take place over the course of a solar year, just over 365 days, with the sun moving a little less than one degree a day around the 360-degree arc of the ecliptic. In ancient Chinese astronomy, the ecliptic was divided into four regions, each of ninety degrees and each corresponding to one quadrant of the sky: the "Azure Dragon" in the east as described above; the "Red Bird" in the south; the "White Tiger" in the west; and the "Murky Warrior" in the north, which is also known as the "Black Turtle." Each one of these "spiritual animals" is composed of seven discrete constellations, known as "lunar lodges," such as the "Horns" and "Tail" of the Azure Dragon mentioned above. These twenty-eight lunar lodges correspond to the spaces that the moon traverses during its monthly rotation around the earth. It is important to note that while some of the groupings of stars correspond to the zodiacal constellations of Western astronomy, they do not do so systematically, but rather have their own unique logic. That being said, it is likely that the system derived from the twenty-eight *naksatras* of Indian astronomy, which in turn were derived from ancient Mesopotamian astronomy.

While it is possible that some of these lunar lodges are mentioned already in the classics of *Poetry* and *Changes*, suggesting that this system of twenty-eight lunar lodges was established already by the first centuries of the first millennium BCE, the earliest certain artifactual evidence of the system is seen in the ornamentation on a lacquer hamper discovered in 1977 in the tomb of Lord Yi of Zeng at Leigudun, Suixian, Henan. As in the case of the much earlier tomb at Puyang, this design prominently features the dragon and tiger to the east and west. However, between them, in a circle, is written the names of the twenty-eight lunar lodges, and in the middle of them, is a depiction of the Dipper, i.e., the Big Dipper and the North Star. The Dipper was thought to rotate through all of the other stars, pointing to the seasons and thus establishing the calendar.[3]

Somewhat later, similar depictions were used to correlate astronomical phenomena and the days and months, apparently in an attempt to foretell future events. Several examples of a "diviners' board" that was used to track the stars have been found. One such board was discovered in 1977 in a tomb at Fuyang, Anhui. It consists of two pieces: a square bottom board (representing earth), on which were written the names of the twenty-eight lunar lodges, as well as the heavenly stems and earthly branches, which were used for counting days. On top of this square board was a round disk (representing heaven). It too has the twenty-eight lunar lodges written around its perimeter, as well as the twelve months of the year. Finally, in the middle of the disk, corresponding to the top of heaven, are the seven stars of the Northern Dipper. This round disk of heaven would have been rotated on the square board of earth to point to the stars, the months and the days.[4]

The importance of the Dipper in these depictions of the stars points to a second basic feature of ancient Chinese astronomy: its circum-polar orientation around the North Star, about which the Big Dipper and all the other stars appear to revolve. So integral to Chinese notions of the night sky was the North Star that even Confucius (551–479) integrated it into his political philosophy of the ruler doing little more than setting a proper example for his subjects:

To govern through virtue can be compared to the North Star; which occupies its place while all of the stars support it.[5]

Figure 14.1 Han-dynasty wall carving depicting Tai Yi, the Great One, riding in the chariot of the Northern Dipper; from *Jin shi suo* (1821).

It is possible that Di, the Shang high god or gods, was identified with the celestial pole, and it is certain that the later high god Tai Yi or the Grand One had his heavenly home there. A Han-dynasty wall carving depicts Tai Yi riding in the chariot of the Northern Dipper (i.e., the four stars that make up the dipper proper), while all the animals and his subjects pay obeisance around him.

The stars would also come to be seen as gods, or in some cases people would become stars. One of the foundational myths of China doubtless was an attempt to explain the night sky. The myth concerns a battle between the Yellow Emperor and an adversary named Chiyou, depicted in later sources as having a metal head in the shape of a bull, a human torso, but the hindquarters of a bear. Through the course of ten years of battle, Chiyou is said to have caused a great fog to descend upon the battlefield, blinding the Yellow Emperor until he invented the "south-facing chariot," considered in China to be the invention of the compass, allowing him finally to defeat Chiyou. The "south-facing chariot" is but a mythological rationalization of the Dipper, pointing the way to the directions and, in some ways, the beginning of time. As for Chiyou, despite his loss in this battle, he was subsequently worshipped as the God of War, depicted as a comet blazing through the sky.

The story from the "Canon of Yao" of the brothers Xi and He, who were put in charge of the stars and teaching the people about the seasons, was also depicted in later texts as a battle in the sky; although the names are different, the story of brothers set apart from each other and destined never to meet is the same. The *Zuo Tradition* preserves the following story set in the year 541.

> The lord of Jin was ill, and the Elder of Zheng sent Zi Chan to Jin to pay him a visit and to ask about the illness. Shu Xiang asked him about it, saying: "As for our lord's illness, the diviners say that Substance Submerging and Terrace Nag are hexing him, but none of the scribes know them; dare I ask who these gods are?" Zi Chan said: "In antiquity, the emperor Gao Xin had two sons, the elder named Obstruction the Elder and the younger named Substance Submerging. They lived in a vast forest, but couldn't abide each other, daily seeking out shields and battle-axes with which to attack each other. The succeeding emperor (Yao) did not approve and moved Obstruction the Elder to the Mound of Shang to preside over (the constellation) Chronogram. The men of Shang have based themselves on this, and thus Chronogram is the Shang star. He moved Substance Submerging to the Great Xia (the area of the state of Jin) to preside over the star Triaster. The men of Tang have based themselves on this, in order to serve the Xia and the Shang."[6]

It is interesting to note that the two gods Obstruction the Elder and Substance Submerging are simply the constellations known in the west as Scorpio and Orion. Their banishment to the east and west respectively is but a mythic explanation of the natural fact that these two constellations never appear together in the night sky: as Scorpio arises in the east, the constellation Orion sets (or, in Chinese mythological and astronomical terminology, 'submerges') in the west. It is interesting too that their mutual antagonism, to the extent of seeking out weapons to do battle with each other, finds a counterpart in the Greek myth of the god Orion, who after doing battle with a giant scorpion plunged into the sea.

Some battles of ancient China that actually did take place on the ground were also seen to be prefigured in the sky. One very rare astronomical event, a conjunction of the five naked-eye-visible planets (Mercury, Venus, Mars, Jupiter, and Saturn), which takes place only every five hundred or so years, coincided repeatedly with the rise and fall of new dynasties. Such planetary conjunctions occurred in 1953 and 1576 BCE, just before the beginning of the Xia and Shang dynasties respectively. Finally, in 1059 BCE, another such conjunction took place, just years before Zhou overthrew the Shang dynasty. Later texts correlate it in turn with the passing of the Mandate of Heaven. This foundation of Chinese political philosophy was thought literally to have been written in the stars.

CHAPTER 15
ESSAY ON THE EARTH

The history of ancient China is inextricably connected to the geography of the East Asian landmass. The climate and landscape influenced everything from agriculture and hunting to city planning and warfare, with great diversity across the different regions of the area. One might think that the geography of China today is a good indication of what it was like in antiquity; as the great poet Du Fu (712–770) wrote upon surveying the destruction of the Tang-dynasty (618–907) capital of Chang'an after a civil war: "The nation is destroyed; the mountains and rivers remain." However, while the mountains and rivers of antiquity may remain, their appearance and their influence over the lifestyles of the people were radically different from what they are today.

One of the earliest accounts of ancient China's geography is a chapter of the *Exalted Scriptures* entitled "Tributes of Yu"; it recognizes nine distinct regions, each with its own distinctive flora and fauna and also different lifestyles, from the leather clothing worn in the north to the salt and sea products of the eastern seaboard to metal and jade from the Yangzi River delta. Although this text bears all the traits of legend, its depiction of the geographical diversity of ancient China is surely accurate. The territory of China is bordered by various seas in the east; vast steppe land to the north and northwest, much of the western steppe now desert; and high mountains in the south and southwest. The mountains to the west, the Himalayas and the Tibetan Plateau, constitute the world's highest landmass. Two of China's major river systems originate in these mountains: the Yellow River, known in ancient China simply as the River (*He*), which winds through all of north China; and the Yangzi, originally also known as the River, but with a different word (*Jiang*) that is probably of Austroasiatic origin, and then later qualified as the Long River, which runs in a more or less west-to-east line across what is today central China before emptying into the East China Sea at Shanghai. Throughout much of ancient Chinese history, the Yangzi River served as an indistinct border of the cultures that coalesced into Chinese civilization.

Essays

The *Classic of Mountains and Seas* and other texts recount a myth explaining why China's mountains rise up in the west and why the rivers flow to the east: this is said to be the result of a war between Zhurong, the god of fire, and Gong Gong, a rebel with a metal head and human torso—apparently another version of the myth of the battle between the Yellow Emperor and Chiyou that explains the correlation between the stars and the seasons. Like Chiyou, Gong Gong too was defeated. In anger, he is said to have butted his head against Incomplete Mountain, the western pillar holding up the sky; when this pillar broke, the earth tilted up and the heavens tilted down in the west, with the result that the rivers flowed down to the lower land and ultimately into the seas in the east.

In fact, at about the time that Gong Gong is supposed to have butted Incomplete Mountain —between 5000 and 3000 BCE, the seas were at their highest point following the age of the glaciers, and the shoreline, especially in north China, was much farther to the west than it is at present. Gradually, over the course of the millennia, silt carried downriver by the Yellow River filled in the coastal area. The Yellow River is so named because of the tremendous quantity of silt that it carries, giving it a muddy yellowish-brown color. The River originates in the Kunlun Mountains of western China, the current province of Qinghai, and then carves a channel through the loess soil of western China's Gansu and Ningxia provinces, loess referring to the easily eroded particulate soil of the area, before turning almost due south, forming the border between the two major provinces Shanxi, the name of which means West of the Mountains, and Shaanxi, West of the Pass. Then encountering the Qinling Mountains at the border between the present provinces of Shaanxi and Henan, the River makes a great bend to the east, beginning its flow through the North China Plain from whence it eventually empties into the eastern sea. The silt has caused the riverbed to rise over time, such that in its lower reaches it actually flows above the surrounding plains, diked on both sides to keep it within its channel. The River has often breached these dikes, not only causing devastating floods but even regularly carving out new channels, sometimes to the north and sometimes to the south of the mountainous Shandong peninsula. These floods doubtless led to the myth of the great ancient flood that was finally tamed by Yu the Great, pulling down mountains and dredging out channels.

In fact, much of China was much wetter in antiquity than it is today. Until about the thirteenth century BCE, the climate of north China was considerably warmer and moister than it became thereafter. Even then, the climate was dominated by summer monsoons, with moisture drawn in from the seas as the warm air of the central land mass rises and creates a vacuum; most of the precipitation for the entire year would fall in the summer months. In the winter, the winds reverse, blowing air—cold and dry, and laden with dust—from Inner Asia over northern China. As the world has cooled, areas of Inner Asia have become deserts. On the other hand, the dust blown over north China has formed its characteristic loess soil, which produces extremely fertile farm land.

Not only has this loess soil been eroded by the Yellow River and its numerous tributaries, but the process of erosion has also been exacerbated by the intensive agriculture practiced there since later Neolithic times. Already in the Warring States period, writers described the landscape as being denuded of vegetation, the *Mencius* describing a mountain in the area of present-day Shandong as having lost its original beauty.

> The trees on Ox Mountain were once beautiful indeed, but because it is in the outskirts of a great country axes chopped them down. Can this be considered beautiful? With this, with the breaths of the days and nights and the precipitation of the rain and dew it is not that no new shoots grow there, but it is just that the cows and sheep graze there and that is why it is all bald like this. When people see its baldness, they assume it never had forests on it, but could it be that this is the nature of the mountain?[7]

Scholars once believed that this process of deforestation was due to the climate change that had taken place over the course of the millennium or so preceding the time of Mencius (*c.* 385–303). After all, north China was once home to elephants and rhinoceroses, animals now found only much farther south. However, just as Mencius assigned responsibility for the deforestation of Ox Mountain to human activity, so too would it now seem that these animals were driven from the Yellow River valley not so much by climate change as by the effects of human settlement on their habitat. In another passage, Mencius credits the Duke of Zhou, one of the fathers of the Zhou dynasty, with driving off the wild animals: "The Duke of Zhou ... drove off the tigers and leopards, rhinoceroses and elephants, and everyone was greatly delighted."[8] The people may have been delighted, but the environment paid a heavy price.

It was not just tigers and leopards, rhinoceroses and elephants that were driven to extinction as Chinese civilization developed in the north China plain. The area once boasted a remarkable diversity of animals, with aurochs and musk-oxen, various species of tigers and bears, and smaller mammals of all sorts; with rivers and streams teeming with fish and such other aquatic animals as turtles and toads, and also salamanders; and birds of all sizes and colors. Unfortunately, throughout most of China's heartland, only the birds survive, their ability to fly putting them above the depredations of mankind.

Some indication of the number of these wild animals and their proximity to human habitation is shown by one Shang-dynasty oracle-bone inscription about the king going on a hunt; the verification—that is, the record of what really happened—states:

> Crack-making on *yiwei* (day 32): "Today the king will hunt at Guang and make a catch." He really did catch two female tigers, one auroch, twenty-one deer, two boars, one hundred and twenty-seven Sika deer, two tigers, two hares, and twenty-seven pheasants.[9]

The catch supplied the court with exotic meat to offer to the ancestors and for its own consumption. Nevertheless, these wild animals were not hunted to extinction. Rather, they became endangered as their habitat was changed. The land was repurposed for agriculture, and cattle and sheep and pigs were domesticated in great numbers. For instance, just one bone workshop excavated at Anyang, the Shang capital, contained thirty-four tons of bones; archaeologists estimate that this represents the remains of 113,000 cattle. Two other such workshops have also been found there. The gradual disappearance of the many species of deer in turn led to the decline of tigers and leopards, and all sorts of other animals of prey, including both brown bears and Asian black bears, who lost their natural source of food. It was almost certainly not the Duke of Zhou who drove them off to ensure the safety of the people.

Hunting and the domestication of cattle, sheep and pigs was just a part—and only a small part, at that—of the way human civilization changed the environment in China. The rise of agriculture played a much greater role. Well into the Neolithic period, people survived—and survived well—on what they could get from hunting and fishing, and from foraging for wild plants, only somewhat supplemented by a single annual crop of millet. By the second millennium BCE, the time of the Xia and Shang, agriculture came to provide more and more of the people's dietary needs. Not only were the native forests cut down and replaced with fruit trees, but the marshy grasslands were drained and turned into fields of grain. While these fields now reliably produced surpluses, allowing for the rise of civilization, paradoxically the people became less healthy: skeletal remains from early Neolithic villages show that the people then were taller and their teeth freer of caries than their descendants in the later Neolithic and Bronze Ages, whose diet came to be dominated by their eating of boiled grains.

The various species of millet were the most important crops, the main types being broomcorn millet and foxtail millet. Both of these bear seeds protected by hard hulls that allow them to be stored for several years, fostering a sedentary lifestyle. These millets came to be supplemented with other grains, such as wheat and rice, as well as with crops such as soybeans. Wheat seems to have been introduced to China from the West in either the third or second millennium BCE, perhaps during the time of the Shang dynasty; indeed, the word for "to come," apparently in the sense of "imported," was originally written with the pictograph for "wheat." Nevertheless, because it was originally adapted to the dry summers and wet winters of the Mediterranean region, it did not become common in China until the Han dynasty (202 BCE–220 CE), when farmers finally developed strains that would flourish in the Chinese climate.

Cattle and sheep arrived in China, also from the west, at about the same time as wheat; probably they all came on the same wave of contact through Central Asia. As noted above with respect to the bone workshops excavated at the Shang capital of Anyang, these domestic animals were soon abundantly present in the vicinity of human settlements. However, while elites certainly consumed plentiful amounts of meat of all kinds, it would seem that the common people did not. Indeed, for all of their contribution to the development of that elite culture, these and other animals (dogs and pigs had lived in synergy with humans since the early Neolithic) probably had adverse effects on most people, for instance facilitating the communication of disease between species. An "Essay on the Earth" should properly consider more than just mountains and rivers to consider the influences of those environments on the people who inhabited them; I have tried here to give some indication of these influences, with the caveat that they were exceedingly diverse and changeable over time—even over the course of the two millennia that are the focus of this book.

CHAPTER 16
ESSAY ON RITUAL

A famous statement in the *Zuo Tradition* says that "The great affairs of state are ritual and warfare." "Warfare" would seem to need no definition; it will be the subject of the next chapter. However, central as "ritual" was to early Chinese civilization, it may be a concept more or less foreign to modern readers; in any event, our modern understanding of ritual is not nearly as expansive as was that of ancient China. Ritual (*li*) of course had to do with the various activities that we normally consider as religious: in ancient China these often centered on prayers and offerings to the ancestors. These involved great expenditures of wealth, both for the production of the implements of ritual—especially the tens of thousands of bronze vessels made to hold the offerings, and also for the offerings themselves, primarily meat and grain, but also such luxury items as silk and jade. Other offerings were made to a vast array of gods and in conjunction with almost every facet of life: when constructing a building, when setting out on a journey, when afflicted with a toothache, and also both before and after battles. Indeed, the "ritual" of the great affairs of state probably concerns primarily the religious activities surrounding warfare. Nevertheless, it is not wrong to take the broadest possible view of ritual. By the end of the period under consideration in this book, the notion of ritual had expanded to encompass everything that is right and proper in civilization. The Confucian philosopher Xunzi (*c.* 316– 217) equated ritual with morality:

> One may ask what is the origin of ritual? I say: Man is born with desires, and if he desires something and doesn't get it, he'll be unable to stop from seeking it. If there are no limits or degrees to his seeking, then he'll be unable to stop from fighting for it. With fighting then there is disorder, and with disorder then there is impoverishment. The past kings hated disorder, and therefore established ritual propriety to keep them apart, and to provide for men's desires and what they seek. They made it so that desires did not impoverish things, and that things

did not extend beyond the desires, the two being held in a steady equilibrium. This is the origin of ritual.[10]

In this view, ritual is what made civilization possible.

For Xunzi, the "past kings" would refer first and foremost to Yao and Shun, prior to the time of dynastic rule. However, while most of the thinkers of the Warring States period did indeed attribute the origins of ritual to Yao and Shun, there is very little in either the historical or the archaeological record with which to trace this. Instead, it is with the inscriptions on the oracle bones and bronze vessels of the late Shang dynasty with which we can properly begin. The oracle-bone inscriptions reveal that the Shang kings—or at least the last nine of them beginning with King Wu Ding (r. *c.* 1225–1189)—performed divinations before undertaking almost any activity. This was certainly true of Wu Ding, the topics he divined about including the weather, the harvest, birth-giving of wives, illnesses of various kinds, warfare, the king's own travels, and so on. These divinations were prayers that the activity that the king proposed to undertake would be successful. Divinations made use of the plastrons of turtles (i.e., the flat underbelly of the turtle) or scapula bones of oxen (while the scapula bone in humans is the pair of thin-bladed bones in the back, in an ox it is the wide bone that runs down the two front legs, essentially the thigh-bone), presumably with the understanding that they would serve as messengers to the ancestors and the spirit world being petitioned. The bone or shell was prepared with a series of hollows. At the time of divination, a hot brand was placed into the hollow, causing a stress crack to appear on the opposite side; it was this crack that was interpreted to be the answer to the divination.

The divination itself was presented as a command to the turtle. When the Shang oracle bones were first discovered, at the turn of the nineteenth century, and for many scholars still today, these commands were understood as questions; after all, how else might one conduct a divination? And there is classical support for this view, with one definition of divination being that "it is to resolve doubts." Thus, according to this interpretation, the most common type of divination, which simply concerns the next week, should be understood as:

Divining: Will the (next) ten-day week be without misfortune?

Nevertheless, most Western scholars of oracle-bone inscriptions now argue that the commands are expressed both grammatically and conceptually as statements, and should be understood as statements of desire. According to this view of divination, the weekly inscription should be understood instead as:

Affirmed: The (next) ten-day will be without misfortune.

Rather than open-ended inquiries about future events, this would be a prayer that those events would transpire as desired. Later records of divination from throughout the Zhou dynasty have demonstrated that this view of divination is almost certainly correct. It was one of the most basic rituals entailing communication between the king—as a representative of the people—and the ancestors.

Regardless of which interpretation of divination during the Shang dynasty one might adopt, there is no question that Shang religion was primarily a family affair. Not only was divination directed toward the king's ancestors, but so too were the offerings, which divinations show were made in great profusion. With only a few exceptions, these offerings could only be made by the king or by members of the royal family. The high god of the Shang pantheon, Di on High (Shang Di), was apparently conceived of as a high ancestor, or perhaps a corporate notion of the ancestors collectively. Bronze inscriptions, which began to appear toward the end of the Shang dynasty, show that other individuals as well worshipped their own ancestors, directing sacrifices to them just as the royal family did to its ancestors.

When the Zhou conquered Shang in 1045, they introduced a new high god: Heaven (*Tian*). This may reflect a religious influence from Central Asia, but it would seem that there was also a political motivation behind it. Just as the arc of heaven covers all under it, so too was the god Heaven conceived of as covering all people, not just the royal family as in the case of Di. The Zhou king soon came to be called the Son of Heaven (*Tianzi*). Although King Wen, the "Cultured King" (r. 1099/1056–1050), had died before the Zhou conquest, he was regarded as the royal family's high ancestor. As subsequent kings died one after the other, they were installed in an ever-expanding ancestral temple, to the left and right in alternating generations. Both the earliest poems in the *Classic of Poetry* and bronze inscriptions from the period show this ancestral temple to have been the focal point of much of Zhou life— both religious and political. One simple hymn, "It is the Command of Heaven," shows well the relationship between Heaven and King Wen.

> It is the command of Heaven; Oh so stately, never ending.
> *Wuhu!* Illustrious, Is the purity of the Cultured King's virtue.
> Enter and shower upon us, That we may receive it.
> Grandly favor us, oh Cultured King, May your grandchildren make it
>   strong.[11]

Figure 16.1 Altar set from early Western Zhou dynasty; Metropolitan Museum of New York 24.72.1–14.

At the beginning of the Western Zhou period, the royal family, as indeed other families as well, was still a rather close-knit unit, with a limited number of members living in the capital. Bronze vessels from that time suggest that the focus of the temple was a small altar, on which was placed all of the vessels—primarily wine vessels—used in the sacrifice. One example of such an altar is housed in the Metropolitan Museum of New York; another was unearthed recently at Shigushan, near the city of Baoji, Shaanxi.

It is likely that all the male members of the family would have gathered together around this altar to celebrate the offering jointly. An interesting insight has been suggested by Jessica Rawson, former keeper of the British Museum in London: the extraordinarily detailed ornamentation on early Western Zhou bronzes reveal more and more the closer one inspects them. This would have had the effect of drawing the concelebrants of these offerings to gather around the altar. Another hymn from the *Classic of Poetry* describes the scene, as they sung in unison; it is entitled "We Offer."

We offer, we sacrifice, They are sheep, they are cows.
May it be that heaven accepts them.
It is proper that we model the Cultured King's statutes,
Daily making tranquil the four quarters.
And so the blessed Cultured King, Has now received and enjoyed
    them.

May we from morning until night
Stand in awe of Heaven's might, And protect it here and now.[12]

As time passed and the royal family expanded and dispersed, it would have become more and more difficult for the entire family to join together in this way around a single altar. By the middle of the Western Zhou, about 900, there was a dramatic change in the number and style of bronzes that were placed in the ancestral temple. Although many bronzes have been unearthed from tombs, and therefore presumably reflect the mortuary context, there have been other discoveries of caches of bronzes, mainly in the Zhou homeland—known as the Zhouyuan—located between the modern cities of Xi'an and Baoji, that provide evidence of the bronzes that would have been used in the ancestral temples. The bronze vessels were deposited in these caches for safekeeping at the very end of the Western Zhou when the Zhou homeland was being overrun by foreign invaders; the bronzes in them almost certainly had been those used in the ancestral temples, and so provide evidence of how rituals in the temples were performed. Once such cache was unearthed in 1975 at the village of Zhuangbai in the Zhouyuan. It held 103 bronze pieces in all, from at least five generations of a single family, the Wei family. Forty-four of these vessels and bells were produced for a single generation of this family, a man named Xing, who lived in the first half of the ninth century. Fig. 16.2 shows most of these. There are two things in particular to note about this collection. First, at the top of the figure are eight tureens (*gui*), which were used to make grain offerings. These eight tureens are virtually identical, and the ornamentation on them is also quite uniform; there is nothing in particular about the décor that would draw one closer to look at it. Indeed, we can imagine that all eight vessels would have been arrayed across one side of a very long altar, as they are often displayed in Chinese museums with complete sets. Although not included among Xing's bronzes, it is almost certain that these tureens would have been complemented on the other side of the altar with nine caldrons (*ding*), similarly arrayed. The second thing to note about the bronzes from this cache is the many bells at the bottom of the figure. Bells were first made in southern China, and were introduced to the Zhou homeland only a century or so before the time of these bells made for Xing. Ancient Chinese bells produced two separate tones an octave apart, but a single bell could not be used for a musical performance. It was necessary to have an array of bells of different sizes, which would produce different notes. Usually these arrays were in multiples of four bells. They would have been suspended from a rack placed to one side of the altar. Not figured here, but certainly present on the other side of the altar would have been a similar rack of chime-stones, also graduated in size so as to produce different notes. It was doubtless the need to make these musical instruments in sets that suggested to the Zhou people of the time that their offering vessels might also be cast in sets.

Visualizing the ancestral temple from which this collection would have come will suggest two further deductions about how the offerings to the ancestors in it were doubtless performed. First, playing the bells and chime-stones was not just a matter of striking them; they had to be struck at exact points, producing different notes. This was not something that just any member of the family could do. It required specially trained musicians. Second, the array of tureens and caldrons would have stretched across an altar twenty meters or more long, far too long for the members of the family

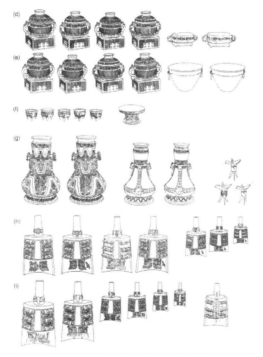

Figure 16.2 Bronzes of Wei Bo Xing, from Zhuangbai, Shaanxi; *c.* 870; from Jessica Rawson, "Western Zhou Archaeology," in Michael Loewe and Edward L. Shaughnessy ed., *The Cambridge History of Ancient China: From the Beginnings of Civilization to 221 B.C.* (New York: Cambridge University Press, 1999), 377 Fig. 6.6; drawing by Ann Searight; used with permission.

to gather around. What is more, the closer to the altar those family members would draw, the less they would see; one would have to stand at a distance in order to take in the entire scene. This suggests that specially trained priests would have stood at the altar performing the offerings on behalf of the family. This is a radically different conception of ritual, so different that it has come to be termed the Western Zhou Ritual Reform (in fact, some have termed it a Ritual Revolution). Another hymn from the *Classic of Poetry* seems to date from after this Ritual Reform. Called "Now Presenting," it describes the reformed concelebration of the ancestral sacrifices.

Now visiting the serving king, Seeking out his insignia:
Dragon banners all aflutter, Harmonic bells all resounding.
The bridles' leather has gilding, Resplendent with valiant brilliance.
Led to visit the shining father, To be filial, to make offering,
To strengthen longevity, Forever going to protect them.
May the august grant many blessings; Valiant and cultured serving lords
Succor us with many blessings. Giving continued splendor in pure grace.[13]

No one, not even the Zhou kings (perhaps especially not the Zhou kings), was exempt from obligations to his ancestors. One of the very few bronze vessels made on behalf of a reigning Zhou king illustrates well the continuing relationship with one's ancestors. This vessel, the *Hu gui*, discovered in 1980, was made for King Li (r. 857/853–842/828), who refers to himself in the inscription by his personal name Hu. The inscription includes a long prayer to his ancestors (curiously stating that they lived in the court of the god Di, normally associated with the ancestors of the Shang royal family).

Hu makes (this) giant sacrificial treasured gui-tureen, with which vigorously to aid my august cultured and valorous grandfather and deceased father. May they approach the prior cultured men, may they constantly be in the court of Di on High, ascending and descending, continuously visited with the august Di on High's great and felicitous mandate, with which commandingly to protect our family, my position and Hu's person.[14]

For King Li and others in the Western Zhou dynasty, the key word was *xiao*, which originally referred to the offerings to the ancestors and the relationship between a son and his deceased father. However, by the time of Confucius, *xiao* had developed into perhaps the core Confucian virtue, typically translated as "filial piety." For Confucius, this went well beyond just supplying offerings to the ancestors, or even to one's parents while they were still alive. Instead, it was conceived of as a psychological attitude, as the following quotation of Confucius shows.

> Zi You asked about filial piety. The Master said, "Nowadays it is those who are able to provide (for their parents) that are said to be filial. Even dogs and horses can be provided for. If not with respect, how is it any different?"[15]

Another aspect of filial piety and ritual practice involved the need for a son to mourn the death of his father for three full years.

> The Master said, "If, for three years, one does not diverge from his father's way, he can be said to be filial."[16]

At the beginning of this essay, I quoted the Confucian philosopher Xunzi as theorizing that ritual was established to divide people into their proper roles in society. This ritual system conceived of the family as the basis of society, which was established in the first place by the bond between father and son. This three-year mourning period, during which a son was to retire from active life and live a life devoid of all social adornment—wearing mourning garments, living in a grass hut, eating coarse porridge, sleeping on a mat of twigs with a clump of earth as a pillow—may sound excessive, but according to Xunzi twenty-five months of mourning was moderate.

> One may ask what is the three-year mourning period? I say: It is a cultural pattern set up on the basis of weighing the emotions. It is designed to show that one belongs to the group and to distinguish between those near and far, honored and humble; it cannot be increased or decreased. That is why it is said that it cannot be avoided or changed. When a wound is deep, it takes many days to heal; where there is great pain, it is slow to get better. That the three-year mourning period is a cultural pattern set up on the basis of weighing the emotions is because it is the extreme of pain. The mourning garments and the cane of the mourner, the hut where he lives, the gruel he eats, the mat of twigs and pillow of earth, these show the intense pain of his grief.

The three-year mourning period is over in twenty-five months; though the grief and pain are not yet gone and one's thoughts of the departed are not yet forgotten, still the ritual stops it at this. Could it be that seeing off the dead would end, but we return to life in moderation.[17]

As the other statement quoted at the beginning of this essay said, ritual was indeed one of "the great affairs of state."

CHAPTER 17
ESSAY ON WARFARE

Beginning in the late Neolithic period, roughly at the time that Yao and Shun were supposed to be ruling China (i.e., the century or two on either side of 2000 BCE), substantial walls began to be erected around settlements all across north China. These were different from the low barriers that mark earlier Neolithic settlements, which apparently were intended to protect the settlements from wild animals; these walls were obviously intended to defend against attacks by other human beings. This is the first evidence, indirect though it is, of widespread warfare in ancient China.

It is only when we move forward to the historical age—the late Shang dynasty—that we have more direct evidence of warfare. There is a great deal of it, both artifactual and inscriptional. The artifactual evidence includes tens of thousands of weapons of various types. The most eye-catching, about which much more will be said below, are horse-drawn chariots that have been found buried near the royal tombs at Anyang. However, far and away the most common weapon is called a dagger-axe (*ge*), a pointed slashing weapon mounted at the end of a long wooden haft. Superficially like a spear, the dagger-axe was wielded in a very different—and more efficient—manner; it was the standard-issue weapon for both foot-soldiers and also one of the three combatants who rode in chariots. One other combatant in the chariots was equipped with a reflex bow, and there is considerable archaeological evidence of bows and especially arrows—in the form of bronze and stone arrowheads (the bows themselves have not survived well in archaeological contexts). However, while bows and arrows were certainly used as long-range projectile weapons (at least one skeleton found in a Shang burial of ritual victims had a bronze arrowhead embedded in his leg), the more common long-range weapon was probably a sort of sling; although none of these have been found, round balls that would have been launched from them have been found at archaeological sites all over north China. The Biblical story of David and Goliath suffices to show the lethal nature of such slung projectiles.

The inscriptional evidence complements the artifactual evidence. The Shang kings, and especially King Wu Ding (r. *c.* 1225–1189), divined about nearly every aspect of life, including of course warfare, both offensive and defensive. One of the most famous oracle-bone inscriptions of all, first published in 1914, just a decade after the first notice of these oracle bones, and subsequently illustrated in almost every account of them, concerns an attack on the Shang by two western enemies called the Earth Land and Spade Land.

> Crack-making on *guisi* (day 30), Que affirmed: "In the next ten-day week there will be no harm." The king prognosticated and said: "There is a curse. It is expected that there will be hardship coming." Reaching the fifth day *dingyou* (day 34), there really did come hardship from the west. Zhi Guo reported saying: "The Earth Land campaigned in our eastern suburbs, conquering two cities. The Spade Land also invaded our western suburbs and fields.[18]

Hundreds of other divinations concern subsequent hostilities between Shang and its allies and these two enemies and their allies. Among those leading the Shang campaigns against them was Consort Hao (Fu Hao), one of King Wu Ding's wives, and the mother of one of his sons who would later become king.

> Crack-making on *xinsi* (day 18), Zheng affirmed: "If this spring the king raises men and calls out to Consort Hao to attack the Earth Land, we will receive aid in it."[19]

The king too led some of the Shang attacks, though apparently not directly against the Earth Land or the Spade Land, but rather against one of their allies.

> Crack-making on *guichou* (day 50), Xuan affirmed: "The king will ally with Xi to attack Ba Land."[20]

Most of the inscriptions record just the original divination, which is a sort of a prayer, expressing the desire that the Shang would be successful, and so do not usually indicate the result. Thus, it is hard to know many details about the battles, even who won and who lost, not to mention numbers of soldiers involved and the tactics used. One divination does propose raising thirteen thousand troops, but this is probably anomalous, if it was even carried out. Some inscriptions bear verifications, after the fact accounts of what really did happen. Two record Shang losses, in one case ten men, in another case fifteen and sixteen men in two separate attacks. There is some evidence that the war against the Earth Land and Spade Land was protracted, continuing over the course of some five years and extending back and forth across what is today southern Shanxi province, just to the west of the Taihang Mountains west of the Shang capital at Anyang, though it is likely that the battles were intermittent. It is certainly unlikely that armies were kept in the field for long periods of time.

After the time of King Wu Ding, because of changes in the scope and purpose of divination, warfare appears less often as a topic. This probably does not mean that fighting itself was any less common. However, it may be the case that the numbers of people involved in battle increased. A hundred or so years after King Wu Ding's war with the Earth Land and Spade Land, one of the longest inscriptions of the entire period concerns another battle between Shang and a coalition of enemies, probably also located to the west of the Shang capital. Unfortunately, only about one-third of this piece survives, making it very hard to read. Fortunately, however, the surviving portion is from the verification. It is probably not surprising that it records a decisive Shang victory.

> ... Minor Vassal Qiang allied to attack, capturing Rou of Wei ... 24 men, 1,570 of Er, 100+ of Fan ... horses, two chariots, 183 ?, 50 quivers of arrows, ... herewith making an offering to Da Yi, sacrificing Yin, the leader of Shen ... Fan to Zu Yi, and sacrificing Rou to Zu Ding. Ran said: The capital bestows ...[21]

Some readers focus on the sacrificial offering of the leaders of the enemy states to different Shang ancestors. However, for the topic of warfare, the number of captives would seem to be indicative of a larger scale to the battle than was the case in the Earth Land war, and perhaps more important still is the mention of capturing two chariots. While, as mentioned above, some artifactual evidence of chariots has been unearthed at Anyang, this is the only explicit mention of them being used in battle (as opposed to hunting) in the Shang oracle-bone record.

The question of the chariot looms large over all discussions of ancient Chinese warfare. The chariot is the largest and most sophisticated piece of equipment of the age, requiring skilled carpentry and metallurgy, not to mention the ability to train horses and to learn to drive and fight from a moving vehicle. Chinese legends variously attribute the invention of the chariot to the Yellow Emperor (Huang Di) or to Xi Zhong, a figure said to have lived at the beginning of the Xia dynasty. Paradoxically, other legends credit the domestication of the horse to Xiang Tu, said to have lived toward the end of that dynasty. None of these legends has any basis in fact. It is now clear that the chariot was imported into China from areas further west, in the trans-Caucasus region of Central Asia, only at about the time of Shang king Wu Ding. Indeed, prior to that time horses were also unknown in China; the horse and chariot arrived as a unit.

Many scholars argue that the chariot was the decisive weapon of antiquity: playing a role analogous to the tank in twentieth-century warfare. Other scholars argue that it was too cumbersome to have contributed any tactical advantage to an army, at best serving as an elevated and mobile command platform. As we will see, there is justification for both of these viewpoints, though they both see only part of the ancient battlefield.

In the inscription quoted just above, the form of which anticipates the long inscriptions on some Western Zhou bronze vessels, the explicit record of the capture of horses and chariots is very important for the history of the chariot in China. It is noteworthy that these chariots were used by a confederation of enemies located to the west of Shang. Perhaps more important (though this would need to be qualified because of the fragmentary nature of the inscription), despite the capture of several chieftains and over fifteen hundred men, that only two chariots were captured perhaps indicates that chariotry had not yet become a prominent part of the military, whether of the enemies or of the Shang. As a new invention—and an imported one at that—the chariot doubtless required a considerable amount of time before people learned to take full advantage of its potential. But ancient China covers a long period of time, and the evidence is that during the Zhou dynasty it became more and more important.

An argument can be made that it was chariots that allowed the Zhou to overthrow the Shang in 1045. Certainly, one of the poems of the *Classic of Poetry*, known as "The Great Brightness," allots a prominent role to them at the battle of Shepherd's Wild (Muye).

The Shepherd's Wild so vast, so vast, Sandalwood carts gleaming, gleaming,
And teams of four pounding pounding. It was Major Exalted Uncle,
The one who raised up eagle-like. Cool was that Martial King,
Spreading out to attack great Shang, Meeting the morning clear and bright.[22]

Of course, there is doubtless a great degree of poetic license in this description. However, there is good evidence that by the end of the Western Zhou, c. 800, armies were using many more than just two chariots in battle. One of the best pieces of evidence comes in the inscription on a bronze vessel, the *Duo You ding*, made to celebrate a Zhou victory in battle over the Xianyun, a western enemy. The inscription is almost cinematic in its retelling of several battles the two sides fought and their aftermath.

> It was the tenth month; because the Xianyun had just arisen and broadly attacked the Jing Garrison, (which) reported back to the king, who commanded the Martial Duke: "Dispatch your premier men to advance and pursue at Jing Garrison."
>
> The Martial Duke commanded Duo You to lead the duke's chariotry to advance and pursue at Jing Garrison. On *guiwei* (day 20), the enemies attacked Xun, taking captives. Duo You westwardly pursued. On *jiashen* (day 21) morning, striking at Mai, Duo You again cut off heads and manacled prisoners; in all, using the duke's chariotry to cut off the heads of two hundred and . . . five men, manacling twenty-three prisoners, capturing 117 teams of the enemy's chariotry, and taking back the captives of the men of Xun. And then striking at Gong, (he) cut off the heads of thirty-six men, manacled two prisoners and captured ten teams of chariotry. Following the vanguard, (he) pursued and struck at Shi. Duo You again cut off heads and manacled prisoners. Then (he) raced in pursuit as far as Yangzhong; the duke's chariotry cut off the heads of 115 men and manacled three prisoners. It was only that the captured chariots could not be taken and so were burned, with only the horses driving the wounded and returning the recovered Jing Garrison captives.
>
> Duo You then presented the captives, scalps and prisoners to the duke. The Martial Duke then presented (them) to the king, who addressed the Martial Duke saying: "You have pacified the Jing Garrison; I bless you, awarding you lands and fields." On *dingyou* (day 34), the Martial Duke was at the Presentation Palace and commanded Xiangfu to summon Duo You, (who) then entered the Presentation Palace. The duke personally addressed Duo You saying: "I initiated the business, (but) you were victorious and unflawed, and have completed the business, with much booty. You have pacified the Jing Garrison; (I) award you one jade-handled ladle, one set of bells, and one hundred catties of finest bronze."

Duo You dares to respond to the duke's beneficence, herewith making this offertory caldron with which to befriend and to assist him; may sons' sons and grandsons eternally treasure and use it.[23]

The combined Xianyun casualties recorded for the three battles described here are 356+ killed, 28 captured, and 127+ chariots captured. It would be tempting to see in the almost exact 1:3 ratio of chariots captured to men killed to think that the Xianyun chariots were manned by three soldiers, as we know the Zhou chariots were. This may well be true. However, the record after the last battle that "the chariots could not be taken and were burned" suggests that the total number of chariots captured was even greater than 127. What is more, this inscription suggests only that the Zhou managed to drive off the Xianyun, not that they annihilated the entire force; many other chariots must have gotten away. And we can expect that the Zhou employed an even greater number of chariots. This would seem to have been two chariot armies facing off against each other.

The subsequent Springs and Autumns period was surely the high tide of chariot warfare, when even the small state of Zhu, a state of no particular significance, is said to have had 600 chariots in its army. To take just the pivotal battle of Chengpu in 632, when the state of Jin and its northern allies turned back a confederation of states led by Chu in a battle that is often seen as having saved northern China from southern domination, records of the battle in the *Zuo Tradition* say that the Jin army included 700 chariots. We can imagine that the opposing Chu army had a similar number. Among the Jin allies, the states of Qi and Song are elsewhere said to have put 800 and 460 chariots into other battles, and the Chu allies Lu and Wei employed 1,000 and 300 respectively. Even if we suppose that many of these numbers are exaggerated, still a conservative estimate for the armies of the ten different states engaging in this momentous battle would put the number of chariots on the battlefield at between 4,000 and 5,000. A modern Chinese military historian has estimated that a chariot occupied 16 square meters standing still. If we assume just half of this conservative estimate for the number of chariots, they would have required forty square kilometers just to deploy, not to mention the amount of space that would have been taken up in their charges against each other.

While chariot warfare continued to be the norm for the remainder of the Springs and Autumns period, two innovations that occurred in China toward the end of the period would render chariots all but obsolete. In some ways, these two innovations worked at cross-purposes, but in both cases they fundamentally transformed warfare. The first led to the rise of the infantry as the most important component of all armies. The second led to a wholly new component of armies: cavalry.

The earlier of the two innovations was the mechanical crossbow. Whereas the hallowed reflex bow, which had been a staple weapon of Chinese armies since at least the Shang dynasty, was a powerful weapon, able to pierce a defender's leather armor at a distance of 70 meters, it required considerable skill both to produce and to use. Indeed, archery was one of the six skills that a nobleman was supposed to master, and there were elaborate rituals involving archery contests. On the other hand, the mechanical crossbow could be mass produced and anyone who could aim and pull a trigger could surpass even the best of the old-fashioned archers. The crossbow pellets could reach the riders on chariots well before they came within their own striking distance, greatly diminishing the threat of that foremost of earlier weapons.

With foot-soldiers now armed with greater killing power than the old chariot forces, armies in the subsequent Warring States period grew larger and larger. This rise in the infantry was only partly driven by the introduction of the crossbow. Doubtless much more important was a rise in the population of the time, itself driven by the introduction of iron plows that produced a great increase in agricultural production. By the end of the period, armies would reach into the hundreds of thousands of soldiers, sometime remaining in the field for months at a time. This in turn entailed an important change in the leadership of the armies. Professional soldiers are well aware that wars are won or lost by successful management of logistics. Soldiers that are hungry or sick do not fight.

In China, this gave rise to professional generals, including those who at least purportedly wrote manuals of warfare. The most famous of these was Sun Wu, better known as Sunzi (544–470), and his *Art of War*. According to Sunzi because warfare at this time required the mobilization of all the resources of a state, it should only be undertaken after thorough consideration and planning. He states regularly that the best warfare is that which never takes place, the best victory that which takes over the opponent's state intact.

> In general, the method for using warfare is that preserving the enemy's state intact is best, destroying it comes next.[24]

But when the army was finally put into the field, it was the general's responsibility to choose the proper battlefield, one that would give his own army the advantage and put the enemy army at a disadvantage. For Sunzi, the art of war was entirely a matter of strategy; tactics were a much less important consideration.

The second great innovation in warfare at the time, not reflected in Sunzi's *Art of War*, was cavalry. By the beginning of the fifth century, mounted warriors already appeared on the periphery of China, and by the late fourth century, Chinese armies also adopted this form of fighting. While this spelled the definitive death knell for chariots, which devolved once again into the elite command platforms that they evidently had been during the Shang dynasty, cavalry never assumed great importance in battles within China proper. It was only along the Central Asian frontier that Chinese armies were all but forced to fight cavalry with cavalry, a fight for which Chinese armies were not well suited.

It is often said that in ancient China wars were fought "to display the chivalric behavior of the participants." People regularly cite as an example of this chivalry an account in the *Zuo Tradition* for 638 in which Duke Xiang of Song (r. 650–637) refused to engage the army of Chu in battle before it had fully prepared.

> In winter, in the eleventh month, on the first day of the month *jisi*, the Duke of Song and the Chu army did battle at the Hong River. The Song army had already formed ranks, but the Chu army had not yet crossed the river. The Song Supervisor of the Horse said, "They are numerous while we are few. Let's attack them while they have not yet completed the crossing." The duke said, "That is not proper." When the Chu army had finished crossing but had not yet formed ranks, the Supervisor of the Horse again reported it to him. The duke said, "It is not yet proper." Only after the Chu army had formed ranks did he attack them. The Song troops were defeated in a rout, the duke was wounded in the thigh, and the palace guards were slaughtered there. The people of the capital all blamed the duke. The duke said, "A gentleman does not wound twice, nor does he take prisoners of those with graying hair. When people of old engaged in warfare, they did not take advantage of defiles and ravines. Although I, the unworthy one, am but the remnant of a lost state, I would not drum an attack against those who have not formed their ranks."[25]

It is doubtless the case that warfare became a bloodier exercise in the Warring States period than it had been in the Springs and Autumns period, not to mention the Shang and Western Zhou before that. Nevertheless, even in those earlier periods, archers shot metal-tipped arrows and foot-soldiers fought for their lives. Duke Xiang may well have exhibited such chivalrous behavior, but he was routinely derided for it by his own countrymen and he was held up as an example of how not to fight. It was surely no exaggeration when Sunzi, who might be called the first professional soldier in China, began his *Art of War* with the following statement:

> Warfare is the great affair of state, the place of life and death, the way of survival or annihilation. It is essential that it be examined.[26]

Soldiers did indeed die. One of the poems of the *Verses of Chu* is called *Martyrs for the State*. It is a fitting conclusion to any treatment of warfare, whether in ancient China or anywhere or anytime else.

Having taken up Wu halberds and strapped on rhinoceros armor,
The chariots scraped against each other's axle-caps, and the short
    weapons joined.
Their banners blotting out the sun, the enemy was like a cloud,
The arrows falling crisscross, the soldiers fought to the fore.
Having surmounted our lines, having broken through our ranks,
The left horse dead in the harness, the right slashed and wounded.
Spiking the chariot wheels and tethering the horses,
The jade mallets beat and the drums were sounded.
The seasons of heaven fell, and the awesome spirits were angry.
You were brutally wiped out, abandoned on the distant plain.
You set out not to come back; you went not to return,
The flat plain abrupt and the road too distant.
With long swords on your belts and Qin bows under your arms,
Your bodies and heads may have been severed, but your hearts are
    unimpeachable.
Truly were you brave, acting with martial valor,
To the end firm and strong, insurmountable.
Your bodies may have died, but your spirits are numinous,
Your souls have become the heroes of the ghosts.[27]

CHAPTER 18
ESSAY ON GOVERNMENT

There is very little that can be said of the earliest forms of government in China. Of course, there are legends that the sage-kings Yao and Shun ruled through force of personal character, and that when they reached old age they abdicated in favor of their most worthy ministers, Shun in the case of Yao, and Yu the Great in the case of Shun. These legends say that Yu too attempted to abdicate, but in the end was succeeded by his son Qi, thus initiating the Xia dynasty and China's pattern of kingship passing from father to son. Traditional histories—and some modern ones too—try to fill in the blanks of this period by analogy with later times, but there would seem to be little point in this.

Even when we enter the historical age proper during the late Shang dynasty, not much more can be said about the government, notwithstanding the tens of thousands of oracle-bone records. It is possible on the basis of these records to deduce the genealogy of the kings of the entire dynasty, and not just of the nine kings for which time written records exist, and it seems likely that these kings did wield ultimate power—at least within their own limited spheres of influence. The king about whom we know the most, Wu Ding (r. *c.* 1225–1189), seems to have ruled together with royal family members, primarily "princes" and a shifting confederation of allied states, and was able to raise troops and to call on officers known as the Many Artisans and Many Horse, perhaps in charge of labor and the military respectively. He also had scores of diviners in his service, divination being one of the important royal activities. Many craftsmen worked in special workshops throughout the capital, doubtless through royal patronage, specializing in bronze-casting, pottery making, and bone-working. What is more, by at least one count Wu Ding had available to him as many as eighty-four different consorts, who presumably served to consolidate the political confederation that he had established. Most of these women came from other states or other peoples, and sometimes it is even possible to suggest where their homes may have been located. However, nothing more can be said about those states, and traditional Chinese views of history do not consider them to have been Chinese, even though they were all assuredly located within the greater North China plain.

It is only with the Zhou dynasty, which overthrew the Shang in 1045, that it becomes possible to describe something of the government organization. The Zhou government, apparently like the Xia and Shang governments before it, was centered upon the king. At the beginning of the dynasty, the Zhou seem to have largely followed the Shang model, though they did so more systematically, deputing royal princes and relatives to oversee the eastern lands that they had just conquered. This is often referred to as a form of feudalism, in which these royal princes and relatives owed fealty and tribute to the Zhou king, but were free to govern their own individual territories.

Shortly after the establishment of the dynasty, the Zhou developed a doctrine which held that the king ruled by divine right; this is usually referred to as the Mandate of Heaven, the Zhou king being referred to as the Son of Heaven. The earliest explicit reference to this doctrine, at least in paleographic sources that date to the period, is seen in the inscription on the *Da Yu ding*, one of the most important bronze inscriptions from the first half of the Western Zhou. It begins:

It was the ninth month; the king was at Ancestral Zhou and commanded Yu. The king approved of saying: "Yu, illustrious King Wen received the Heaven-blessed great mandate. At (the time) King Wu succeeded Wen and made the state, (he) ridded it of evil, extended it over the four quarters, and governed their people. Among the managers of affairs, he suppressed wine; none dared to get flushed. Having offerings and sacrifices, none dared to get sloshed. Therefore, heaven respectfully looked upon him and treated (him) as a son, and greatly protected the former kings . . . to have the four quarters."

The inscription goes on to commemorate Yu's appointment to "stand beside" the king:

"You early had great service. It was when I had assumed my elementary education; you did not press me, your ruler, the one man. Now it is that I assume the model and follow King Wen's upright virtue, and as King Wen commanded the two and three governors, now it is that I command you, Yu, to assist Rong respectfully to secure virtue's continuance. Diligently morning and evening enter to remonstrate, and making offerings hasten to be awed by heaven's awesomeness. The king said, "*Wuhu*! (I) command you, Yu, to take as model your ancestral grandfather Duke Nan." The king said, "Yu, then assist and stand beside me, overseeing the Supervisors of the Military. Be diligent and quick in punishments and law-suits; morning and evening assist me, the one man, to uphold the four quarters and when I inspect the people and borderlands received by the former kings."[28]

Concomitant with the Mandate of Heaven in which the king was regarded as the son of heaven, it is important to recognize that the Zhou government was based upon kinship, just as Yu here is commanded to "take as your model your ancestral grandfather Duke Nan." The ancestral temple was the focal point of the royal family, to be sure, but also of all of the different families and lineages that made up the state. It was not only where the important bronze vessels were kept and where offerings to the ancestors were made, but also where much of the government administration was conducted. Kinship would continue to be the foundation of that government for at least the next half a millennium.

Within the royal domain itself, essentially centered on the two capitals at modern-day Xi'an, Shaanxi, and Luoyang, Henan, early Zhou rule seems to have been relatively ad hoc, what Max Weber characterized as a "patriarchal" form of government, in which a few close advisers to the king attended to whatever business was required, whether civil or martial (if such a distinction even made sense at the time). This pattern began to change by the beginning of the second century of Zhou rule, when King Mu (r. 956–918) undertook first to reorganize the military, appointing officers of fixed rank, with some indication of an explicit chain of command. Little by little, whether during the reign of King Mu himself or those of his immediate successors, this structure was extended to include also civil officers. There were three main divisions of the government, under the Supervisors of the Horse, Labor, and Lands. There was also a royal secretariat, responsible for communicating the king's commands and for maintaining written records. There is some indication that local jurisdictions mirrored this bureaucratic structure to some extent. It is also at the time of King Mu that later tradition says a written law code was first promulgated, but the text cited as evidence of this, the "Punishments of Lü" chapter of the *Exalted Scriptures* is almost certainly from a later date.

Inscribed bronze vessels that provide the best evidence that we have for the later Western Zhou government show that the incipient bureaucracy established at this time persisted, at least in the capital regions. There is less evidence to know how the areas beyond the capitals were governed. There is little evidence that the rulers of these erstwhile colonies reported back to the king as feudal bonds would have required them to do, though marriage bonds were continued between the royal family and the rulers of the colonies founded by non-Zhou allies, such as the state of Qi, which had been established under the Grand Duke Wang, a member of the Jiang family and the leader of the Zhou army during its conquest of Shang. The only evidence that the Zhou king entered into the affairs of any of the local states came in the 860s when King Yi (r. 865–858) sent a royal army into Qi, and then in the 810s when King Xuan (r. 827–782) intruded in the succession of Lu. Both of these interventions seem to have been counter-productive, the intervention in Lu ultimately ending up destabilizing that state. The other states apparently went their own way. By the time the Western Zhou came to an end in 771, these states were already practically independent, a status that would soon be recognized by the weakened Zhou kings in their new capital at Luoyang.

The first important development in government of the subsequent Springs and Autumns period took place in the state of Qi, just about one hundred years after the end of the Western Zhou. There are two features of geography which, added to Qi's non-Zhou heritage, may have contributed to it introducing innovations in government sooner than the other independent states. First, Qi occupied most of the Shandong peninsula, far to the northeast of even the eastern Zhou capital at Luoyang, and also more or less isolated from most of the other eastern states. Second, and perhaps more important, Qi was one of the larger states, encompassing a varied topography; it stretched from marine salt flats along its eastern seaboard to fertile plains in its northwest and mountains in the southwest. These different zones supported different life-styles and required different local governance. At the time of Duke Huan (r. 685–643), Qi experimented with a new government structure. The state was divided into seven counties (*xian*), each of which was sub-divided into three districts (*xiang*), thus making for twenty-one districts in all. The word *xian* for "county" means "to suspend," and suggests individual threads hanging from a central support. Each of these counties and districts was administered by its own officers, and each had its own tax burden and requirement to contribute men to the army. At least in theory, the officers were to be judged on the basis of performance, and to be promoted or demoted accordingly. This structure, generally credited to Duke Huan's chief minister Guan Zhong (*c.* 730–645), made Qi the most powerful state of the time. Duke Huan was recognized by the Zhou king and the rulers of the other states as *ba*, a term often translated as "hegemon," but which probably originally meant "senior" or "elder" in the sense of the first born within a generation. Thus, the *ba* was the first among equals; i.e., "premier." According to the kinship principles underlying the Zhou political structure, fictive though the relationships may have been, the *ba* was thus the primary support and protector of the Zhou king.

Qi's administrative structure based on counties quickly spread to the other states of the time, especially the large states of Qin, Chu and Jin. There is some evidence that at almost the same time as in Qi, the state of Qin made counties of four newly conquered territories, but this seems not to have been extended throughout the entirety of that state. Somewhat later, the southern state of Chu also made newly conquered lands into counties, and then expanded the system to encompass the entire state. The state of Jin also adopted the county system beginning about the time of Duke Wen (r. 636–628). A century later it is said to have had forty-nine separate counties, each of which was tasked with contributing one hundred chariots to the state's combined military force, suggesting that these reforms involved both civil and military administration.

As the large states gradually absorbed smaller states, and as they sought new ways to integrate these new territories into their own government structure, they also realized that those structures required reorganization. For instance, in 621, Jin reorganized its military, reassigning the commanders. One of the commanders, Zhao Dun (also known as Zhao Xuanzi; d. 601), who had traveled with the previous ruler Duke Wen during his long exile, was praised as being especially capable; this capability was identified as "the benefit of the state." For this reason, Zhao Dun was put in charge of the Jin government, a major new development; after this time, although states continued to be ruled by the nobility, the administration would be in the hands of prime ministers, who could be either noblemen themselves or, more and more, commoners. According to the *Zuo Tradition*, Zhao Dun immediately set about "producing statutes; rectifying laws and crimes; handling lawsuits and punishments; directing the pursuit of those who had absconded and instituting the use of pledges and contracts; putting in order the old and stagnant, and ranks based on ritual; extending regular offices and bringing out those who had been obstructed or were in obscurity." When he had completed these reforms, he commanded that they "be put in practice throughout the state of Jin as constant laws."

The promulgation of "constant laws"—or at least of a written law code—is often credited to—or blamed upon—Zi Chan (also known as Gongsun Qiao; d. 522), a minister active in the government of the state of Zheng. In 536, he is said to have had the state's legal code cast onto a bronze caldron or caldrons.

According to the *Zuo Tradition*, the prime minister of Jin, Shu Xiang (d. *c.* 528), objected to this act, sending Zi Chan a lengthy letter in which he argued that from ancient times the good working of the government depended solely on the virtue of the ruler. By putting laws into writing, as Zi Chan had done, this would eliminate the role of the ruler, and would end up making the people litigious. Shu Xiang ended the letter predicting that Zi Chan would bring his state of Zheng to ruin. Despite this prediction, twenty-three years later, generals of Jin would cast a similar caldron, though this one of iron, inscribed with their own penal code, an act for which they were in turn criticized by none other than Confucius (551–479). What is more, far from bringing Zheng to ruin, Zi Chan's reforms were quite successful. When he assumed control of Zheng, it had long since ceased to be an important state. However, even though it was located at the very crossroads of the central China plain, with enemies all about, his reforms succeeded in strengthening the state sufficiently that it managed to outlive even the great state of Jin.

Zhao Dun's promotion from a military leader to having responsibility for the entire government was not unusual, much of the reorganization of the governments at this period coming about as a result of changes in warfare and military thinking. Many of these were driven in turn by technological changes. The sixth century BCE saw the definitive onset of the Iron Age in China. While bronze had long been used for ritual goods, now iron tools and weapons began to be available on a wide scale. One tool in particular brought about important demographic changes: the ox-drawn iron-bladed plow allowed new lands to be opened and old lands to be furrowed more deeply and more effectively than theretofore, greatly increasing crop yields; this quickly led to a substantial increase in population, which in turn allowed the increasingly larger states to muster ever larger armies. These larger armies were outfitted with iron weapons that were both less expensive to produce and more effective than bronze weapons. Among these weapons was the newly invented mechanical crossbow, with a mass-produced trigger mechanism. The crossbow required much less training for the masses of new soldiers to master than had been the case with the traditional reflex bow. Not only this, it was lethal at far greater distances than the reflex bow, and it soon rendered the horse-drawn chariot obsolete; drivers and the warriors on the chariots could be killed at a distance before they ever threatened the ranks of infantry. From this time on, instead of battles featuring perhaps a thousand or so chariots, each carrying three elite and highly trained warriors (the driver, the archer, and a defender bearing a dagger-axe), armies—reaching into the hundreds of thousands of soldiers—now consisted primarily of foot-soldiers, control of which was entrusted to expert generals such as Sunzi, the author of *The Art of War*.

While *The Art of War* includes some discussion of battlefield tactics, the great majority of the book concerns the administration of the state and the logistical demands of getting armies to the battlefield and keeping them there. These concerns were shared with the civil administration, which was charged with maximizing agricultural production to support the armies. When the first treatises of government were written, toward the beginning of the fourth century, agriculture and warfare would come to be seen as the two "handles" of government. The first of these treatises, unfortunately long since lost, is said to have been the *Classic of Laws* by Li Kui (455–395). Li Kui was appointed prime minister of Wei in 422, under that state's founding ruler, Lord Wen of Wei (r. 445–396). While the book did, to be sure, contain a written law code that would serve as the basis for the later Qin and then Han law codes, much of it was devoted to the topic of agriculture. Li Kui apparently argued that the traditional system of manorial lands belonging to noblemen and worked by quasi serfs was inefficient, and should be replaced by small-scale farms worked by single families. Two other policies would also have profound and long-lasting influence, and not just in the state of Wei. The first of these was his "Law of Even Grain Prices," by which the state would buy grain in good years to store in state granaries, to be released in years of famine, thus stabilizing the price of grain and ensuring farmers a steady market for their goods. Some 2,400 years later, this policy would be adopted in the United States under President Franklin Delano Roosevelt's Secretary of Agriculture Henry A. Wallace (1888–1965; Secretary of Agriculture 1933–1940), establishing what he called the "Ever Normal Granary," a series of price supports that has since been adopted throughout the world. The second of Li Kui's influential policies was his insistence on merit in the selection of officials. This too was taken up well beyond just the state of Wei. Just as the armies required specialists to be able to arm, to feed, and to control the masses of new soldiers, so too did the civilian governments require specialists to keep track of the people living under their charge, and to extract from them the requisite tax and labor to support the armies. In the states of Chu and Qin, the newly established counties came to be headed by "governors" who were drawn not from the nobility of the state but rather were chosen on the basis of their ability. This turn from noble rank to recognition by ability was reflected also in the philosophical writings of the time. A set of chapters of the *Mozi* was entitled "Exalting the Worthy" (*Shang xian*), a term also consistent with the views of Confucius (551–479) and his followers.

It is said that a half century after Li Kui wrote his *Classic of Laws*, the book was carried by Shang Yang (*c.* 390–338) when he left Wei to go to Qin. Shang Yang, the putative author of the *Book of the Lord Shang*, is probably most remembered for the establishment of what came to be called Legalism, and for his strict enforcement of laws in the state of Qin. However, he was also instrumental in using the reins of government to develop agriculture, and staffing that government with a bureaucracy chosen for its skills, rather than its noble pedigree. The entire population was registered, and adult males were individually responsible for a household tax or head tax. On the other hand, the population was organized into affinity groups of five, ten, and fifty households. He also instituted a policy whereby members of these affinity groups had responsibility for each other's conduct. If any single individual committed a crime, the entire group was responsible for reporting the infraction, and the property of the criminal would be confiscated and shared with the other members of the group. The military was organized in a similar fashion, with members of the unit mutually sharing in its success, or being similarly punished for its failure. These reforms quickly made Qin the strongest state of all the remaining independent states, with security within and military power brought to bear against those other states.

Qin's nearest neighbor to the east was the state of Han, one of the three successor states to the former great state of Jin. At the same time that Shang Yang was chancellor of Qin, the Han government was administered by a man named Shen Buhai (d. 337). He contributed notions of bureaucracy to the theory of government known as Legalism, stressing the need for impersonal—and thus impartial—rule. He argued that since it is impossible for a ruler to know all of his subjects personally, it is necessary for him to group them into classes and deal with them through officials. On the other hand, the ruler must never allow any one official to become too powerful. Shen Buhai likened the government to a wheel: the ruler was the hub, empty and essentially motionless, while the many ministers should "act together like the spokes." One important innovation of this bureaucratic model is that officials were paid a salary for their service rather than living off the labor of peasants attached to awards of land; the amount of salary paid came to indicate the rank of the official. This innovation was soon adopted by all of the other states as well. For instance, by the late third century, the state of Qin extended this salary system to all government employees. Among the government records written on bamboo strips and found in 1975 at Shuihudi, Hubei is the following instruction:

Government secretaries and runners receive a half bushel of polished grain, a quarter pint of sauce, and leeks and onions for soup. Those of the fifth rank and above are fed according to their rank. Relatives of runners receive a half bushel of husked grain, while servants receive a third of a bushel.[29]

Over the next century, the various states competed with each other to attract the most qualified officials and generals, who traveled from state to state offering their services. However, it was the state of Qin that implemented Legalist policies most effectively and became the preeminent power, eventually conquering all of the other states and unifying the empire. In 221, after completing the conquest, the First Emperor of Qin (r. 246/221–210) convened a meeting of his principal advisers to consider how to rule the vast newly conquered lands. Most of the advisers recommended looking to the past for precedent—to the early Zhou dynasty when royal relatives were deputed to rule over the territories. However, one adviser, Li Si (c. 280–208), argued against this policy, and recommended that these newly conquered territories should also be ruled from the capital, in the same way as the territory of Qin had been ruled. Accepting this argument, the First Emperor divided the land into thirty-six commanderies (jun). Fully half of these had previously existed as commanderies, six in Qin itself, and twelve others in the various conquered states. This was an administrative structure that has remained in place, at least in principle, down to the present day.

It is now possible to see how the administration of this vast empire worked. In 2002, archaeologists in the city of Liye, Hunan discovered some 37,000 bamboo strips that had been deposited in a well at the end of the Qin dynasty. This is now regarded as the most important archaeological discovery of Qin remains after only the discovery of the terracotta warriors buried near the tomb of the First Emperor. During the Qin dynasty, Liye was the county seat of Qianling county of Dongting commandery, and these strips constituted part of the archive of the local government. They demonstrate a great deal of detail about that local government, but perhaps most important they also show how the imperial government functioned. Laws and edicts were promulgated in the capital, and copies were sent to each of the commanderies, which in turn were required to send copies to each county in its jurisdiction, and so on even to areas below the county level. This required an enormous bureaucracy, which was one of the Qin government's greatest legacies to later Chinese civilization. The empire was conquered by the sword, but it was ruled by the writing brush.

CHAPTER 19
ESSAY ON LAW

As is often the case for ancient China, the earliest evidence of law—or at least of the administration of punishments—is seen in the oracle-bone inscriptions of the Shang dynasty. There is evidence of four of what would come to be a series of five mutilating punishments. In all four cases, the punishment is portrayed in the pictograph corresponding to the word for the punishment. Only in the last case is the oracle-bone form of the graph directly antecedent to the present-word, and even in that case the word now has a different meaning.

- 劓 "to cut off the nose," the character combining a nose and a knife, corresponding to the modern character *yi* 劓

- 𠂆 "to amputate the leg," the character combining a frontal view of a person with one foot missing and a hand holding a saw, corresponding to the modern character *yue* 刖

- 斀 "to castrate," the character combining a penis and a knife, corresponding to the modern character *zhuo* 剢

- 伐 "to decapitate," the character combining the blade of a dagger-axe going through a man's neck, corresponding to the modern character *fa* 伐 "to attack"

The fifth of the mutilating punishments, the lightest of the five, was tattooing the face, the character for which is seen in later Zhou-dynasty bronze inscriptions: 墨 (corresponding to the modern character *mo* 墨 "ink; inky"), the mark on the face clearly visible, as it would have been on the person so marked for life as a criminal.

As is also often the case, it is during the Western Zhou period that we encounter the earliest expressions of what would later become fundamental principles of Chinese civilization. Notions of law are no exception. Most histories of Chinese law begin with the "Pronouncement to Kang" chapter of the *Exalted Scriptures*. It purports to be an announcement to Kangshu Feng, the youngest main-line son of King Wen of Zhou (r. 1099/1056–1050), when he was appointed to oversee the former capital territory of the Shang dynasty, just a few years after the Zhou conquest of the Shang. Chinese historians debate whether the king who made the address was King Wu (r. 1049/1045–1043) or the Duke of Zhou (d. *c.* 1030) speaking on behalf of the young King Cheng (r. 1042/1035–1006), but it is likely that the address took place after the deaths of those two founding fathers, and certainly after the Zhou suppressed the Shang people's rebellion against Zhou rule.

There are several fundamental principles that Feng is told to uphold. First, given that he is overseeing the people of the former Shang capital, he is told to consider the laws of the former dynasty, and to follow them when they are proper. More important, he is to consider whether crimes are committed intentionally or by accident, and to adjust the punishment accordingly. A small crime, if committed intentionally, was to be punished harshly, but even a great crime, if committed accidentally, was to be treated leniently. Of even more interest, crimes within a family were also within the purview of the ruler: a son who transgressed against the dictates of filial piety or a father who did not treat his son properly were seen as throwing into disorder the "righteousness of Heaven"; they were beyond pardon. In a similar vein, teachers and government officials were to be held to an especially high standard. The king says that he "detests" any action that corrupts the young or takes advantage of the common people.

The document is too lengthy to quote in its entirety. The portion concerning the law as we might understand it reads as follows:

> The king said: "*Wuhu*! Feng, respectfully understand your punishments. When men have small crimes that are not accidental, but carried to the end, intentionally acting contrary to the statutes, even though their crimes be small, you must put them to death. But in the case of great crimes not carried to the end, but done accidentally or by mischance, if they confess their guilt, you must not put these to death.... It is not for you Feng to punish or put men to death; do not randomly punish or put men to death. It is not for you Feng to cut off the nose or ears; do not randomly cut off the nose or ears.... In deciding to imprison someone, deliberate upon it for five or six days or even for ten days; do not blindly imprison someone.... All those people who are guilty of their own accord, who rob and steal, are villainous and traitorous, who kill and take others' property, blindly unafraid of death; there are none who do not detest these."

The king said: "Feng, of the most vile and detestable, what could be more so than being unfilial or unbrotherly. A son who does not respectfully serve his father greatly wounds his father's heart. Or a father who is unable to love his son brings pain to his son. . . . In pitying these, if we in government do not arrest the criminals, the righteousness that Heaven has given our people will be greatly disordered. You must quickly follow King Wen to determine their guilt, punishing them without pardon. In following the great laws, how much more so those who teach others: the governors, minor ministers, the regulators, responsible for distributing and broadcasting the laws, meeting with great praise from the people; if they do not consider or use them, they afflict their ruler. These then lead others to be wicked; it is they I detest. You should quickly follow what is proper and put them to death."[30]

The conception of law as expressed in the "Pronouncement to Kang" depends almost exclusively on the discretion of the ruler; it was apparently up to the ruler even to decide what constituted a crime and what did not. Another chapter of the *Exalted Scriptures*, also purports to date to the Western Zhou period, though to a period a hundred or so years later than the "Pronouncement to Kang." This is the "Punishment of Lü" ("Lü xing"), which spells out the various punishments appropriate for different crimes. This code is supposed to date to the reign of King Mu of Zhou (r. 956–918), and he has been roundly criticized for divorcing the law from the personal virtue of the ruler. He is even more criticized because the text includes ways that the mutilating punishments can be avoided by paying fines, essentially allowing the rich to commit crimes with impunity. However, it is almost certain that this text dates to a later period, probably toward the end of the Springs and Autumns period, when several states began to codify their law-codes and even to inscribe them onto bronze or iron vessels.

There is other evidence that really does come from the Western Zhou period. It too was inscribed on bronze vessels of that period. But these are not systematic law codes. Rather, they are the occasional records of actual law cases. Because of the nature of bronze vessels, which were cast to commemorate successes in the life of an individual—such as appointments at the royal court or victories in battle—records of criminal cases are quite rare. In one case, however, we can see that the paying of a fine to avoid a mutilating punishment really did take place at this ancient period. The *Ying yi* dates to the late Western Zhou dynasty, probably just before or after 800. Its inscription records a verdict against someone referred to as "Shepherd," who apparently broke an agreement that he had with Ying, the person who cast the vessel, and thus almost certainly the person who won the lawsuit. It is interesting that Shepherd was initially sentenced to be whipped and branded, but this punishment was then commuted to a lesser whipping and the payment of a fine. In the end, it seems that the sentence was reduced just to the payment of a fine.

It was the third month after the dying brightness, *jiashen* (day 21), the king was at the Upper Palace of Pang. Elder Yangfu then reached a verdict, saying: "Shepherd, ah, how could you have gone so far! You have dared to sue your captain, and you have even been duplicitous regarding your former oath. And now you have again gone against your oath, so far as to go over the wall to meet with Ying promising to bring these five men, and now you have again gone against your oath. You must again abide by your words and your oath. Would that it can be proper. I ought to whip you 1,000 times and cut your face, but now I greatly pardon you, and will whip you 500 times and fine you 300 catties." Elder Yangfu then made Shepherd again swear an oath saying: "From now on if I dare to trouble your minor or major officers or if your captain again accuses you, then I will cause you to be whipped 1,000 times and to cut-and-ink your face. Shepherd then swore the oath in order to report to Officer Xiong and Officer Hu at Hui. Shepherd's verdict and oath completed, he was fined bronze. Ying herewith makes this sacrificial ewer.[31]

In another case, the *Fifth Year Qiu Wei ding*, the inscription of which was translated in Chapter Four above, provides the record of yet another lawsuit between two individuals: Qiu Wei, the patron of the vessel, and a States-lord Li. According to Qiu Wei's suit, States-lord Li had promised to turn over to Qiu Wei five different fields, but States-lord Li apparently reneged on the deal. The case was heard before a jury of five person, most of whom are known from other bronze inscriptions of the period as important senior officers of the court. After a brief interrogation, they determined that States-lord Li was required to relinquish the fields as agreed, their boundaries stipulated. It is interesting to note that his son and several of his assistants were also required to treat Qiu Wei to a banquet, as a way of sealing the deal. In later Chinese history, banquets were routinely held to formalize agreements.

As mentioned above, by the close of the Springs and Autumns period, law codes began to be formalized, and even inscribed on bronze or iron vessels such that they were immutable and available for all to see. The first state to have done this, in 536, is said to be the small state of Zheng, under the leadership of its prime minister Zi Chan (d. 522). Zi Chan was harshly criticized for this by Shu Xiang (d. 528), the prime minister of the larger state of Jin, who argued that in antiquity the law was embodied in the virtue of the ruler, quoting the *Classic of Poetry* (*Shi jing*) as saying:

> A proper model the Cultured King,
> The ten thousand countries the proof.[32]

According to Shu Xiang, the sage-kings of old, such as King Wen (r. 1099/1056–1050) had been able to consider all the circumstances of a case in making their decision on a case-by-case basis, unrestrained by an overly literal interpretation of the law. By introducing written law, the people would come to distrust their rulers and become ever more litigious. Many historians also see this as a transfer of power from the nobility to the common people. While all of this is doubtless true, it is also true that King Wen had died over five hundred years before this time, and that by the time of Shu Xiang there were no longer any sage-kings in whom to trust. And so, in 513, the state of Jin itself cast a vessel, said to have been of iron, inscribed with its own legal code. This code is supposed to have been the text of the *Book of Punishments*, the writing of which is credited to Fan Xuanzi (d. 548) some half century earlier.

Over the course of the following Warring States period, every state that was still independent promulgated similar law codes, whether they cast them in metal or not. In Wei, Li Kui (455–395) is said to have written the *Classic of Laws* shortly after being appointed prime minister in 422. Although this book has long been lost, early quotations suggest that it was divided into three parts: "Formal Statutes," "Miscellaneous Statutes," and "Statutes Concerning Losses." The Formal Statutes included crimes against others: Robbery, Assault, Imprisonment, and Arrests; the Miscellaneous Statutes concerned personal behavior: Deceit, Illegal Entry into Cities, Gambling, Fraud, Immodesty, Lewd Behavior, and Overstepping One's Position; the Statutes Concerning Losses apparently concerned what we would today term inventory control. It is said that when Shang Yang (*c.* 390–338) left his native state of Wei to go to Qin in about 360, the one book he took with him was this *Classic of Laws*; it would become the foundation of Qin's own legal code.

Shang Yang's reforms in Qin pertained to every aspect of the Qin government, including of course the legal system. The book he is credited with writing, *The Book of the Lord Shang,* has a fully elaborated theory of law, and is generally regarded as the founding text of the political philosophy known as Legalism. It would eventuate in the final dismantling of the former nobility, replacing it with a bureaucracy that was strictly bound to interpreting and administering the laws exactly as they were written, with little room for personal discretion. The best evidence for this legal system was discovered in 1975 in a tomb at Shuihudi, in present-day Hubei province. This area was formerly within the state of Chu, but had been conquered by Qin in 278 and incorporated into the expanding Qin state. The tomb of a mid-level local magistrate named Happy (Xi; d. 217), it included many of the texts that he would have used during his life to adjudicate cases. The most important of these documents is a set of eighteen statutes, covering the following topics: Agriculture, Stables and Parks, Granaries, Currency, Passes and Markets, Craftsmen, Norms for Craftsmen, Equalizing Craftsmen, Labor, the Supervisors of Works, Appointments of Officials, Checking, Noble Ranks for Military Actions, Rations for Passport Holders, Transmission of Documents, Ministers of Finance, Commandants, Dependent States. Almost all of these concern the civil administration of the government, though they also touch on punishment for failure to carry out the statutes properly. One example from the statute on "Checking," which refers to inventory control, will give some indication as to just how detailed these statutes were.

> When a granary leaks and rots the grain, as well as when one piles up grain causing it to go bad, if what is not edible amounts to less than 100 bushels, then reprimand the foreman; if it is between 100 and 1000 bushels, then fine the foreman one set of armor; if it is more than 1,000 bushels, then fine the foreman two sets of armor. Command the foreman and the officers working there jointly to repay the cost of the grain. If the grain is still edible despite having gone bad, then weigh it. Determine the responsibility on the basis of the number of bushels wasted.[33]

As detailed as these statutes were, it was anticipated that there would still be questions about their interpretation. There is another document, the longest of all the legal documents in this tomb, that was called by the archaeologists *Answers to Questions about Laws and Statutes.* These questions ask about various extenuating circumstances. For instance, consider the following scenario:

A stole a cow. When he stole the cow, he was six *chi* tall (i.e., 1.4 m or about 4'7"). After he had been imprisoned for one year, he was again measured, and was found to be six *chi* seven *cun* tall (i.e., 1.57 m or about 5'2"). Question: How is A to be judged? He is considered to be a full "wall-pounder."[34]

It is clear here that A was a juvenile when he stole the cow, but that after spending a year in jail he had reached an adult stature. If he had been judged while still a juvenile, it is likely that his sentence would have been lighter. But because he was already an adult when the final verdict was pronounced, he was thus sentenced as an adult to hard labor.

Another text, *Models for Sealing and Investigating,* reads almost like a set of detective stories, presenting cases of crimes and how the detective proposed to solve the case. Another case involving a cow will illustrate something of the flavor of these cases.

> "A Fight over a Cow": Reported in writing: Constable A of such-and-such village and commoner B brought in one cow; it was a black female, with a long halter and horns. They reported saying: "This is A and B's cow, which had run off. We each recognize it. Jointly bringing it in, we have fought over it." I immediately commanded such-and-such a clerk to examine the cow's teeth (to determine its age); the cow was six years old.[35]

Not all cases provide a resolution. Nevertheless, they can still be remarkably informative about the society of the time. The final case to be considered here concerns slavery and the right of owners to inflict bodily mutilation upon their slaves, almost wantonly.

> "Tattooing a Female Slave": Reported in writing: Constable A of such-and-such village bound and brought in an adult female named C, and reported saying: "I am the headman of alderman B of such-and-such village. C is B's female slave. B has sent A to say: 'C is unruly. I petition to tattoo her and cut off her nose.' Interrogating C, she said: 'I am B's female slave. I have not been charged with any crime.' Prefect so-and-so reports to the chief of such-and-such district: 'Constable A of such-and-such village brought in B's adult female named C, saying: "B commands A to petition to tattoo her and cut off her nose."' Is this as he says or not?" Make certain of the name, affair, and village, any

crimes for which she has been charged, and whether she has been questioned again or not. Report in writing.[36]

There are other cases, unfortunately too long to be considered here, that take up a number of especially difficult cases. In the case of one murder, the detective was required to provide a forensic examination of the body, and a complete description of the crime scene, including footprints. In another, a woman six months pregnant miscarried; it is clear that she was suspected of aborting the fetus. A female bondwoman was made to give her a vaginal examination, while others interrogated other members of the woman's household. Finally, there is another case in which a doctor is called in to examine a man suspected of having leprosy. The doctor's report of his examination leaves no doubt about the diagnosis: "C has no eyebrows. The bridge of his nose is gone, his nostrils are rotted, and when I pricked his nose he did not sneeze." The diagnosis: leprosy.

It is clear from all of these documents buried together with Happy in the tomb at Shuihudi that these legal codes were intended as much to ensure that officials performed their duties correctly as they were to regulate the common people. Indeed, these statutes were an important step in the development of bureaucracy in China, the lasting achievement of Legalism.

CHAPTER 20
ESSAY ON MUSIC

In the Chinese language, there is an intrinsic relationship between "music" (*yue*) and "joy" (*le*), which despite the different pronunciations of the words in modern Chinese, their ancient pronunciations were almost identical, and they are both written with the same character. But more than just the emotional enjoyment one derives from music, it was also understood that music was a form of non-verbal communication between an individual or a group of musical performers and both the social and natural worlds. An early treatise on music, the *Record of Music* begins with the following passage:

> In all cases, music comes to life from the human heart. It is the case that things cause the human heart to be moved. Resonating with things, it takes shape in sounds; the sounds corresponding with each other gives life to changes; and changes producing a pattern is what are called notes. Putting notes side by side and enjoying them, and adding to them shields and halberds, feathers and pennants, is called music.[37]

In addition to the affective derivation of music, this passage entails at least a couple of other points that are basic to it. Music is sound, but it is not just sound; it is only when different sounds—notes, when they are differentiated— are put together into a coherent pattern does sound become music. But even this does not exhaust what music was in ancient China. The "shields and halberds, feathers and pennants" that were to be added to the sounds refer to the costumes that martial and civil dancers wore as they danced to the music; dance too was an intrinsic part of music.

Of course, it was theoretically possible for a single individual to make music in solitude by playing a single instrument, or by simply singing a cappella or even just whistling. However, the full communicative force of music was produced in a social setting, and the social setting that is most often mentioned in ancient Chinese texts was either the ancestral temple or the royal (or ducal) court. One of the earliest descriptions of such a musical performance is the poem "Blind Musicians," which is contained in the *Zhou Hymns*, the most ancient portion of the *Classic of Poetry*. I include the Chinese characters; even those unable to read them will see at a glance that the lines are uniform in having four characters, which I have tried to replicate by translating into a modified iambic tetrameter. This meter, which is characteristic not only of the poetry in the *Classic of Poetry*, but also of much of ancient Chinese prose literature, probably derives from the four-beat meter of the music (or eight beats in two lines), the underlying rhythm of which was supplied by bells and drums. The visual appearance of the Chinese characters may not suggest this percussive aural dimension, but perhaps the English translation captures to some extent their sounds. Another feature of poems in the *Classic of Poetry* is that they frequently use onomatopoeic reduplicatives to describe the sound of the music: here "booming-booming (*huang-huang*) for the sound of the pan-pipes and flutes. This linguistic feature is seen first on inscriptions of bells themselves.

有瞽有瞽,	Blind musicians, blind musicians,
在周之庭。	In the court of the house of Zhou.
設業設虡,	Setting out stands, setting out racks,
崇牙樹羽,	With looming hooks and standing plumes,
應田縣鼓,	Responding snares and hanging drums,
鞉磬柷圉。	Hand-drums, chime-stones, bongos, clappers,
既備乃奏。	Being ready they then perform.
簫管備舉,	Pan-pipes and flutes ready and raised,
喤喤厥聲,	Booming-booming are their sounds
肅雝和鳴,	Blended in harmonious call,
先祖是聽。	This is what the ancestors hear.
我客戾止,	Our guests arrive in a jumble,
永觀厥成。	Long observing their completion.[38]

Set in the ancestral temple, musical performances were an ideal means of social communication. Performed after the sacrificial offerings had been made to the ancestors, it was thought that the music would carry the prayers up to those ancestors. Whether the ancestors would hear them or not, the visitors to the temple would certainly find an impressive spectacle. Imagine having just observed the food and wine offered to the ancestors, and then participating in a banquet in which those offerings were then consumed by the guests. Then, with the dishes cleared away, the musical entertainment would begin. The stage would have been set in advance: the bells and drums and chime-stones, the mainstays of the earliest orchestras, were hung from their racks to either side of the main stage, carefully calibrated in different sizes so as to produce different notes. Other instruments were placed to the fore: mouth organs, bamboo flutes and string instruments; these would carry the melody. In front of these instruments and between the bells and drums would be ranks of dancers, all dressed in their finest robes and moving in unison. Another poem from the *Classic of Poetry*, called "Thorny Brambles," describes the scene. Too lengthy to quote in its entirety, the first stanzas describe the sacrifice and the banquet; the last two stanzas then describe the musical entertainment.

> Ceremonies being finished, The bells and drums having sounded,
> The pious grandson takes his place.
> The presiding priest brings the report:
> "The spirits are all drunk." The august corpse is now to rise.
> The bells and drums escort the corpse, The divine guard comes in return.
> The many aides and lords' ladies Clear the dishes without delay.
> The many uncles and brothers Make ready to feast on their own.
> Musicians all enter to play, To make secure fortune to come.
> Your meats having been presented, None resentful, all celebrate.
> Being drunk and being sated, The young and old touch heads to ground.
> Spirits enjoyed the food and drink, Granting our lord longevity.
> Very kindly, very timely, May he keep them until the end.
> With sons' sons and grandsons' grandsons Never failing to extend them.[39]

Songs such as "Thorny Brambles" would come to be regarded as the classical music of ancient China. But this was not the only music of the time. Once when Mencius (*c.* 385–303) was having an audience with King Huicheng of Wei (r. 369–334, 334–319), the king said to him: "I don't understand the music of the kings of old; I only like popular music." Mencius attempted to turn the conversation to a lesson in good government, but the king's preference points to ways some music changed in the several hundred years from when the *Classic of Poetry* was composed until the time of King Huicheng. Songs, apparently now driven by the lilting melodies of flutes and zithers rather than the somber pounding of bells and drums, could grow to great lengths and could move from the ancestral temple to the halls of court.

Essays

The following brief passage from a long song called "Summoning the Soul" included in the collection *Verses of Chu* describes a song and dance performance that seems to have ended in an orgy. Perhaps it is not so unusual that King Huicheng would enjoy popular music.

> The delicacies still not cleared, the female musicians take their places.
> Arraying the bells and setting the drums, they launch into the latest songs.
> "Crossing the River," "Plucking the Water-Chestnut," Starting up "Holding Up the Water-Lily."
> Beautiful people all drunk, Rouged faces are all flushed.
> Flirtatious smiles and fleeting glances, Eyes wave from one to another.
> All made up in gauzy silks, The beauty is truly rare.
> Long hair piled on high, So many bright colors aclash.
> Two rows of eight costumed dancers, Start up the "Dance of Zheng."
> Sleeves like swaying reeds, Bodies dipping to the floor.
> Pan-pipes and zithers join wildly, The drums booming out.
> The halls of court thunder and shake, As they start up "Whirling Chu."
> The songs of Wu and tunes of Cai, Now presenting the "Great Pitch."
> Men and women sitting together, All tangled in a heap.
> Hat-strings and sashes come undone, Whirling around all mixed up.[40]

This is not to say that classical music did not have its own sensual quality. The most famous poem—song—in the *Classic of Poetry* is the very first one in the collection; it is called "J-o-i-n, the Osprey." It begins with the call of one osprey to another, which leads the male protagonist to think of his lover. Beginning with a brief description of some aspect of nature—birds and animals, plants and trees—and then following this with the main topic of the poem, almost invariably human relationships and human emotions, is a common feature of poems in the *Airs of the States* section of the *Classic of Poetry*, and would continue to characterize much of Chinese poetry also in much later times. Some modern readers regard these references to nature as more or less meaningless, intended only to set the rhyme scheme to be used in the poem. This is a serious misreading of what in Chinese intellectual history is often referred to as "correlative thought," which sees an intrinsic relationship between the natural and human realms. When Confucius (551–479) encouraged his disciples to study the *Classic of Poetry* in order to be able "to recognize the names of birds and animals, plants and trees," his interest was almost surely not pedantically biological. Instead, he believed that birds and animals, plants and trees are part of the same world order as family members and statesmen. Some animals are crafty, while others can be tamed; some plants are bitter, while others are sweet. According to Confucius, the better we understand nature, the better we will understand human society as well. Indeed, in some senses, the poets and musicians of ancient China transcribed the sounds of nature into their poetry and music. In "J-o-i-n, the Osprey," the call the osprey makes is written with Chinese characters, *guan guan*, which mean "join together"; indeed, they might even be rendered more crudely as "bang bang." The poem climaxes with the banging of bells and drums, usually understood as a celebration of the marriage of the protagonist and his lover. The Chinese characters again show something of the structure of the poem.

"J-o-i-n, the Osprey"

關關雎鳩，	在河之洲。	*J-o-i-n J-o-i-n*, chirped the osprey, On the island of the river.
窈窕淑女，	君子好逑。	Shy and slender is the chaste girl, For the lord's son a loving mate.
參差荇菜，	左右流之。	Up and down the water lilies, To the left and right drifting them.
窈窕淑女，	寤寐求之。	Shy and slender is the chaste girl, Awake and asleep seeking her.
求之不得，	寤寐思服。	Seeking her but not getting her, Awake and asleep wishing to pair.
悠哉悠哉，	輾轉反側。	Longing, ah, longing ah, Tossing and turning to and fro.
參差荇菜，	左右采之。	Up and down the water lilies, To the left and right picking them.
窈窕淑女，	琴瑟友之。	Shy and slender is the chaste girl, With harp and lute befriending her.
參差荇菜，	左右芼之。	Up and down the water lilies, To the left and right choosing them.
窈窕淑女，	鐘鼓樂之。	Shy and slender is the chaste girl, With bell and drum delighting her.[41]

Bells and drums were clearly the premier instruments of ancient Chinese music, the bells in particular requiring great expenditures—and great expertise—to be produced. One of the unique features of the earliest Chinese chime bells, already evident beginning in the mid-Western Zhou, is that they had two distinct tones, an octave apart, depending on where they were struck. Since the bells were graduated in size, they each produced different tones. Later music came to be based on a pentatonic scale, the five tones being called *gong*, corresponding to *do* in American musical notation; *zhi: sol*; *shang: re*; *yu: la*; and *jue: mi*. Musicians soon realized that each of the five tones was related to the other tones by a single interval, which in Western music is termed a fifth: *zhi* was a fifth above *gong*, *shang* a fifth above *zhi*, *yu* a fifth above *shang*, and *jue* a fifth above *yu*. The entire scale could be generated by the numerical ratio of 3:2 in terms of the frequency of vibration. That is to say, if the length of a string of a zither or a hollow bamboo tube of a flute were shortened by one-third, it would produce a pitch one fifth higher than the first, and so on. Since this ratio would extend over more than two octaves, another way of producing tones within a single octave would be to alternate between ratios of 2:3 and 4:3. In a hypothetical construction, if we started with a string or tube 81 cm long producing a C, this would give four other strings or tubes of 54 (G), 72 (D), 48 (A), and 64 (E) cm.

When an orchestra played together, it was necessary to tune this pentatonic scale to a pitch standard (*lü*), to adjust for the different instruments that may not all have been made with the same lengths of strings or tubes. A chapter of the *Springs and Autumns of Mr. Lü* called "Ancient Music" attributes the discovery of different pitches to someone named Ling Lun, a minister to the Yellow Emperor (Huang Di), who lived in the third millennium BCE. It says that Ling Lun could distinguish the cries of phoenixes, with the males producing six pitches and the females six other pitches. The Yellow Emperor is then said to have ordered that a set of twelve bells be cast to harmonize the five tones according to these pitches. The twelve pitches are called *Wuyi* (corresponding to A in the Western scale), *Yize* (G), *Ruibin* (F), *Guxi* (E), *Taicu* (D) and *Huangzhong* (C) of the male pitches, and *Yingzhong* (B), *Nanlü* (A), *Linzhong* (G), *Zhonglü* (F), *Jiazhong* (D), and *Dalü* (C) of the female pitches. These two sets of six pitches alternate between the male and female pitches, one full tone apart in their order, though the female pitches were considered subordinate to the male; therefore, it was also common to speak in terms of just six pitches.

Needless to say, the story of Ling Lun producing these pitches from the cries of phoenixes is a creation myth. Bells were not used in sets until the ninth century BCE, and even then Western Zhou bell sets may not have been based on the pentatonic scale, since they included only four tones per octave, lacking *shang: re*. This does not necessarily mean that this earliest music did not use a pentatonic scale; the bells doubtless provided the deep structure of the music, and there may well have been other instruments, such as pan-pipes and flutes—as mentioned in the poem "Blind Musicians"— that made use of the full scale. However, it is the case that the earliest evidence of pitch standards does come from inscriptions on bells: sixty-four bells found in the tomb of Lord Yi of Zeng. The inscriptions on these bells provide a full set of musical notations for the tones the bells were capable of playing; it is particularly interesting that while the notations conform to the music of the state of Zeng, the inscriptions also provide translations of the names of the tones in the different states of the time. The notes are indicated as a relationship between the pitch and the tone; for instance, the notation "*gong* of *guxi*" refers to a bell on which an A-tone produced a C-pitch. With such a massive set of bells, they could play over three full octaves.

Music was not just correlated with nature; it was also seen to be in tune with the politics of the time. One of the chapters of the *Record of Ritual* is called the "Record of Music." It begins by differentiating between "sounds" and "notes" and "music," regarding music as the highest expression of human relationships.

> In general, musical notes are born from the hearts of humans. Music connects human relationships. This is why the birds and beasts know sounds but do not know musical notes, while the masses of people know musical notes but do not know music. Only the gentleman is able to know music.

The "Record of Music" continues by correlating the five tones of the pentatonic scale with social ranks: *gong*, "the ruler"; *shang*, "the minister"; *jue*, "the people"; *zhi*, "events"; and *yu*, "objects."

> If the five notes are not disordered, then there will be no dissonant pitches. If *gong* is out of order, then there is chaos; it is because the ruler is arrogant. If *shang* is out of order, then it is aslant; it is because the ministers are corrupt. . . . If all five tones are out of order, then they intrude upon each other in turn; this is called *lento*. Like this, the state will be lost in no time.[42]

In the actual performance of music, *gong*, correlated with the ruler, was the primary tone of a composition, the "tonic" from which the other four tones would be generated and the main theme to which the piece would return after visiting the other tones. In theory, when music was performed properly, it had the potential to transform society. The Confucian philosopher Xunzi (c. 316–217) wrote an "Essay on Music" in which he argued that music could bring about harmony in the world.

> When music proceeds, the will is clarified; when ritual is refined, conduct is perfected. The ears and eyes are discerning and bright, the blood and *qi* harmonious and balanced. It changes the airs and alters customs, and all under heaven is tranquil, the beautiful and good delighting each other.[43]

Harmony is a musical quality, but also a social quality. Confucius drew on both senses to make one of his most famous sayings:

> The Master said: "The gentleman harmonizes but does not copy; the petty man copies but does not harmonize."[44]

A musical composition that played the same note over and over again would not be beautiful music. So too, people just copying the behavior of others makes for a boring—and ultimately disharmonious—society. Relations work best when we each sound our own note, though set to the same key.

CHAPTER 21
ESSAY ON BRONZE

Of all of the arts that the craftsmen of ancient China practiced with very great skill, such as pottery making, jade carving, silk weaving, and lacquer designs, the supreme art was doubtless that of the bronze casters. It is not a coincidence that most of ancient Chinese history occurred during the period routinely referred to as the Bronze Age. Bronze was employed throughout the entire period in making the implements of both ritual and warfare, routinely said to be "the great affairs of state," and it is prominently displayed throughout the museums of the world.

Bronze is an alloy of copper and tin. In ancient China, lead was usually added as well. The casting of bronze vessels began in central China early in the second millennium BCE, some thousand or more years later than its first appearance in West Asia. Although the origin of Chinese bronze casting is debated in China, with many archaeologists still arguing for indigenous invention, it is increasingly clear that at least the idea of smelting ores to produce a liquid that would then harden into a new shape, if not the technique of casting bronze vessels themselves, came into China from the west. The earliest items made of cast bronze in what is today China, knives and jewelry cast in flat stone molds or perhaps bivalve molds, are found in the western provinces of Xinjiang and especially Gansu, appearing as much as one thousand years before bronze is first seen in China proper. The first bronze vessels to appear in the Central Plains of China were found at the Erlitou site, very near the city of Luoyang in northern Henan province. Although there is also a debate about the identification of this Erlitou Culture, archaeologists and historians in China routinely regard it as the capital of the Xia dynasty, and this is certainly consistent with its location and date, around 1700–1600. These earliest vessels, which appear somewhat crude by later standards, would quickly develop into some of the most beautiful bronze pieces seen anywhere in the world.

While knives and jewelry could be cast in flat stone molds or simple bivalve molds, the casting of even the simplest vessel required a much more

Figure 21.1 Early Western Zhou bronze *zun*-vase; Metropolitan Museum of Art, New York; 24.72.4.

elaborate technology. In the West, from the earliest times, bronze-casting made use of the "lost-wax" method of casting, which began with a model of the desired vessel or implement made in clay and coated with wax, around which still more clay was packed with an opening at the bottom. This whole assemblage was then heated, causing the wax to melt and flow out of opening at the bottom of the assemblage, while the clay baked into a hard outer shell, which would then serve as a mold. Molten bronze was then poured into the opening, filling the void inside the mold left by the melted wax. Once the assemblage cooled, and the molten bronze had hardened, the clay mold was then broken apart, leaving just the desired vessel or implement in bronze. By contrast, from the very earliest times in China the casting of bronze vessels was achieved with a technique referred to as piece-mold casting. This began with making a model of the desired bronze vessel in semi-hard clay; if any décor was desired on the exterior of the vessel, this might be added to the model at this time. Next, a mold, also made of clay in several pieces, was fitted around this model. This mold, which could be taken apart and then fitted

Figure 21.2 Early Western Zhou-dynasty *you*-wine warmer; *c.* 1050 BCE; Metropolitan Museum of Art, New York; 24.72.3a, b.

back together again, would accept the shape of the model, as well as any ornamentation that had been applied to it; other ornamentation could be applied directly to the interior of the mold, when it was opened. The model would then be removed from the mold assemblage, placed on a base, and its outer layer would then be shaved off, to the desired thickness of the intended bronze vessel. This sounds like a very cumbersome procedure; in fact, it was probably not much more difficult than using a vegetable peeler to peel the outer layer of a potato or a carrot. Once this layer of clay had been removed from the original model, the remaining clay would then become the core of the casting assemblage. The mold was then placed again around the model, which was now the core of the assemblage, with an opening or openings into which molten bronze could be poured and out of which the gasses produced by the bronze could escape. The molten bronze would fill the space between

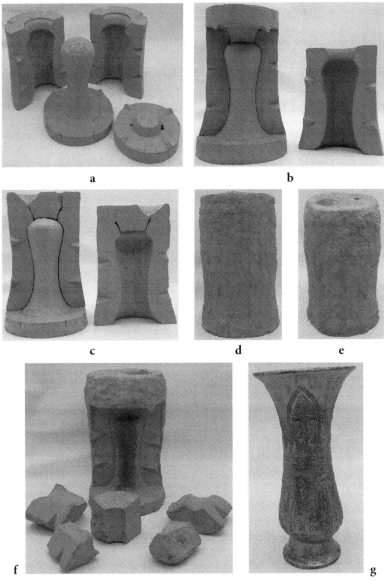

a   b

c   d   e

f   g

Figure 21.3 Models showing the process of piece-mold casting for a bronze *zhi*-beaker; courtesy of Lian Haiping, Shanghai Museum.

the core and the mold. When it cooled, the mold could then be opened, inside of which would be the bronze vessel, together with the décor that was on the mold. Strangely enough, although it seems logical that these mold assemblages could be reused to make multiple vessels, they seem never to have been re-used; instead, they were broken apart and discarded. The various steps in the process are shown in the Figure 21.3.

Cumbersome though this process would seem to be, it took advantage of a long tradition of pottery making in China, and provided the ancient bronze-casters with at least one great advantage over the lost-wax casting method: they had access to the inside of the mold assemblage, and so could add extremely elaborate and detailed ornamentation to the vessel, as seen in bronze vessels from the early Western Zhou dynasty, about 1000 (Figures 21.1., 21.2). One constraint that the piece-mold technology imposed upon the bronze casters: to be able to take the mold pieces apart and fit them back together again, they needed to be symmetrical about the core. This produced an aesthetic in China that valued symmetry, both in the shape of vessels, and also in their décor.

Bronze vessels were used in sacrifices to the ancestors, whether to warm wine or to cook meat or grain. They also came to carry inscriptions, first very simple inscriptions with just a clan sign or the name of the ancestor to whom sacrifices would be offered. However, over time, the inscriptions would grow longer and longer. While in later times, inscriptions would sometimes be carved into the cold metal with a knife, ordinarily—and certainly from the earliest times—the inscriptions were cast directly into the vessel, usually on the inside, though in the case of some types of vessels or musical instruments, the inscription might appear on the outside. The insertion of these inscriptions entailed yet another step in the complicated procedure of casting a vessel. The text to be inscribed would be incised into clay. This would then be impressed with another slab of clay, producing a relief version of the text originally inscribed into the clay. Then a space would be excavated in the model (i.e., the original core) of the casting assemblage, and this slab of clay carrying the inscription would be inserted into that space. When the vessel was then cast, the inscription would appear on the inside of the vessel, the text being reversed yet again, such that it would appear intaglio (i.e., as if incised) in the vessel.

This same technique could be used to produce inscriptions of any length. By the late Shang dynasty, inscriptions of twenty or thirty characters began to be produced. These usually commemorated an award by the Shang king to the patron for whom the vessel was cast; the vessel was usually dedicated to an ancestor. Throughout the Western Zhou dynasties, inscriptions grew longer and longer, by the end of the period reaching

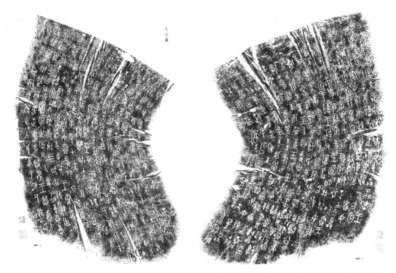

Figure 21.4 Inscription on *Mao Gong ding*; from Luo Zhenyu (1866–1940), *Sandai jijin wencun* (*Repository of writings on auspicious bronzes of the Three Dynasties*) (Shanghai: 1936), 4.46–49.

almost 500 characters in the *Mao Gong ding*, a vessel cast about 800, and commemorating a royal award to the patron: Yin, the Duke of Mao.

Two or three centuries after the time of the *Mao Gong ding*, during the Springs and Autumns period, bronze-casters of China finally began to experiment with lost-wax casting, though even then and thereafter they would use the technique only occasionally, usually preferring to use the time-honored technique of piece-mold casting. The first pieces made with lost-wax casting still show the casters' preference for symmetry.[45] However, it was only a matter of a short time before bronze casters took full advantages to create fantastic creature in every imaginable shape.[46] This would bring to full flower the art of bronze-casting in ancient China.

CHAPTER 22
ESSAY ON WRITING

The preface to *Discussing Pictographs and Analyzing Compound Graphs*, China's earliest dictionary, describes the invention of writing in the following manner:

> In antiquity when Baoxi, Tamer of Beasts, ruled all under heaven, he looked up and observed the images in the heavens, looked down and observed the patterns on the earth, examined the markings of birds and animals and the properties of the earth, and near at hand taking from his own body and at a distance taking from the many things thereupon first made the eight trigrams of the *Changes* in order to suspend patterns and images. Coming to Shennong, the God of Agriculture, he knotted cords by way of governing and systematized the affairs. As the many occupations proliferated, ornament and artifice sprouted. Cangjie, the scribal officer of the Yellow Emperor, saw the tracks and footprints of birds and beasts and knowing that their different patterns could be differentiated, for the first time invented writing.[47]

This suggests that Chinese writing was originally pictographic, based on "the tracks and footprints of birds and beasts," or rather on the shapes of the birds and beasts themselves. The earliest writing in China, the oracle-bone inscriptions of the Shang dynasty, contains hundreds of examples of pictographs. Figure 22.1 shows just a few obvious examples drawn from the animal kingdom.

Whereas pictographs can only depict tangible objects, we speak about much more than this: actions, ideas, directions, names, and so forth, that are not so directly represented. Thus, the *Discussing Pictographs and Analyzing Compound Graphs* dictionary distinguished five other types of characters in addition to pictographs: "pointing at things characters," "combining ideas characters,"

"elephant"　　"cow"　　"sheep"　　"horse"　　"deer"　　"fish"　　"bird"

Figure 22.1 Pictographs of animals seen in Shang oracle-bone inscriptions.

"shape-sound characters," "loan characters," and "explaining each other characters." The first two of these are essentially also pictographic in nature, though their depictions depend on the combination of two or more elements; all of these might best be categorized as "characters that express meaning."

The category "combining ideas characters" is often called "ideographs." While this term is sometimes used—quite incorrectly—to describe all Chinese characters, the oracle-bone inscriptions show that it too was a powerful tool in the toolkit of the inventers of the Chinese script, with additional hundreds of such characters known. The following are just a few examples. The iconicity of the characters may not always be immediately apparent to readers unfamiliar with early Chinese writing; however, in all cases the components are quite conventional and would be well recognized by all readers of the script.

- "to follow" (the modern character *cong* 从 (i.e., 從), the character combining two "men," one following the other
- "back; north" (the modern character *bei* 北 (and by extension *bei* 背), the character combining two "men" back to back
- "to reach" (the modern character *ji* 及), the character combining a "man" and a "hand" reaching him from behind
- "to capture" (the modern character *fu* 孚), the character combining a "child" with a "hand" grabbing it from above
- "to give birth" (the modern character *yu* 毓, the fuller form of *yu* 育), the character combining a "mother" and an upside-down "child" together with added dots indicating amniotic fluid
- "sickness" (the modern character *ji* 疾), the character combining a "bed" and a "man," often with added dots apparently indicating "sweat" from a fever
- "to open" (the modern character *pi* 闢), the character combining a "door" with two hands pushing out
- "to ascend" (the modern character *zhi* 陟), the character combining two "feet" going up a "mound"

"to descend" (the modern character *jiang* 降), the character combining two inverted "feet" going down a "mound"

"to plant" (the modern character *yi* 埶), the character combining a "man with two hands extended" grasping a "tree" over "earth"

"evening" (the modern character *mu* 莫 or *mu* 暮), the character combining a "sun" with four "trees" or "grass"

"morning" (the modern character *zhao* 朝), the character combining a "sun," "moon," and "grass," indicating the time when both the sun and moon are visible in the distance

"to see" (the modern character *jian* 見), the character combining an "eye" with a "person"

"to gaze" (the modern character *wang* 望), the character combining an "eye" directed upward from a "person"

"to attend to (eating); right away" (the modern character *ji* 即), the character combining a "food bowl" with a "kneeling figure" before it

"to finish" (the modern character *ji* 既), the character combining a "food bowl" with a "kneeling figure" whose "mouth" is turned away from the food bowl

"to feast" (the modern character *xiang* 鄉), the character combining a "food bowl" with two "kneeling figures" facing the food bowl

"to crow" (the modern character *ming* 鳴), the character combining a "mouth" and a "bird"

"to bark" (the modern character *fei* 吠), the character combining a mouth and a "dog"

"to smell; to stink" (the modern character *chou* 臭), the character combining a "nose" and a "dog"

The number of such "combining ideas characters" could be multiplied many times over. At the earliest stage of the language, the oracle-bone inscriptions of the Shang dynasty, their iconic meaning is usually unmistakable, as in the case of the "horse" or "deer," though this iconicity tends to get lost at later stages of writing. Other cases, such as *ming* 鳴 "to crow" and *fei* 吠 "to bark," which combine a "mouth" (口) component with the pictograph of a "bird" (鳥) or "dog" (犬), rely on the combination of ideas more than pictography.

The third type of "characters that express meaning" is called "pointing at things characters." It was once thought that there were very few examples of this category, typical examples being the graphs ⌣ and ⌢ differentiated by a single stroke above or below a line indicating the horizon to mean "above" or "below," now written as 上 and 下; or 末 and 本 for the "crown of a tree" and "roots of a tree" respectively with a line indicating the part of the tree ("tree" being written in modern Chinese characters as 木). Now it is known that many other characters were formed more or less in the same way, as the following examples taken from the human body show:

- 𝟤 "forearm" (the precursor to the modern character *hong* 厷), a circle on the arm beneath the hand (i.e., *you* 又) marking this part of the arm

- 𝟤 "elbow" (the precursor to the modern character *zhou* 肘), a noticeable bending at the end of the forearm (i.e., *you* 又), with an additional mark indicating the point of focus

- 𝟤 "to kneel" (the precursor to the modern character *gui* 跪), a mark beneath the knee of a kneeling figure (*jie* 卩 or 㔾)

- 𝟤 "armpit" the precursor to the modern character *ye* 腋), the dots indicated under the arms of a figure standing frontally (i.e., *da* 大)

The several examples here in which the "pointing at things character" is indicated as the precursor of a modern character means that a character was first written in one form and subsequently came to be written in a different form (often referred to in Chinese as "ancient-and-modern characters") provide good examples of another important category of characters: "loan characters." These are characters where the sound of a word that can be drawn with a pictograph is "borrowed" to write a homophonous word that would be difficult to depict. This is the rebus principle, known not only from modern television game shows (as in 𝟤 Reader, 𝟤 ♡ 𝟤), but also in all other ancient writing systems. These loan characters were already routinely employed in the Shang oracle-bone inscriptions, as for instance in using the pictograph of the "nose" 𝟤 (i.e., *zi* 自) to indicate the homophonous preposition "from," or the pictograph of a "basket" 𝟤 (now pronounced *ji* and written 箕) to write the pronoun "he, she, it" which was homophonous at that time (it is now pronounced *qi* and written 其). The number of these loans is somewhat masked in the later language because in many cases, as in the case of *ji* 箕 "basket" and *qi* 其 "he, she it," or in the case of 𝟤 for "armpits," which is now written as *ye* 腋 (adding a component to it indicating that it has to do with "meat" or "flesh"), while the original character is used only for the word "also" (*yi* 亦), the "borrowed" meaning has entirely supplanted the original meaning attached to the pictograph, and a new character has been invented to write the original meaning.

These loan characters or rebus writing allowed an extraordinary breakthrough in Chinese writing. Imagine the difficulty in inventing a pictographic or conceptual character for "it," which surely must count as one of the most basic words in any language. However, once it was realized that sound could be utilized in writing, this opened the door for the next great development: characters that would combine meaning and sound to write words that might otherwise be difficult, or even impossible, to distinguish. For instance, it is a simple matter to depict a fish as 𩵋, or a tree as 朩. However, whereas it might also be possible to differentiate pictographically between a palm tree and a pine tree, how easy would it be to do so between a beech and a walnut tree? Similarly, we can certainly visualize the difference between a shark and a swordfish, for instance, but a trout and a bass look quite a bit alike. Simply borrowing the sound for "trout" (in Chinese *zun*) from the pictograph 尊 meaning "wine vessel; esteemed" (originally a pictograph of two hands holding up a wine vessel, now written *zun* 尊) would have been one option, however it might not have always been easy to disambiguate the word for "trout" from that for wine vessel, or even for a type of "pheasant," also pronounced *zun*. To differentiate these different words, the inventers of the Chinese script quickly modified the rebus principle, combining the component carrying the sound with another component that contributed the basic semantic category. Thus, for "trout," a "fish" 魚 component was added to the component 尊 representing the sound *zun*, giving the composite character 鱒. Similarly, a "bird" 鳥 component was combined with the same phonographic component to write the word for "pheasant": 鷷. This is what traditional Chinese paleographers term "shape-sound characters." It would prove to be the decisive development in the development of the Chinese script. Once it began to be exploited fully, it became possible to write any word in the Chinese language. By the Zhou dynasty, just a few centuries after the Shang dynasty, most new words were created according to this principle, and more than 90% of the characters in modern dictionaries are "shape-sound characters." Indeed, the category is so pervasive that it would be almost superfluous to provide examples of it.

CHAPTER 23
ESSAY ON LITERATURE

Since the Han dynasty, the *Classic of Changes* (*Yi jing*), also known as the *Zhou Changes* (*Zhou Yi*) has been ranked as the first of the Chinese classics. Originally written and used as a manual of divination, by the Warring States period thinkers had transformed it into a text of natural philosophy and wisdom. It is composed of two parts: the first part has sixty-four brief texts arranged around "hexagrams" (symbols made up of six lines, either solid or broken), while the second part is a series of commentaries that explain the meaning of the text.

Legge, James. *The Yi King*. Volume 2 of *The Sacred Books of China: The Texts of Confucianism*. 2nd edition. The Sacred Books of the East 16. Oxford: Clarendon, 1879.

Wilhelm, Richard. *The I Ching or Book of Changes*. Translated into English by Cary F. Baynes. Introduction by Carl G. Jung. Bollingen Series 19. Princeton: Princeton University Press, 1950.

Rutt, Richard. *The Book of Changes (Zhouyi): A Bronze Age Document*. Richmond: Curzon, 1996.

Shaughnessy, Edward L. *Unearthing the* Changes: *Recently Discovered Manuscripts of the* Yi jing *(I ching) and Related Texts*. Translations from the Asian Classics. New York: Columbia University Press, 2014.

Takashima, Ken-ichi. *Studies of Fascicle Three of Inscriptions from the Yin Ruins*. 2 vols. Institute of History and Philology, Academia Sinica, Special Publications 107. Taipei, 2010.

Schwartz, Adam C. *The Oracle Bone Inscriptions from Huayuanzhuang East: Translated with an Introduction and Commentary*. Library of Sinology 3. Mouton: DE Gruyter, 2020.

Cook, Constance A. and Zhao Lu. *Stalk Divination: A Newly Discovered Alternative to the I Ching*. New York: Oxford U. Press, 2017.

Harper, Donald. "A Chinese Demonology of the Third Century B.C." *Harvard Journal of Asiatic Studies* 45.2 (1985): 459–498.

The *Classic of Scriptures* (*Shu jing*), also known as the *Exalted Scriptures* (*Shang shu*), purports to include the earliest writings in the Chinese literary tradition, stretching from the time of Yao and Shun through the early Springs and

Autumns period. It is supposed to have included one hundred texts, selected by Confucius from among all ancient texts as the most important texts. Unfortunately, most of these were subsequently lost, with only twenty-eight chapters reconstituted during the early Han dynasty. Later, in the early fourth century of the common era, "ancient script" versions of the lost chapters were presented at court and were accepted as authentic. It was only in the early Qing dynasty (eighteenth century) that these were definitively proven to be spurious.

Legge, James, tr. *The Shoo King or the Book of Historical Documents*. Volume 3 of *The Chinese Classics*. 2nd edition. Oxford: Clarendon, 1861. Rpt. Hong Kong: Hong Kong University Press, 1960.
Karlgren, Bernhard. "The Book of Documents." *Bulletin of the Museum of Far Eastern Antiquities* 22: 1–81. Rpt. Göteborg: Elanders, 1950.
Palmer, Martin, et al. *The Most Venerable Book: Shangshu, also Known as the Shu Jing: The Classic of Chronicles*. London: Penguin, 2014.
Shaughnessy, Edward L., *The Tsinghua University Warring States Bamboo Manuscripts, Volume One: The* Yi Zhou Shu *and Pseudo*-Yi Zhou Shu *Chapters*. Beijing: Tsinghua University Press, 2023.
Cook, Constance A., and Paul R. Goldin, eds. *A Source Book of Ancient Chinese Bronze Inscriptions*. Revised edition. Early China Special Monograph Series 8. Berkeley, 2020.

The *Classic of Poetry* (*Shi jing*), also known as *Mao Poetry* (*Mao Shi*), is the oldest collection of poetry in China, with 305 poems that were composed after the beginning of the Zhou dynasty (*c.* 1000) down to about 600. The poems are divided into three major types: Hymns, including the earliest pieces in the collection, these were sung in the ancestral temple; Odes, divided between Major and Minor, these generally praised the exploits of the founders of the Zhou dynasty and important figures in its later history; and Airs of the various states, folk songs of thirteen different states that became independent after the collapse of the Western Zhou dynasty. Poetry served throughout the entirety of the Zhou dynasty as the preeminent form of literary expression. The most important subsequent collection was the *Verses of Chu* (*Chu Ci*), said to have been authored by Qu Yuan and other figures from the late Warring States state of Chu.

Legge, James. *The Shih King, or, Book of Poetry*. Sacred Books of the East, Volume 3. 19871. Rpt. Hong Kong: Hong Kong University Press, 1960.
Waley, Arthur. *The Book of Songs*. London: Allen & Unwin, 1937. Rpt. with a Preface by Joseph Allen. New York: Grove Press, 1996.
Karlgren, Bernhard. *The Book of Odes*. Stockholm: Museum of Far Eastern Antiquities, 1950.

Staack, Thies. "Reconstructing the *Kongzi shilun*: From the Arrangement of the Bamboo Slips to a Tentative Translation." *Asiatische Studien/ Études asiatiques* 64.4 (2010): 857–906.

Mattos, Gilbert L. *The Stone Drums of Ch'in*. Monumenta Serica Monograph Series 19. Nettetal, Germany: Steyler, 1988.

Hawkes, David. *Ch'u tz'u: The Songs of the South, an Ancient Chinese Anthology*. Oxford: Clarendon Press, 1959. Second revised edition: Harmondsworth: Penguin Books Limited, 1985.

Sukhu, Gopal. *The Songs of Chu: An Anthology of Ancient Chinese Poetry by Qu Yuan and Others*. New York: Columbia University Press, 2017.

The *Springs and Autumns* (*Chunqiu*) is a spare annalistic history of the state of Lu covering the period from 722 through 481. It is traditionally said to have been written by Confucius, but few modern scholars give much credence to that tradition. It has been recognized as a classic in the first place because of its nature as a work of history, and it is now clear that most if not all states in ancient China had their own annalistic histories, and a few have now been unearthed. It has also long been contended that the book includes subtle wording that reveals Confucius's evaluation of historical actors and events. This has led to a robust commentarial literature. Three such early commentaries, the *Zuo Tradition* (*Zuo zhuan*), the *Gongyang Tradition* (*Gongyang zhuan*), and *Guliang Tradition* (*Guliang zhuan*), have been recognized as classics in their own right. The *Zuo Tradition* in particular is the most important source for the history of the Springs and Autumns period.

Legge, James. *The Ch'un Ts'ew, with the Tso Chuen. The Chinese Classics* V. London: Trübner, 1872. Rpt. Hong Kong: Hong Kong University Press, 1960.

Durrant, Stephen; Li, Wai-yee; Schaberg, David. *Zuo Tradition (Zuozhuan)*. Seattle: University of Washington Press, 2016.

Van Auken, Newell Ann. *Spring and Autumn Historiography: Form and Hierarchy in Ancient Chinese Annals*. New York: Columbia University Press, 2022.

Legge, James, tr. *Zhushu jinian* James Legge, *The Chinese Classics*, vol. III, *The Shoo King or Book of Historical Documents*. Oxford: Clarendon, 1861. Rpt. Hong Kong: Hong Kong University Press, 1960, Prolegomena, Ch. IV, "The Annals of the Bamboo Books," pp. 108–176.

Miller, Harry, tr. *The Gongyang Commentary on The Spring and Autumn Annals: A Full Translation*. New York: Palgrave Macmillan, 2015.

Gen Liang, tr. *A Forgotten Book: Chun Qiu Guliang Zhuan*. Singapore: World Scientific, 2011.

Zhao, Ye. *Spring and Autumn Annals of Wu and Yue: An Annotated Translation of Wu Yue Chunqiu*. Translated by Jianjun He. Ithaca: Cornell University Press, 2021.

Milburn, Olivia. *The Glory of Yue: An Annotated Translation of the Yuejue shu*. Leiden: Brill, 2010.

Milburn, Olivia. *The Spring and Autumn Annals of Master Yan*. Leiden/Boston: Brill, 2016.

Pines, Yuri. *Zhou History Unearthed: The Bamboo Manuscript* Xinian *and Early Chinese Historiography*. New York: Columbia University Press, 2020.

The three ritual classics, *Ceremonies and Rituals* (*Yi li*), *Record of Ritual* (*Li ji*), and *Zhou Rituals* (*Zhou li*), together constitute the fifth of the traditional Five Classics. The *Ceremonies and Rituals*, probably dating to the Warring States period, describes the rituals appropriate to the *shi* "sire" class of the population. The *Record of Ritual* is a heterogeneous text including chapters of several different genres; although the book was not edited in its final form until the Han dynasty, it is clear that much of it dates from the Warring States period, and manuscript versions of some of the chapters have even been unearthed in recent decades. The *Zhou Rituals*, originally known as the *Zhou Offices* (*Zhou Guan*), is the one classic that has not yet been translated into English. It purports to describe the structure of government implemented by the Duke of Zhou at the beginning of the Zhou dynasty; in fact, the book is generally recognized as a late ideal that was never actually put into practice.

Steele, John C. *The I-li: or Book of Etiquette and Ceremonial. Translated from the Chinese With Introduction, Notes and Plans*. London: Probsthain & Co., 1917.

Legge, James. *The Lî Kî (Book of Rites). Sacred Books of the East*, volumes 27 and 28. Oxford: Oxford University Press, 1885.

During the last period of his life, Confucius was surrounded by a large group of disciples to whom he imparted his vision of the way life should be lived. By shortly after his death in 479, these disciples began to transmit his teachings in written form. The *Analects* (*Lunyu*) purports to be a record of his sayings to those disciples, and in large part that is just what it is. It is often regarded as the earliest work of philosophy in the Chinese tradition. Later generations of followers of the Confucian way developed this philosophy in divergent ways. Mencius and Xunzi, in particular, have had great influence on later Chinese philosophy.

Legge, James. *Confucian Analects, the Great Learning, and the Doctrine of the Mean. The Chinese Classics* Vol. I. London: Trübner, 1861. Rpt. Hong Kong: Hong Kong University Press, 1960.

Waley, Arthur. *The Analects of Confucius*. London: George Allen and Unwin, 1938. Rpt. New York: Alfred A. Knopf, 2000.

Lau, D. C. *Confucius, The Analects (Lun yü)*. Harmondsworth: Penguin Books, 1979.

Ames, Roger T. and Henry Rosemont Jr. *The Analects of Confucius: A Philosophical Translation. A New Translation Based on the Dingzhou Fragments and Other Recent Archaeological Finds*. New York: Ballantine, 1998.

Brooks, E. Bruce, and A. Taeko Brooks. *The Original Analects: Sayings of Confucius and His Successors, 0479–0249*. New York: Columbia University Press, 1998.

Legge, James. *The Hsiâo King. Sacred Books of the East*, Vol. III. Oxford: Oxford University Press, 1879.

Ames, Roger T. and Henry Rosemont. *The Chinese Classic of Family Reverence: A Philosophical Translation of the Xiaojing*. Honolulu: University of Hawaii Press, 2009.

Legge, James. *The Works of Mencius. The Chinese Classics*, Vol. 2. Oxford: Clarendon Press, 1861.

Lau, D. C. *Mencius*. London: Penguin Books, 1970. Rpt. *Mencius (New Bilingual Edition)*. Hong Kong: Chinese University Press, 2003.

Van Norden, Bryan. *Mencius: With Selections from Traditional Commentaries*. Indianapolis: Hackett Publishing Company, 2008.

Bloom, Irene. Ed. Philip J. Ivanhoe. *Mencius*. New York: Columbia University Press, 2009.

Dubs, Homer H. *The Works of Hsüntze*. London, Probsthain & Co., 1927.

Watson, Burton. *Hsün-tzu: Basic Writings*. New York: Columbia University Press, 1964.

Knoblock, John. *Xunzi: A Translation and Study of the Complete Works*. 3 vols. Stanford: Stanford University Press, 1988–1994.

Hutton, Eric L. *Xunzi: The Complete Text*. Princeton: Princeton University Press, 2014.

Cook, Scott. *The Bamboo Texts of Guodian: A Study and Complete Translation*. 2 vols. Cornell East Asia Series 164–165. Ithaca, N.Y., 2012.

Daoism is a way of thought that takes the Way (*dao*) of nature as the model for life. Within this general notion, there are various permutations. The first exposition of the philosophy is usually credited to Laozi, traditionally thought to have been an elder contemporary of Confucius. He is supposed to have written a book, referred to either as *Laozi* or *Classic of the Way and Virtue* (*Daode jing*), the version of which available to us today has about 5,000 characters in eighty-one chapters, though early manuscript copies that were unearthed about thirty years ago contain only about a third of those chapters. Later thinkers also grouped under the label Daoist include most prominently Zhuangzi, who lived in the latter half of the fourth century; his book is not only philosophically profound, but also one of the masterpieces of Chinese literature.

Legge, James. *The Sacred Books of China: The Texts of Taoism*. Rpt. New York: Dover Publications, 1962.

Chan, Wing-tsit. *The Way of Lao Tzu (Tao-te ching)*. Indianapolis: Bobbs-Merrill, 1963.

Lau, D.C. *Tao-te-ching*. London: Penguin Books, 1963.

Henricks, Robert G. *Lao-Tzu Te-Tao Ching: A New Translation Based on the Recently Discovered Ma-wang-tui Texts*. New York: Ballantine, 1989.

Essays

Henricks, Robert G. *Lao Tzu's* Tao Te Ching: *A Translation of the Startling New Documents Found at Guodian.* Translations from the Asian Classics. New York: Columbia University Press, 2000.

Watson, Burton, trans. *The Complete Works of Chuang Tzu.* New York: Columbia University Press, 1968.

Graham, A.C. *Chuang-tzŭ: The Inner Chapters.* London and Boston: George Allen & Unwin, 1981. Rpt., Indianapolis and Cambridge, Mass.: Hackett, 2001.

Cleary, Thomas. *Wen-tzu: Understanding the Mysteries.* Boston: Shambhala, 1992.

Graham, A.C. *The Book of Lieh Tzu.* London: John Murray, 1961.

Brindley, Erica F., Paul R. Goldin and Esther S. Klein. "A Philosophical Translation of the *Heng Xian.*" *Dao* 12 (2013): 145–151.

After the death of Confucius, an army of disciples coalesced around Mo Di or Mozi, a thinker who advocated a situational ethics intended to create the greatest good for the greatest number of people. This included advocating for "universal love," which rather than a notion of free love stressed the need for impartiality in all human relationships. This entailed rejecting even the priority of family relationships, which was the core of Confucius's teaching. By the late fourth century, Mozi's teaching was said to have been extremely popular. However, in later centuries it was largely forgotten.

Watson, Burton tr. *Mo-tzu: Basic Writings.* New York: Columbia University Press, 1963.

Johnston, Ian. *Mozi: A Complete Translation.* Hong Kong: Chinese University Press, 2010.

Knoblock, John, and Jeffrey Riegel. *Mozi: A Study and Translation of the Ethical and Political Writings.* China Research Monograph 68. Berkeley: Institute of East Asian Studies, University of California, 2013.

The political theory known in the West as Legalism (*Fajia*) developed in stages beginning in the middle of the Warring States period. It is especially associated with the state of Qin, which enthusiastically adopted its principles of bureaucratic government, but elements of the thought were to be found in most of the political theories of the time, and it continued to play an influential role in Chinese governing for many centuries to come.

Duyvendak, J. J. L. *The Book of Lord Shang: A Classic of the Chinese School of Law.* London: Arthur Probsthain, 1928. Rpt. Chicago: University of Chicago Press, 1963.

Pines, Yuri. *The Book of Lord Shang: Apologetics of State Power in Early China.* New York: Columbia University Press, 2017.

Creel, Herrlee G. *Shen Pu-hai: A Chinese Political Philosopher of the Fourth Century B.C.* Chicago: University of Chicago Press, 1974.

Emerson, John. *Shen Dao: Text, Translation, and Study.* N.p.: Éditions Le Real, 2012.

Watson, Burton tr. *Han Fei Tzu: Basic Writings*. New York: Columbia University Press, 1964.

Liao, W. K., trans. *The Complete Works of Han Fei Tzu*. 2 vols. London: Arthur Probsthain, 1939.

Kern, Martin. *The Stele Inscriptions of Ch'in Shih-huang: Text and Ritual in Early Chinese Imperial Representation*. American Oriental Series 85. New Haven, 2000.

Hulsewé, A.F.P. *Remnants of Ch'in Law: An Annotated Translation of the Ch'in Legal and Administrative Rules of the 3rd century B.C. Discovered in Yün-meng Prefecture, Hu-pei Province, in 1975*. Leiden: E.J. Brill, 1985.

Caldwell, Ernest. *Writing Chinese Laws: The Form and Function of Legal Statutes Found in the Qin Shuihudi Corpus*. New York: Routledge, 2018.

The School of Names (*Ming jia*) or Logicians was a minor group of thinkers who proposed logical conundrums apparently intended to show the folly of formulating rational argumentation. One of the most famous logicians was Hui Shi, a friend and intellectual adversary of Zhuangzi, but he left only a short series of paradoxes. The book *Gongsun Longzi* is often regarded as the prime remaining example of this thought.

Perleberg, Max. *The Works of Kung-sun Lung tzu*. Hong Kong: The Local Printing Press, 1952.

Johnston, Ian. "The *Gongsun Longzi*: A Translation and an Analysis of Its Relationship to Later Mohist Writings." *Journal of Chinese Philosophy* 31.2 (2004): 271–295.

Harbsmeier, Christoph. "A Reading of the Guodian 郭店 Manuscript *Yucong* 語叢 1 as a Masterpiece of Early Chinese Analytic Philosophy and Conceptual Analysis." *Studies in Logic* 4.3 (2011): 3–56.

There were many other thinkers whose thought is not easily assigned to one school or another. Most later Chinese bibliographies and analyses assign them to the category "Miscellaneous" (*Za*) perhaps also to be regarded as "Syncretist."

Rickett, Allyn W. *The Kuan-tzu, A Repository of Early Chinese Thought*. Hong Kong: Hong Kong University Press, 1965.

Rickett, Allyn W. *Guanzi: Political, Economic, and Philosophical Essays from Early China*. Princeton: Princeton University Press, 1985.

James I. Crump. *Chan-kuo ts'e*. Ann Arbor, Mi.: Center for Chinese Studies, University of Michigan, 1996.

Knoblock, John, and Jeffrey Riegel. *The Annals of Lü Buwei: A Complete Translation and Study*. Stanford, Calif.: Stanford University Press, 2000.

Fischer, Paul. *Shizi: China's First Syncretist*. New York: Columbia University Press, 2012.

Defoort, Carine. *The Pheasant Cap Master: A Rhetorical Reading*. Albany, N.Y.: SUNY Press, 1997.

Essays

One of the most important categories of literature in ancient China concerns the arts of war. The most important of these works is *Sunzi's Art of War* (*Sunzi Bingfa*), which is sometimes regarded as the oldest military treatise in the world. It has been translated many times, and has been seen to have implications far beyond the ancient battlefield.

Giles, Lionel. *The Art of War: The Oldest Military Treatise in the World*. 1944. Reprinted as *Sun Tzu on the Art of War*. London: Kegan Paul, 2001.

Griffith, Samuel B. *Sun Tzu: The Art of War*. Oxford: Clarendon, 1963.

Mair, Victor. *The Art of War: Sun Zi's Military Methods*. New York: Columbia University Press, 2007.

Sawyer, Ralph. *Sun Tzu: Art of War*. Boulder: Westview, 1994.

Ames, Roger T. *Sun-tzu: The Art of Warfare. The First English Translation Incorporating the Recently Discovered Yin-ch'üeh-shan Texts*. New York: Ballantine, 1993.

Sawyer, Ralph, trans. *Sun Pin: Military Methods*. Boulder: Westview, 1995.

Caldwell, Ernest. "Promoting Action in Warring States Political Philosophy: A First Look at the Chu Manuscript *Cao Mie's Battle Arrays*." *Early China* 14 (2014): 221–258.

Other texts from ancient China include descriptions of the natural world, especially of geography. The most important example of this genre is *The Classic of Mountains and Seas* (*Shan Hai Jing*). Other writings might best be described as environmental treatises, advising the proper use of natural resources, and spelling out the repercussions of their misuse.

Birrell, Anne. *The Classic of Mountains and Seas*. Harmondsworth: Penguin, 1999.

Strassberg, Richard. *A Chinese Bestiary: Strange Creatures from the Guideways Through Mountains and Seas*. Berkeley: University of California Press, 2002.

Cheng Te-k'un. "The Travels of Emperor Mu." *Journal of the North China Branch of the Royal Asiatic Society* 64 (1933): 124–142; 65(1934): 128–149.

Barnard, Noel. *The Ch'u Silk Manuscript: Translation and Commentary*. (Monographs on Far Eastern History 5). Canberra: Australian National University, 1973.

Li Ling. *The Chu Silk Manuscripts from Zidanku, Changsha (Hunan Province)*. Lothar von Falkenhausen and Donald Harper tr. 2 vols. Hong Kong: Chinese University of Hong Kong Press, 2020, 2023.

Pines, Yuri. "Political Mythology and Dynastic Legitimacy in the *Rong Cheng shi* Manuscript." *Bulletin of the School of Oriental and African Studies* 73.3 (2010): 503–529.

HEREDITARY HOUSES

CHAPTER 24
THE HEREDITARY HOUSE OF LU

The hereditary house of the state of Lu looms large in the historical consciousness of ancient China, indeed much larger than its relatively limited geographical extent and military power ever warranted. This prestige derives primarily from two features of its history. First, it was founded, at least nominally, by the Duke of Zhou (d. *c.* 1032), son of King Wen of Zhou (r. 1099/1056–1050) and younger brother of King Wu of Zhou (r. 1049/1045–1043), and—for a time—apparently regent for King Wu's young son, King Cheng of Zhou (r. 1042/1035–1006). Although the Duke of Zhou did not actually take up rule in Lu, which is located in the southwestern part of present-day Shandong province, far to the east of the Zhou capital in the Wei River valley of what is today Shaanxi province, he was always looked back upon as the high ancestor of the state. A second reason for the prominence of Lu is that it was the state where Confucius (551–479) lived most of his life, and where he was supposed to have put into final form the *Springs and Autumns* (*Chunqiu*), an annalistic historical account of the state from 722 until 481.

The establishment of Lu, as in the case of almost all the colonies in the eastern part of the Zhou realm, was intimately connected with the Wu Geng rebellion shortly after the Zhou conquest of Shang. When King Wu died just two years after the conquest, the Duke of Zhou, who was in residence in the Zhou capital, announced that he would be in charge of the government in place of King Cheng, who is often described as being still in diapers. The Duke of Zhou was the fourth of ten sons of King Wen and his principal consort Tai Si. The eldest son, Bo Yi Kao, had died prior to the conquest. Then came Fa, better known as King Wu. After King Wu, the third son was Guanshu Xian; the fourth Dan, the Duke of Zhou; fifth, Caishu Du; and so on through the youngest Danji Zai. The reason that the Duke of Zhou was in the capital, but not his elder brother Guanshu Xian is because Xian, together with the fifth son Caishu Du, had been sent to the former Shang capital to oversee the Shang people there. When they learned that the Duke of Zhou had taken command of the Zhou government, they naturally treated it as a sort of *coup d'etat,* and so joined together with Wu Geng, the son of the last king of Shang, Di Xin (r. 1086–1045), to rebel against this act. The Duke of Zhou in concert with King Cheng and the Duke of Shao then launched a second conquest campaign, according to most traditions killing Wu Geng and Guanshu Xian and sending Caishu Du into exile. According to the standard historical tradition, the Duke of Zhou then continued in charge of the government for several years before eventually returning command to King Cheng, when he had become old enough to rule.

The Wu Geng rebellion certainly did take place; there is a bronze vessel cast for the Grand Protector (*Tai Bao*), the Duke of Shao, that commemorates his role in suppressing this rebellion. Interestingly, the inscription does not mention the Duke of Zhou, but gives credit to the king "The king attacked Luzi Sheng (i.e., Wu Geng) and suppressed his rebellion." Much of the rest of the story concerning the Duke of Zhou almost certainly did not take place, at least not in the way that the standard story suggests. He may well have precipitated the rebellion by seizing control of the government, but it was not just his brothers Guanshu Xian and Caishu Du who resented this. There are strong hints throughout the historical tradition that King Cheng also resented this usurpation, as did, most probably, the Duke of Shao, who was the king's "protector" in fact as well as in title. There are other hints, or even explicit statements, that when the Duke of Zhou returned power to the king, he himself went into a sort of exile. It seems likely that this exile was in the area of Lu. There is another bronze vessel, known as the *Ran fangding,* from this same period that is currently in the collection of the Asian Art Museum of San Francisco and that describes the Duke of Zhou as leading an attack against three different eastern peoples.

> It was when the Duke of Zhou was on campaign attacking the Eastern Peoples, the Elder of Feng, and Pugu, all of which he destroyed. The duke returned and sacrificed a bird in the Zhou temple. On *wuchen* (day 5), he drank Qin-spirits. The duke awarded one hundred strands of cowries to Ran, who herewith makes this precious caldron.[1]

The Eastern Peoples lived throughout the southern part of modern Shandong province as well as western Jiangsu and northern Anhui; they had been a nemesis even to the former Shang state, and would continue to be a threat to the Zhou kings for the remainder of the Western Zhou period. Feng and Pugu can be located with more certainty. They were both located very near to where the capital of Lu was located: at modern Qufu, Shandong. There is another bronze vessel that doubtless also derives from this same military campaign, this time against yet another polity in the same area: Gai. The inscription is not lengthy, but it is important because it mentions both the Duke of Zhou and a person named Qin, which was the name of his son who is supposed to have become the first lord of Lu.

> The king attacked the Lord of Gai. The Duke of Zhou conspired with Qin to pray. Qin offered flesh in praying. The king awarded (him) bronze, one hundred measures; Qin herewith makes this treasured vessel.[2]

Qin went to Lu to become the first lord of the state, and is said to have ruled there for forty-six years. According to one account, it was three years after taking up his post before he returned to the Zhou capital to report. When asked why he was so slow, he said that it had taken that long to make the local inhabitants conform to Zhou ways. In fact, from archaeological excavations conducted at Qufu, Shandong in the 1960s and 1970s, it is clear that the area in which Lu was located had long been inhabited; evidence from graves in and near Qufu suggests that the city was distinctly segregated, with an underclass buried according to Shang burial practices and furnished only with pottery vessels, and a ruling class buried according to Zhou practices furnished with bronze vessels. Over time, however, Zhou practices prevailed. The contours of the city walls could be reconstructed, suggesting that the city came closest of all ancient cities to the classical standards outlined in the later ritual classics.

The history of the state of Lu is also the most fully recorded among all of the states of the time, with the names and lengths of reign of each of the lords of the state recorded throughout the Western Zhou period. However, until the time of King Xuan of Zhou (r. 827–782), these records do not indicate anything more than who succeeded who; sometimes succession passed from father to son, sometimes from elder brother to younger brother, without any apparent standard. At the very beginning of King Xuan's reign, Duke Wu of Lu (r. 825–817) succeeded his elder brother, Duke Zhen (r. 855–826). In the spring of of 817, the already aged Duke Wu together with his sons Kuo and Xi went to the Zhou capital to pay their respects to the king. King Xuan became smitten with the younger son Xi and ordered that he be named Duke Wu's heir apparent. Despite remonstrations at court against this breach of precedent, when Duke Wu died that same year, King Xuan did appoint Xi as lord, to be known as Duke Yi (r. 816–808). King Xuan's ministers argued that the king's intrusion into the normal succession of the state would surely bring about turmoil. They were right about that. Nine years later, Bo Yu, the son of the elder brother Kuo, together with the people of the state assassinated Duke Yi. This prompted King Xuan to invade the state to overthrow Bo Yu, installing yet another younger brother of Duke Yi as the new lord of the state. *Records of the Historian* states laconically that "from this time on, the many lords rebelled against the king's commands."

The century or so after the time of King Xuan, and particularly the half century after his son King You (r. 781–771) was killed, bringing the Western Zhou period to an end, are something of a dark age in the history of ancient China. Records resume in 722, with the *Springs and Autumns* of Lu and its complement *Zuo Tradition*, which narrate the history of the state of Lu—year by year—for the next 242 years (or 247 years in the case of the *Zuo Tradition*). The *Springs and Autumns* is a sparse annalistic record, noting events in the state, and often in other states as well, especially when they impinged on the affairs of Lu. The *Zuo Tradition* is a much fuller historical accounting, especially for the second half of the period, providing considerable context for the events of the time. In addition to its unique value as a historical source, the *Zuo Tradition* is generally regarded as one of the masterpieces of the Chinese literary tradition. So important are the *Springs and Autumns* and *Zuo Tradition* for the history of this period that dates within the period are generally given according to the twelve rulers of Lu, and no longer by the Zhou kings. One thing to note, however, is that although these rulers are routinely referred to in these sources as "dukes" (*gong*), and it is routine to refer to them as such, and I will do so here as well, in fact "duke" is a posthumous appellation referring to any deceased ruler; during their lives, the rulers of Lu had the title of "lord" (*hou*). The only rulers of the time who had the title of "duke" during their lives were those of the small state of Song, ruled by descendants of the kings of the former Shang dynasty.

Both the *Springs and Autumns* and *Zuo Tradition* begin in 722 with the first year of Duke Yin. As was the case a century before, his succession was irregular. Duke Yin was the son of a secondary consort, and ruled as a regent for a younger brother, the future Duke Huan (r. 711–694). Given the confusion of having two different lords alive at the same time, there was a plot to do away with the younger brother. When Duke Yin refused to join the conspiracy, he was assassinated himself, making way for Duke Huan. Just as Duke Huan's reign began with a murder, so too did it end with his own murder. He was killed while accompanying his wife, Wen Jiang, on a visit to the neighboring state of Qi, her natal state. While there, she had an affair with her own brother, Duke Xiang of Qi (697–686). When Duke Huan objected to her behavior, she told her brother, who had Duke Huan murdered. This would not be the last such episode among the rulers of these two neighboring states.

Duke Huan was succeeded by his son Duke Zhuang (r. 693–662), whose reign coincided with the beginning of the reign of the great Duke Huan of Qi (r. 685–643). Duke Huan of Qi was acknowledged as the first of the "premiers" (*ba*) of the Springs and Autumns period, and Lu too was able to benefit from the period of peace and stability that he brought about. Nevertheless, despite Duke Zhuang's own relatively successful reign, the reign did not end well, with the succession once again problematic. On his deathbed, he asked two of his brothers for advice as to who should succeed him. One brother, by a different mother, Prince Ya, recommended his own full brother Prince Qingfu, while another brother, Prince You, recommended Duke Zhuang's son Ziban. In the course of this debate, Prince You killed Prince Ya, while Prince Qingfu arranged for the murder of Ziban. Prince You first fled the state, together with another of Duke Zhuang's sons, the future Duke Min (r. 661–660), but then returned to have Duke Min installed as ruler. His reign did not last long, as he was soon murdered by Prince Qingfu, who, however, was then forced to flee in exile himself. The last man standing was yet another son of Duke Zhuang, who was installed as Duke Xi (r. 659–627). While Duke Xi did manage to have a lengthy reign of thirty-three years, and even to die a natural death, his reign saw the final decline in the power of the actual rulers of Lu. The houses of the three princes most intimately involved in the succession struggle after the death of Duke Zhuang came increasingly to dominate the affairs of state. The houses are usually referred to as the "grandson" (*sun*) lineages, differentiated by order of birth: the Zhongsun lineage (also known as the Meng lineage) deriving from Prince Qingfu, the Shusun (or Shu) lineage from Prince Ya, and the Jisun (or Ji) lineage from Prince You.

Duke Xi was followed by lords Wen (r. 626–609), Xuan (r. 608–591), Cheng (r. 590–573) and Xiang (r. 572–542). By the time that Duke Xiang succeeded, at the tender age of four years old, most real power was in the hands of the the three "grandson" houses, and especially that of the Jisun lineage under the long-lived Ji Wenzi (*c.* 651–568). Under Ji Wenzi's son, Ji Wuzi (d. 535), the Lu army was reorganized into three divisions, one each under each of the three houses, such that Duke Xiang was left without any power at all. While the tales of sex, lies and power in the *Zuo Tradition*'s account of the domestic affairs in Lu are always entertaining, and the behavior of the three houses has long been studied in China for how to behave—or, more often, how not to behave—affairs in Lu were of little import in the greater world of Zhou China. Even the *Zuo Tradition* seems more concerned during this hundred-year period with the rise of the state of Jin and its competition with the southern state of Chu.

By the beginning of Duke Zhao's reign (r. 541–510), Jin had lost its preeminence in the lower Yellow River valley to Chu, though by the end of that lengthy reign Chu had already squandered its power and was in the course of being replaced—at least temporarily—by its newly arising eastern neighbor Wu. Within Lu itself, when Duke Zhao attempted to challenge the three "grandson" lineages, they joined together to drive him into exile. Their cooperation did not last long, as they soon reverted to fighting among themselves.

The story of Duke Zhao's exile, which occurred in 517, is said to have been foretold by the appearance earlier in that year of a type of mynah bird or grackle that had never before been seen in northern China. This omen recalled to the music master a children's song that had been popular about a century earlier. As shown by the translation of James Legge (1815–1897), the Scottish missionary who contributed so much to our understanding of ancient China through his translations of the Confucian classics, the movements of the grackles were correlated with the movement of Duke Zhao.

Here are grackles apace! The duke flies in disgrace.
Look at the grackles' wings! To the wilds the duke flings, A horse one
    to him brings.
Look how the grackles go! In Kan-how he is low, Wants coat and
    trousers now.
Behold the grackles' nest! Far off the duke doth rest. Chow-fu has lost
    his state, Sung-foo comes proud and great.
O the grackles so strange! The songs to weeping change.[3]

The *Zuo Tradition* account of Lord Zhao's reign is replete with other such stories, providing a rich tapestry of sixth-century BCE Chinese cultural history, a particularly important time since it largely coincides with the life of Confucius (551–479). The first mention of Confucius comes in the seventh year of Duke Zhao (535), though it anticipates an event that would take place seventeen years later. In 535, while on a diplomatic visit in the state of Zheng, Meng Xizi, the head of the senior Zhongsun lineage, embarrassed himself by bungling matters of ritual and state protocol. Upon his return to Lu, he set about looking for a teacher of ritual. In 518, on his deathbed, he decreed that his sons Yue, better known as Meng Yizi, and Heji (Nangong Jingshu) should become students of Confucius. To this, Confucius is said to have said:

> One who is able to correct his mistakes is a gentleman. The *Poetry* says: "A gentleman can serve as a standard, as a model." Meng Xizi can be a standard, a model, to be sure![4]

As Confucius became older, he is quoted more and more often in the *Zuo Tradition*, often offering evaluations of statesmen in other states, such as Zi Chan of Zheng (d. 522), or criticizing Shu Xiang of Jin (d. 528) for casting the law-code of state on the side of an iron caldron, predicting that it would cause the people to become litigious.

The final two lords included in the *Springs and Autumns* and *Zuo Tradition* are Duke Ding (r. 509–495) and Duke Ai (r. 494–468). Unlike the *Zuo Tradition*'s fulsome descriptions of events during the reign of Duke Zhao, its coverage of these two reigns is quite spare, often simply noting a military campaign here or there. However, there were many military campaigns to be noted. As the two major powers of the preceding century, Jin and Chu, lost their power, warfare became even more frequent, setting the scene for the onset of what is usually referred to as the Warring States period. Toward the end of his reign, Duke Ai, like Duke Zhao before him, was forced into exile by the three lineages, though he was eventually able to return home. He was followed by nine further lords of state, who persisted for over two hundred years, about which very little is known; it is obvious that Lu was but a pawn in the chess match among the seven great powers of the day. Finally, in 256, it was annihilated. Unlike the other states of the time that were exterminated by the western state of Qin, Lu was brought to an end by the southern state of Chu. But for Lu the result was the same. As Sima Qian (145–89) said in concluding his account of the state: "Its rituals of bowing and yielding are worth following, but oh how perverse was its conduct of affairs!"

CHAPTER 25
THE HEREDITARY HOUSE OF YAN

The state of Yan, strategically located at the northern entrance to the great north China plain, anchored in the foothills of the Taihang Mountains to the west, the Yanshan Mountains to the north, and the Bay of Bohai of the Yellow Sea to the east—essentially where modern Beijing is located, was one of the first of the eastern colonies founded by the Zhou rulers. Although it survived more or less quietly throughout much of Zhou history, it did in fact survive, being one of the last of the states to be vanquished—in 226—in the course of the final Qin campaign to unify the surviving warring states. The name continues to echo in modern China history, though often written as Yen instead of Yan. Yenching University (*ching*, *jing* in pinyin Romanization, meaning "capital") was one of the first modern universities founded in China; its campus, located in the northwestern suburbs of the city, was later given over to Peking University, which still occupies it, though some of the old buildings were recently re-appropriated for the newly established Yenching Academy. The name is often heard as well in the United States, by way of the Harvard-Yenching Institute, founded in 1928 as a separate foundation administered by Harvard University. And those who have visited Beijing will doubtless know of Yanjing Beer, the popular local brew.

The indigenous people of the area had long had cultural contact with the Shang court at Anyang, but there is no evidence that Shang political control reached so far north. This situation would change shortly after the Zhou conquest of Shang, when the Zhou conquerors established Yan as their northernmost colony. After the untimely death of King Wu of Zhou (r. 1049/1045–1043), and the difficult succession of his young son King Cheng of Zhou (r. 1042/1035–1006), Shi, the Duke of Shao, a son of King Wen of Zhou (r. 1099/1056–1050), albeit by a secondary consort, joined together with his younger half-brother Dan, the Duke of Zhou to serve as the "protectors" of the young king. Like the Duke of Zhou, who was only nominally appointed to rule the eastern colony of Lu, the Duke of Shao—the Grand Protector— was appointed to rule Yan, represented there by his eldest son. The Grand

Protector remained in the Zhou capital, where he exercised considerable power; in fact, he long outlived the Duke of Zhou, and would go on to be the *eminence grise* behind the king not only throughout King Cheng's reign but also well into the following reign of King Kang (r. 1005–978).

The tradition that the Duke of Shao had been appointed to found the Zhou colony at Yan was confirmed in 1986 by bronze vessels excavated from a tomb at the site of Liulihe, just southwest of Beijing. The short inscription on one of these bronze vessels, known as the *Ke he*, seems to record the initial command to the Duke of Shao's son, Ke.

> The king said: "Grand Protector, it is your intelligence and your sweet-wine that you have offered to me, your ruler. I greatly respond to your offering, commanding Ke to be lord at Yan, administering the Qiang, Ma, Cuo, Yú, Yù, and Wei." Ke came to Yan, and sent in soil and his supervisors, herewith making this treasured offertory vessel.[5]

The site at Liulihe included an extensive cemetery and also the remains of a walled city surrounded by a moat, all dating to the early Western Zhou. Roof tiles in the Zhou metropolitan style suggest that there were palace structures inside the walls as well as the colony's own bronze foundry. Three tombs in the cemetery were furnished with the two ramps indicative of a ruler's tomb; unfortunately, two of them had been looted before the arrival of modern archaeologists. The other one produced the bronzes the inscriptions of which recount Ke's coming to rule Yan. That inscription recorded that Ke was to rule over six different indigenous peoples, and different burial practices in the cemetery do seem to show that Yan was a multi-ethnic state.

Archaeological evidence at Liulihe is overwhelmingly concentrated in the early Western Zhou. One of the two looted tombs of rulers of the state probably belonged to a lord Zhi, known from looted bronze vessels in various museum collections. The inscription on one of these bronzes, the *Yan Hou Zhi ding*, shows that he made the long trip back to the Zhou capital, Ancestral Zhou (Zongzhou):

> Zhi, Lord of Yan, first presented service at Ancestral Zhou. The king awarded Zhi twenty double-strands of cowries, whereby he makes for (his mother) Si this treasured offertory vessel.[6]

Unfortunately, the cemetery at Liulihe seems to have ceased being used after these first three generations, and no subsequent early capital site has been found. The history of the state in *Records of the Historian* supplies hardly any other information. After the time of Grand Protector Shi, it records simply that nine generations later, at the time that King Li of Zhou (r. 857/853–842/828) fled into exile, the lord of Yan was Lord Hui. Thereafter, even though the names of the rulers are given, the only records are to correlate their reigns with those of other rulers; almost nothing is known of the internal history of the state for more than five hundred years.

In 316, King Kuai of Yan (r. 320–316, d. 312), having grown old and seeking to emulate the sage-kings of antiquity Yao and Shun, abdicated in favor of his chief minister Zi Zhi, and deposed his own son, the crown prince Ping. This was in line with a philosophical and social movement at the time to "exalt the worthy" (*shang xian*), but for the kings of the day—and especially those of the neighboring states, it posed an existential threat to their own right to rule—and to transmit their rule to their sons. Some sense of this threat can be seen in the inscription on the *Zhongshan Wang Cuo ding* bronze vessel, which was discovered in 1974 at Pingshan, Hebei. The vessel was cast for King Cuo of Zhongshan (r. *c.* 327–310), a small, non-Chinese state located in that area, which is not far from Yan. Most of the lengthy inscription deals with the domestic affairs of Zhongshan, but the beginning refers emphatically to the events that were just then taking place in Yan.

> It was the fourteenth year, King Cuo of Zhongshan made a caldron bowl, the inscription saying: "*Wuhu*, the proverb is not remiss indeed. I have heard: For a snake, it is better to sink into the depths than to sink among the people. Previously Yan's Ruler Zi Kuai was profoundly conscientious and broadly informed, long serving as the people's ruler, defending against the things under heaven. Nevertheless, he was confused and dazzled by Zi Zhi and lost his country, becoming reviled by all under heaven. How much more so would it be the case with me, a young ruler![7]

In 314, Ping, the erstwhile crown prince, rebelled against Zi Zhi. King Xuan of Qi (r. 319–301) took advantage of the civil war in Yan to attack and annex the state, initially installing a puppet ruler. However, this invasion brought about yet another rebellion. When the Qi army withdrew, King Wuling of Zhao (r. 325—299 B.C.) moved in to establish a younger son of King Kuai as King Zhao of Yan (r. 311–279). In the course of the rebellions and counter-rebellions surrounding this attempted abdication, the noble lineages of the state were thoroughly stripped of whatever power they still had. King Zhao was able to take advantage of this political vacuum to impose land and military reforms and to attract worthy ministers from other states. By 284, the state had become sufficiently wealthy to join together with Qin, Chu and the three former Jin states to attack Qi, forcing King Min of Qi (r. 300–284) to flee south, where he was captured and killed by the Chu army. Yan, being the only local army, entered the Qi capital of Linzi, capturing all of the treasures of the state.

The last event in which the state of Yan was a major actor came in 228. Two years earlier, Qin had begun its final campaign to defeat all of the remaining independent states, first conquering Han and, then, in 228, Zhao. That put the Qin army on the doorstep of Dukang, the fertile southern plain of Yan. The Yan army was under the command of Huan Yi (d. 227), who had formerly served Qin but then had left for Yan when he lost favor in Qin. Huan Yi realized that the Yan army was no match for the Qin army. He then launched a plot with Jing Ke (d. 227), a nobleman from Wei who had similarly fled to the north to Yan, whereby Jing Ke would assassinate King Zheng of Qin, the soon-to-be First Emperor, Qin Shi Huangdi (r. 246/221–210). The plan was for Jing Ke to gain admission to King Zheng by offering him the head of Huan Yi, who agreed to commit suicide so that the plan might work. Jing Ke did gain admission, and nearly succeeded in stabbing King Zheng, but in the end failed; he was killed, and King Zheng then turned his fury on Yan, conquering it in 226.

Figure 25.1 Han-dynasty wall carving of Jing Ke's attempted assassination of King Zheng of Qin; from *Jin shi suo* (1821).

CHAPTER 26
THE HEREDITARY HOUSE OF QI

Located in the northern part of present-day Shandong province, between Lu
to the south and Yan to the north, the state of Qi was another of the hereditary
houses established shortly after the Zhou conquest of Shang. Like the state of
Lu and Yan, it too was one of the last independent states to be conquered by
Qin in its drive to unify the empire. However, unlike Lu and Yan, which
despite their moral or strategic value were always of more or less minor
political and economic importance, Qi would grow into the major power of
northeastern China, and for a period of time in the early seventh century
was recognized as the foremost of all the independent states. Also, unlike Lu
and Yan, which were founded by blood relations of the Zhou royal house, Qi
was founded by Jiang Ziya, also known as Shi (General) or Lü Shangfu,
though he is perhaps best known to history as Tai Gong Wang, the Grand
Duke Expected; his various names indicate that he was a member of the Lü
lineage of the Jiang family, one of the major families of Zhou China and one
that often intermarried with the royal family of Zhou.

According to legend, Tai Gong Wang was a butcher from the coastal area
of eastern China, living in obscurity after having been cast out, late in his life,
by his wife. Disgruntled with the immoral rule of Di Xin (r. 1086–1045), the
last king of the Shang dynasty, he traveled west to the area of Zhou. It is said
that he was fishing in the Wei River, when Ji Chang, the pre-dynastic ruler of
the Zhou people better known as King Wen (r. 1099/1056–1050), who
himself was on a hunting expedition, encountered him there. Recognizing
him as a sage who would help Zhou win power, King Wen immediately
appointed him as Grand Duke, and gave him the name Wang "Expected."
Although King Wen died before Zhou could overthrow the Shang, the Grand
Duke continued to serve Wen's son, King Wu (r. 1049/1045–1043). King Wu
appointed him to lead the Zhou army, perhaps because as an easterner he
was thought to have inside knowledge of the Shang army and its tactics.
Zhou did win a decisive victory at the battle at Muye, bringing the Shang

dynasty to an end. The poem "Great Brightness" of the *Classic of Poetry* writes of his "eagle-like" role in this battle:

> The legions of the Yin and Shang, Their joining was like a forest.
> Arrayed upon the Shepherd's Wild, It was our lords who were aroused.
> God on High looked down upon you, There was no doubt in your hearts.
> The Shepherd's Wild so vast, so vast,
> Sandalwood carts gleaming, gleaming, And teams of four pounding pounding.
> It was the general Shangfu, The one who raised up eagle-like,
> Chilling the heart of that King Wu, Spreading out to attack great Shang,
> Meeting the morning clear and bright.[8]

It is impossible to say to what extent the Grand Duke was responsible for the Zhou victory. Nevertheless, he has become enshrined as the patron saint of generals, and numerous military manuals credit him as the author, though this is certainly fictional. It is interesting that the most famous of these works on the art of war, called the *Six Quivers* (*Liu tao*), was long suspected of being a late forgery, but in 1972 a fragmentary copy was found in a tomb at Yinqueshan, Linzi, Shandong, which is to say within the territory of the state of Qi; this shows that the text is in fact quite ancient, even if not quite so ancient as the Grand Duke.

The Zhou victory won and the new dynasty proclaimed, the first person that King Wu appointed to establish a new colony in the east, even before the king's brothers, was none other than the Grand Duke Wang. His colony, known as Qi, was to be at Yingqiu, just to the east of the present-day city of Zibo, Shandong. Although Zibo is now quite far removed from the sea, at the beginning of the Zhou dynasty, with the coastline much further to the west than is currently the case, it would have been on or near the Bay of Bohai. As such, it quickly became rich through seafood and salt. Because of this strategic location, the initial establishment of the state here was not uncontested, Qi having to fight off attacks from the native Eastern Peoples.

The Grand Duke Wang is said to have lived to be over one hundred years old, though of course there is no way to know whether this is true or just part of his legend. He was succeeded by his son Lü Ji, subsequently to be known as Duke Ding of Qi, who is mentioned once in the *Exalted Scriptures* for having returned to the royal court to participate in the installation of King

Kang as the third king of the Western Zhou. After the time of Duke Ding, there is little information about the state for the next hundred years or more. There are a few bronze inscriptions that record that Qi contributed troops to various campaigns against the Eastern Peoples, but none of these is mentioned in traditional sources. However, beginning in the middle of the ninth century, the state seems to have lurched from one crisis to another. First, the ruler of the small neighboring state of Ji is said to have slandered Duke Ai of Qi to the Zhou king, King Yi (r. 865–858), and King Yi ordered Duke Ai to be boiled in a bronze caldron. Although this has the smell of legend about it, there are bronze inscriptions from this time that suggest the royal court did in fact move to involve itself in the internal affairs of Qi, which apparently were quite complicated. Duke Ai was replaced by a younger half-brother, Duke Hu, but Hu was in turn hated by another younger full-brother of Duke Ai, who led his partisans against Duke Hu, killing him and driving his followers into exile; this was Duke Xian. With this, a state of divided allegiances persisted for several decades. Full-blown civil war broke out again about 820. Duke Li (r. 824–816) is described as cruel, prompting the son of Duke Hu to return from exile to kill him, though this son of Duke Hu was himself killed in the battle. With this, Qi once again largely passes out of historical accounts for well over another century, though it must have passed this time of relative obscurity by enriching itself.

Qi re-enters history early in the seventh century, with the succession to power of Duke Huan (r. 685–643), named Jiu. Duke Huan's succession was not at all auspicious. *Records of the Historian* says of his predecessor and elder half-brother, Duke Xiang (697–686): "Duke Xiang drunkenly killed Duke Huan of Lu (r. 711–694), raped his wife, killed and executed many without reason, was lewd with the women, and many times cheated the great ministers." Finally, Duke Xiang was assassinated in a palace coup, though the assassin, by the name of Wuzhi, which means Ignorant, was also killed in turn. Meanwhile, fearing that disaster would reach him as well, Jiu went into exile at Lu, the natal home of his brother. There he was put under the care of one Guan Zhong (*c.* 730–645). With the assassination of Duke Xiang and the death of Wuzhi, Jiu returned to Qi. His more than forty years of rule would be one of the most illustrious reigns in all of Chinese history.

Once Duke Huan was in power, Guan Zhong is said to have organized the state into a hierarchical administrative structure. The state was divided into seven counties (*xian*), each of which was sub-divided into three districts (*xiang*), thus making for twenty-one districts in all, with each district sub-divided into ten marches (*lian*), each march into four villages (*li*), each of which contained five groups of ten families. This structure was reflected as well in the organization of the Qi army: each group of ten families was responsible for contributing five soldiers, each village one chariot, each march a legion of two hundred troops, and each district a regiment of two thousand troops. Theoretically at least, the Qi army could put 45,000 men and 800 chariots into the field, making it the largest and best organized army of the time.

Meanwhile, the small states along the central course of the Yellow River were being threatened by the newly rising southern state of Chu. Seeking the protection of the larger and richer state of Qi to the north, these central states—Song, Chen, Wèi, Zheng, Xu, Cao, Cai, and Lu, as well as other still smaller states—signed mutual defense treaties at a pair of interstate meetings in 681 and 680, guaranteed by Qi. The second of these meetings was attended as well by a representative of the Zhou king, who confirmed the privileged place of Duke Huan among all the lords, recognizing him as "Premier" (*ba*), the first among all the lords. Over the next almost forty years of his reign, Duke Huan presided over ten more interstate meetings. Some of the meetings were held for the express purposes of launching military campaigns, others merely to discuss topics of mutual concern, and the various states paid contributions to Qi for its leadership.

In 645, after forty years of serving Duke Huan, Guan Zhong died. Before he died, Duke Huan asked for his advice as to which minister should succeed him; Guan Zhong advised against all of the leading candidates. After his death, Duke Huan nonetheless appointed three of the people Guan Zhong advised against. This was but the first of his mistakes, as they immediately set up monopolizing power among them. Two years later, Duke Huan died in his own turn, leaving behind a complicated family situation. He had three principal consorts, but none of the three had given birth to an heir. He also had six other consorts who he treated as if they were principal wives. Each of these six consorts had given birth to sons. Duke Huan and Guan Zhong had originally named Zhao, the son of a woman from the state of Zheng, to be crown prince, but had sent him to Zheng's neighbor state Song for safe-keeping. Back in Qi, another consort from the state of Wèi and the palace eunuchs convinced the dying duke to replace Zhao with her son Wugui. This caused the five sons still in the state to fight among themselves over the succession, the different factions blocking access to the ducal palace. Duke Huan died in the tenth month of 643, but with no one able to enter the palace the body lay untouched for sixty-seven days; when he was finally examined, maggots were crawling out of the body. And this was not the worst of it. Wugui took his place as duke, but Duke Xiang of Song (r. 650–637), at the head of an army, escorted the original crown prince Zhao back to Qi. Alarmed, the people of Qi put Wugui to death; his reign lasted all of three months. But when Zhao was about to take power, the other four sons attacked him, and he had to flee once again to Song. Song attacked again, finally placing Zhao in power; he was known as Duke Xiao (r. 642–633). Duke Huan was finally buried in the eighth month of the year, some ten months after he had died.

Qi would never recover from this fraternal succession battle. A century later, the heirs of the Grand Duke Wang would lose power entirely. In 534, Tian Wuyu (also known as Chen Huanzi; fl. 571–532), a descendant of the lords of the south-central state of Chen, was appointed high minister; three generations later, in 485, another member of the Tian family, Tian Heng (also known as Chen Heng, Chen Chang and Tian Chengzi; fl. 481), murdered the heir apparent of Duke Dao (r. 488–485). In 481, he murdered the young puppet ruler Duke Jian (r. 484–481) and took effective control of the state himself. From this time on, the state was ruled by the Tian family, first in fact, and then by the end of the century in name also; the subsequent period is usually referred to in histories as the Tian Qi, in contrast to the earlier Jiang Qi. A story in the *Zuo Tradition* says that as early as 672 this was predicted by a divination using the *Zhou Changes*, better known in the West as the *Classic of Changes*. It is not easy to understand all of the interpretations of this divination, but the story provides some sense of the developing philosophy around the *Zhou Changes*.

> Duke Li of Chen was born of a woman from Cai. Therefore, men of Cai killed Wufu and established Duke Li (as ruler). He fathered Jingzhong. When (Jingzhong) was young, the Scribe of Zhou used the *Zhou Changes* to have an audience with the Lord of Chen. The Lord of Chen had him divine by milfoil (about Jingzhong), meeting *Guan* ䷓ "Looking Up"'s *Pi* ䷋ "Negation," and said: This says:
> > Looking up at the kingdom's radiance. Beneficial herewith to be hosted by the king.
> >
> Will this one not come to replace Chen's rulers? If not here, it will be in a different state. If not by himself, it will be his descendants. 'Radiance' is distant and shines from something else. *Kun* ☷ is 'Earth,' *Xun* ☴ is the 'Wind,' and *Qian* ☰ is 'Heaven.' 'Wind' becoming 'Heaven' above 'Earth' is 'Mountain.' Having the resources of a mountain, and shining on it with heavenly radiance is to reside above 'Earth'; therefore,

it says, 'Looking up at the kingdom's radiance. Beneficial herewith to be hosted by the king.' The court's goods are displayed by the hundreds, presented with jades and silk. The beauties of heaven and earth are all complete among them. Therefore, it says: 'Beneficial herewith to be hosted by the king.' And yet there is 'looking up' in it, and therefore I said it will be with his descendants. The 'Wind' moves and strikes upon the 'Earth,' therefore I said that it will be in another state. If it is in another state, it surely will be of the Jiang family. The Jiangs are the descendants of Grand Peaks. Mountain peaks then match Heaven. Among things, nothing can be of equal greatness. When Chen declines, this one will flourish."

Coming to the time when Chen was first being lost, Chen Huanzi for the first time was great in Qi. Later when (Chen) was lost, Chen Heng gained the government.[9]

By the middle of the fourth century, Qi finally regained some of its former stature, engaging with the remaining independent states, sometimes as ally, sometimes as enemy. In 335, after winning several major battles over the preceding decade, Lord Wei (r. 356/334–320) entered into an alliance with Lord Huicheng (r. 369/334–319) of Wei, the preeminent power of the time, to recognize each other by the title "king" (*wang*). From this time on, the rulers of Qi were known as "kings." King Wei's successor, King Xuan (r. 319–300), is well known for his patronage of many visiting scholars, including especially Mencius (*c.* 385–303). He is also supposed to have housed these scholars at what is usually referred to as the Jixia Academy, a sort of early think tank. Qi became the center of the intellectual world of the time. One of King Xuan's grandsons, Lord Mengchang (also known as Tian Wen; d. 279) is said to have had in his service three thousand retainers who had come from throughout all of the independent states of the time.

In one of the conversations between King Xuan and Mencius, the king said that he had been advised to tear down the Bright Hall, and asked whether he should do so. Mencius's answer spoke to the question of true "kingship," obviously a sore point for a king whose father had more or less arbitrarily arrogated the title. Mencius told him that the Bright Hall was the seat of government, and if he wanted to exercise "kingly" government, he ought not tear it down. This led the king to ask of "kingly government." Mencius said:

In ancient times, when King Wen ruled Mount Qi, the tillers provided one-ninth (of their produce in tax) and the government servants inherited their salaries. At the passes and markets, goods were checked but not taxed, fish traps were not prohibited, and the guilt of criminals did not extend to their family members. King Wen always thought first to use the government to extend humaneness to widows and widowers, the elderly without children, and orphans, all the poor people of the world with nowhere to turn. The *Poetry* says: "Fortunate are the wealthy ones, Woeful are those who are alone."[10]

When the king expressed his admiration for this sentiment, Mencius, said: "If milord appreciates this, then why don't you put it into practice?" The king responded that he had weaknesses for wealth and sex, to which Mencius responded by urging the king to share what he had with the people, such that no one in the state was without enough to eat or someone to love. If he could do this, he would be a true king, just as King Wen (r. 1099/1056–1050) had been.

The question of true kingship was also at the heart of the major crisis of King Xuan's reign. Shortly after he had succeeded to power, King Kuai of Yan (r. 320–318, d. 314), wishing to emulate Yao and Shun, the sage-kings of still older times, abdicated, deposing his own son, the crown prince Ping, in favor of his chief minister Zi Zhi. King Xuan feared that this precedent would call into question the fundamental legitimacy of dynastic rule, and so he took advantage of civil disorder in Yan to attack and occupy the state. This occupation turned disastrous for Qi. When the Qi army was forced to withdraw King Wuling of Zhao (r. 325–299 B.C.) moved to fill the vacuum in Yan, installing a younger son of King Kuai as King Zhao of Yan (r. 311–279). Over the next three decades, with the good rule of King Zhao, Yan became wealthy and powerful. In 284, it joined together with all of the powerful states of the time to attack Qi, forcing King Min of Qi (r. 300–284) to flee south, where he was captured and killed by the Chu army. With that, Yan entered the Qi capital of Linzi and captured all of the treasures of the state. Although Qi would persist until 222, the last of the independent states to be conquered by Qin, it would never again regain the power that had been its under the rule of Duke Huan, four and a half centuries earlier.

CHAPTER 27
THE HEREDITARY HOUSE OF JIN

There is a story told about the young King Cheng of Zhou (r. 1042/1035–1006) toward the beginning of his reign when he was still a young boy: playing with his younger brother Shu Yu (Shu meaning "Junior"), he told him that he was awarding him rule of a state. The royal scribe asked on what day this would happen. The king responded that they were just playing and that he didn't really mean it. The scribe responded: "For the Son of Heaven there are no playful words. What he says the scribe will write it, the ritual masters will fulfill it, and the musicians will sing of it." With that, Shu Yu was made to rule the state of Tang, a small area to the east of the Yellow River and the Fen River in what is today southwestern Shanxi province. This was the precursor to the state of Jin, which in subsequent centuries would become the most important state of the Springs and Autumns period. This is clearly a just-so story, intended to show the gravity of the ruler's responsibility and the probity of the historian's work. In fact, it is almost certain that King Cheng was already an adult when he came to power, and Shu Yu, though certainly younger, was doubtless also an adult. His appointment to develop a colony in the Fen River valley was part of the greater Zhou strategy of ruling the territories that they had just conquered. The Fen River valley was a strategic location between the Zhou homeland and the former Shang capital area, and had been the scene of considerable fighting during the reign of Shang king Wu Ding (r. c. 1225–1189) and probably also thereafter. It was important that it be governed by someone trustworthy, and who could be more trustworthy than a brother.

In the early 1990s, archaeologists from Peking University located a cemetery in the area, just outside of the city of Houma, Shanxi, that they identified as containing the tombs of the early lords of Jin. Unfortunately, tomb robbers found some of the tombs before the archaeologists did. Toward the end of the decade, the archaeologists believed that they had finished their work, with seventeen tombs arrayed in two more or less neat rows, representing eight generations of lords and their wives (one of the lords' tombs was accompanied by tombs of two wives). Unfortunately, in the spring of 1998, tomb robbers struck again, blasting their way into a tomb that was located at the far end of the cemetery between the top and bottom rows of tombs. When the archaeologists finally salvaged what they could of the tomb, they found that it was the earliest of all tombs in the cemetery. They found the bottom portion of a square caldron that had otherwise been obliterated by the dynamite blast. By a stroke of rare luck, it was precisely the portion of the vessel that carried the inscription. The vessel was made for Shu Yu.

> It was the fourteenth month, the king performed a libation offering, greatly inscribing a prayer at Cheng Zhou. Completing the prayer, the king called out to convene his sires, and awarded Shu Yu with a skirt and jacket, chariot and horses, and thirty double-strands of cowries, (for which Shu Yu) dares to respond to the king's beneficence, herewith making (this) treasured offertory vessel; may for ten thousand years it extol the king's making radiant his sire.[11]

This matches to some extent a record in the *Zuo Tradition*, recounting the award made to Shu Yu to be the first lord of Jin. However, despite being the founder of the state, it was not Shu Yu, but rather his son Xie who moved the administrative seat to Jin. This move too has now been corroborated by a recently unearthed bronze vessel. Unfortunately, this vessel too was unearthed by tomb robbers, and purchased in 2005 by the National Museum of China on the antique market in Hong Kong. The inscription uses a style of date-notation that had been in use in the earlier Shang dynasty, referring to a king commanding a Bo (Bo meaning "Senior" or "First Born") of Tang to be lord in Jin. Since Shu Yu was not "first born," this Bo of Tang must be his son; the "twenty-eighth year" must refer to later in the reign of King Cheng, probably 1008.

> Yao Gong makes for his wife Yao this *gui*-tureen, meeting with the king's commanding Tang Bo to be lord in Jin. It is the king's twenty-eighth year.[12]

These recent discoveries do not add much to what is known of the first years of the state of Jin, but they do show something about the role of archaeology—and, unfortunately, of tomb robbers—in unearthing some of the material remains of that early history. Indeed, the excavations at the

Houma cemetery provide almost the only information about the early lords of the state; the "Hereditary House of Jin" chapter of *Records of the Historian* does no more than note the names of Xie and the next four rulers of the state.

It would not be until late in the Western Zhou period that Jin would become involved in Zhou politics, first perhaps inadvertently, and then more deliberately. In 842, King Li of Zhou (r. 857/853–842/828) was forced to flee into exile. The place he went, Zhi, along the Fen River in Shanxi province, was either within or very near to Jin territory; whether he went there with the active support of Jin or not cannot now be known. However, after this time Jin comes to be mentioned more and more for its support of the Zhou kings. In the thirty-third year of the reign of King Xuan of Zhou (r. 827–782), the Jin lord Su (also known as Lord Xian) accompanied the king on a lengthy campaign far to the east, in present-day Shandong province. Afterward, he was given awards at the Zhou eastern capital at Luoyang, a campaign and awards that he would commemorate on a rack of bells: the *Jin Hou Su bianzhong*. About this time, Jin also fought several battles to the north of its state seeking to defend against Warrior attacks into the Zhou heartland. These succeeded in buying only a few years. In 771, the final Western Zhou king, King You (r. 781–771) was killed and the capital was sacked. King You's court had been riven by factionalism, with Jin arrayed against Guo, its neighbor on the southern side of the Yellow River, and Zheng, which was just then relocating to the east of Guo. There was a period of about twenty years when there were two claimants to the Zhou kingship, and no king residing in either of the two capitals; King You's younger brother Yu Chen claimed to rule at Guo, while King You's son by his original queen Yi Jiu sought refuge among his maternal relatives. Finally, in 750, Chou, Lord Wen of Jin (r. 780–746) killed Yu Chen at Guo and then escorted Yi Jiu to the Zhou eastern capital at Luoyang, where he would reign for another thirty years as King Ping (r. 770–720). Lord Wen was also celebrated with a ceremony at the capital, being awarded a command the text of which was preserved as one of the chapters of the *Exalted Scriptures*.

Unfortunately for Jin, when Lord Wen died, it too broke into factions. Lord Wen was succeeded by his son, Lord Zhao (r. 745–739), who ruled at the Jin capital Yi. Lord Wen's younger brother, Cheng Shi was given the city of Quwo, where he reigned over a separate polity, posthumously known as Huan Shu (r. 745–731). When Lord Zhao was assassinated in 739, Huan Shu attempted to enter the capital to take control of the entire state, but the people of the capital area revolted against him, and he was forced to withdraw again to Quwo. The main-line "lords" (*hou*) of the state and the Quwo branch of the family continued to contend for power for the next several decades, with the two factions repeatedly attacking each other. In 730, Cheng Shi's son Zhuang Bo (r. 730–716) succeeded to power in Quwo. In 724, he himself stabbed the ruler of the capital, Lord Xiao (r. 739–724), to death, and again attempted to take control there, but he too was rebuffed. With the succession of Duke Wu in Quwo (r. 715–679/677), the tide began to shift decisively in favor of the Quwo rulers. In 679, Duke Wu finally succeeded in taking the capital and killing the last of the direct line rulers, Duke Min (r. 706–679). Duke Wu took the plunder from the city and presented it to the Zhou king, King Xi (r. 681–677). In return, King Xi recognized Duke Wu—and thus the Quwo lineage—as the legitimate rulers of Jin. This would not be the end of civil wars in Jin, by any stretch, but at least it resolved this first conflict. Indeed, similar problems would begin with the reign of Duke Wu's son, Duke Xian (r. 676–651). It involves many personal names, the relationships among which need to be kept straight. The names make it difficult to follow, but the plot is easy: male lust, female ambition, and fraternal conflict, though virtue wins out in the end.

In the fifth year of his reign, 672, Duke Xian launched an attack against the northern Li Warriors, in the course of which he captured one of their women: Li Ji, making her one of his consorts. A few years later, he moved against the Jin nobility, killing many of them, with others fleeing into exile in Jin's former nemesis Guo. He himself constructed a new capital at Jiang, where a few years later still, Li Ji gave birth to a son, Xiqi. Duke Xian had already sired three sons, the mother of the eldest of them, Shensheng, was a daughter of the "premier" among the rulers of the independent states: Duke Huan of Qi (r. 685–643); the other two sons, Chong'er, and Yiwu, were born of two different women from another "barbarian" state of the north: the Di (Distant Ones). To make room for Xiqi, the duke sent these three sons to live in three separate cities of the state. Over the next several years Li Ji publicly praised Shensheng, but privately slandered him to the duke's most influential advisors, Li Ke and Xun Xi, seeking to have her own son named the prince-in-waiting. Shensheng finally resolved the problem by committing suicide. With this, the two younger brothers, Chong'er and Yiwu, realizing that they would be the next targets of Li Ji's machinations, fortified the cities in which they were living. This angered their father Duke Xian, who attacked both cities. Chong'er fled in exile to the Di, while Yiwu initially successfully resisted the attack, but eventually was also forced into exile.

Chong'er's exile, which lasted nineteen years, is one of the great stories of Chinese history. It took him through most of the independent states of the time, first in north China, then to Chu in the south, and finally to Qin in the west. Almost everywhere he went he and his band of supporters impressed their hosts with their abilities. The supporters included men from the Zhao and Wei lineages, which, together with another lineage—the Han—would eventually divide Jin into three separate states. But that would not happen for another two hundred years. In the meantime, much would take place within the ducal house in Jin.

In 651, Duke Xian died, in the ninth month of the year. Li Ji immediately enlisted the aid of Xun Xi in naming Xiqi to be the next duke. However, before this could take place, another minister, Li Ke, killed Xiqi. Xun Xi then named another young son of Duke Xian, Zhuozi, who was a son of Li Ji's younger sister and who was still a toddler, to be duke, with himself as regent. Li Ke again inserted himself, killing both Zhuozi and Li Ji. He allowed Xun Xi to commit suicide. Li Ke, now in a position to name the next duke, invited Chong'er to return from exile; Chong'er declined to do so. Li Ke then invited Yiwu to do so, which he accepted, being known posthumously as Duke Hui of Jin (r. 650–637). His reign would be characterized throughout by the intrigue and duplicity with which it began.

Duke Hui's first command was that Li Ke, his ostensible patron, commit suicide, which he did. Four years later, he managed to so offend Duke Mu of Qin (r. 659–621), who was married to his sister, that Qin invaded Jin and took Duke Hui prisoner. At the urging of his wife, Duke Mu spared Duke Hui's life, allowing him to return to Jin. Once returned to power, hearing that ministers wished to replace him with his older brother Chong'er, he sent assassins to the Di to try to kill Chong'er. The assassins were not successful. In the meantime, Duke Hui sent his son, Yu, to Qin as a hostage, intended to guarantee that he would not again deceive Duke Mu of Qin. Duke Mu again treated him generously, giving him one of his daughters in marriage. However, in 638, hearing that his father Duke Hui was ill and dying, Yu secretly escaped from Qin to return to Jin; his wife, the daughter of Duke Mu of Qin, refused to accompany him. Duke Hui died in the next year, and Yu became duke of Jin, known posthumously as Duke Huai (r. 637). His reign did not last long. Duke Mu of Qin, outraged that he would escape from his hostage situation, and especially that he would leave his wife behind, invited Chong'er to Qin, giving him in marriage the same daughter as well as four other daughters. With the support of the Qin army, Chong'er crossed the Yellow River, finally returning to Jin territory. He met the Jin army of

Duke Huai at Gaoliang, and defeated them in battle, killing Duke Huai, whose reign lasted only a few months.

With that, Chong'er's nineteen-year exile had come to an end, and at sixty-two years of age he finally took his place as duke of Jin, to be known posthumously as Duke Wen (r. 636–628). He moved immediately to reorganize the Jin government and especially its depleted military, forming it into three armies, each division of which was led by the senior members of the six major lineages of the state. In addition to strengthening Jin's own military strength, Duke Wen also drew on the relationships he had developed during his exile to forge alliances with other states. What is more, in the second year of his reign, he came to the rescue of the Zhou king, King Xiang (r. 651–619), who had been driven out of the capital by his own brother. Duke Wen led a group of states to return the king to the capital. Needless to say, this put the Zhou king very much in his debt.

Over the preceding two decades, the southern state of Chu had taken advantage of the death of Duke Huan of Qi and the chaos in Jin to expand toward the north. In 633, it attempted to extend this expansion still further, invading the state of Song, an ally of Jin. Duke Wen reconstituted his coalition to come to the aid of Song. In the next year, the Jin coalition, with forces of Qi and Qin serving as the principal support of all three armies of the reconstituted Jin military, decisively defeated the Chu army and its allies at the battle of Chengpu, somewhere near where the present-day provinces of Henan and Shandong meet. The battle, which took place on the fourth day of the fourth month of 632, the day *jisi* of the cycle of sixty days, is often said to have been the most important battle of the Springs and Autumns period; it is certainly the battle most fully described in the *Zuo Tradition*, including both the pre-battle preparations and also the tactics employed by both sides.

With its army defeated and its alliances shattered, Chu withdrew to its Yangzi River homeland and did not again threaten the northern states for several generations. The following month, Duke Wen hosted King Xiang of Zhou at a place called Jiantu, and presented him with the Chu captives: one hundred chariots and one thousand foot-soldiers. The king awarded Duke Wen a grand chariot, a red bow and 100 red arrows, a black bow and 1,000 black arrows, sweet-wine, a ladle, and 300 bodyguards; these gifts are very much like the gifts recounted in bronze inscriptions from the period. More important, the king appointed Duke Wen as the premier among the leaders of all the states.

Already aged when he came to power, Duke Wen reigned for only another four years after being named premier. However, this was a status that the rulers of Jin would maintain for almost a century to follow. The history of the state through Duke Ding (r. 511–475) saw ups and downs, but in general proceeded smoothly. Beginning with the following reign, that of Duke Chu (r. 474–458/52), Jin's rulers would confront one crisis after another that would eventually cause the state to break apart.

Despite Duke Wen's great accomplishments, his reorganization of the Jin government and military would come back to haunt Jin almost two centuries later. Duke Wen drew upon leading members of different Jin lineages, most of them people who had followed him throughout his exile, and rewarded them with their own territorial power bases. Six of these lineages—Wei, Zhao, Han, Xun, Zhonghang, and Fan—would develop into independent powers in their own right. By the fifth century, in a pattern reminiscent of the independent states vis-à-vis the Zhou king, these six lineages had become more powerful than the Jin rulers. In 458, Zhibo, the leader of the Xun lineage and the most powerful figure in the state at the time, joined forces with the Wei, Zhao and Han lineages to divide up the territories of the other two: Zhonghang and Fan. With this, Duke Chu, fearing that Zhibo would next move on him, fled in exile to Qi, the long-time ally of the Jin rulers. Meanwhile, Jin devolved into civil war. There is some evidence that there were two people each claiming to be Duke Chu's successor, such that there may have been three different reign years simultaneously in use. This has caused the traditional histories not only to confuse the chronology of the period, but even who was ruling—or trying to rule—the state. What is clear is that in 453, Wei, Zhao and Han turned on Zhibo and killed him, dividing the territory of his own Xun lineage among themselves. This act—and thus this year—is often regarded as the beginning of the Warring States period. For Jin, it was the beginning of the end. The state survived through four more dukes, but just barely. Indeed, one of them, Duke You (r. 433–416) was stabbed to death by his own wife while he tried to rape her. Finally, in 403, the three surviving lineages—Wei, Zhao and Han—divided the state among them. They would all be major powers of the Warring States period, each writing its own chapter among the hereditary houses of the period.

CHAPTER 28
THE HEREDITARY HOUSE OF WEI

The hereditary house of Wei, one of the three states into which the great state of Jin had divided in 403, ostensibly traced its heritage back to one Bi Gao, a figure who took part in the Zhou conquest of Shang and was subsequently awarded rule of a local territory at Bi, located just to the southwest of the Zhou capital at present-day Xi'an, Shaanxi. Although Bi Gao continued to serve the Zhou kings Cheng (r. 1042/1035–1006) and Kang (r. 1005–978), and a command to him was even preserved as one of the chapters in the *Exalted Scriptures*, the *Records of the Historian* suggests that his descendants lost their land and ended up living among the northern "barbarians." Inscribed bronze vessels from the Western Zhou period suggest that this is not true at all, and that the Bi family retained considerable influence throughout the entire period. In 1966, a pair of early bronze *gui*-tureens that were cast for Bi Gong himself to commemorate an award made to him by one of these early Zhou kings was discovered in the Zhou homeland at Qishan, and numerous other vessels from throughout the entirety of the Western Zhou have been discovered over the centuries. One, the *Yu Hu ding*, discovered in 1992, suggests that the Bi family was still located just to the south of the capital.

On the other hand, the most recent discoveries suggest that the Bi family was also active further to the east of the Zhou capital. In 2006, several vessels were discovered in Jiang County, Shanxi, the inscriptions of which record that a Bi daughter had been married to the ruler of a state called Peng, thought to have been a non-Zhou state located there. More recently still, in 2007 a *ding*-caldron cast by a Ke the Elder of Bi was unearthed at Liangdaicun, along the north-south stretch of the Yellow River in eastern Shaanxi. The vessel was cast either at the very end of the Western Zhou or perhaps after the Zhou western capital had been lost, and was dedicated to his "high ancestor who had received the mandate, Duke Bi." It is unclear whether this means that the Bi family had ties throughout the middle Yellow River valley, or if they moved east along with the Zhou kings only at the very end of the Western Zhou period. In any event, traditional histories pick up the story of the Bi family again in 661, when a figure named Bi Wan is said to have ridden in the chariot of Duke Xian of Jin (r. 676–651), serving as his spearman. Duke Xian defeated three small states located in the Fen River valley of Shanxi province: Huo, Geng and Wei, and awarded rule of Wei to Bi Wan in recognition of his service. A diviner at the court of Duke Xian predicted that the descendants of Bi Wan would certainly become very great, since his name Wan means "10,000" or a "myriad," while Wei means "lofty." Bi Wan's own divination about whether to serve the Jin lords or not was also auspicious, indicating that he would certainly prosper. In fact, Wei would become one of the greatest states of the Warring States period. This probably does not mean that this prediction and divination were prescient; instead, they were probably created after the fact to explain the rise of the state. Nevertheless, Bi Wan's descendants did become great.

When Duke Xian died a decade later and control of Jin descended into chaos among his many sons, Bi Wan threw his support to Chong'er, who would eventually become duke: Duke Wen of Jin (r. 636–628). From their base in Wei, Bi Wan and his descendants would continue to be among the six ministers serving the Jin rulers for more than a century. Toward the end of the sixth century, power in the state shifted decisively away from the Jin rulers themselves and toward these six ministers. In 514, their positions as heads of government were formalized by Duke Qing (r. 525–512). Over the next two generations, Wei would make common cause with Zhao and Han, two of the other six ministers, to attack the other three: Fan, Zhonghang and Xun. In 458, fighting among these local powers would drive Duke Chu (r. 474–458/52) into exile, with different factions supporting different pretenders to rule. This strife culminated in 453, when Wei, Zhao and Han would join together to annihilate Xun, killing its leader Zhibo, who had been the power behind Duke Chu. The three lineages divided up his territory and control of Jin effectively passed to them. This year is often seen as the beginning of the Warring States period.

The beginning of Wei history as an independent state properly begins with Lord Wen of Wei (r. 433–496), during whose long reign Wei consolidated its power as the preeminent of the three states. Although Jin had effectively divided into the three states of Wei, Zhao and Han, Lord Wen succeeded for the most part in keeping the three states working in concert with each other. Wei, in particular, became the most powerful state in north China, attacking Qin to the west and reclaiming the fertile land to the west of the

Yellow River that Jin had lost to Duke Mu of Qin (r. 659–621). At this time, Wei even attacked the non-Chinese state of Zhongshan to the east of the Taihang Mountains in present-day Hebei province. In 404, Lord Wen achieved his greatest success. In that year, the state of Yue, which was a rising power in southeastern China, agreed to a treaty with the northern states of Qi and Lu to counter the power of the Jin states. To celebrate this treaty, the ruler of Yue visited Lu, where a triumphal parade was staged, with him riding in a chariot driven by the lord of Lu and assisted by the lord of Qi. Offended by this, Lord Wen of Wei, joined by the other two Jin states, and entering the "long wall" there attacked Qi, defeating Duke Kang of Qi (r. 404–386). This victory is noteworthy for three different reasons. First, the reference to the Wei, Zhao and Han armies passing through a "long wall" in both a contemporary bronze inscription, the *Biao Qiang zhong*, and also in the recently discovered Tsinghua manuscript *Annals*, is the first reference in any Chinese literature to what would become the Great Wall of China. Second, the allied Jin armies signed two separate treaties acknowledging Qi's defeat: one with Duke Kang of Qi, who would be the last ruler of Qi's original ruling family, and one with Tian He, the leader of the family that would supplant the ruling family and go on to rule Qi for the next 175 years. Third, the Jin allies then went on to present the Qi captives to the king of Zhou, King Weilie (r. 425–402); the king then recognized the the rulers of Wei, Zhao and Han as "lords" (*hou*). This marked the end of the state of Jin, which had survived and prospered for more than six centuries, even though several of the centuries were wracked by civil war.

Lord Wen is looked back upon by Chinese historians as a particularly capable ruler, doubtless because in reforming the government he entrusted the reforms to three capable ministers: Li Kui (455–395), Wu Qi (440–381), and Ximen Bao (dates unknown). While the contributions these men made in Wei have been overshadowed in the grand sweep of Chinese history by more illustrious ministers in other states, they all played important roles, not only in making Wei the strongest state of its time, but also in showing the way for other states to become strong. If Shang Yang (d. 335), who in the middle of the fourth century would become chief minister in Qin, is usually regarded as the father of the school of thought called Legalism and the administrative and economic reforms associated with it, Li Kui should be regarded as its grandfather. Indeed, in the earliest bibliography of Chinese literature, a book bearing the name *Li Kui* and said to have been written by him, comes at the very beginning of the section on Legalism. His economic theory stressed the importance of agriculture, and especially the role of the single family as the basic unit of production. He urged that land be measured in standard sized plots to maximize tax income while still allowing sufficient income for the peasants to live. While an echo of his agricultural policy would be heard in the reforms instituted by Shang Yang in Qin, it is also possible to see in it the famous well-field policy mentioned in the work of Mencius (*c.* 385–303). This well-field policy takes its name from the Chinese character for "well": 井; it is said to describe a land management system in which eight households would individually till their own separate plots, those around the perimeter of the square, but would join together to till the central square, the harvest of which would be paid to the state as a tax. Li Kui is also said to have written a book on the law: the *Classic of Law*. Although the book has not survived, descriptions of it suggest that it was the first extended code intended to ensure civil security. It was organized in six separate sections: bandits, brigands, prisons, arrests, miscellaneous punishments, and extenuating circumstances. Shang Yang is said to have taken a copy of this *Classic of Law* with him when he went to Qin, and it is clear that it influenced the development of law there, and through that also law throughout later Chinese history.

Wu Qi is ranked together with the earlier Sun Wu (*c.* 544–496), better known as Sunzi, as the two great military geniuses of ancient China; indeed, their names are often linked as "Sun Wu" (Wu being Wu Qi's surname, a different character from Sun Wu's given name). He was originally from the old state of Wèi (not to be confused with this state of Wei), located in the northeastern part of present-day Henan province, but at a young age commanded the Wei army in its reconquest of the area to the west of the Yellow River, over which he was given control. After making a name for himself in Wei, he moved on to the southern state of Chu, where he also achieved great success, but also made numerous enemies. It was there that he was assassinated. Two anecdotes about him in the later military classic *Wei Liaozi* illustrate well his military philosophy. The first says that on the eve of a battle, his officers offered Wu Qi a sword; he rejected it, saying "To command the troops and direct their blades is the role of the commander; to wield a single sword is not his role." The second says that at the battle, he ordered his army to await his command to attack. One bravo, unable to restrain himself, rushed out and attacked the enemy line, killing two men with whose heads he returned to his own lines. Wu Qi ordered that he be executed for having disobeyed the original order. This second anecdote recalls a story about Sunzi, who the King of Wu tested by ordering that he train his harem. When the women of the harem repeatedly failed to follow orders, Sunzi ordered that the king's favorite two consorts be executed for failing to instill discipline. Although the king was dismayed with this order, Sunzi insisted that it be carried out. Afterwards the women of the harem obeyed every order without hesitation. These anecdotes are doubtless much embellished, but they have long been used to explain the important role of the commander in Chinese military theory.

Ximen Bao, the third of Lord Wen's principal advisers, was in charge of important infrastructure projects, especially the building of a network of twelve canals that were used especially for irrigation, bringing the water of the Yellow River to the area of southwest Shanxi, the heartland of Wei, making it the most fertile land of the time. The irrigation network was still in use during the Han dynasty, some three hundred years later, at which time it was said of him that "his name was known to all under heaven and his moisture flowed to later generations."

Lord Wen is also famous for being a friend and patron to such paragons of virtue and learning as Zi Xia (b. 507), Tian Zifang (*c.* 369–286) and Duan Ganmu (*c.* 475–396). Zi Xia, famous as the most scholarly of Confucius's personal disciples, was in turn the teacher of Li Kui, Wu Qi and Ximen Bao. Tian Zifang is said to have been Lord Wen's teacher of philosophy, while Duan Ganmu resisted almost every attempt to draw him into the government, but through that became ever more famous. Still, his friendship with Lord Wen contributed to the lord's success. It is said that in 401, a Qin army was about to attack Wei, when a Qin adviser reminded the duke of Qin of Duan Ganmu's presence in Wei; Qin withdrew its army in recognition of Duan's virtue.

Lord Wen died in 387, and was succeeded by his son Ziji, better known as Lord Wu, the Martial Lord, of Wei (r. 395–370). Despite the posthumous name by which he is known, not only was his short reign not marked by any notable military successes, he seems to have been defeated in every battle that he led. What is more, the alliance that his father had achieved with Zhao and Han, the other two successor states of Jin, would dissolve under Lord Wu. For instance, in 380, Zhao joined with Chu, Jin's old nemesis now under the command of none other than Wu Qi, Wei's former general, to attack Wei; Zhao occupied much of eastern Wei, while Chu took all of its territories south of the Yellow River. This alliance between Zhao and Chu would introduce a new form of diplomacy and military alliances, in which countries would join together temporarily to gain one advantage or another, knowing full well that some years later they might very well be enemies.

Another failure of Lord Wu was his failure to name a successor prior to his death. He had two sons, the elder named Ying, and younger Gongzi Huan. After Lord Wu's death, Gongzi Huan went to Zhao to enlist its aid in installing him. Han joined together with Zhao to take advantage of the succession crisis in Wei to invade, dealing the Wei army a crippling defeat and taking Ying prisoner. Despite this initial success, the two states disagreed over how to proceed. Zhao wanted to kill Ying, and make Huan the puppet ruler, while Han argued that killing Ying would cause the people of Wei to regard them as butchers, and thought it best to let the two brothers divide the state between them. In fact, when the two allies withdrew their armies, Ying was released, killed his younger brother, and became lord of Wei, known to history as Lord Huicheng of Wei (r. 369–335), or better known by his subsequent title King Hui of Liang (r. 334–319). His lengthy reigns were marked by numerous notable events, making him arguably the most famous of all leaders of the Warring States period.

Lord Huicheng had a checkered career as a military leader, with some notable victories but also many defeats. His achievements as a political strategist were more positive. In 361, he moved the capital of the state from Anyi, in the western part of the state along the north-south stretch of the Yellow River far to the east at Daliang, south-southeast of present-day Kaifeng, Henan; this had the effect of taking it out of danger from attacks by Qin, and to place the capital in the very center of the north China plain. In the next year, he opened the Wild-Goose Canal, linking the Yellow River near present-day Zhengzhou with the Huai River in Anhui province; to the northeast, it also connected with the Ji River of Shandong province. This had the effect of connecting all of the major rivers of the region, and was a precursor of the Grand Canal that linked the Yellow River and the Yangzi River that was completed almost a thousand years later. From this time on, the state was often referred to as Liang rather than Wei. At this time too, he also exchanged several cities with Zhao and Han, having the effect of consolidating Wei territory and making it easier to govern and easier to defend. He also engaged in numerous meetings with rulers of other states. For him, this culminated in his declaration of kingship in 334, which the other states recognized. Thereafter, he reigned for sixteen years as King Hui of Liang.

King Hui is now perhaps best remembered as the patron of the famous Confucian philosopher Mencius, who visited his court very late in his reign and whose book features several notable conversations between the two men. One of the more memorable of these conversations provides insight into both men.

King Hui of Liang said, "My attitude towards my country is to put all of my heart into it. If the area Within the River has a famine, I move the people to the area East of the River and move its grain to Within the River, and if the area East of the River has a famine I do likewise. When I examine the governors of neighboring states, there is none as conscientious as I am, yet the populations of those states don't decrease while mine doesn't increase. Why is this?"

Mencius replied, "Milord loves warfare, so let me illustrate it with warfare. Exuberantly drumming the men into battle, if once the weapons have crossed your men throw away their armor and dragging their weapons run off, some running a hundred paces and stopping, while others stop after fifty paces. How would it be if those who ran fifty paces laughed at those who had run a hundred?"

"That wouldn't be OK! Just because they didn't run a hundred paces, they too ran off."

Mencius said, "If Milord understands this, then don't look for your people to be more numerous than those of your neighbors."[13]

In fact, in all five of the conversations between King Hui and Mencius, King Hui comes off as a vain man, singularly concerned with his public image. While these conversations were clearly intended to show off Mencius's perspicacity and wit, it probably does not get King Hui too wrong. After King Hui died, in 319, Mencius stayed on to advise his son, known as King Xiang'ai (r. 318–296), but left shortly thereafter, explaining that the king "does not look like a ruler" and there is "nothing in him that inspires awe." It has not helped King Xiang'ai's historical reputation that Sima Qian in *Records of the Historian* completely mistook his identity, dividing him into two separate kings, the first, King Xiang, being confused with the sixteen-year reign of his father as king, and a second, a King Ai, whose twenty-three-year reign was actually that of King Xiang'ai. Perhaps it is just as well since his reign was marked by no great accomplishments. Instead, there was a great deal of back and forth fighting and negotiation with Qin, but to no real effect.

The situation only deteriorated during the reign of his son, King Zhao (r. 295–277). During the first nine years of his reign, *Records of the Historian* records defeat after defeat at the hands of Qin.

In King Zhao's first year, Qin plucked our Xiang City. In the second year, we fought with Qin, but it did not benefit us. Third year, we aided

Han to attack Qin, but the Qin general Bai Qi defeated our army of 240,000 men at Yique. In the sixth year, we gave Qin four square miles of our area East of the River. Mang Mao tricked us. Seventh year, Qin plucked sixty-one of our cities large and small. Eighth year, King Zhao of Qin became the Western Emperor and King Min of Qi became the Eastern Emperor, though a month later they both resumed using the title of "king." In the ninth year, Qin plucked our cities Yuan and Quyang.[14]

During the reign of his son, King Anxi (r. 276–243), the situation did not improve. In 266, Wei suffered the indignity of being attacked by Qi from the north and Chu from the south, having to request aid from their old enemy Qin. Qin provided the aid, since it did not want Wei's territory and riches to fall into the hands of its rivals Qi and Chu. The last two kings of Wei, King Jingmin (r. 242–228) and his son Wang Jia (r. 227–225), did not fare any better. In 225, Wei was one of the first of the old states to fall completely to Qin, being incorporated into the growing Qin empire as a single prefecture.

There is probably no single lesson to learn from the history of this hereditary house other than that all such houses eventually fall. It is not a bad lesson to remember.

CHAPTER 29
THE HEREDITARY HOUSE OF ZHAO

The hereditary house of Zhao, one of the three houses that the once great state of Jin divided into in 403, ostensibly had the longest pedigree of the three houses, even if it was the only one that did not belong to the same family as the Jin rulers: it traced its heritage back to the ancestors of the Ying family, the family of which the most notable branch was the rulers of Qin, at the time of the Shang dynasty. After the Zhou conquest of Shang, Zhao is supposed to have switched its allegiance to Zhou, though no members of the family appear in the historical record for this period until the fourth generation. This was a figure known as Zaofu, who is credited with being the charioteer of King Mu of Zhou (r. 956–918). The *Biography of the Son of Heaven Mu*, a text written on bamboo strips that was discovered in 279 CE in an ancient tomb in what is today Ji County, Henan, purports to record a journey that King Mu made to the Kunlun Mountains in the west, in present-day Qinghai, where he is said to have met with the Queen Mother of the West (Xi Wang Mu). It mentions Zaofu prominently; unfortunately, being an unearthed text, there are some breaks in the wording.

> The Son of Heaven commanded that the team of eight steeds be hitched, the right inside being . . . Roan and the left being Green Ears, the right outrider being Crimson Ji and the left being White Propriety. The Son of Heaven was in charge of the chariot, Zaofu was the driver, . . . was Righthand Man.
>
> . . .
>
> On *guiyou* (day 10), the Son of Heaven commanded that the team of eight steeds be hitched, Zaofu being the driver of the team of four of Roan Racer. They campaigned southwards floating along, crossing the Distant Road, ascending the Great Mountains, and crossing over the River in the south. They had galloped a thousand *li* and then entered into Ancestral Zhou. The officers presented the blood of a

white swan for the Son of Heaven to drink and to wash the Son of Heaven's feet. Zaofu then prepared the blood of a sheep for the charioteers of the team of four.[15]

The tomb in which the *Biography of Son of Heaven Mu* was found was closed in 299 BCE or just slightly later. Thus, although the text is not a true history of King Mu's travels, it certainly dates no later than the fourth century BCE. Another text that was found in the same tomb has long been called the *Bamboo Annals*. It has more claim to being an actual record of events of the time. While it too mentions the Queen Mother of the West, it rather more believably mentions that Zaofu was King Mu's charioteer in a battle against the Xu Warriors of the east, a military campaign that seems to be reflected in bronze inscriptions from the time. The *Bamboo Annals* also mentions that in the sixteenth year of King Mu's reign (941), the king enfeoffed Zaofu with the territory of Zhao.

For six generations after the time of Zaofu, the heads of the house of Zhao are supposed to have continued to serve the Zhou kings as charioteers. But with the defeat of King You of Zhou (r. 781–771) and the loss of the Zhou homeland, Shu Dai is said to have left this service and relocated to Jin, where he served Lord Wen of Jin (r. 780–746). Another six or seven generations later, at the time of the domestic unrest caused by Duke Xian (r. 676–651) and his consort Li Ji (d. 651), yet another head of the Zhao house, Zhao Shuai (d. 622), left his homeland to travel abroad, though in this case his exodus would be temporary: Zhao Shuai joined Chong'er, who would eventually become better known as Duke Wen of Jin (r. 637–628), on his nineteen-year peregrination around the then Chinese world. Much of Duke Wen's success, both in his travels and after his return to Jin, is credited to the good counsel he received from Zhao Shuai.

While Duke Wen and his entourage were traveling, they first spent several years with the Di, the "Distant" peoples to the north of Jin. While there, the Di made presents of two girls to Chong'er and to Zhao Shuai; surprisingly the elder of the two, Shu Wei, was offered to Zhao Shuai. With her, Zhao Shuai had a son: Zhao Dun (c. 650–601). Prior to leaving Jin, Zhao Shuai had been married to a woman of Jin, with whom he had sired three sons. When he returned, his Jin wife welcomed the Di wife, and offered to treat Shu Wei as Shuai's principal consort, and Zhao Dun as heir, her own three sons serving him. When Zhao Shuai died, in 622, he was enshrined in the ancestral temple with the posthumous temple name Zhao Chengji. His son Zhao Dun would go on to succeed him as prime minister of Jin, controlling the government over the course of the following two reigns, leading troops in battle and representing Jin at interstate assemblies.

When Duke Xiang (r. 627–621) died in 621, the crown prince was quite young. Zhao Dun proposed making Duke Xiang's younger brother Yong the successor. However, he was persuaded against this by the queen mother, and despite his better judgment allowed the crown prince to succeed; this was Duke Ling (r. 620–607). Whereas Zhao Dun earned a reputation for being capable in government and humane in his treatment of the people, Duke Ling was quite the opposite. The two men eventually became estranged. When Duke Ling let it be known that he wished to execute Zhao Dun, Dun fled and was harbored among the people. At that point, a kinsman assassinated Duke Ling and invited Duke Xiang's younger brother Yong to become lord; this was Duke Cheng (r. 606–600). During most of the brief reign of Duke Cheng, Zhao Dun continued in control of the government. However, in 601 he died, enshrined with the posthumous name Zhao Xuanmeng. He was succeeded as head of the family by his son Shuo. However, Duke Cheng died the next year, and the fortunes of the family took a turn for the worse.

At the beginning of the reign of Duke Jing (r. 599–581), control of the government fell to two other great ministers, Han Jue and Tu'an Jia, the first a supporter of the Zhao family, while the latter blamed Zhao Dun for having assassinated Duke Ling, even though he had not been in the capital at the time. Tu'an Jia eventually gained the upper hand, and executed all of Zhao Dun's family members: not only his son, Zhao Shuo, but also his three half-brothers by Zhao Shuai's first wife. Tu'an Jia did not kill Zhao Shuo's wife, who was pregnant at that time. However, when he heard that she had given birth to a son, he ordered that the son too be killed. Through various subterfuges, the son managed to survive, living in the mountains. Some fifteen years later, as Duke Jing lay dying, Han Jue revealed to him that Zhao Shuo's son was actually alive; this was Zhao Wu. Duke Jing allowed him to return, and together with Han Jue, they exterminated Tu'an Jia's family, and the original Zhao lands were returned to him.

The next several decades saw several new lords of Jin, each reigning for just a short time. Meanwhile, the six families of the great ministers of the state grew increasingly powerful; these were the houses of Zhao, Han, Wei, Fan, Zhonghang, and Xun. These six families would contend with each other for power for over a century. For several decades before and after 500, Zhao, in the person of Zhao Jianzi (d. 476), gained ascendancy among the six families. Throughout this period, he served as prime minister to the Jin lords, and in 497 finally managed to drive the heads of the Zhonghang and Fan families into exile, absorbing their land into that of Zhao. Several years later, Zhibo, the head of the Xun family, attacked the state of Wèi. Zhao Jianzi sent his son Wuxu to assist in the attack. However, one night Zhibo got drunk and poured ale all over Wuxu. Although Wuxu resisted his assistants desire to kill Zhibo for this act, nevertheless from that day forward he harbored resentment against him. When a few years later Zhao Jianzi died, Wuxu became the head of the Zhao family, known as Zhao Xiangzi (d. 425, though this date is uncertain, since the chronology of the state of Jin at this time is hopelessly confused). At this time, the remaining four families continued to contend for power, Zhibo joining with Han and Wei to attack Zhao. Although this attack was initially successful in causing Xiangzi to flee the capital, he subsequently conspired with Han and Wei to join forces against Zhibo and Xun. In 453, the three families succeeded in defeating Xun, absorbing all of its land. From this time on, Jin was controlled just by the three families Zhao, Han and Wei.

When Zhao Xiangzi died, there was a succession battle between a nephew of his, Huan, and his younger brother Jia, though it should be noted that historical sources disagree about these attributions. Jia succeeded in driving the nephew into exile for a short period of time, himself ruling the family and its land for just one year. In the midst of this turmoil and fraternal warfare, there is evidence that he mobilized the men of the Zhao family to swear allegiance to him. In 1965, some four hundred sacrificial pits were excavated just outside of Houma, Shanxi, the heartland of the Zhao family. In these pits were more than five thousand fragments of jade and stone inscribed with oaths or covenants in which members of the family swore allegiance to Jia. These oaths were entirely formulaic, generally written in red ink, and copied over and over again for each individual member of the family. The following example for a man named Chao is typical.

If Chao dares not to split open his belly and heart in serving his master, and, if he dares not to exhaust his strength following Jia's covenant, and the commands of the Ding Palace and Ping Altar, and, if he dares then to cause [name] and [name] to change, causing them not to guard the two palaces, and, if he dares to have the intention of restoring Zhao Hu and his sons and grandsons, and [list of enemy names], to the lands of the Jin state, along with the masses who broke the covenant, my lord, may you brightly and terribly watch him, and wipe out his family.[16]

Although Jia was posthumously ennobled as Zhao Huanzi (r. 424), after his death Zhao Xiangzi's nephew Huan was installed as head of the family. Then in 403, when the three houses of Jin—Zhao, Han and Wei—were formally recognized as independent states, Huan was retrospectively credited as the founding ruler of the state: Lord Xian (r. 423–409). Some years later, in the first year of Lord Jing (r. 386–375), the state moved its capital to Handan, a city which still goes by that name in southwestern Hebei province. In 376, just before he died, Lord Jing joined together with Han and Wei to exterminate what little remained of the once great state of Jin, dividing up the remaining territory among them. This would not be the last time these three related states cooperated with each other, but the history of the next one hundred and fifty years would more regularly feature contention among them. This history is a blur of first one state attacking another, then a few years later joining together with that state to attack yet another state, or joining together to swear a covenant that they would then subsequently break. Through it all, Zhao managed to maintain its capital (at least for the most part; it was briefly occupied by Wei in 347, though control of the city reverted to Zhao two years later) and expanded its territory, growing—together with Wei—to be one of the major powers of the fourth and third centuries.

There is little to be gained from narrating the back-and-forth of the almost non-stop battles in which Zhao was engaged during this time. However, two related engineering accomplishments bear mention. Zhao is credited with pioneering the building of defensive walls along its borders with neighboring states; these were the direct predecessors to the eventual Great Wall of the Qin dynasty. Also, in 332, when under attack by the armies of Wei and Qi, it defended itself by breaching the dikes along the Yellow River, flooding the opposing armies. This is the first record of this defensive technique, which would be used again and again in later Chinese history, often to devastating effect.

In 326, when Lord Su (r. 349–326) died, the five states Wei, Qin, Chu, Qi and Yan are said to each have sent contingents of ten thousand troops to participate in the funeral. Together with Han, the survival of which, given its location surrounded by Qin to the west, Chu to the south, Wei to its east, and Zhao to its north, was always precarious, these five states, together with Zhao, would be the major powers of the next century. In the next year, the Zhao ruler followed the examples of the rulers of the other states in taking on the title of "king": King Wuling (r. 325–299). King Wuling's reign was also marked by a notable military development: having been harassed repeatedly by the mountain peoples living to the north and east of Zhao, peoples who employed a sort of mobile, guerilla style of warfare, in 307, King Wuling decreed that the Zhao army would deploy a cavalry division dressed in "Hu" (Hun) clothing, essentially a matter of wearing pants. He also had the troops trained in being able to shoot a bow and arrow from horseback, in the way pioneered by the indigenous peoples of the north. Prior to this time, officers led troops riding into battle in chariots and dressed in formal court robes. This was true not just of the Zhao army, but of the armies of all the central states. This was a reform that met with resistance from many of the military officers, but King Wuling insisted, arguing that it was necessary to change with the times. The general question of the tension between ancient precedent and modern innovation was also a topic much discussed by the philosophers of the day, especially the Confucian moralists and Legalist reformers. In the end, of course, Wuling's cavalry reforms were a great success, and were soon imitated by all of the other major powers.

In 299, just over forty years of age, King Wuling abdicated in favor of a younger son Zhao He, to be known as King Huiwen (298–266). In doing this, he was imitating King Kuai of Yan (r. 320–316, d. 312), who in 316 had abdicated in favor of his chief minister Zi Zhi, hoping thereby to emulate the sage-rulers of antiquity Yao and Shun. However, perhaps because in doing so King Kuai had deposed his own son, the crown prince, his action was viewed as an existential threat by the rulers of the other states, whose rule was always passed within the ruling family, if not necessarily from father to son. While King Wuling's abdication in favor of a younger son was not met with a similar reaction from the other states, it did provoke a fraternal succession struggle from Zhao He's elder brother, Zhao Zhang. When Zhao Zhang was unsuccessful in his bid to overthrow Zhao He, he was given sanctuary by none other than his father, the erstwhile King Wuling, now known simply as the "Ruler Father." This provoked a counter-attack from elder members of the royal family, who killed Zhao Zhang. These elders of the family, still upset with the prior military reforms, then laid siege to Wuling's palace, effectively accusing him of having "gone barbarian." After more than three months of siege, Wuling finally starved to death. As in the celebrated case of Duke Huan of Qi (r. 685–643), almost three hundred and fifty years earlier, when people finally entered the palace, King Wuling's body was discovered covered in vermin. As *Records of the Historian* says of this episode, "both father and son died, the laughing stock of all under heaven; how sorrowful it was!"[17]

Under King Huiwen, the familiar pattern of shifting alliances and attacks against the other of the six states continued. As the power of Qin grew ever greater, Zhao would first join it in attacking other states further east, and then fearing being overrun in turn would then join with the eastern states to resist Qin. The alliances were regularly guaranteed by an exchange of hostages. One such hostage in Zhao was Yiren, the heir apparent to King Zhaoxiang of Qin (r. 306–251) and the eventual King Zhuangxiang of Qin (r. 250–247). While in Zhao, Yiren came to know Lü Buwei (d. 238), a wealthy merchant who would eventually leave Zhao for Qin, where he would go to become grand councillor. Lü Buwei presented Yiren with one of his own consorts, with whom Yiren had a son: Zheng; Zheng would become in his own turn first King Zheng of Qin (r. 246–221) and then the First Emperor (r. 221–210).

Warfare between Qin and Zhao was perhaps the most brutal of all the warfare of the Warring States period. In 262, King Zhaoxiang of Qin sent his great general Bai Qi (c. 332–257) to invade the northern part of the state of Han, the part of the state to the north of the Yellow River just south of Zhao. Realizing that it was no match for Qin, Han simply ceded the land to Zhao. Qin then turned its attention to Zhao. The two armies met at Changping Pass, located at present-day Gaoping, Shanxi. Occupying the high ground and having the shorter supply line, the Zhao army dug in, seeking to wait out the Qin army. Qin was persistent. The two armies faced off for over two years. Finally in 260, King Xiaocheng of Zhao (r. 265–245), dissatisfied with the lack of progress in the battle, replaced the Zhao general Lian Po with the young and inexperienced Zhao Kuo (d. 260). Zhao Kuo was the son of Zhao She (d. c. 265), who just ten years earlier had dealt another Qin army a decisive defeat. However, Zhao Kuo was not cut of the same cloth. It is said that whenever he played chess with his father, he invariably beat him, but the father was not impressed by this, knowing that there was a great difference between a game and real war. When the Qin general Bai Qi heard that Zhao Kuo had taken over the Zhao army, he feigned a retreat, withdrawing the bulk of the army a short distance but leaving a strong force of cavalry behind. With this, Zhao Kuo came out of the defensive fortifications in which the army had been secure for two years and launched a frontal attack on the Qin army, only to have the Qin cavalry circle to his rear and cut his supply lines. Meanwhile, the bulk of the Qin army counter-attacked both flanks of the Zhao army. Surrounded, the Zhao army dug in once again, but this time without food or water. It held out for forty days before Zhao Kuo himself was killed in a desperate attempt to break the siege. The rest of the army, said to have been 400,000 strong, finally surrendered. Bai Qi ordered the entire force to be executed except for 240 youths, who were instructed to return to the Zhao capital to spread the news of the defeat. In fact, over the centuries, bones have continually surfaced at the site of the battle, most recently in trenches with bodies buried one after another; it is thought that this is evidence that the Zhao army was buried alive.

Having won this great victory at Changping, Bai Qi pressed on in the next year to attack north into the heartland of Zhao. Satisfied with the initial gains and promised by King Xiaocheng of Zhao that Zhao would give six cities in the area to Qin, King Zhaoxiang ordered him to halt the campaign. However, when King Xiaocheng reneged on the promise, giving them to the northern neighbor Qi instead, and then called on all of the other states—Han, Wei, Yan and Chu—to join together in a grand alliance against Qin, Qin returned to the offensive, however under a new general, Wang Ling, since Bai Qi now urged that the campaign be broken off, fearful that the Zhao coalition was too strong to be defeated. Wang Ling pressed the attack, reaching all the way to the Zhao capital city Handan, which he promptly set under siege. When 100,000 Chu troops and 80,000 Wei troops arrived to reinforce the main Zhao army, it became clear that there was no hope that Qin could take the city. In 257, after two years of siege, the Zhao-Wei-Chu coalition emerged from the city to attack the Qin army, defeating it and forcing it to surrender.

Having battled almost continuously for almost five years, both Qin and Zhao were exhausted. It would be another several decades before they resumed the rivalry. But thirty years later, in 228, Handan finally fell, all but bringing an end to the state of Zhao.

CHAPTER 30
THE HEREDITARY HOUSE OF HAN

The hereditary house of Han was one of the three states that were recognized when the once great state of Jin was divided in 403. Not only did the creation of the state of Han derive from civil war in Jin, but the very establishment of the house, almost three hundred and fifty years earlier, also resulted from yet another civil war in the state. When Lord Wen of Jin (r. 780–746), the titular founder of the state, died, he was succeeded by his son, Lord Zhao (r. 745–739), who ruled at the Jin capital Yi. At the same time, Lord Wen's younger brother, Cheng Shi, was given the city of Quwo, which he ruled as a separate entity, posthumously known as Huan Shu (r. 745–731). When Lord Zhao was assassinated in 739, Cheng Shi attempted to enter the capital to take control of the entire state, but the people of the capital area revolted against him, and he was forced to withdraw again to Quwo. The two factions—the main-line "lords" (*hou*) of the state and the Quwo branch of the family— repeatedly attacked each other over the next several decades. In 730, Cheng Shi's son Zhuang Bo (r. 730–716) succeeded to power in Quwo; six years later he himself stabbed Lord Xiao (r. 739–724) to death, and again attempted to take control of the capital. However, he too was rebuffed by the people of the capital. This stalemate began to shift when Zhuang Bo's son Duke Wu (r. 715–679/677) succeeded to power in Quwo. In 709, Duke Wu led yet another attack on the capital at Yi. In this attack, the driver was his own uncle, the younger brother of Zhuang Bo; his name was Han Wan. This attack was successful, at least temporarily, causing the lord in the capital, Lord Ai (r. 717–710) to attempt to flee. However, Lord Ai was captured, and Duke Wu had Han Wan execute him. For his services, Han Wan was given the territory of Han, the southern part of the state.

Nothing more is known of the state of Han until 597, when Jin was riven with yet further civil unrest. For most of the last two decades of the seventh century, the Jin government was under the control of Zhao Dun (d. 601), the head of the Zhao family. When he died, control fell to two other great ministers, Han Jue and Tu'an Jia, the first a supporter of the Zhao family, while the latter was an ardent opponent of the Zhaos. Tu'an Jia eventually gained the upper hand, and executed all of Zhao Dun's family members. However, he did not kill the wife of Zhao Dun's son, who was pregnant at the time. She eventually gave birth to a son. With the protection of Han Jue, this son survived to adolescence. Fifteen years later, as the boy was coming to adulthood, Han Jue brought him back to the capital and together they exterminated Tu'an Jia's family. From this time on, the houses of Han and Zhao would be intimately related, and would often be allied against one or more of the other six powerful families in Jin: Zhao, Han, Wei, Fan, Zhonghang, and Xun.

The next mention of Han in the history of Jin does not occur for still another century. By the beginning of the fifth century, the Zhao family had again gained ascendancy in the state, the head of the family, Zhao Jianzi (d. 476), holding paramount power. In 491, the Zhao and Han families joined together to attack the Fan and Zhonghang families, driving the heads of the families into exile and dividing their lands between their own families. In 453, the Zhao and Han families again joined together, this time also with the Wei family, to attack the Xun family, exterminating it and absorbing its lands as well. By this time, the territory held by the three remaining families—Zhao, Han, and Wei—far exceeded that of the Jin lords themselves, and they held all the power in the state. Finally, at the end of that century, in 403, the territories of the three families were recognized by the Zhou king as independent states. Although the Jin lords would survive for a few decades longer, for all practical purposes the state of Jin had ceased to exist. From this time on, it was the "three Jin" states—Han, Zhao and Wei—that occupied the center of Warring States China.

In the late 1920s or early 1930s, a set of at least fourteen bronze bells known as the *Biao Qiang zhong* was discovered just outside of Luoyang, Henan. Most of these bells ended up in Japan and are currently housed at the Senoku Museum in Tokyo (though two bells are also in the collection of the Royal Ontario Museum in Toronto, Canada). Made for a man named Biao Qiang, the bells carry an inscription that not only mentions the establishment of Han as an independent state, but also provides the first mention of a "great wall" built by the state of Qi, in modern Shandong province. Although the date at the beginning of the inscription—"twenty-second year"—does not mention which ruler it refers to, the events recorded thereafter leave no doubt that it is the reign of King Weilie of Zhou (r. 425–402): i.e., 404.

It was the twenty-second year, Biao Qiang served as a warrior for his ruler. The Han lineage was the supreme leader in the campaign against Qin and attacked Qi, entering into the Great Wall. We first met up at Pingyin. Bringing to bear all of the force of the troops, I took Chujing, and was rewarded by the Han lineage, and commanded by the Duke of Jin, having audience with the Son of Heaven. I herewith brightly record it in the inscription. Having been valiant in both martial and civil affairs, may eternal generations never forget Biao's bells.[18]

These bells were discovered in the heartland of the state of Han, very near where the Zhou kings had their capital. But just as this location did not prove to be sustainable for the Zhou kings, it also proved precarious for Han. Bordering Qin on the west, Chu on the south, Zhao to its north, and Wei to its east, it was the most exposed of the major states of the time. For instance, records for the first two years of the reign of Lord Zhao (r. 362–333) read "Qin defeated our western mountains," and "Second year, Song took our Huangchi; Wei took Zhu." For the state to survive in such an environment required a government superior to those of the other states. In 355, Lord Zhao appointed Shen Buhai (d. 337) to be chancellor of the state. Shen Buhai had been a native of the old state of Zheng. However, shortly after Han's formal establishment in 403, it conquered Zheng and moved its capital to the old city of Zheng, present-day Zhengzhou, Henan. With that, Shen Buhai too was absorbed into the Han government. Living in the eastern part of the state, close to the border with Wei, Shen Buhai would have been familiar with the government reforms introduced there some years earlier by Li Kui (455–395). Li Kui was the supposed author of a book called *Classic of Law*, in which he argued, among other things, in favor of meritocracy and against the old system of noble entitlement, with an emphasis on staffing the government with capable officials. It is said that Li Kui's philosophy of government was the main influence on Shang Yang (c. 390–338), who was the major architect of the government reforms in the mid-fourth century that made the state of Qin into the major power of the next century and more, and who was in turn the supposed author of the *Book of the Lord Shang*. It is said that when Shang Yang left the state of Wei for Qin in 361, he took with him Li Kui's *Classic of Law*, and used it as the blueprint for his reforms. In Han, located between Wei and Qin, Shen Buhai instituted similar reforms, and he too is supposed to have authored a book, known simply as *Master Shen*, which however has long been lost. Still, enough early quotations of the book survive to gain at least some glimpse of his government philosophy. It is often characterized as being based on "technique" or "method" (*shu*), and this seems to be short-hand for "bureaucracy." However, whereas bureaucracy is usually seen as focusing on the members staffing it—and it is true that Shen Buhai too counselled staffing the government with capable officers—he placed the emphasis instead on the ruler. A Han-dynasty annotated bibliography of ancient literature characterized his book in the following way:

> The philosophy of Master Shen is called "form and name." "Form and name" is to use names to require substance, thus honoring the ruler and humbling the minister, exalting superiors and restricting inferiors.[19]

This notion of "form and name" was a means whereby the ruler could control the personnel serving under him, requiring that the "form" of their performance match the "name," that is, the specifications of their office. An early quotation of the book *Master Shen* portrays the ruler as a sort of puppet-master:

> The *Master Shen* says: "The ruler must have clear laws and correct properties. It is like suspending a balance and weight to measure the light and heavy, which is what is used to unify the many ministers.[20]

Just as the point from which the balance is suspended does not move, so too, according to Shen Buhai, once the government apparatus was working correctly, the ruler would have no need to move, which is to say to intervene in its workings. Another early quotation explains this, drawing on the legendary example of the sage-ruler Yao.

> Yao's governing was just to clarify the laws and examine the commands and nothing more. The sage-ruler relies on laws and does not rely on intelligence, relies on method and does not rely on persuasion. The Yellow Emperor's rule of all under heaven was to put laws in place and not to change them, causing the people to be content with those laws.[21]

Shen Buhai used another term to explain what was required of the ruler: *wuwei*. This is a term that has long perplexed translators. It can mean "non-action," and this is certainly one aspect of Shen Buhai's sense. But it has a more nuanced sense of "non-motivated action": that the ruler ought not use his personal inclinations to affect an outcome. *Wuwei* is a term that Shen Buhai may have borrowed from Daoist philosophy, or perhaps Daoist philosophy borrowed the term from him; most likely, it is a term that was in general use throughout Warring States China (and perhaps even earlier), but that different thinkers understood in slightly different senses. For Shen Buhai, *wuwei* was to eliminate all arbitrary decisions from government. One final quotation from his book likens the ruler to a mirror or, again, to a balance:

> A mirror reflects the essence without doing anything, and the beautiful and ugly are all apparent in it. A scale finds the balance without doing anything, and the light and heavy are obtained of themselves.[22]

Shen Buhai's notion of *wuwei* would have a great influence a century later on the writings of Han Feizi (*c.* 280–233), and through them on most subsequent Chinese governments. But unlike Han Feizi—and also unlike Shang Yang before him—the other great philosophers credited with the political philosophy known as Legalism, philosophers who met an untimely and violent death because of their own attempts to influence rulers, Shen Buhai lived to an old age and died a natural death, in 337.

In 322, Lord Xuanhui (r. 332–312) followed the practice of the rulers of the other major states in declaring himself "king" (*wang*). Unfortunately, he had forgotten the principles Shen Buhai advised for the ruler. In 317, he allowed Han to get caught up in the struggle between Qin and Chu, the two major powers to the west and south of Han respectively. Knowing that Qin was planning to attack Chu, he first committed to an alliance with Qin. But then, in the midst of the intrigues, he allowed himself to be persuaded by Chu to switch allegiance and join with Chu. This of course angered Qin, which turned its might on Han. Finally, in 312, the year of King Xuanhui's death, he did join with Qin in attacking Chu, winning a great victory. But this victory would prove to be transitory. The following years brought an almost unending series of attacks on Han by both Qin and Chu; when attacked by Chu, Han would seek relief from Qin, or when attacked by Qin would seek relief from Chu, but more often than not the relief was not forthcoming. Finally, in 234, under assault from Qin, King An (r. 238–230) sent Han Feizi, a nobleman of the state and the great theorist of Legalist philosophy, to Qin to try to persuade King Zheng of Qin (r. 246/221–210), the future First Emperor of Qin, to relent. Although King Zheng appreciated Han Feizi's philosophy of government, through the intrigues of Han Feizi's former classmate Li Si (280–208), Han Feizi was forced to commit suicide in the very next year. Three years later, in 330, Qin attacked Han once again, taking King An prisoner and absorbing all of the remaining Han territory into the expanding Qin empire. The state that had come into existence through warfare went out of existence in the same manner.

CHAPTER 31
THE HEREDITARY HOUSE OF CHU

According to *Records of the Historian*, the hereditary house of Chu, arguably the greatest power of the entire Eastern Zhou period, began with Zhuanxu, a grandson of the legendary Yellow Emperor (Huang Di). Three generations later, his great grandson Chong Li is said to have had great merit as the Regulator of Fire under the emperor Di Ku, and so Di Ku named him the Zhu Rong (Prayer of Fusion). When Chong Li then failed to suppress the disturbance caused by Gong Gong, Di Ku had him executed and replaced with his younger brother Wu Hui, who was also named as Zhu Rong. This Zhu Rong would come to be worshipped in Chu texts of the Warring States period as the high ancestor of the Chu people; sacrifices were routinely offered to him first and foremost. This Zhu Rong is said to have had six sons, the youngest of whom was named Ji Lian (Cadet Connection). *Records of the Historian* notes laconically that the house of Chu descended from him. A recently unearthed manuscript of the Warring States period entitled *Residences of Chu*, which recounts the many capital cities of the state of Chu over the course of the centuries, provides more detail about Ji Lian:

> Ji Lian first descended upon Roan Mountain, arriving at the Exhausted Cave. He went forward out of Lofty Mountain, and dwelled upon its slope. Going upstream along the Wide River, he saw the children of Whorling (Pan) Geng living upon Square Mountain. One daughter was named Ancestress Zhui. She held tight to his leading visage, her beauty acknowledged throughout the four quarters. Ji Lian heard that she was available and followed and reached her at Whorling. And then she gave birth to the elder son Ying and the second-born Yuan.[23]

This suggests a relationship between the progenitors of Chu and the rulers of the Shang dynasty. On the other hand, a poem from the "Shang Hymns" section of the *Classic of Poetry* entitled "Soldiers of Yin" describes a Shang attack on Chu, bringing it into submission under the Shang state.

Piercing were those soldiers of Yin, Rising up and attacking Jing Chu,
Deeply entering their blockades, Rounding up the legions of Jing,
Cutting off their places of life: The threads of the grandsons of Tang.[24]

Whether through marital relations or military conquest, there is a long
tradition that the state of Chu goes back in time to the Shang dynasty.

The poem "Soldiers of Yin" refers to the Chu people by the double name
"Jing Chu." Both *chu* and *jing* refer to a type of hard thorn-wood, the latter
word being also the name of Jing Mountain, located in the northwestern
part of modern Hubei province near where the state of Chu had its
beginnings. The *Residences of Chu* manuscript also provides a rationale for
why the state got its name. After the account of Ji Lian's marriage to a
daughter of the Shang king Pan Geng, the text continues with another
marriage of Ji Lian, though he is now referred to by another name, Xue
Xiong, to one Ancestress Lie.

Xue Xiong slowly transferred to the Great Temple, where he met
Ancestress Lie upstream along the Zai River; her appearance was of
whispering ears. Then he married her and she gave birth to Dou the
Third and Li the Youngest. The birth of Li was not smooth, as he
emerged from her side. Ancestress Li was hosted by Heaven, where
Magician Xian healed her side with a stick of thorn-wood (*chu*), and
that is why until today the people are called Chu.[25]

The state was referred to as Chu, while the rulers came from the Xiong
lineage, which seems to have had a bear as its totem.

According to *Records of the Historian*, after Ji Lian there is a gap in the
genealogical records of Chu rulers for the remaining two centuries of the
Shang dynasty, with the statement that sometimes the state was located in
the central kingdoms and sometimes among the Man and Yi "barbarians."
The genealogy picks up again with the beginning of the Zhou dynasty, when
Xiong Yi was rewarded for his services to King Cheng of Zhou (r. 1042/1035–
1006) by being established at Danyang, in the upper or middle reaches of the
Han River valley in what is now southwestern Henan and northwestern
Hubei. Following this, another five generations follow with nothing more
than the names of Chu rulers.

Inscribed bronze vessels from the Western Zhou period fill in some of
this gap, indicating in particular that Zhou and Chu were at least occasionally
at war with each other. The most important of these wars took place in the

early tenth century, when King Zhao of Zhou (r. 977/975–957) personally commanded the Zhou armies in a campaign against Chu. For the Zhou, the campaign was a catastrophe, with the king drowning in the Han River and the Zhou armies being decimated. We do not have Chu records concerning this event; presumably they would have seen it as a great victory. A century or so later, Chu joined with the Southern Huai Peoples, a confederation of southern and eastern peoples, to attack the Zhou heartland, reaching almost to the Zhou eastern capital at Luoyang before finally being repulsed. This Zhou "victory" is recounted in the inscription on the *Yu ding*. The inscription makes clear that the Zhou army was no match for the Chu and Huai Peoples invaders, but had to rely on a warlord, the Martial Duke, to save their own capital.

After another century or so, taking advantage of great turmoil among the now fully independent states of north China, which were experiencing assassinations, civil wars, and attacks back and forth, Chu took its first step toward expanding to the north. In 706, during the reign of King Wu of Chu (r. 740–690), the first ruler of the many states to arrogate the title of "king" (*wang*) theretofore formally reserved for just the Zhou king, it attacked Zeng (known in traditional texts as Sui), one of the oldest Zhou states, which was located just to the north of Chu's own capital region. Although Zeng was not brought fully under Chu control until the reign of King Wu's son, King Wen (r. 689–677), it would serve thereafter as a loyal ally of Chu, often acting very much in concert with later Chu rulers. King Wen pressed his expansion farther and farther north, bringing other old Zhou states into its alliance, including the state of Cai, which had been founded by one of the sons of King Wen of Zhou, and threatening also the state of Zheng in the very heart of the Yellow River valley. With this, Chu was recognized as one of the largest and most powerful states of all, and King Wen's successor (after a brief interregnum), King Cheng (r. 671–626) was renowned for his virtue and generosity—at least at the beginning of his reign.

In 656, Chu's expansion finally brought it into contact with what was then the strongest state of north China, the state of Qi. Qi was then ruled by Duke Huan (r. 685–643), the first of the many lords to be widely recognized as "premier" (*ba*)—first among equals. Although Qi's campaign, led by Duke Huan's famous minister Guan Zhong (723–645), is portrayed in the *Zuo Tradition*, as one of chastisement, with Guan Zhong essentially scolding Chu for misbehaving, in fact it is clear that it resulted in a standoff between the two superpowers of the day. The story of their encounter is both amusing and illustrative of inter-state relations.

In the fourth year, in spring, the Lord of Qi took the armies of the many lords to invade Cai. Cai collapsed. Subsequently they attacked Chu. The Prince of Chu sent an envoy to speak with the general, saying: "Your ruler dwells near the northern sea, while I, the unworthy one, dwell near the southern sea. Given these airs, even our horses and cattle will not couple, so I would not anticipate that you would wade into our territory. Why have you done so?" Guan Zhong replied, "In the past Duke Kang of Shao commanded our former ruler the Grand Duke, saying, 'As for the princes of the five lords and nine premiers, it is really for you to chastise them in order to assist the house of Zhou.' . . . Your offerings of bundled cogon-grass did not arrive, so that the king's sacrifices were not supplied, and there was nothing with which to filter the ale. This is what I, the unworthy one, have come to complain about. Moreover, King Zhao campaigned to the south but did not return. I would like to ask about this as well." The envoy responded, "It was our lord's fault that the tribute did not arrive. Would we dare not to supply it in the future? As for King Zhao's not returning, milord should ask about that on the banks of the river."[26]

Having sufficiently "chastised" Chu, the Qi army then withdrew.

Just over a decade later, first Guan Zhong and then Duke Huan of Qi both died, bringing Qi's period of hegemony to an end. While Chu would have dearly loved to be recognized as its successor, it would be thwarted in this by another of the old northern states: Jin. Jin's rise at this time, under the leadership of Chong'er—posthumously known as Duke Wen of Jin (r. 636–628), is one of the great stories of the Springs and Autumns period, appropriately told elsewhere in this history. In 637, after traveling for eighteen years throughout north China, including among both Chinese and non-Chinese states, Chong'er came finally to Chu, where King Cheng entertained him with the respect due to a head of state before sending him back north with many presents. This goodwill between the two rulers would be remembered, but only in the breach. In 632, Chu was requested to intercede in a succession struggle in the state of Qi among the several sons of Duke Huan. This brought it further north than it had ever before been. When it then attacked the state of Song, ruled by descendants of the former Shang dynasty, Song turned for assistance to Jin, now ruled by Chong'er. With this, King Cheng wished to break off the attack on Song, and to return to Chu. However, the general in command of his army, Prince Yu (d. 632), insisted on pressing the attack. King Cheng left him with a small force, which was soundly defeated by a coalition of states under the leadership of Jin at a place called Chengpu, located in the southwestern part of present-day Shandong province. Infuriated with the defeat and Prince Yu's insubordination, King Cheng had him put to death. The battle of Chengpu is often regarded as the high-water mark of Chu expansion, and the decisive event cementing northern rule of China. In fact, this was by no means the last battle between Chu and Jin, the two states trading victories over the next several decades.

The series of excellent rulers beginning with King Wu and ending with King Cheng was now followed by a string of weak, or even evil, rulers, beginning with King Cheng's grandson, King Zhuang (r. 613–591). The first five years of his rule were marked by his own licentious behavior and inattention to government business. Then, after reforming himself, the rest of his twenty-three years of reign brought one war after another. Yet another story in the *Zuo Tradition* provides some indication of King Zhuang's arrogance. One campaign north brought him to the outskirts of the Zhou capital at Luoyang. When King Ding of Zhou (r. 606–586) sent an envoy bearing gifts for King Zhuang, King Zhuang is said to have asked about the size and weight of the bronze caldrons at court, the symbols of royal legitimacy. The royal envoy responded that their significance resided in virtue, and not in their size, recounting how the caldrons were first cast during the Xia dynasty, but then when that dynasty lost its popular mandate to rule, were transferred to the founder of the Shang dynasty; when the last Shang rulers in their own turn lost the mandate, the caldrons were then transferred to the Zhou. The envoy allowed as to how the house of Zhou was in decline, but it had not yet lost the Mandate of Heaven, and it was not acceptable for the Chu king to inquire after these symbols of legitimate rule.

The next generations brought about the nadir of Chu governance. Perhaps the worst of the Chu kings was King Ling (r. 540–529). Originally known as Prince Wei, he was the second son of King Gong (590–560) and younger brother of King Kang (r. 559–545). This made him also the uncle of Jia'ao (r. 544–541), King Kang's son, who succeeded to power upon the death of his father. However, shortly thereafter Prince Wei had him murdered together with his two sons, and took over as king himself, ruling for twelve years. During this time, he was extremely ambitious, in 538 bringing the rulers of the northern states, including the great state of Jin, together for a conference where he hoped to be named premier. This was unsuccessful. Nevertheless,

King Ling continued to expand northward, attacking the old Zhou states of Chen and Cai. The attack against Cai was led by his own brother Qiji, who captured the Cai heir-apparent. King Ling ordered that Qiji be made Duke of Cai, and that the Cai heir-apparent be sacrificed to the gods. In other examples of King Ling's arrogance, he determined that his consorts were not sufficiently prominent for his status, and so took a new consort from Jin; he then quickly moved to install her as his queen.

In 529, fearing the rise of the eastern state of Wu, the capital of which was then located near Wuxi in present-day Jiangsu province, the king turned his attention away from the north and personally led a campaign against the state of Xu, which commanded the route between Chu and Wu. A story in the *Zuo Tradition* for this year reflects the king's mindset at this time. According to this anecdote, King Ling had a turtle-shell divination performed, in which he announced "I wish to gain all under heaven." When the result turned out not to be auspicious, he is said to have thrown the turtle away and to have cursed heaven, screaming "If you do not give me even this trifling thing, I will certainly take it for myself." Not only did he not take it for himself, while he was on campaign in Xu, his youngest brother Qiji led a coup against him, occupying the Chu capital, killing King Ling's two sons, and installing his elder brother Bi as king. Deserted by his army and unable to find any support among the common people, King Ling eventually committed suicide. However, unaware that the king was no longer alive, and fearful that he would return to the capital, his brother Bi also committed suicide. With this, the youngest brother Qiji assumed the kingship, ruling as King Ping (r. 528–516).

King Ping restored stability in Chu, but only for a short while. Unfortunately, his reign sowed the seeds for one of Chu's great calamities. The first of these seeds of discontent concerned his crown prince, Jian. Seeking a bride for Jian, he dispatched the assistant tutor to the crown prince to the state of Qin to request a daughter of Duke Ai of Qin (r. 536–501). When the assistant returned, King Ping found the bride-to-be so beautiful that he took her as his own consort; they soon had a son, who was named the new crown prince. The former crown prince Jian then went into exile, while his principal tutor, a man named Wu She remained in the capital remonstrating against the king's behavior. The king soon tired of the criticism, and condemned Wu She to be executed unless his two sons, Wu Shang and Wu Zixu, would come to the capital and be executed in his place. Wu Shang was regarded in the state as a paragon of filial piety, while Wu Ziyu was known for his political cunning. The filial Wu Shang went to the capital to accept his fate, but the cunning Wu Zixu did not. Wu Zixu eventually made his way to the still farther southern state of Wu, where his exploits would become one of the great stories of the late Springs and Autumns period.

In 516, King Ping died and was in fact succeeded by the son of his consort from Qin; this son, who would be known as King Zhao (r. 515–489), was just a young boy at the time. Wu Zixu, already employed as an advisor to King Liao of Wu (r. 526–515) urged the king to launch a surprise attack against Chu. When this attack failed, King Liao's nephew assassinated him, assuming power in Wu as King Helü (r. 514–496). Ten years later, Wu again attacked Chu, this time with much greater success, at least initially. After several battles, the Wu army entered the Chu capital, and King Zhao was forced to flee to its neighbor Sui, also known as Zeng. Wu Zixu, accompanying the Wu army, dug up the grave of King Ping of Chu, who had executed his father and elder brother, and whipped the corpse three hundred times. Nevertheless, the Wu army was ultimately unsuccessful in capturing King Zhao; the siege at Sui was lifted when Duke Ai of Qin, King Zhao's maternal grandfather, sent an army to rescue him. This would set the stage for continuous relations between Qin and Chu, sometimes as allies, but much more often as adversaries.

For the next century and a half, Chu seems to have stayed out of relations with its northern neighbors, at least for the most part. However, even though the various northern states eclipsed it in terms of military power and diplomatic influence, Chu remained the largest state in terms of territory and a state to which others would turn for alliances. By the middle of the fourth century, Chu was no longer seen as the principal menace to the central states; that distinction would now be accorded to Qin, which had grown increasingly powerful due to the reforms instituted during the reign of Duke Xiao (r. 361–338) by his famous chancellor Shang Yang (c. 390–338). Through much of this time, Chu and Qin maintained their previous alliance. At the beginning of the reign of King Huai of Chu (r. 329–299), the four major states—Chu, Qin, Qi and Wei—met and swore a non-aggression covenant. However, in 319, the eastern states broke the covenant and attacked Qin, with Chu in the lead. The alliance army entered the Hangu Pass, the gateway to Qin, but then withdrew as they met with Qin resistance. In 314, King Hui of Qin (337/324–311), planning to attack the far northern state of Qi, one of Chu's allies, sent his diplomat Zhang Yi (373–310) to Chu to persuade Chu to break the alliance with Qi and join together with Qin. Zhang Yi offered Chu 600 *li* (about 300 kilometers) of land in Shangyu, territory that Chu had long coveted. King Huai was delighted with this offer, and then sent an ambassador to Qi to break their alliance. With that, Qi turned around and joined Qin in an alliance against Chu. What is more, Zhang Yi reneged on his previous offer, claiming that he had said six *li*, not six hundred. In 313, Qin invaded Chu, fighting a major battle at Danyang, in the Han River valley; Chu was routed, losing some eighty thousand soldiers, seventy generals, and also its commandery in the area. With this, King Huai mobilized his entire army to counter-attack Qin. The Chu army reached the Wei River valley, the outskirts of the Qin capital region, but then was repulsed. It is interesting that in the Northern Song dynasty (960–1127 CE) three stones known as the *Cursing Chu Prayer* were unearthed in the former territory of Qin. They had been inscribed at the time of this war between Qin and Chu, with prayers to the Qin gods, pleading for aid in the battle. The three stones bear almost identical inscriptions, differing only in being addressed to three different gods; that to the god Jue Qiu reads as follows:

The successor king, ruler of Qin, dares to use the Auspicious Jade and Radiant Disk to cause Shao Gu, priest of his ancestor temple, to proclaim and report to the illustrious great god Jue Qiu to reveal the Chu king Xiong Xiang (i.e., King Huai of Chu)'s many crimes. In the past, our former ruler Duke Mu and King Cheng of Chu truly bound their strength and were of the same heart, and the two countries were as one. We were joined in marriage and confirmed through a solemn covenant, saying for generations our myriad descendants would not do anything to each other that was not beneficial. I personally look up to the great god Jue Qiu and pledge myself to him. Now the Chu king Xiong Xiang is deviant and lawless, dissolute and extremely chaotic, promotes overindulgence and intemperance, and has broken the covenant bond. Internally he violates the innocent, murdering pregnant women, imprisoning relatives, arresting its elders and placing them in dungeons and coffins. Externally he makes bold to change his heart, not fearing the august heavenly high god or the great god Jue Qiu's radiantly displayed awesome spirit, but turns his back on all eighteen generations of sworn covenant, leading the troops of the many lords to encroach upon us, wanting to despoil our gods of the soil and to attack our hundred families, seeking to wipe out the august heavenly high god and the great god Jue Qiu's temples, ritual jades, and sacrificial offerings, and so has taken our border cities Xinhuang and Yu, Chang and Qin. I dare not say that this is permissible. Now he again raises all of his masses and expresses his arrogance and anger, decorates his armor and sharpens his weapons, rouses his men and fills out his armies in order to press upon our border region, wishing to recover what he has given us. It is for this reason that Qin's multitudes contribute their property, and the elders bring it to rescue themselves. It is also because we have received numinous virtuous award of the august heavenly high god and the great god Jue Qiu, that we can thwart the Chu army, and also restore our invaded border cities. We dare to enumerate the Chu king Xiong Xiang's turning his back on the covenant and its curse, and inscribe it on the stone tablets in order to make our pledge to the awesome god.[27]

In fact, Qin once again routed Chu. Not only this, the states of Han and Wei hearing of Chu's defeat, promptly invaded Chu, forcing the Chu army to retreat to defend its own homeland.

The next year, King Hui of Qin made a peace offering to King Huai of Chu, offering to divide the commandery of Hanzhong that he had captured from Chu. King Huai dismissed this offer, stating that what he really wanted was the diplomat Zhang Yi, who had tricked him two years before. Zhang Yi agreed to go, trusting that friends there would protect him. The king initially wanted to kill him, but through Zhang Yi's friends was bribed with land and women and musicians to let him go. The famous poet Qu Yuan (d. 343–278) remonstrated with the king, but it was too late. Zhang Yi was gone, and so too was most of Chu's power. In 278, Qin overran most of the state, including the capital, burning the graves of the former kings and incorporating the territory into the expanding Qin realm. The Chu king, King Qingxiang (r. 298–263), escaped to Chencheng in the northeast. Although three more generations of Chu kings were able to resist Qin, more or less, the state was finally exterminated in 223.

Chu was traditionally seen as a distinct cultural entity, a view that modern archaeology has seemed to confirm, with many discoveries from Chu tombs showing a "flamboyant" style of mortuary objects. This unique nature of its culture has also been seen in the poetry of the *Verses of Chu*. Nevertheless, others have argued that the difference between Chu and cultures to the north is more apparent than real, and that the Chu elites partook of the greater Zhou world. It would seem that there is a basis for both of these viewpoints: Chu culture was certainly regarded by the people of the northern states as something different from their own culture, and this view was certainly shared by the people of Chu themselves. On the other hand, the culture was not so very different as to be "barbarian" or "non-Chinese," as some extreme views would have it. Indeed, its contribution to "Chinese culture," which was always developing throughout this period and also thereafter, was as strong, if not stronger, as that of any of the individual states of the north.

CHAPTER 32
THE HEREDITARY HOUSE OF ZENG

Although the state of Zeng is never mentioned, at least by this name, in traditional historical sources, it is one of the best attested states in the archaeological record. Already in the Song dynasty, there is a record of two different bells, both "discovered in Anlu," a city in present-day Hubei province, and both bearing the inscription "It was the king's fifty-sixth year; returning from Xiyang, Yan Zhang, king of Chu, makes these ritual vessels for Lord Yi of Zeng's ancestral temple, to place in Xiyang. May he forever hold them and use them to make offerings." Scholars of the Song dynasty were already able to identify "Yan Zhang, King of Chu" as King Hui of Chu (r. 488–432); not only was he the only Chu king to have reigned as long as fifty-six years, but it is also recorded in *Records of the Historian* that his personal name was "Zhang," just as in the inscriptions. What the scholars of the Song dynasty were unable to do was to identify "Lord Yi of Zeng." There was simply no record either of him or even of the state of Zeng, at least anywhere near the area of present-day Hubei.

This changed dramatically in 1978, when a large tomb was excavated in Suizhou, Hubei, very near Anlu. This was none other than the tomb of Lord Yi of Zeng, who apparently died in 433. This has been hailed as one of the greatest archaeological discoveries of the twentieth century; even now, almost a half century later, this does not seem to be an exaggeration at all. The tomb was divided into four chambers, essentially a subterranean palace. Records written on bamboo slips—still the earliest such bamboo-slip records yet discovered—record that forty-three chariots, donated by lords from throughout the region, took part in the funeral procession that brought the goods to the tomb. The northern chamber was an armory, filled with weapons. The central chamber, essentially the central court, was supplied with numerous bronze ritual vessels, many of them inscribed with the name of Lord Yi of Zeng. The most astounding discovery was a rack of sixty-four chime-bells, still suspended from the original wooden rack. Still more amazing, grouped together with these bells was one other bell, with the same inscription known from the Song dynasty; it was obviously a burial gift from King Hui of Chu to be buried with Lord Yi of Zeng, whose name appears in this inscription as well. The western chamber contained string and wind musical instruments—a chamber music ensemble apparently intended for the lord's private entertainment. Eerily, it also contained thirteen coffins in which there were the remains of thirteen female attendants, presumably the musicians. The eastern chamber held the nested coffins of the lord, as well as another eight smaller coffins with still more female attendants, perhaps his consorts. However, the tomb of his primary wife was separate from his, discovered three years later about one hundred meters away.

This discovery stimulated a debate among scholars about the identification of Zeng and about its history. Surprisingly, this small state apparently unknown in the traditional historical record is the best attested state of all (other than the Zhou royal house itself) in bronze inscriptions from all periods of the Zhou dynasty. It was mentioned in other inscribed bronze vessels discovered already during the Northern Song dynasty (960–1127). In 1118, also at Anlu, Hubei, a cache of six ancient bronze vessels was discovered. These vessels were much older than the bells that King Hui of Chu had made for Lord Yi of Zeng. These earlier vessels bear inscriptions recording that they were cast by someone named Zhong to commemorate a military campaign, under the leadership of Nangong, to suppress a rebellion by an enemy referred to as the Tiger Land (Hufang).

> It was the year that the king commanded Nangong to attack the rebelling Tiger Country. The king commanded Zhong to proceed to the southern countries to connect the road and to establish a royal residence at Kui ... Mountain. Zhong called out to send back a living phoenix to the king, placing it in the treasured vessel.[28]

Nangong has long been identified as Nangong Kuo, a minister who assisted Kings Wen and Wu of Zhou at the very beginning of the Zhou dynasty, and this was the basis for dating these Six Vessels of Anlu to the very beginning of the Western Zhou dynasty. This Tiger Land was apparently located in the area from which the vessels were unearthed. The longest inscription on these vessels begins:

> The king commanded Zhong to proceed to inspect the southern countries to connect the road and to establish a residence at Zeng.[29]

"To establish a residence at Zeng" would seem to refer to the establishment of a state there, the southernmost Zhou colony. Although its position far away from the Zhou capital was always precarious, between the time of this establishment and the death of Lord Yi of Zeng in 433, Zeng not only survived but apparently flourished. Generation after generation, lords of the state and other noblemen sponsored the making of hundreds of bronze vessels, some with inscriptions recounting the history of the state. These have long been recognized in various royal and private collections of bronze vessels, even if no one knew where the state of Zeng was located. The discovery of Lord Yi's tomb in 1978 brought much more attention on the part of archaeologists to the area around Suizhou, and in the decades since that time cemetery after cemetery from throughout the course of the centuries of the first millennium BCE has been discovered. Unfortunately, tomb robbers have beaten archaeologists to many of the tombs, with many bronze vessels from lords and noblemen of the state of Zeng flooding the international antiquities market.

Late in 2010, farmers working at a place called Yejiashan, about twenty kilometers from where Lord Yi's tomb was located, inadvertently opened two ancient tombs. Early the next year archaeologists began excavating the site, eventually opening sixty-five tombs from the early Western Zhou, including three large tombs that seem to be those of early lords of Zeng. One of these lords, named Jian, may have ruled the state shortly after the time of its establishment. In addition to a full range of bronze ritual vessels and a very early set of bronze bells some five hundred years older than those of Lord Yi, many of the tombs were supplied with a great number of weapons. Archaeologists suggest that this is evidence of the still precarious security situation in which Zeng found itself at this time. Some of the inscriptions on the bronze vessels show that it alternately cooperated with and competed with a neighboring state called E, an early cemetery of which was also unearthed in the vicinity. However, other evidence shows that shortly after this time E moved out of the area, while Zeng expanded over the Tongbai Mountains to the headwaters of the Huai River to become the major power in this area "between the rivers" (i.e., the Han and Huai Rivers). Unfortunately, suggestive though the inscriptions are, they do not provide sufficient context to understand the dynamics of these developments.

Some of this history can be discerned from another cemetery, also located in Suizhou, that was excavated only in 2018. This cemetery is located at Zaoshulin, in which four large tombs were excavated. These tombs together contained even more bells than the tomb of Lord Yi: eighty-eight in all. What is more, even though one of them, numbered Tomb 190, had already been plundered by tomb robbers, the archaeologists still recovered from it numerous bronze food and wine vessels, as well as thirty-four bells of different types; their inscriptions show that they were made for yet another lord of Zeng, this one named Qiu. From the shape and ornamentation of the vessels, the archaeologists have dated the tomb to the middle of the Springs and Autumns period, roughly 600. Even though this is more than three centuries later than the cemetery at Yejiashan, the bells carry a lengthy inscription that recounts the founding of the state. It deserves to be translated in full:

It was the king's fifth month, the auspicious day *dinghai* (day 24), Qiu, Lord of Zeng said:

In the past when our illustrious High Ancestor was able to join with the Zhou kings Wen and Wu, good and pure Bo Kuo was ever careful of his virtue in serving the High God, and compliantly embraced many blessings to be at the left and right of the rulers of Zhou. He abundantly extended his sageliness and received those who were not peaceful. Illustrious was his soul, spreading and stirring respect.

The king hosted us in the Kang Palace, calling out to the Manager to command our August Ancestor to be established in the southern land, covering Cai's southern gate, allied with Ying's capital altar, and screening the area to the east of the Han River. The southern region is unbounded. Go on to campaign against the Huai Peoples as far as Fanyang. (The king) said: "King Zhao traveling south, delivered a command at Zeng: "Thoroughly complete our service, being at the left and right of the ruler of Zhou."

(The king) awarded him use of a *yue*-axe, to use to campaign throughout the southern region. Nan Gong's valor and astute sageliness is renowned, causing the high and low to ascend and descend, and protecting and ruling his sons and grandsons.[30]

This inscription seems to resolve one of the conundrums regarding the establishment of the state of Zeng. Its founder is supposed to have been Nangong Kuo, who as noted above is supposed to have been an assistant to the Zhou founders Kings Wen and Wu, but who is also supposed to have been commanded by King Zhao of Zhou, three generations later than even the time of King Wu, to lead a campaign to the south against the Tiger

Country. From the inscription on this set of bells made for Lord Qiu of Zeng, it is now clear that Nangong (which means Southern Palace) was Kuo's clan name, and as such continued to be used by his family. The inscription confirms that Kuo served the Zhou founders and that he was looked back upon as the high ancestor of Zeng, but it was not he who led the campaign that actually established the state in the south. This was done by one of his descendants, also known by the family name Nangong, or sometimes by the homophonous name Nan Gong, Duke of the South.

While Zeng expanded to the north after its initial establishment, any expansion to the south was blocked by the much larger state of Chu, which was centered along the north bank of the Yangzi River. Chu too was an old state, but much larger than Zeng, and one with much greater territorial ambitions. It is clear from the material culture on display in the tomb of Lord Qiu that Zeng was already heavily influenced by Chu culture. Another tomb in this same cemetery, also dated to about 600, contained yet another set of chime bells, the inscription of which shows that they were cast for a woman named Mi Jia (sometimes written Jia Mi). Her surname Mi indicates that she was originally from Chu, and indeed other inscriptions on dowry vessels reveal that she was a daughter of a king of Chu and was married to a lord of Zeng. More than that, the set of chime bells that she sponsored shows that after her husband died at a young age, she took over control of the state of Zeng. The inscription, which begins with a quotation of Mi Jia's husband, probably named Duke Gong, identified as a descendant of Nangong Kuo, the high ancestor of the state, and as a son of a Lord Mu of Zeng, pointing to his illustrious pedigree, suggests that Chu had somehow double-crossed Zeng, such that he was now opposing them despite his being married to a daughter of the king of Chu (though some readers have drawn quite the opposite sense from it). The inscription then goes on to quote Mi Jia herself, showing her to be firmly in control of the Zeng government. Some passages of the inscription are quite difficult to understand, but however it should be understood, it offers a fascinating glimpse into the role of women in intrastate relations.

> It was the king's first month, first auspiciousness, *yihai* (day 12), it was said: "Bo Kuo received the command to follow Yu's traces to rule this southern tributary. I am King Wen's descendant, Mu's eldest son, going on to establish the country in Zeng. I do not dare to do anything shameful. Chu having been duplicitous, we have come to oppose them. Making good our plans, the great mandate does not change."

Our resplendent youngest daughter Jia Mi said: "*Wuhu!* Lord Gong having died early, I protect his borderlands, and conduct control of the Zeng state in order to prolong our Xia. I record his virtuous model and the people's basic rule. Oh-oh jiang-jiang, we being wife and husband, I have diminished the lustre of the lower ruler, and respectfully fearing the departed lords and our great officers, have magnificently enjoyed governance, causing our country and family to arise.

"I select our auspicious black gold and golden ore, herewith myself making these harmonious bells for the ancestral temple, in order to please our beautiful emissaries and fine guests, uncles and elder brothers and our great officers, with which to be filial and to make offering, receiving blessings without limit. Syncopated is their harmony, glowing and gleaming. The great officers, the many sires, and the festival attendants will toast and offer, sing and dance, feast and enjoy the drink and food, awarding us a numinous end and yellowing old-age, with which to receive treasured blessings. May they not change for ten thousand years, down to grandsons and sons all protecting and using them."[31]

Regardless of the relations between Zeng and Chu at the time of Duke Qiu and Mi Jia, within another century the fates of the two states would once again be intertwined, and this time Zeng would come to the rescue of Chu. In just the few years between the discoveries of the Yejiashan and Zaoshulin cemeteries, in 2013 yet another Zeng cemetery—dating to a century or more later than the Zaoshulin cemetery—was discovered, this time at a site called Wenfengta. This cemetery also contained the graves of various lords of Zeng, including one that had four tomb ramps, what is called in Chinese a 亞-shaped tomb. Unfortunately, this tomb had been robbed clean except for the eastern chamber, in which alone were found seventy ritual bronze vessels. These show that the tomb belonged to a Lord Bing, probably the son of Lord Yi, and so dated to around 400. Another tomb was of an earlier Zeng lord, named Yu. He was probably Lord Yi's grandfather, and must have died shortly after 500. Interestingly enough, one of the bronze vessels in Lord Yi's tomb had an inscription showing that it was originally made for Lord Yu, but his name had been scratched out of the bronze and replaced with Lord Yi's name. It is unclear why Lord Yi should have done this; after all, he certainly had the wherewithal to cast a new vessel for himself.

In Lord Yu's own tomb was discovered yet another set of chime bells with an important inscription, claiming that Zeng was instrumental in coming to the rescue of Chu when it was attacked, in 506, and nearly overrun by the eastern state of Wu. This inscription too warrants translation in full.

It was the king's fifth month, the auspicious day *jiawu* (day 31), Yu the Lord of Zeng said:

Bo Kuo (served) God on High, and at the left and right of (kings) Wen and Wu pierced Yin's mandate and pacified all under heaven. The king dispatched a command to Nan Gong to garrison the land between the rivers, and to rule these Huai Peoples, watching over those ruling the Jiang and Xia.

After the Zhou house had become debased, we therewith harmoniously allied with Chu. Wu relying on its multitudes created chaos, campaigning westward and attacking southward, then pressing on Chu. The country of Chu having already grown weak, the mandate of heaven was about to be lost. The majestic Lord of Zeng, complete being his sagacity, personally took hold of the martial work, battling for the Chu mandate and restoring the Chu king. The Lord of Zeng's soul, so beautiful is the Lord of Zeng, stalwart and fearsome, respectful in his offerings and covenants, outwardly militant but embracing and harmonizing the four borderlands. I have continued the Chu success, changing and restoring Zeng's boundaries.

Selecting our auspicious metal, I myself make this vessel for the ancestral temple. The harmonious bells sound radiantly, herewith being used filially to make offering to our august ancestors beseeching long life and the great mandate's prolongation. May pure virtue descend and may I for ten thousand generations with this be exalted.[32]

Unlike the histories of the other hereditary houses, almost all of which are well known in traditional literature, the state of Zeng was all but unknown, and its history can only be reconstructed—little by little—on the basis of inscribed bronze vessels. While the claims made in bronze inscriptions, if not quite exaggerated, almost invariably present only the most favorable historical records. Nevertheless, the suggestion in this bell set made for Lord Yu of Zeng that Zeng played a crucial role in rescuing Chu at the time of this crisis is doubtless true in large measure, and would explain in part why seventy years later King Huai of Chu, who first came to power just over a decade after this crisis, should have given the bronze bell to Lord Yu's grandson, Lord Yi of Zeng, that was found in 1119 and which first brought the name of Zeng to the light of day.

CHAPTER 33
THE HEREDITARY HOUSES OF WU AND YUE

The state of Wu, also known as Gouwu, Gongyu or Gongwu (the latter three names apparently the pronunciation in some language other than Chinese, and the last of these, Gongwu, written with a different character pronounced *wu*), located along the estuary of the Yangzi River in eastern China, emerged like a comet across the screen of China's ancient history. Although it claimed a long and noble pedigree, in fact, it entered into history at a relatively late date, and then also passed out of it quite quickly. However, at the apogee of its power, during the late sixth and early fifth centuries, it burned bright.

Wu claimed to be descended from the Zhou royal family. According to this story, the pre-dynastic ruler of Zhou Gugong Danfu (*c.* 1150) had three sons, Wu the Eldest, Middle Yong, and Royal Cadet. When a son was born to Royal Cadet with auspicious marks on his body (he is supposed to have had four nipples), Gugong Danfu determined that this grandson, whose name was Chang, meaning Flourishing, should one day lead the Zhou people. Chang is better known as King Wen of Zhou (r. 1099/1056–1050). Given the Zhou practice of primogeniture, by which the eldest son would normally succeed the father, and that son's son, and so on, for Chang to become king it was necessary for Wu the Eldest and Middle Yong to somehow give way to Royal Cadet. They did so by going into voluntary exile at the opposite end of what might then have been considered the Chinese world, far to the southeast, locating at present-day Wuxi in Jiangsu province. In fact, this pedigree is almost surely fictional. The earliest inscribed bronze vessels cast for rulers of the state all refer to the state as Gongyu or Gongwu. It was only after the state began to interact on a regular basis with the Chinese states of the north that the name began to be written with the *wu* of Wu the Elder; this was certainly an attempt to make themselves appear more "Chinese." In fact, it appears that they were successful in this adaptation; the Zhou states did in fact recognize Wu as their brethren.

Almost nothing is known of the state for more than five hundred years after the time of the pre-dynastic Zhou rulers Royal Cadet and King Wen, even though many historians believe that archaeology has provided at least some evidence to support this story. In 1954, a tumulus was excavated in Dantu county, Jiangsu, with several bronze vessels, one of them from the early Western Zhou with an inscription commemorating a Lord Ze of Yu being commanded by the Zhou king to relocate to Yi. Because the name Yu 虞 contains the character Wu 吳 (together with another component, *hu* 虍, that indicates the pronunciation), and because Dantu is located just south of the Yangzi River and less than one hundred and fifty kilometers northwest of Wuxi, many scholars assumed that this Lord Ze was a descendant of Wu the Eldest, and that this relocation was from the area of Wuxi to that of Dantu. However, further research suggests that this Yu and Wu are not directly related; rather, Yu refers to a location in Shanxi province on the north side of the Yellow River, and the Yi to which he was transferred was located in the vicinity of the Zhou eastern capital at Luoyang, Henan. Since all of the other bronze vessels found in the tumulus together with this *Yi Hou Ze gui* were from the early Eastern Zhou period, several hundred years after the early Western Zhou, it would seem that this vessel must have been transported south at some point in the intervening years and then buried together with the later vessels.

The next mentions of Wu in the traditional historical record stem from that later Eastern Zhou period. According to the *Zuo Tradition*, in 600, the great southern state of Chu for the first time entered into a covenant with the two states Wu and Yue, both of which were located still further south and east of Chu. Then in 584, during a series of wars between Chu and the northern power Jin, Wuchen, a former Chu minister who had defected to Jin, recommended that Jin open a new front against Chu by sending aid to Wu, whose ruler Shoumeng (r. 585–561) had just the previous year followed the precedent of Chu by taking the title "king." Jin sent Wuchen to teach Wu the northern art of war, focused in particular on archery and chariotry. Over the course of the next seventy-five years, Wu grew into a military power. During this time, Chu and Jin were engaged in almost non-stop combat, wearing each other out in their competition to be the paramount power. Meanwhile, Wu continually harassed Chu on its southeastern flank, sapping that great state's strength still further. On the diplomatic front, during the 570s and 560s, Wu participated in several other multi-state conferences. It was beginning to be recognized as one of the powers of "China."

King Shoumeng died in 561 leaving behind four sons by his primary wife: Zhufan (r. 560–548), Yuji (r. 547–544), Yumei (r. 543–527), and Ji Zha.

Although Shoumeng recognized Ji Zha as the most capable of these sons, and hoped that he would succeed him, Ji Zha did not want to become king and went into hiding to avoid that fate. Thus, the eldest son, Zhufan, became king, succeeded in turn by the next two younger brothers. When the third son Yumei died and ministers sought to have Ji Zha succeed him, Ji Zha once again fled. With no other principal sons to turn to, the ministers had no other recourse but to turn to Shoumeng's eldest son by a consort; this would be known as King Liao of Wu (r. 526–515). It is worth noting that it was only at moments of royal succession that Ji Zha went into hiding. Otherwise, he was active in affairs of state throughout his very long life. He became renowned by representing Wu at diplomatic meetings throughout the northern states and as late as 485, when he was certainly in his eighties, brokered a truce between Chu and the Wu ally Chen by arguing that rulers were better served by virtue than by military arms.

King Liao ruled for just over ten years, but his authority was not accepted by the mainline descendants of King Shoumeng. At the end of his reign, he sought to take advantage of a succession crisis in Chu, Wu's old nemesis. In 516, King Ping of Chu (r. 528–516) died, leaving a young son by a consort that he had taken from the state of Qin; the son would have been only six or seven years old at the time. In Wu, Prince Guang, a son of Yumei, the third of King Shoumeng's principal sons, urged King Liao to take advantage of the uncertain situation in Chu to invade the state, even though there was little chance that such an attack would succeed. When the Wu army was in fact defeated, Prince Guang had King Liao assassinated and assumed power himself. He was known as King Helü (r. 514–496). He would be one of the most famous rulers of the time, bringing Wu to the pinnacle of power.

During the first ten years of his reign, King Helü bided his time, advised by two of the preeminent figures of the time: Wu Zixu (559–484) and Sunzi (544–496). Finally, in 506, Wu again invaded Chu, this time having much greater success, at least initially. The Wu army pillaged the Chu capital Ying, and drove the young Chu king, King Zhao (r. 515–489), into exile at Sui (also known as Zeng). It was said at the time that King Helü had attempted to rape King Zhao's mother, the queen mother, though it is also said that she fought him off with a knife. This would turn out to be one attack too many, and Wu's fortunes in this campaign turned for the worse thereafter. King Helü then pressed the attack on to Sui, where the young Chu king had gone in exile. Wu besieged the state capital, but Sui, a long-time ally of Chu, refused to turn over King Zhao. During the siege, King Zhao of Chu was able to call on his mother's home state of Qin to come to his rescue; infuriated by King Helü's attempt on her virtue, Qin sent a sizable army that defeated the Wu army. Meanwhile, Wu's neighbor to the south, Yue, took advantage of the Wu army being in Chu to attack Wu itself. King Helü had no recourse but to return to Wu with little to show for his original success. After King Helü returned to Wu, the fortunes of Wu became increasingly inter-twined with those of its southern neighbor Yue, such that from here on the history of both states should be told together.

Even less is known about the early history of Yue or Yuyue than is the case for Wu. The name Yuyue, like those of Gouwu, Gongyu or Gongwu for Wu, seems to be a Chinese translation from some Austro-Asiatic language. Many historians hold that a state of Yue, written with a character meaning "battle-axe," is mentioned already in Shang oracle-bone inscriptions, but this is almost certainly mistaken; that Yue was a small polity somewhere to the west of the Shang capital, certainly not to its south. The Chinese character with which Yue came usually to be written means "surpassing," perhaps indicating that Yue was beyond the realm of Chinese culture. Another pronunciation is *viet*, as in the name of Vietnam, which means to the South of Yue. Two features that impressed the northern Chinese are that the people of Yue cut their hair short and tattooed their bodies, both practices that were taboo in the north.

Although there are scattered references to Yue in texts such as the *Zuo Tradition* and *Guanzi* for the eighth and seventh centuries, it is only in the sixth century that the state began to interact with other states, especially Wu. At this time, the capital of Yue was at Kuaiji, near modern Hangzhou in Zhejiang province. This coastal location explains why the people of Yue were frequently associated with water, both for their ability to swim and also for being the first state in China to fight from boats; indeed battles between Wu and Yue were frequently fought on water. But whether on land or on water, the two states fought almost continuously for over half a century. One of the first battles recorded took place in 544, when Wu attacked and defeated Yue. After this defeat, Yue sent an assassin to assassinate King Yuji of Wu. A few years later, the first ruler of Yue to bear the title of king was Yunchang (r. 537–497), whose long reign coincided with three kings of Wu: Yumei, Liao and Helü.

As noted above, in 506, King Yunchang took advantage of King Helü and the bulk of the Wu army being occupied with pillaging Chu and chasing after King Zhao of Chu to invade Wu. This invasion proved abortive when Helü returned to Wu to face the threat. However, despite his attention to this outside threat, domestically Helü is said to have become increasingly autocratic, building pleasure palaces for himself, for which he needed to raise taxes on the common people, and distancing himself from the famous ministers Wu Zixu and Sunzi, who had helped him achieve his earlier successes. In 497, King Yunchang of Yue died of illness, a relatively rare end for rulers of the two countries at this time. King Helü of Wu sought to take advantage of Yunchang's death by attacking that southern neighbor, but his string of reversals continued. Helü was mortally wounded in the battle. Before dying, he made the crown prince, the future King Fuchai (r. 495–473) swear that he would avenge his father's death. Two years later, Fuchai attacked and defeated Yue, taking its King Goujian (r. 496–465) prisoner. Fortunately for Goujian, his adviser Fan Li (fl. fifth century) bribed Bo Pi (d. 473), who had outmaneuvered Wu Zixu to become King Fuchai's prime minister. Bo Pi advised Fuchai to allow Goujian and also Fan Li to live as the king's servants. Throughout their servitude, Fan Li continued to bribe Bo Pi, and within three years, they were both allowed to return to Yue, Goujian to resume his kingship there.

After having defeated Yue and humiliated King Goujian by making him his personal servant, King Fuchai of Wu set his sights on still greater glory. He now turned his attention to the north. In 486 B.C., Wu constructed the Han Canal to connect the Yangzi River with the Huai River to its north, where it also linked with the already existing Hong Canal to provide water transport as far as the Yellow River. Thus able to supply its army in the field, the next year Wu invaded the far northern state of Qi, defeating it at the battle of Ailing. In subsequent years, Wu extended the canal system throughout the heavily populated Central Plain of China. Finally, in 482, Fuchai summoned the rulers of the northern states to a conference at Huangchi. Even Duke Ding of Jin (r. 511–475) realized that the Wu army was all but invincible, and so the states recognized King Fuchai as Premier (*Ba*) among all of the leaders.

King Fuchai's moment of glory would not be long-lasting. By turning his attention to the north and forgetting about the threat in his rear, Fuchai repeated the mistake his father King Helü had made just twenty-five years earlier. Indeed, his former chief minister Wu Zixu, now serving as ambassador in Qi, repeatedly warned him to pay attention to Yue in the south. By that time, Wu Zixu was out of favor in Wu, but his vision of the threat from Yue would soon prove to be prescient. Even while Fuchai was enjoying the pinnacle of success at Huangchi, King Goujian of Yue launched an invasion of Wu, which was defended only by the old and weak under the command of Fuchai's son You (d. 482). The Yue army quickly overran the Wu capital and executed the heir apparent. However, knowing that Yue was still too weak to face the Wu army upon its return, Goujian quickly retreated. But he had made his intentions known, and used the next decade to further strengthen his country.

King Fuchai, again like his father before him, refused to take to heart Wu Zixu's warnings against the state of Yue, and instead turned his attention more and more to affairs of the heart. It is said that during the time that King Goujian and his minister Fan Li had spent in captivity in Wu, Fan Li came to recognize Fuchai's weakness for beautiful women. Upon returning to Yue, he sought out the most beautiful women in the realm, including especially Xi Shi (fl. fifth century), famed in China as one of the most beautiful women of all time, and gave them to Fuchai as presents. With this, instead of building new canals, Fuchai built palaces for his harem and spent his days bewitched by the beautiful Xi Shi. In 476, Yue launched a full-scale invasion of Wu. After a siege that is said to have lasted for three years, Fuchai wished to surrender, asking for the same terms that he had extended to King Goujian just twenty years earlier. Fan Li advised Goujian to refuse this offer. Fuchai was forced to commit suicide, and Yue simply absorbed the state of Wu. Thus came to an end the brief but glorious history of the state of Wu.

Immediately after defeating Wu, Goujian too took his army north across the Yangzi River, convening yet another meeting of the rulers of the various states at Xuzhou, in present-day Jiangsu province. Not only did the rulers of Qi and Jin both attend, but King Yuan of Zhou (r. 475–469) sent Goujian ritual presents signifying that he was now the Premier of all the states, the last ruler to be accorded this status. Goujian transferred his capital even further north to Langye, in present-day Shandong, transporting the treasures of his state on boats navigating the canals that had been built by King Fuchai. One amusing tale accompanies this transfer. It concerns Goujian's great minister Fan Li. Knowing that Goujian could suffer privation well, but fearing that he would be undone by success, Fan Li took his leave of the state, living thereafter as something of a hermit, though in the company of the beautiful Xi Shi.

Yue remained a dominant power throughout the remainder of the fifth century, and survived throughout the entirety of the Warring States period, finally being exterminated in 222, during the final push of the Qin unification. However, it is the reign of King Goujian, and especially his battles with Kings Helü and Fuchai of Wu that entered into the imagination of Chinese readers of all periods. The book *Springs and Autumns of Wu and Yue* has long been a favorite not only for the stories of these three rulers, but also for those of Wu Zixu, Sunzi, Fan Li, Xi Shi and other notable figures. In the case of Wu, it is a story of how quickly success can turn to defeat, and in the case of Yue, how it is possible to turn even the greatest humiliation into the world's greatest recognition.

CHAPTER 34
HEREDITARY HOUSES OF THE EASTERN PEOPLES

From the early Neolithic period through the entirety of China's ancient historical period, numerous peoples lived along China's eastern seaboard, from the present-day province of Fujian in the south all the way to the Korean peninsula in the north. These peoples were never fully assimilated into the classical civilizations of the Central Plains, and were generically referred to by the peoples of the Central Plains cultures as the Eastern Peoples (*Dong Yi*), often translated as Eastern Barbarians. However, this generic terminology masks radical differences among these people, all of whom contributed in very significant ways to the synthesis that would become "Chinese" civilization.

A long history of the Eastern Peoples would begin with the archaeological site at Hemudu, just south of Hangzhou Bay in modern Zhejiang province. The culture affiliated with this type site persisted for more than two millennia throughout China's Neolithic Period, from about 5500 to 3300 BCE, and presents some of the earliest known evidence for rice cultivation. The people lived in communal long houses that were raised on stilts, an adaptation to the watery environment that would also persist well into historical times.

The Hemudu Culture is popularly associated with the Yue culture of China's historical period. In its narrowest sense, "Yue" refers to a state mentioned in such Chinese texts as the *Zuo Tradition* that was centered in what is now northern Zhejiang province, more or less the same area as the Hemudu Culture, and which is known to have existed and interacted with the cultures of China's central plains between the seventh and fourth centuries BCE. Although later Chinese texts created a fictive genealogy for the Yue people stretching back to Yu the Great and the Xia dynasty, earlier texts contemporary with the state of Yue emphasize its foreignness: that the people cut their hair short and tattooed their bodies, lived in houses raised up off the ground (often described as being like birds' nests), and perhaps most important of all spoke a language that was totally unintelligible to people of the central plains. Modern scholars associate this language with either Tai or Austronesian languages (or both), and associate the Yue Culture with cultures stretching across a broad arc from east to west across most of southern China and Southeast Asia in one direction, and another string of cultures stretching south and east from present-day Fujian and Guangdong through Taiwan, the Philippines, and even further afield in the South Pacific. The numerous different cultures in these zones were referred to by Chinese writers sometimes as the "Southern Yue" and sometimes as the "Hundred Yue." In 204, after the fall of the Qin dynasty, Zhao Tuo (240–137), commander of the Qin Southern Seas (Nanhai) region, established the state of Southern Yue (Nanyue). Although it comes after the end of the period covered in this Short History, it deserves mention that in 1983 the tomb of Zhao Tuo's grandson, Zhao Mo (175–124), the second ruler of Southern Yue (r. 137–124), was discovered in the middle of modern Guangzhou; filled with artifacts from throughout the world of the time, it is one of China's great archaeological discoveries. It should be noted too that the name Yue is better known to people today in the pronunciation "Viet"; indeed, Vietnam simply means "South of Yue."

Aside from the states of Wu and Yue, whose meteoric rises and falls in the decades just before and after 500 certainly caught the attention of the other states of the time and captured the imagination of Chinese readers ever since, the peoples generically referred to as the Southern Yue seem never to have had any direct influence on the northern states (though a good argument has been made that they were the ultimate source of the crossbow, the weapon that so decisively changed ancient Chinese warfare about 400). The same is not true of the peoples living north of Wu and Yue and generically referred to as the Eastern Peoples (Dong Yi). Already in the oracle-bone inscriptions of the Shang dynasty, the Peoples of the Huai River valley loom large as an adversary of the last Shang king Di Xin (r. 1086–1045). Di Xin led an almost year-long campaign from Anyang into the Huai River to attack them, the best documented military campaign—at least in terms of the day-to-day movement of the troops—prior to the Han dynasty. With the subsequent Zhou conquest of Shang, the Eastern Peoples became in turn the principal adversaries of the Zhou.

Shortly after the Zhou conquest, as the Zhou royal house deputed its sons and allies to colonize the east, Dan, the Duke of Zhou, was given the responsibility to bring under control the area around Mount Tai in what is today southwestern Shandong. The city of Lu that he and his son established there, at Qufu, Shandong, seems originally to have been inhabited by Shang peoples, but other polities in the area are described generically as Eastern Peoples. Although both bronze inscriptions from the time and also later accounts credit the Duke of Zhou with conquering these polities, they would maintain their identity as Eastern Peoples at least until the time of Confucius. In fact, there is at least some suggestion that Confucius's father was born in Zou, the capital city of the state of Zhulou, an Eastern Peoples state, and that his mother was a member of those people. To whatever extent this heritage may have influenced Confucius himself can only be conjectured.

Further south in the Huai River valley proper, the native people seem never to have been brought under the control of the Zhou, even if the Zhou kings' claim to rule all "under Heaven" is usually understood to have included this area. The antagonistic relationship between the Zhou and the Eastern Peoples is best to be seen in a long series of inscribed bronze vessels from the time of King Mu of Zhou (r. 956–918). While these inscriptions, like almost all bronze inscriptions, which—in the formulation of a later ritual classic— were intended to "praise the beautiful and not to mention the ugly," portray the Zhou army as winning the war, reading all of them together leaves little doubt that the Zhou were on the defensive, fighting to defend the heartland region around their eastern capital Chengzhou, located at present-day Luoyang, Henan. The following vessel, the *Lu Dong you*, has been known since the Qing dynasty.

> The king commanded Dong, saying: "Oh, the Huai Peoples have dared to attack the inner state; you shall take the Chengzhou legions to defend at Xu Garrison." Elder Yongfu praised Lu's accomplishments, and awarded (him) ten strands of cowries. Lu bows and touches his head to the ground, in response extolling the Elder's beneficence, herewith making for his cultured deceased-father Dong Yi this treasured offertory vessel.[33]

In 1975, another vessel, the *Dong gui*, which may have been cast by the same person, was excavated in the Zhouyuan area of Shaanxi province. It is one of the most unusual of all bronze inscriptions in that the patron of the inscription, Dong (written with the same character as the Dong of the *Lu Dong you*), credits his accomplishments to the spiritual aid of his deceased mother. The inscription is somewhat awkwardly worded, vacillating between referring to Dong sometimes in the first person and sometimes in the third person, but it seems to reflect his heartfelt gratitude to his mother.

It was the sixth month, first auspiciousness, *yiyou* (day 22), at the Jing Encampment. The warriors attacked X. Dong led the supervisors and legions to chase after and defend against the warriors at Yu Woods, striking the warring Hu.

My cultured mother strongly and earnestly opened the march, granting firmness to his heart, eternally giving inheritance to his body, and ruling and conquering his enemies. (I) took 100 heads, shackled two chiefs, and captured the warriors' weapons: shields, spears, halberds, bows, quivers, arrows, uniforms, and helmets, in all 135 pieces. (I) captured 114 warrior captives and their uniforms. There was no harm to Dong's body.

Your son Dong bows and touches his head to the ground, in response extolling his cultured mother's fortune and valor, herewith making for his cultured mother of the day Geng this treasured offertory tureen. Help your son Dong for ten thousand years herewith morning and night offer filiality to his cultured mother. May his sons' sons and grandsons' grandsons eternally treasure (it).[34]

While Dong of course claims to have won a great victory (otherwise he would most certainly not have cast a bronze vessel), it is significant that the battle took place at Yu Woods, which was almost certainly located at Yexian, Henan, just twenty-five kilometers southeast of Pingdingshan, Henan. Pingdingshan was the site of a Zhou colony, Ying, founded by a younger brother of King Cheng (r. 1042/1035–1006); it was obviously located there to defend against the Eastern Peoples.

The later "Biographies of the Eastern Peoples" of the *History of the Latter Han*, which draws on local accounts of these people rather than records of the Zhou kings, provides the following statement about this time.

The People of Xu arrogated the title and then led the Nine Peoples to attack Ancestral Zhou, reaching west as far as the Yellow River. King Mu feared that they were about to break through and then divided the many lords of the eastern lands, commanding King Yan of Xu to lead them.[35]

The state of Xu was located precisely in the area of the Yu Woods mentioned in the *Dong gui* inscription. This seems to confirm that the Eastern Peoples' attack reached all the way to the Yellow River. Although this gives credit to King Mu for "commanding King Yan of Xu to lead" the "Nine Peoples," obviously referring to the many different groups of people living in the Huai River valley, it is not hard to imagine that this was simply a Zhou rationalization for their diplomatic recognition of King Yan as the leader of the Eastern Peoples.

Warfare between the Eastern Peoples and Zhou forces continued throughout almost the entirety of the Western Zhou period. Many of the bronze inscriptions describing this warfare show that the battles continued to be fought along the southern approaches to Chengzhou, the Zhou eastern capital. It was only during the first half of the reign of King Xuan (r. 827–782) that the king attempted to restore Zhou control over the eastern territories. One of the poems of the *Classic of Poetry* entitled "The Jiang and Han" celebrates a Zhou campaign into the Huai River Valley. The first three stanzas of the poem claim that Zhou control was everywhere, "Reaching even to the southern sea."

> The Jiang and Han bubbling, bubbling, The warriors crest upon crest.
> It is not for peace, not for sport, It's the Huai Peoples we've come to catch.
> Having sent out our chariots, Having set out our banners,
> It is not for peace, not for rest, It's the Huai Peoples we've come to snatch.

> The Jiang and Han boiling, boiling, The warriors glimmer and gleam.
> Laying out all the four quarters, Reporting success to the king.
> The four quarters being at peace, The king's countries are all secure.
> Now that there is no more fighting, The king's heart is set at ease.

> By the banks of the Jiang and Han, The king commands Hu of Shao:
> That he govern the four quarters, Throughout all of our borderlands.
> It's not long suffering, not piercing; The king's countries to the ends,
> From the borders to the hamlets, Reaching even to the southern sea.[36]

This poem too is almost certainly Zhou propaganda. Another inscribed bronze vessel, the *Jufu xugai*, cast just a few years after the time that the poem "The Jiang and Han" is supposed to describe records another Zhou foray into the territory of the Southern Huai Peoples. Although most contemporary Chinese historians understand this as an embassy to obtain tribute offerings from the Huai Peoples, a straightforward reading of the inscription suggests a very different scenario: that Jufu, the patron of the vessel, was sent to present tribute to the Huai Peoples, in the hope that they would in turn reciprocate with "tribute" of their own. This was yet another form of diplomacy: an early form of international trade.

It was the king's eighteenth year, first month; Nanzhong Bangfu commanded Jufu to approach the many lords of the south and to lead Gaofu to present the Southern Huai Peoples their tax and their tribute, and to be solicitous of the Peoples' customs, such that they would not dare not to respect and be awed by the king's command and in return present us their presents and their tribute. We then arrived at Huai, and of the small and large countries none dared not completely to respond to the king's command. In the fourth month, returning as far as Cai, (I) make this set *xu*-tureen; may Jufu for ten thousand years eternally use it with much beneficence.[37]

The final group of eastern peoples to be considered here, even if only very briefly, lived far to the north, and claimed heritage that has been much contested, both in China and especially in Korea. According to Chinese legends, late in the reign of King Di Xin of the Shang dynasty, as the king grew increasingly violent, his uncle Jizi went off into exile in what is today Korea. In China, Jizi's legendary association with the Shang dynasty served as justification for the later colonization of Korea during the Han dynasty. On the other hand, in Korea, Jizi, or in Korean pronunciation Kija, has long been viewed as the founder of the Old Chosŏn dynasty (n.d.–108 BCE), the earliest known state in Korean history. Almost nothing is known of the early history of the state. According to the most credible account, it was only in 194 that Wei Man, a refugee from the northern Chinese state of Yan fled to Chosŏn and became ruler there. Since Wei Man's usurpation is both outside the territory of ancient China and outside the temporal bounds of this short history, it can be mentioned just in passing. However, it is interesting to note that Korean scholars debate among themselves the ultimate derivation of the Chosŏn people: from the nobility of the Chinese people, or from the Eastern Peoples. And a credible argument can be made that it was only after the Chosŏn dynasty became powerful in its own right that Chinese people adapted the legend of Jizi going into exile there to claim their own authority over it. Whatever the actual relations between the peoples of the Korean peninsula and areas to the west that are now part of China may never be known, but that their ethnicity is still debated is an important reminder of the importance of ancient history.

CHAPTER 35
HEREDITARY HOUSES OF THE WESTERN PEOPLES

The vast areas in the west of present-day China, from Inner Mongolia in the north, Xinjiang and Qinghai in the far west, Sichuan and the Tibetan Plateau in the center, and Yunnan in the south, were largely *terra incognita* to the people of ancient China. However, not only were these areas most certainly not unpopulated wildernesses, each of them in its own way had enormous influence on the development of Chinese civilization. Indeed, without the input of the western peoples, China would have been a far different place than it was.

Just as peoples living along ancient China's eastern seaboard were referred to generically as the Eastern Peoples (*Dong Yi*), often translated as Eastern Barbarians, so too were the many peoples living in the west referred to generically as Western Warriors (*Xi Rong*), also often translated as Western Barbarians. In China's ancient historical period, the term "Western Warriors" was most often used to refer to the semi-nomadic peoples inhabiting the broad stretch of Central Asia from Mongolia in the north through western Gansu and Qinghai, and it was these peoples who had the greatest influence on the development of China's classical civilization. Nevertheless, the west was home to many other people, including many who were never mentioned in Chinese historical sources, but who have now re-appeared through archaeological discoveries.

It was once common to view civilization as having begun in the Ancient Near East and to have radiated out from there. By the late nineteenth century, theories of pan-Babylonian diffusion had reached even China. In 1894, Terrien de Lacouperie (1844–1894), a professor of comparative philology at the University of London, published the book *Western Origin of the Early Chinese Civilization from 2,300 B.C. to 200 A.D.*,[38] in which he argued in the late third millennium BCE, the Bak people, a tribe of Elamite descent, wandered out of Chaldea and made its way to China, introducing "some 370 items of civilization" to China. Surprisingly, two of China's greatest scholars of the time, Zhang Taiyan (1869–1936) and Liu Shipei (1884–1919) accepted the thesis that the Bak people were so named in China because they were white (*bai* in modern Chinese, but the pronunciation of which was something like *bak in the Han dynasty) and that the Yellow Emperor (Huang Di), the mythological progenitor of the Chinese people, was so called because of his blond hair. When, two decades later, archaeological excavations at Anyang, Henan, the site of the last capital of the Shang dynasty, revealed an advanced civilization with the earliest evidence of writing in China, beautiful bronze vessels, and horse-drawn chariots, scholars in China argued for an indigenous development of civilization in China, and these early notions of diffusion were dismissed as some of the worst examples of imperialistic Orientalism, which in fact they were. Nevertheless, more recent archaeological discoveries suggest that at least some of the key features of Chinese civilization did come from the west, perhaps brought, at least in part, by blond-haired peoples.

In the far west of what is today the People's Republic of China lies the province of Xinjiang, the "New Border," which became part of the Qing empire only in the middle of the eighteenth century. The southern half of Xinjiang is known as the Tarim Basin, which now forms the Taklamakan Desert. Since the dry desert air is a natural preservative of organic material, over the last twenty-five years hundreds of naturally mummified human remains have been found throughout the Tarim Basin, such as at Gumugou (dated to about 2000 BCE), Xiaohe (1800) and Beifang (1700). Dating more or less to the period of this book, about 2000 BCE to 200 CE, these mummies, many dressed in felt and woolen clothing similar to that worn in cultures much further to the west, have attracted great attention because they are clearly Caucasoid in appearance. One of these, known as the "Beauty of Xiaohe," was found in 2006. Although the young woman died almost four thousand years ago, the extreme conditions of the desert have preserved and mummified her body, so much so that her facial features and even her reddish-brown hair and eyelashes are still to be seen.

Moving somewhat to the east of Xinjiang, one finds along the upper Yellow River valley of western Gansu and eastern Qinghai provinces hundreds of settlements of the Qijia Culture. Dating to just before and after 2000 BCE, this is the earliest Bronze Age culture in China, pre-dating the Erlitou Culture. It has clear connections with the Seima-Turbino Complex, a more or less contemporary Bronze Age culture widely distributed across southern Siberia and the trans-Altai region. To the east, the Qijia Culture also has demonstrable connections with the Erlitou Culture, unearthed in the 1960s and 70s in Yanshi, Henan, just east of Luoyang. This culture features the earliest bronze vessels cast in central China, and because the culture largely coincides in time (roughly 1800–1600) and space (northern Henan and southern Shanxi provinces) with the area that is supposed to have been the homeland of the Xia dynasty, Chinese archaeologists and historians routinely identify it with that dynasty. This connection has been suggested too because of the myth that Yu the Great, the founding father of the Xia dynasty, cast Nine Caldrons at the beginning of the dynasty. These caldrons, symbolic of political power and legitimacy, were said to have been transmitted from dynasty to dynasty, until they were eventually lost at the end of the Zhou dynasty; images of the First Emperor of Qin trying to fish them out of the Si River were a popular motif during the Han dynasty.

When the excavations at Anyang in the late 1920s and 1930s revealed a mature Bronze Age culture, most archaeologists and historians—and certainly most Chinese archaeologists and historians—turned away from the diffusionist theories that had been popular just a few decades earlier. Nevertheless, with new discoveries of ever earlier bronze cultures far to the west of central China, it is now almost certain that the idea of smelting ore into molten metal—if not the casting of bronze itself—was certainly

Figure 35.1 Stone engraving of the First Emperor of Qin attempting to retrieve the Caldrons of Yu from the Si River; from *Jin shi suo* (1821).

imported from the west. This was perhaps the most consequential import, though it was by no means the only one.

Another Bronze Age culture in western China that archaeologists in the 1930s, or even in the 1960s and 70s, could never have imagined was unearthed in 1986 in Guanghan, Sichuan, just outside the modern city of Chengdu. This was found at the site Sanxingdui. There is evidence that the site was enclosed within a massive city wall, 40 meters wide at the base. Within the walls, archaeologists found two sacrificial pits containing gold, bronze, jade, and pottery artifacts, as wells as hundreds of ivory tusks from elephants. While some of the bronze vessels at the site were similar to bronze vessels seen in the more or less contemporary Erligang Culture of central China, the culture usually associated with the early and middle portion of the Shang dynasty, the gold masks and bronze statues from the site were unlike anything seen theretofore in China. One colossal standing figure, in particular, standing some seven feet high was unprecedented.[39] However, the culture seems to have disappeared without a trace soon after the city was built about 1300. Nevertheless, it certainly reveals a very mature and sophisticated culture, more than sixteen hundred kilometers to the southwest of Luoyang.

Another eight hundred or more kilometers to the south would bring us to the territory of the Dian Culture. Excavations at Shizhaishan, just south of Kunming, Yunnan, in 1956 revealed yet another early bronze using culture, dating roughly from the fifth century through the end of the Western Han dynasty. This culture, too, features bronzewares that are entirely unusual within the Chinese cultural tradition. The most amazing of these bronzes are drums, the covers of which have three-dimensional depictions of such scenes as mounted warriors, hunting, tigers attacking oxen, or human sacrifices. These drums are closely connected with the Dong Son Culture of Vietnam to the south.

While the cultures surveyed above almost certainly did not exist in isolation, either from each other or from the various cultures of central China, they were all completely unknown to traditional historians. However, there were other peoples living to the west of China who loomed very large in the consciousness of the Chinese of the time—and also thereafter. The first of these to appear in Chinese texts is the Devil Land, who are mentioned in both the *Classic of Changes* as being engaged in warfare with the Shang king Wu Ding (r. *c.* 1225–1189) and in the *Bamboo Annals* somewhat later in the Shang dynasty. This name is almost certainly a generic term for all of the non-Chinese peoples living along the middle course of the Yellow River, in

Figure 35.2 Lid of a bronze drum of the Dian Culture, *c.* 400 BCE; photo by Zhou Yuwei, used with permission.

the northern parts of Shaanxi and Shanxi provinces, and into Ningxia. Although this name was still in use as late as the early Western Zhou dynasty, seen for instance in the *Xiao Yu ding* inscription, which celebrates a Zhou victory in which more than 13,000 prisoners were taken, by late in the dynasty the name came to be replaced by two different names: Xianyun and Dog Warriors (Quan rong). It is likely that these names refer to the same people, "Xianyun" (the characters for which in standard Chinese script feature the "dog" signific) doubtless being a transliteration of the name that the people used for themselves, and "Dog Warriors" being a Chinese translation of that name. By this time, these Dog Warriors were pressing into the very heartland of the Western Zhou capital region in the Wei River valley, as shown by many bronze inscriptions and poems in the *Classic of Poetry*. In 771, they overran the capital and killed King You (r. 781–771), the last king of the Western Zhou, forcing the Zhou court to relocate eastwards. While traditional Chinese historians explain the Zhou loss of the west by way of domestic considerations (including especially the king's deposing of his queen and the crown prince in favor of a secondary consort and her own son), the intermittent warfare between the Dog Warriors and the Zhou over the preceding half century suggests that more systemic forces were at play. There are records that the Zhou homeland was suffering from persistent drought at this time, and other suggestions that it was at this time that the steppe-land of Central Asia was drying out, causing the pastoral peoples of the zone to move about searching for new pastures. According to one scenario, these peoples would have bumped into one after another, sort of like billiard balls, leading finally to the Dog Barbarians bouncing into the Zhou capital. Whatever the validity of this explanation, it is certain that climate change had a profound effect on the people of the time.

The period from the eighth century through the fourth century BCE was characterized by mature pastoralism—cattle herding—all across the steppe-land of Central Asia, including the Northern Zone of China, a great arc extending from Xinjiang, Gansu, Ningxia, Inner Mongolia, and also into the mountainous regions of Shanxi and Hebei provinces. The peoples of these areas closest to central China were generically known as *hu*, sometimes specified as the Eastern Hu or Forest Hu, etc., or as *di*, a word that seems to mean distant or far-off. They are often mentioned in Chinese histories, alternately raiding the northern and western outposts of the Chinese states or trading goods with them. Among their trade goods, perhaps the most important were horses. Already from the earliest evidence of horses in China—first seen in the excavations of horse-drawn chariots at the Shang dynasty site at Anyang, it is clear that both horses and chariots were imported from areas to the west, ultimately from the trans-Caucasus region of present-day Russia. The horse, in various applications, would soon become the most important force in Chinese armies. It is known from Western Zhou bronze inscriptions that battles between the Zhou and the Dog Warriors were largely fought on chariots, and at least the first half of the subsequent Springs and Autumns period saw a high-tide of chariot warfare among the central Chinese states. It was the nomadic peoples of Central Asia who first gave up their chariots in favor of riding astride on their horses, which is not at all the natural act that movie Westerns would seem to depict. In central China, it was not until 307 that King Wuling of Zhao (r. 325–299) decreed that the Zhao army would deploy a cavalry division dressed in "Hu" clothing, essentially a matter of wearing pants. Prior to this time, officers led troops into battle in chariots and dressed in formal court robes. Although this reform met with resistance from many of the military officers, it was soon imitated by all of the other major powers.

From this time on, the central Chinese states came to be more and more intimately aware of the nomadic peoples of Central Asia. In addition to defending against them with their own cavalry forces, the northern-most of the Chinese states—Qin, Zhao and Yan—began to build walls along their northern borders. At the same time that Qin was conquering all of the Chinese states, it was also expanding northwards, colonizing the Ordos region of northern Shaanxi and Ningxia in 215. This in turn caused dislocation among the peoples living there, now known as the Xiongnu, often regarded as genetically related to the Huns who invaded Europe six hundred years later. In 209, the Xiongnu leader Maodun (r. 209–174) killed his father Touman and unified the various tribes into a confederation that would go on to be a powerful counterforce to the Han dynasty, the Chinese successor to the short-lived Qin dynasty. But that is a story for a later history.

BIOGRAPHIES

CHAPTER 36
BIOGRAPHIES OF YI YIN AND FU YUE

Ji Zhi, better known to history as Yi Yin, is reputed to have been a close advisor of Cheng Tang, the founder of the Shang dynasty. As such, he would have lived in the first half of the sixteenth century. He is said to have been born in present-day Ji County, Henan, a member of the Youshen state, though there are also traditions that he was born either in Shandong province or in Luoyang. The "Yin" of his name refers to the official position that he is supposed to have had after the establishment of the Shang dynasty, it means "governor," more or less equivalent to the later position of prime minister, which one tradition says that he held for more than fifty years, through the first five reigns of the dynasty. It is recorded in the *Bamboo Annals* that he died at the age of 100 in the eighth year of the reign of King Wo Ding (*c.* 1525), though, as we will see, this is part of a different tradition concerning Yi Yin. Oracle-bone inscriptions from later in the dynasty indicate that he was worshipped together with Cheng Tang.

Legend has it that a woman was picking mulberries beside the Yi River (in present-day Henan) when she found a baby in a hollow mulberry tree. The mother had become pregnant when she dreamt that a god told her to leave home to avoid a flood; looking back upon her flooded town as she was leaving, she herself was turned into a hollow mulberry tree, from which the baby was later retrieved. Presented to the king of Youshen, he was raised in the kitchens, and therefore has entered into Chinese legend as the patron saint of cooking. Although his cooking skills are praised in many ancient texts, there are no specific recipes; he is said to have regarded water as the first and most important ingredient in cooking, and that the entire process of turning ingredients into food is a form of transformation that takes place in the caldron. He is supposed to have intuited his government doctrines from this skill at harmonizing flavors.

Growing up, Yi Yin is also said to have been a brilliant student of history, such that Cheng Tang, prior to attacking the Xia king Jie, three times went to

Youshen to seek instruction from him. Yi Yin was then in a sexual relationship with Meixi, the deposed first wife of Jie; from this relationship he had inside knowledge of the Xia state, which he then used to help Cheng Tang defeat Xia. Although little is known about any specific military advice he provided, he is credited with knowing about—spying—on the Xia dynasty before the battle, and for trickery. This has led to his being regarded in Chinese legend as the patron saint of military "intelligence services."

Other traditions credit Yi Yin with divine healing powers, probably deriving from his knowledge of the macrobiotic properties of different foods. According to the *Mencius*, he lived at a time before the connection between heaven and earth had been severed, and so he was able to speak for heaven. In this role, he was regarded as the first of the "magicians" (*wu*, often translated as "shamans") of the Shang dynasty, figures who had magical abilities to know the future and to cure disease. For this, he has also been regarded throughout Chinese tradition as the patron saint of medicine, and especially of acupuncture.

Needless to say, all of this is the stuff of legend. His biography, such as it can be pieced together from much later texts, is distinctly contested. According to the orthodox historical tradition, as exemplified by *Records of the Historian*, after the death of Cheng Tang, Yi Yin continued serving as governor for the next two kings, Wai Bing and Zhong Ren. When Zhong Ren was succeeded by Cheng Tang's grandson Tai Jia, Tai Jia refused to follow the ways of Cheng Tang. To teach him a lesson, Yi Yin sent him to live beside Cheng Tang's grave, while he himself ruled the country in his place. During this time, Tai Jia is supposed to have studied the precepts of government that Yi Yin passed on to him. Three years later, Tai Jia acknowledged his faults, and Yi Yin then relinquished government to him, though still remaining as his loyal advisor. During this time, Yi Yin is credited with being the author of several chapters in the *Exalted Scriptures*. For his part, Tai Jia reformed his ways such that all of the people paid their allegiance to him and he established a great peace.

There is an alternate tradition regarding Yi Yin's relationship with Tai Jia. This is seen in the *Bamboo Annals*. According to this text, after Yi Yin sent Tai Jia into exile he proclaimed himself Son of Heaven. When Tai Jia subsequently returned from exile he killed Yi Yin and reclaimed the kingship for himself.

Neither of these two competing narratives about the role Yi Yin played in the government of the early Shang, if any, can be substantiated by contemporary evidence. Both of them would seem to be deeply informed by debates that engaged political theorists of the Warring States period. For instance, Confucius stressed the important role that ministers should play in government, and Mozi even argued for a sort of meritocracy which, taken to its extreme, would eclipse the hereditary rights of the nobility. However, when, as a demonstration of his own "humility," Zi Kuai, king the northern state of Yan, was persuaded in 316 to abdicate in favor his chief minister Zi Zhi, this practical experiment in meritocracy ended very badly. Within two years, neighboring states, fearing that this precedent would threaten their hereditary rights, attacked Yan, killing both Zi Kuai and Zi Zhi. This episode is famously recounted in the work of the contemporary Confucian philosopher Mencius, who was just then serving as an adviser to King Xuan of Qi; Mencius vigorously encouraged King Xuan to attack Yan and restore its monarchical rights. The orthodox tradition concerning Yi Yin as the loyal minister voluntarily returning power to Tai Jia after he had reformed his ways almost certainly reflects Mencius's philosophy. On the other hand, the account in the *Bamboo Annals* doubtless reflects the viewpoint of Zi Kuai and Zi Zhi.

In the "Record of Arts and Letters" of the *Han History*, Yi Yin is credited as the author of the military text *Yi Yin*, and a collection of tales called *Persuasions of Yi Yin*. He is thought to be the author of the medical texts *Classic Recipes of Soup Fluids*, and *Materia Medica of Soup Fluids*, the word for "soup" being, perhaps not coincidentally, the same as the name of the founder of the Shang dynasty. He is also the subject of numerous unearthed manuscripts, including those found at the Han-dynasty tomb Mawangdui as well as among the Tsinghua University manuscripts.

Fu Yue was a legendary adviser to the Shang king Wu Ding (r. c. 1225–1189), the putative recipient of one of the "command" chapters of the *Exalted Scriptures*: the "Command to Yue." According to the story, at the time that Wu Ding came to power, the Shang was in a period of prolonged decline. Hoping to restore the fortunes of the state, Wu Ding dreamt that he was visited by a holy man who would help him rule the country. When he awoke, he examined his various advisers at court, but none of them resembled the figure in his dream. He had a portrait drawn of the image, and sent people throughout the land to search for a match. At the time, Fu Yue was toiling as a wall-builder at a place called Fu Cliff (said to be along the Yellow River in the southwest of present-day Shanxi province), in the land of a ruler called Shi Zhong. He is said to have had an unusual physique, with shoulders raised up looking like the wings of a bird; this made him easily recognizable. When he was brought to King Wu Ding, the king confirmed that he was the figure he had seen in his dream. Fu Yue also recounted a similar dream, matching that of the king. With that, the king appointed him as his premier, and also put him in command of the Shang army. As premier, he advised Wu Ding to exercise restraint in sacrifices to his ancestors. As the leader of the army, he was commanded to attack the state of Shi in which he had been found, which he did successfully. Wu Ding went on to enjoy a lengthy reign, and is said to have restored Shang to its former glory, including especially bringing the area of modern southern Shanxi province under Shang control.

Fu Yue is not mentioned at all in the tens of thousands of oracle-bone inscriptions known from the time of King Wu Ding. However, there is a figure from the time named Ya Que, who led Shang armies into the area of the Yellow River near where the state of Shi and Fu Cliff are supposed to have been located. Indeed, some scholars even claim that there are inscriptions recording that Ya Que attacked a state called Shi. Because of this, it has been suggested that Ya Que is none other than Fu Yue, thus providing a historical basis to the legend.

Tenuous though this attribution is, Fu Yue's importance for Chinese history has little or nothing to do with whether he actually lived. In the Warring States period, when the theory of sagely ministers advising rulers reached a high tide, Fu Yue was one of the most commonly cited examples, being mentioned in almost all of the philosophical and historical texts of the period. What is more, as mentioned above, a chapter of the *Exalted Scriptures* was devoted to him, and this chapter—said to have been in three parts—was also quoted by several texts of the period. Unfortunately, the *Exalted Scriptures* was lost at the end of the Warring States, often said to have been burned in the Qin "burning of the books." The text of the *Exalted Scriptures* that was reconstituted a generation or two after the fall of Qin, the so-called New Text version, did not include this "Command to Yue," even though the title was included in the known contents of the text. Not only that, an ancient manuscript version said to have been discovered another couple of generations later in the Han dynasty, the so-called Old Text version, also did not contain the chapter. Nonetheless, in the early fourth century CE, a complete text of the *Exalted Scriptures* was presented at court, and it did indeed include a "Command to Yue," also in three parts. This contained passages concerning Fu Yue found in the various Warring States texts that quoted the "Command to Yue," and so seemed to be authentic.

This text of the *Exalted Scriptures* was accepted as authoritative and went more or less unquestioned for some fifteen hundred years. In the eighteenth century, scholars demonstrated reasons why much of this text—very much including the "The Command to Yue" chapter—was questionable, and for the last two centuries or more the authenticity of the *Exalted Scriptures* has been the most important topic in Chinese textual history. The debate over the authenticity of the received text of the "The Command to Yue" was finally resolved in 2010, with the first publication of a corpus of manuscripts from the Warring States period that are now in the collection of Tsinghua University in Beijing. One of the texts in this corpus is in three parts; it is called "The Command to Fu Yue," and is almost certainly the earliest version of this text now extant. While the description of Fu Yue is more or less the same as in the received "The Command to Yue," the rest of the text is completely different. This almost certainly shows that at least this one chapter of the *Exalted Scriptures* is a late forgery, and suggests as well that the other fifteen chapters that were added to the text in the fourth century CE are also forgeries of that period. To understand the significance of this debate within the Chinese classical tradition, imagine that the book of *Genesis* in the Hebrew *Bible* was shown to be a fourth-century CE forgery. Thus, Fu Yue has again become a figure of great importance in China.

CHAPTER 37
BIOGRAPHY OF CONSORT HAO

Among the numerous persons mentioned in Shang-dynasty oracle-bone inscriptions, the one that has attracted the most attention from both specialists and the general public is Consort Hao (Fu Hao). One of the numerous wives of King Wu Ding (r. c. 1225–1189), she appears as the topic of hundreds of divinations, which show her as very much at the center of affairs at the Shang court. Some of these divinations concerned her birth-giving, as we might expect of a woman, royal or otherwise, and it seems clear that she was the mother of at least one of Wu Ding's sons who became king, probably Zu Geng (r. c. 1188–1179). However, many other divinations show clearly that she took full part in several of the military campaigns of Wu Ding's reign, both raising troops and also leading them into battle. The first publication of these inscriptions drew added attention, coinciding as it did with the global women's suffrage movement and a nascent women's liberation movement even in China.

The inscriptions concerning Consort Hao were also the focus of the most important debate among modern historians of the Shang dynasty. This debate concerns the methodology of dating the oracle-bone inscriptions, and as such is far too complicated to review in full here. It will have to suffice to say that divinations about her belong to two different types of inscriptions: one type that can certainly be dated to the reign of King Wu Ding, and one type that could either belong to the same time or to another reign or pair of reigns almost one hundred years later. For fifty or more years after the first efforts to date these inscriptions, the leading view was that the second type of inscription should date to the later period, and thus that there were two different people of the same name: Consort Hao. According to this view, power at the Shang court oscillated between two different factions: one that it termed the Old School, characterized by the inscriptions certainly dateable to the reign of King Wu Ding, and another termed the New School, pioneered by one of Wu Ding's sons, who introduced new rituals to the court. These scholars argued that in addition to the new rituals, the New School would

Figure 37.1 Statue of Consort Hao at Yinxu (Waste of Yin) archaeological site; Anyang, Henan; photo by Zhou Yuwei, used with permission.

have brought in an entirely different cast of personnel, but that when power reverted to the Old School, descendants of the people who had served at Wu Ding's court came back to power. In a modern context, this might be comparable to the Clintons and Bushes exchanging power in the United States, but over the course of a century rather than just a few decades.

In the early 1970s, new discoveries of oracle bones at Anyang showed that this periodization was fundamentally flawed. While there was certainly something of a theological reform that took place under one of the sons of Wu Ding, and thus the notion of an Old School and New School still has merit, after this reform there was no oscillation back to the Old School. With respect to the two different types of inscriptions concerning Consort Hao, it was demonstrated that both of them dated to the time of Wu Ding, and thus that there was only one person named Consort Hao. But even these discoveries would elicit scholarly debates, debates that are still ongoing in some quarters of Chinese historical studies.

The earliest mention of Consort Hao in the oracle-bone inscriptions, in a type of inscription known as the Shi-group, dating to perhaps 1210, concerns her giving birth:

Crack-making on *jiashen* (day 21), affirmed: "Consort Hao will have a child." Eighth month.[1]

More divinations about her giving birth would follow. Verifications to some of these divinations show that she gave birth to at least two girls, and there is indirect evidence that she gave birth to at least one boy—a boy who would go on to be the king to succeed Wu Ding: Zu Geng.

It was by the last stage of oracle bones from Wu Ding's reign, perhaps two decades later in time, that Consort Hao is mentioned numerous times in the context of military campaigns. The following two divinations were both recorded on a single turtle-shell from this period, perhaps about 1195.

Affirmed: "The king will command Consort Hao to ally with Archer-Lord Gao to attack Ren."

Crack-making on *xinwei* (day 8), Zheng affirmed: "Consort Hao will ally with Zhi Guo to attack Ba Land, the king attacking from Eastern Fen and defending Fu Hao's position.[2]

The campaign against Ba Land seems to have been the opening salvo in a lengthy war—perhaps lasting as long as five years. Although it seems to have begun with Shang attacks against Ba Land and two other statelets probably located in what is today southwestern Shanxi province, this seems to have precipitated attacks against Shang by two larger powers located farther to the north: the Earth Land and Spade Land. At least at the beginning of the hostilities with Earth Land, Fu Hao was still very much involved in the Shang attack.

Crack-making on *xinsi* (day 18), Zheng affirmed: "If this spring the king raises men and calls out to Consort Hao to attack Earth Land, we will receive aid in it." Fifth month.[3]

However, as the war against Earth Land and Spade Land continued over the course of the next three years, even though hundreds of divinations were performed about Shang attacks against them, Consort Hao was never again mentioned. Instead, we find a number of inscriptions that seem to suggest that she had died. These are not unproblematic. Most of them are very short, and several are broken into small fragments. More important, we ought always to remember that divinations were performed prior to an event, and merely reflected what the Shang king wished to happen; only in cases when there is an after-the-fact verification can we be sure that something really did happen. Finally, several of these inscriptions rely on comparisons with what we think we know about the Shang kings' relations with the ancestors (and ancestresses) in order to be understood. Nevertheless, taken together, they seem to show that Consort Hao had died.

> Affirmed: "As for the king's nightmare, it is not Consort Hao causing harm."[4]

> ... on *xinchou* (day 38), we will offer Consort Hao sacrifice.[5]

> Crack-making on *jimao* (day 16), Bin affirmed: "It is God (Di) who has taken Consort Hao in marriage."[6]

The last of these inscriptions, suggesting that Di, the Shang high god, had taken Consort Hao in marriage, may have been an honor for her, though it may also have caused King Wu Ding's nightmare.

In 1975, Consort Hao re-entered the global consciousness when her tomb was unearthed just outside of the Shang royal palace precincts in Anyang, Henan. The mouth of the tomb had been covered by a layer of pisé, a form of stamped-earth that was used for wall building and for the foundations of buildings; presumably it was the foundation of a temple erected over the tomb. When it hardens, pisé becomes as hard as concrete. In this case, it had the happy effect of protecting the tomb from tomb robbers, such that it was undisturbed until being opened by the archaeologists of the Institute of Archaeology of the Chinese Academy of Social Sciences. In fact, it was the first tomb of any significance at Anyang that had not previously been robbed. What they found was astonishing. Although the tomb itself was only of medium size, its furnishings were surely fit for a queen. It contained over 400 bronze vessels and weapons, many of the vessels of the greatest artistic perfection; 600 jade pieces, some of them obviously already more than a thousand years old when they came into Consort Hao's possession; and over 7,000 cowrie shells, an object of value in ancient China. More than sixty of the bronze vessels bore inscriptions, many of them with the name "Fu Hao," showing that this was indeed her tomb.

Prior to this discovery, the periodization of Shang bronze vessels had been the subject of the same sort of periodization debate as outlined above for oracle bones. The prevailing view was that the ornamentation on the vessels had developed at a more or less constant slow pace, with the most ornate vessels being produced only at the end of the dynasty. What is more, most scholars believed that the earliest inscriptions on bronze vessels also dated to the very end of the dynasty, some hundred years after the time of King Wu Ding. When Consort Hao's tomb was first excavated, the advanced ornamentation on the vessels and especially the inscriptions on them caused many archaeologists, relying on the old periodization of oracle-bone inscriptions, to suspect that this Consort Hao must be the queen of a later Shang king. However, for archaeologists in China, the best indicator of archaeological date is the day-to-day pottery found in tombs, and not such luxury items as bronze and jade. The pottery in Consort Hao's tomb showed conclusively that it dates to the time of Wu Ding after all. This required a reconceptualization of the development of bronze casting in the Shang dynasty. It was necessary to conclude that rather than developing at a constant slow pace, there must have been an explosion of new styles introduced to the Shang artisans late in the reign of Wu Ding. It seems likely that at least some of this innovation was prompted by the Shang contact with western peoples during their expansion to the west of the Taihang Mountains, an expansion that had been led—at least in part—by Fu Hao herself. Thus, Consort Hao was instrumental in her own time in the fortunes of the Shang court, and she has been just as instrumental in the modern understanding of that court.

CHAPTER 38
BIOGRAPHIES OF LUZI SHENG AND THE
THREE HUMANE MEN OF SHANG

Luzi Sheng, also known as Wangzi (Prince) Sheng, Wangzi Lufu, and posthumously by the temple name Wu Geng, is reputed to have been the son of Di Xin, the last king of the Shang dynasty. When Di Xin was killed in the course of the Zhou conquest of Shang, Luzi Sheng became the titular leader of the Shang people. There is conflicting evidence of what happened after the conquest. The standard account in later historical sources, such as *Records of the Historian*, says that two or three younger brothers of King Wu of Zhou—Guanshu, Caishu, and perhaps Huoshu—were deputed to the Shang capital area to serve as "overseers" of the Shang people. According to these accounts, when King Wu died suddenly just two years after the conquest, yet another royal brother, the Duke of Zhou, who had remained in the Zhou homeland, declared himself to be in charge of the Zhou government. The brothers overseeing the Shang regarded this as a usurpation on the Duke of Zhou's part, and joined together with Luzi Sheng and the Shang people to rebel against the Duke of Zhou. However, their revolt was unsuccessful. The Duke of Zhou, together with yet another half-brother, Grand Protector Shi, the Duke of Shao, led a second conquest campaign, suppressing the revolt, and killed Wu Geng and at least one of the royal Zhou brothers.

This standard account is so entrenched in the minds of most historians that it is hard to imagine a different scenario. And yet a recently unearthed manuscript, called by its editors the *Annals*, does suggest just such a different scenario. It states:

> After King Wu of Zhou had conquered the Shang, he sent the three overseers to the Shang capital. When King Wu died, the Shang city rose in rebellion, killing the three overseers and establishing Luzi Sheng.[7]

This suggests that the three younger brothers of King Wu were killed by the Shang people they were sent to oversee, and implies at least that Luzi Sheng took command of them in actuality. Other evidence that has been unearthed would seem to be consistent with Luzi Sheng taking over the governance of the post-conquest Shang people, if only briefly. The *Tai Bao gui*, a beautiful bronze vessel that was commissioned by Grand Protector Shi and that is now in the Freer Gallery of Art in Washington, D.C., bears an inscription that begins:

> The king attacked Luzi Sheng, suppressing his rebellion. The king sent down a campaign command to the Grand Protector. The Grand Protector was able to be respectful and without flaw.[8]

The "king" of this inscription is almost certainly the young King Cheng, who succeeded his father King Wu after Wu's death. According to this inscription, it was King Cheng and Grand Protector Shi who put down Luzi Sheng's revolt. That the inscription does not mention the Duke of Zhou, said in most traditional historical accounts to have led the campaign against the revolt, does not mean that he did not participate in it, but it does at least call into question his leadership of the campaign.

Other inscribed bronze vessels seem to have been cast for Luzi Sheng himself. One late Shang-dynasty or early-Western Zhou bronze is made for a "Luzi" and dedicated to a "Father Ding." If this Luzi is Luzi Sheng, it too would call into question one of the important aspects of the traditional biography of Luzi Sheng. That biography stresses that Luzi Sheng was the son of Shang king Zhòu, the king defeated and killed by King Wu of Zhou. The Shang kings were all known posthumously not by their given name, but rather by the day of the ten-day week on which they received sacrifices. King Zhòu is invariably known as Di Xin, *xin* being the eighth of the ten days. On the other hand, the *Luzi Sheng gong* inscription says that Luzi Sheng's father received sacrifices on the day *ding*, the fourth day of the week. Thus, he could not have been King Zhòu's own son. However, his status as a "prince" indicates that he was some king's son.

That Luzi Sheng was named by the Zhou conquerors to be the titular head of the Shang people would seem to attest to his senior status among that people. Three other figures, traditionally referred to as the "Three Humane Men of Shang," might otherwise have had some claim to that leadership role. These were Jizi Xuyu, Bizi Gan, and Weizi Qi. According to later historical sources both Jizi Xuyu and Bizi Gan were sons of Shang king

Wen Ding, the grandfather of King Zhòu such that Jizi and Bizi were the king's uncles, while Weizi Qi is supposed to have been a son of King Di Yi, King Zhòu's father, such that he was King Zhòu's brother or half-brother (indeed, perhaps even an elder brother, albeit by a secondary consort). The reason that these three figures are known as the Three Humane Men of Shang is that they are supposed to have remonstrated against King Zhòu's misrule, though to no avail. Indeed, all three of them suffered for their attempts. Bizi is said to have been executed on King Zhòu's order (in a particularly gruesome manner, having his heart cut out), Weizi was sent into exile, and Jizi was imprisoned in the Shang capital. According to the famous *Shi Qiang pan* bronze vessel, the inscription of which recounts a sketch history of the first seven kings of Western Zhou, Weizi's descendants moved to the Zhou homeland and became hereditary scribes to the Zhou kings. As for the third of the three humane men, Jizi, traditional histories say that he did outlive King Zhòu. According to those accounts, when King Wu of Zhou defeated the army of King Zhòu at the battle of Shepherd's Wild, one of his first actions upon entering the Shang city was to send Grand Protector Shi to release Jizi from prison.

The biography of Jizi just barely begins with his release from prison upon the Zhou conquest of Shang. Again, according to later traditions, rather than being grateful for his release, he was ashamed to be in the debt of the enemy of his people. For this reason, he attempted to go into exile far to the north of the Shang capital. When King Wu heard this, he appointed Jizi to be the ruler of this land, to be known as Chaoxian or, as it is better known, at least in Korea, Chosŏn. With this, Jizi, or as he has come to be known in Korea, Kija, has come to be seen as the founding father of Korea. Needless to say, this attribution is very much tied to nationalistic sentiments, with Chinese sources from the Han dynasty using it to claim Korea for the Chinese state, and Korean sources, much later, to be sure, using it to claim the great antiquity of the Korean state, especially as opposed to that of Japan. While many modern historians, including also Korean historians, viewed the story of Jizi or Kija as a fairy tale, a modern archaeological discovery has caused many of them to reconsider. In the 1970s, many bronze vessels were unearthed in the Daling River valley of Liaoning province, the Chinese province bordering on North Korea. One of the bronzes bears an inscription saying that it was cast for one "Jizi." Could this be evidence that Jizi founded a state well to the north of the former Shang state?

One of the reasons for introducing these three figures, the stories about whom probably owe more to later moralistic historiography than to actual events, is for what they suggest about Luzi Sheng. Since Jizi is explicitly said to have been a son of King Wen Ding, that it was Luzi Sheng who was then appointed to be the titular leader of the Shang people might mean that he too was at least of the same generation as Jizi, which would be consistent with the *Luzi Sheng gong* being dedicated to his father of the Day Ding. Regardless of who Luzi Sheng's father may have been, his rule over the Shang people did not last for long. As the *Tai Bao gui* recounts, the Zhou suppressed the rebellion that put him in place, and then Luzi Sheng and most of the Shang people passed almost entirely from the historical record.

CHAPTER 39
BIOGRAPHY OF MOUFU, DUKE OF ZHAI

Zhai, often mispronounced as Ji and later referred to as She (though also mispronounced as Ye), was a small state located in present-day Xingyang county, Henan province, between Kaifeng and Zhengzhou, where the Yellow River empties into the Central Plain flood basin. According to the *Zuo Tradition*, it was one of six states established by sons of the Duke of Zhou (d. *c.* 1033), and rulers of the state continued to be influential in the local politics of the state of Zheng well into the Springs and Autumns period. Lords of this state were especially influential at two different periods in Zhou history: first, during the middle of the Western Zhou period, when they served as close advisers to the Zhou kings Zhao (r. 977/975–957) and Mu (r. 956–918), and then again in the early Springs and Autumns period, by which time the state had been absorbed into the larger neighboring state of Zheng. Of all the figures associated with the state, none was more important than Moufu (d. 936), who was its head throughout the first half of King Mu's reign. This was a particularly perilous moment in Western Zhou history, following upon a disastrous military defeat in 957, when King Mu's father, King Zhao, was defeated in the course of an attack on the southern state of Chu, losing his own life and much of the Zhou army. Later texts suggest that King Mu was as prone to dangerous undertakings as his ill-starred father had been, but that Moufu, the Duke of Zhai, strived to restrain the king's worst impulses.

Several bronze inscriptions from throughout the latter part of the early Western Zhou mention a Duke of Zhai, one of them, known as the *Nüe ding*, suggesting that he was the supreme commander of the Zhou army. Another inscription, on the *Ling ding*, describes an unnamed Zhou king traveling by chariot to a palace at Zhai, with someone named Zhai Junior (Zhai Zhong) riding in the chariot together with him. While the identities of both this Zhou king and Zhai Junior are uncertain, it seems likely that they were King Zhao and a son of the then reigning duke of Zhai; in any event, the relationship certainly bespeaks a close relationship between these two figures. Of course, bronze vessels were not cast to commemorate King Zhao's defeat and death, but the event is mentioned, albeit obliquely, in the traditional historical record, with several passages mentioning that a Duke of Zhai accompanied the king, some of them adding that this duke also lost his life at the time, drowning in the Han River.

Other, only slightly later, bronze inscriptions show that King Mu quickly set about reorganizing the Zhou military soon after succeeding his father. Some of this must have been forced upon him. Not only had the Zhou army been decimated in King Zhao's southern campaign, but early in King Mu's reign it also faced attacks from the Eastern Peoples, attacks that reached into the very heartland of the Zhou eastern capital. However, some other military activity was apparently driven by the king's own initiative. Several Warring States texts that were unearthed in the third century CE from a tomb in present-day Jixian, Henan, very near to where the state of Zhai was located, contain information—probably partly historical, partly legendary—about this period of King Mu's reign. One of these texts, known as the *Biography of Son of Heaven Mu*, describes a long-distance journey undertaken by the king and his army, setting out from the eastern capital at modern Luoyang, Henan, proceeding north along the Taihang Mountains between Henan, Hebei and Shanxi, and then following the Yellow River into Central Asia. While most of this "biography" simply recounts the travels of the king, one passage relates that he met and enjoyed a relationship with the Queen Mother of the West (Xi Wang Mu); it is this passage for which the *Biography of Son of Heaven Mu* is most famous.

The *Biography of Son of Heaven Mu* mentions several times that another Duke of Zhai traveled with the king; this Duke of Zhai was named Moufu. This Moufu is also mentioned prominently in another text that was discovered in the tomb at Jixian: the *Bamboo Annals*. The first mention comes in the eleventh year of the king's reign (946), saying that he was named to be *qingshi*, probably equivalent to prime minister. According to the same text, two years later he accompanied the king on his journey to the west described in *Biography of Son of Heaven Mu*, even though other texts record that he advised against it. Finally, the *Bamboo Annals* mentions that Moufu died in the twenty-first year of King Mu's reign, now given the posthumous title of the Cultured Duke of Zhai.

King Mu's journey to the west, and especially his meeting with, and apparent romance with, the Queen Mother of the West, are certainly the best-known contents of the *Biography of Son of Heaven Mu*. However, there is one chapter that was tacked on to the end of the text that was apparently originally a separate text, which one early editor called *The Death of Cheng Ji, the Lover of King Mu of Zhou*. This text purports to describe a different royal romance that apparently took place at this time. The text recounts how on a royal hunting trip in the eastern domain, very near the Duke of Zhai's home, the king met and fell in love with a woman named Cheng Ji. Her name indicates that she was from a very small state in the area called Cheng, and also that she was from the same extended family as the king. This is important because according to ancient Chinese tradition, relationships between males and females of the same family were regarded as incestuous, no matter how distant the relationship may have been. Despite this taboo, the king had a pleasure palace constructed for her, called Doubled Jade-Disk Terrace. Unfortunately, shortly thereafter Cheng Ji became ill and died. The king commanded that she be buried with the honors of a queen and then went into mourning, the text describing him as so despondent that he would not even meet with the various heads of state who had come to pay their condolences. *The Death of Cheng Ji, the Lover of King Mu of Zhou* concludes with a common soldier criticizing the king: "From of old there has been life and death; how could it be different only with a sweetheart."[9]

Even though *The Death of Cheng Ji, the Lover of King Mu of Zhou*, like the *Biography of Son of Heaven Mu* and *Bamboo Annals*, was found in a tomb dating to just slightly after 300 BCE, and thus is certainly ancient, most readers regard it as fiction, some literary historians even treating it and the *Biography of Son of Heaven Mu* as the beginnings of the Chinese fiction tradition. Another text, almost certainly found in the same tomb and almost certainly also relating to Cheng Ji's death, is certainly fictional; it is almost certainly the earliest known example of a genre that would come to be known "stories of the strange." There is much about it that is very strange indeed.

> King Mu of Zhou's Queen Jiang went to bed during the day and became pregnant. [Yue:] Cheng Ji was favored, and stole and raised [the baby]. Killing fourteen blackbirds, she smeared it with pig blood, and put it with Queen Jiang, who thereupon reported to the king about it. The king was alarmed, and opening the books prognosticated it saying:
>
>> The wings of the mayfly, Fly and gather on the window.
>> As for the wild goose's stopping, The younger brother cannot bring
>> order to it.

> The august numen has descended to perform an execution; Would
> that it return to its place.

He asked the Scribe of the Left about it, and Scribe Bao said: "Insects flying and gathering on the window means that the sun has lost its place; it is that that petty person was not capable of raising the lord's son." Scribe Liang said: "This means that the palace relative will retain his body; only after returning it to the mother will you get peace. Inscribe and store it [i.e., the record of the divination], and its benefit will be incited." The king together with the Commandant of the Secretariat inscribed and stored it in the coffers. After three months, Cheng Ji died. On the seventh day she returned, and spoke about the situation saying: "The past queen angered me greatly, saying: 'You are a barbarian slave; why have you stolen the lord's son and not returned him to his mother? I will discard your great punishment when the king's son is in power.'"[10]

This story of the king's romance with Cheng Ji is relevant to the biography of Moufu, the Duke of Zhai, because there is yet another ancient text that purports to record his final advice to King Mu, given while he was on his deathbed. One version of this text has long been known as a chapter in the *Leftover Zhou Scriptures*, which is supposed to be a collection of ancient writings left over after Confucius had finished editing the *Exalted Scriptures*. An ancient manuscript of this text, bearing the title *The Duke of Zhai's Testamentary Charge*, was recently discovered, dating to about the same time as the *Biography of Son of Heaven Mu* and *Bamboo Annals*. One passage of the text contains Moufu's most pointed advice to the king.

> You ought not because of favored consorts hurt your good queen. You
> ought not because of small plans defeat great considerations. You
> ought not because of favored sires hurt the great officers, ministers
> and deputies. You ought not bring family to advise your house, to
> suppress and not care for those outside it.[11]

This passage would be good advice to any king, or indeed any head of a family. However, it seems to take on special meaning when considered in light of King Mu's romance with Cheng Ji. If so, perhaps there is more than a kernel of truth in all of these fictional accounts, and Moufu, the Duke of Zhai, really did live, more or less as the texts say.

CHAPTER 40
BIOGRAPHY OF LU, THE ELDER OF JING

Lu, Elder of Jing and Supervisor of the Horse, most often referred to as just Elder of Jing, is mentioned in about twenty different bronze inscriptions of the middle Western Zhou period (though often not with his full name or full title), including some of the longest and best-known inscriptions of the time. He was clearly the most important figure in the government, other than the king himself, and was the patriarch of a family that would continue to be important for the next 150 years. Nevertheless, the name is totally unknown in the received textual tradition; everything we know about him has to be pieced together on the basis of these bronze inscriptions.

The only bronze vessel on which the Elder of Jing is referred to by his full-name and title was discovered in 1963 in Wugong County, Shaanxi, very near to the Zhou homeland known as the Zhouyuan; it is known as the *Shi Yun gui*. Although only the cover of the vessel survives, it is decorated with two facing long-tailed birds, showing that it was almost certainly made during the reign of King Mu of Zhou (r. 956–918). The inscription records that the king visited the Palace of the Army's Supervisor of the Horse, where "Lu, Elder of Jing and Supervisor of the Horse" served as the guarantor, the "right-hand man," to someone name Captain Yun, who received the king's command to supervise the military officers of the city. The inscription is entirely formulaic and would not have attracted much attention if it hadn't provided the key to identifying the Elder of Jing.

Some forty years later, in 2005, the National Museum of China purchased in a Hong Kong antiques gallery a bronze vessel that had obviously been robbed from a tomb some years earlier. This bronze vessel, bearing the same ornamentation of facing long-tailed birds as seen on the *Shi Yun gui*, commemorates the appointment of Lu as Supreme Commander of the Horse. Without the *Shi Yun gui*, there would have been no way to know that this Lu was none other than the Elder of Jing. Although the inscription on this vessel is also more or less formulaic, it is crucial for understanding his career.

It was the twenty-fourth year, ninth month, after the full moon, *gengyin* (day 27), the king was at Zhou and approached the Grand Chamber, assuming position. Supervisor of Crafts Yin entered at the right of Lu, standing in the center of the court facing north. The king called out to the foreman of the Maker of the Slips to read the command to Lu, saying: "Succeed to your grandfather's responsibility, serving as Supreme Supervisor of the Horse. You will then remonstrate and judge assiduously, taking as salary ten *lüe*. I award you red kneepads, a somber jade pendant, a metal chariot with metal reins and pennant. You will then be on guard morning and night, not neglecting my command, and you will begin the offerings."

Lu bowed and touched his head to the ground, daring in response to extol the Son of Heaven's grace, herewith making for my cultured grandfather the Somber Elder this treasured tureen. May Lu for ten thousand years have grandsons and sons eternally to treasure and use it.[12]

The date at the beginning of the inscription, "the twenty-fourth year, ninth month, after the full moon, *gengyin* (day 27)," corresponds to August 20, 933 BCE. To be named Supreme Supervisor of the Horse, essentially the Minister of War or the Chairman of the Joint Chiefs of Staff, Lu must have been reasonably mature. However, from the other bronze inscriptions in which he appears, it is clear that he lived through the remainder of King Mu's reign, all of the reign of King Mu's son, King Gong (r. 917–900), and into the first years of his grandson, King Yih (r. 899–873).

As in the case of the *Shi Yun gui* above, in many of the inscriptions in which the Elder of Jing appears, his role is as guarantor for military figures, many of whom bear the title "Captain" (*shi*). Even in one case in which the appointee does not have the title Captain, the *Dou Bi gui*, the ceremony takes place in the Great Chamber of Captain Xi, and Dou Bi is commanded to "oversee the bows and arrows of the Supervisor of the Horse of the State's Lord of Youyu," apparently a kind of regional warlord. In another vessel, the *Chang Xin he*, the Elder of Jing joins in an archery contest, surely a prerogative of military figures.

It was the third month, first auspiciousness, *dinghai* (day 24); King Mu was at the Lower Yu Residence. King Mu offered the sweet-wine and approached the Elder of Jing and the Grand Priest's shooting. King Mu praised Chang Xin and took (him) to come to approach the Elder of

Jing. The Elder of Jing was respectful and not deceitful. Chang Xin was praised for (his) accomplishments and dares in response to extol the Son of Heaven's incomparable grace, herewith initiating the making of this offertory vessel.[13]

That the Elder of Jing took part in the archery contest in front of the king already shows his considerable prestige. That the king would seek him out and introduce Chang Xin to him is unprecedented among other inscriptions of the time.

In several bronze inscriptions from the following reign of King Gong, the Elder of Jing assumed a new responsibility: as a judge of court cases, especially those involving land disputes. These inscriptions are especially important for the early history of both business transactions and also of law suits. In the first of these, dated to the third year of King Gong's reign (915), the Elder of Jing was just one of a jury of five judges. In later inscriptions, he would be listed as the first of the judges, presumably indicating his leadership of the jury. The earliest of the vessels, the *Qiu Wei he*, provides valuable information about land prices: someone named Shuren, Elder of Ju, first sold ten fields to Qiu Wei, the maker of the vessel, the price being a single jade tablet valued at eighty strands of cowries, and then subsequently sold him another three fields, the price of these being "two red tiger-skins, two deer knee-pads, and one painted skirt," their price being twenty strands.

It was the third year, third month, after the growing brightness, *renyin* (day 39); the king erected the pennant at Feng. Shuren, Elder of Ju, took a presentation demi-tablet from Qiu Wei, at eighty strands of cowries its value. He gave up ten fields. Ju then took two red tiger-skins, two deer knee-pads and one painted skirt, at twenty strands of cowries. He gave up three fields. Qiu Wei then respectfully reported to Elder Yifu, the Elder of Rong, the Elder of Ding, the Elder of Jing and the Elder of Shan, who then commanded the Three Supervisors: Supervisor of Lands Wei Yi, Supervisor of the Horse Shan Yu, and Supervisor of Works Yirenfu conjointly to give the fields at Bin and Fu. Wei's young son Zhi met Zhu Qi to feast him.

Wei herewith makes (for) my cultured deceased-father Hui Meng this treasured basin. May Wei for ten thousand years eternally treasure and use it.[14]

Other inscriptions show that the Jing lineage, of which the Elder of Jing seems to have been the patriarch (even though the *Lu gui* inscription indicates that his own grandfather was Supervisor of the Horse before him), occupied a network of lands and cities to the west of the Zhou homeland in the Zhouyuan, along the Beishan mountain range in northeast Qianyang, northern Fengxiang, and northeastern Linyou counties of Shaanxi. Indeed, the cadet branch of the extended family had its family cemetery just across the Feng River from the Zhou capital at Hao; it was excavated in the 1980s, turning up hundreds of tombs. Unfortunately many of these had been looted in antiquity, but they still give some indication of both the extent and wealth of the family.

There is evidence that toward the end of the Western Zhou period, the family lost its original land holdings to the west of the Zhou homeland and the retainers on it absconded to other families. One of the most famous vessels of all, the *Da Ke ding*, dated to about 800 during the reign of King Xuan (r. 827–782), contains the following command to Ke,

Ke, previously I had commanded you to bring out and take in my commands. Now I am extending and increasing your command, awarding you plain knee-pads, a tri-corner hat, and a centered jade. I award you fields at Ye; award you fields at Bi; award you the Jing family's attached fields at Yun, with their vassals and women; award you fields at Kang; award you fields at Yan; award you fields at Bo Plains; award you fields at Han Mountain; award you scribes and minor vassals, chimists and flutists, drummers and bellmen; award you the registers of men raised by and attached to Jing; award you Jing men (who) have fled to Dong. Respectfully morning and night herewith serve. Do not neglect my command.[15]

The award of so many Jing-family lands and retainers to Ke seems to have spelled the end of the Jing lineage. Nevertheless, Lu, Elder of Jing and Supervisor of the Horse, during the reign of King Mu, played an important role in consolidating the power of the dynasty at a critical time in its life.

CHAPTER 41
BIOGRAPHY OF YIN JIFU

Yin Jifu, also known as Xi Jia or Xibo Jifu, would seem to have been one of the most well-rounded individuals of the late Western Zhou period, a man of military, administrative and literary accomplishments. Nevertheless, although he is mentioned in a few literary sources, his name is today known only to specialists in the history of the period.

Yin Jifu is mentioned in the *Bamboo Annals* under the fifth year of King Xuan's reign (r. 827–782), as leading an attack against the Xianyun, the western peoples who fifty years later would be the primary force to overthrow the last of the Western Zhou kings, King You (r. 781–771). There is evidence that Yin Jifu's attack was successful in repelling the Xianyun threat to the Zhou capital region, since he commemorated his victory by casting a bronze vessel (using his alternate names Xi Jia and Xibo Jifu). In recognition of this victory, the king not only awarded him four horses and a chariot, but also put him in charge of the finances for the entire eastern portion of the Zhou domain, stretching from the eastern capital at present-day Luoyang all the way to the lands held by the Southern Huai Peoples— probably including parts of the present provinces of Henan, Hubei, Shandong, and Anhui.

> It was the fifth year, third month, after the dying brightness, *gengyin* (day 27); the king for the first time went to attack the Xianyun at Tuhu. Xi Jia followed the king, cutting off heads and manacling prisoners, being victorious without defect. The king awarded Xi Jia four horses and a colt chariot. The king commanded Jia to govern and supervise the taxes of the four regions of Chengzhou as far as the Southern Huai Peoples.
>
> The Huai Peoples of old were our tribute money men; they ought not dare not to produce their tribute, their taxes, their presented men, and their wares. They ought not dare not to approach the encampments and approach the markets. If they dare not to follow the commands,

then enact punishments and strike and attack them. If it be our many lords and hundred families who dare not bring them to market or dare to send in barbarian and illicit wares, they too are to be punished.

Xibo Jifu makes this basin; may he have long life for ten thousand years without limit, and sons' sons and grandsons' grandsons eternally to treasure and use it.[16]

There is also a poem in the *Classic of Poetry* entitled "In the Sixth Month" that seems to concern this same campaign against the Xianyun, describing Yin Jifu as both "cultured and martial." Called "In the Sixth Month," it is an excellent example of the sort of narrative poetry that developed at just about the time that Yin Jifu lived.

In the sixth month, bustling about, The war carts had been made ready.
The four stallions raring to go, Loaded with the standard duties.
The Xianyun were greatly ablaze, Because of this we were harried.
The king went out on campaign To set right the royal domain.

Side by side the four black stallions, Their training was by the standard.
It was in that the sixth month, That we completed our duties.
Our duties being complete, We were on the march for thirty miles.
The king went out on campaign, To assist the Son of Heaven.

The four steeds were tall and sturdy, Their great size so majestic.
Broadly did we attack the Xianyun, Offering up our best effort.
Both earnest and in good order, We upheld the duties of war.
We upheld the duties of war, To settle the royal domain.

The Xianyun were by no means weak, Having occupied all of Jiaohuo.
Invading Hao, they reached the verge, As far as the north of the Jing.
With woven patterns of bird emblems, The white banners were all agleam.
The ten largest war chariots, Went ahead to open the road.

The war chariots riding smooth, Low in the front, high in the back.
The four steeds had gone straight ahead, Gone straight ahead upon command.
Broadly did we attack the Xianyun, As far as the great plain.

Jifu, both cultured and martial, Is a model for all the countries.
Jifu feasts and is so happy, Having received many blessings.

He comes in return from Hao, Our march has been a long, long time.

Giving drinks to the many friends, Along with roast turtle and minced carp.

And who is it that is with him. Zhang Zhong, the filial and friendly.[17]

The *Preface to the Poetry*, a Han-dynasty text that describes the contexts in which the 305 poems of the *Classic of Poetry* were created, credits the authorship of four other poems to Yin Jifu; if these credits are to be believed, this would make Yin Jifu the most prolific poet of his time. In two cases, these attributions are based on statements in the poems themselves, in which Yin Jifu takes credit for making the poem. The poem "Throngs of People" is one of these. It concerns one Zhong Shanfu, who two years after Yin Jifu had cast his bronze vessel, was commanded by King Xuan to take an army to defend the eastern state of Qi.

Heaven gave birth to throngs of people, With their emblems, with their standards.

The people hold fast to the norms, And fine virtue is what they love.

Heaven reflects upon the Zhou, Its radiance reaching down below,

Protecting this Son of Heaven, And giving birth to Zhong Shanfu.

The virtue of Zhong Shanfu, Mild and giving is his standard.

Of commanding manner and visage, Careful in every detail.

The old lessons are his pattern, Awesome manner is his power.

The Son of Heaven approves of him, The bright commands he spreads about.

The king commanded Zhong Shanfu: Be a pattern to the hundred aides,

Continue your ancestor's work Of protecting the king's person.

Take out and in the king's commands, Serving as the king's throat and tongue,

Spreading the governance abroad, Energizing the four quarters.

So solemn are the king's commands, It is Zhong Shanfu who presents them.

Whether the states approve or not, It is Zhong Shanfu who brightens them.

Being both bright and also wise, Thereby he protects his person.

Morning to night never slacking, In his service of the One Man.

People also have a saying: If it is soft then chew it up,
If it is hard then spit it out. It is only Zhong Shanfu
Who neither chews up the soft, Nor spits out the hard.
Neither rude to orphans and widows, Nor in awe of the strong and
   mighty.

People also have a saying: Virtue is as light as a feather,
But few are those who can lift it. When I properly think about this,
There is just Zhong Shanfu to lift it, Even without anyone's help.
When the fabric of state has holes, There is just Zhong Shanfu to mend
   it.

Zhong Shanfu sets out on the road, The four stallions are so robust,
The marching men are so rapid, Each one worried he won't keep up;
The four stallions pounding, pounding, The eight bit-bells clanging,
   clanging.
The king commanded Zhong Shanfu To wall off that eastern country.
The four stallions with heads raised high, The eight bit-bells jingling-
   jangling.
Zhong Shanfu's on the way to Qi; Would that he be soon to return.
Jifu is he who made this chant, Stately as the purest breeze.
May Zhong Shanfu always cherish it, Thereby bringing joy to his
   heart.[18]

It is often said that poetry serves as a mirror reflecting our truest values.
It is doubtless the case that in this poem Yin Jifu portrayed his colleague as
he himself wished to be portrayed. The poem also reflects much about the
late Western Zhou view of the world.

CHAPTER 42
BIOGRAPHY OF BAO SI

The Chinese political theory of the Mandate of Heaven generally manifests itself in history in terms of a purported dynastic cycle, in which the founding father of a dynasty is described as perfectly virtuous at a time when the last king or kings of the preceding dynasty are evil incarnate. This is supposed to have been true of the evil King Jie of the Xia dynasty, who was overthrown by the King Cheng Tang (r. sixteenth century) of the Shang dynasty, and even more so of the paradigmatically evil King Zhòu of Shang (i.e., Di Xin; r. 1086–1045), who was overthrown in his turn by kings Wen (1099/1056–1050) and Wu (r. 1049/1045–1043) of the Zhou dynasty. An all too common concomitant feature of these early dynastic changes is that at least some of the evil behavior of the last kings of dynasties is blamed on women. In the case of King Jie, it was his consort Mo Xi; in the case of King Zhòu, it was Da Ji.

The Chinese on-line encyclopedia *Baidu* gives the following description of King Jie of Xia:

> King Jie was culturally and martially complete and with his bare hands was able to straighten iron hooks, but he was licentious beyond all bounds and vicious without morals. He was arrogant and lazy, corrupt in his lifestyle, employing the great power and wealth of the masses to construct his palaces and jasper gardens, drafting in beautiful women from every area to fill his rear quarters.[19]

It also provides the following painting to illustrate this depravity. The colophon reads:

> Not attending to court affairs, dallying with Mo Xi,
> Turning everywhere to wine, besotted with foolishness.
> Coming to when Tang of Shang took up weapons,
> He was chased out, awakening too late.

Figure 42.1 King Jie of Xia with his consort Mo Xi and others; from Wang Yunwu ed., *Gu Lie nü zhuan* (Shanghai: Shangwu yinshuguan, 1936).

Of all of the women blamed for the falls of dynasties, none is so infamous as Bao Si, who is blamed in large measure for the fall of the Western Zhou. According to the "Basic Annals of Zhou" chapter of *Records of the Historian*, in the third year of the reign of King You of Zhou (r. 781–771), the king became enchanted with Bao Si. When she then gave birth to a son named Bo Fu (also known as Bo Pan), the king deposed his original queen, the daughter of the ruler of the more or less important state of Shen, and also her son, the heir apparent, and made Bao Si his queen and named Bo Fu the heir apparent. Needless to say, this infuriated the Lord of Shen and also precipitated a crisis among the related states.

Records of the Historian goes on to relate the following story about Bao Si.

Of old when the Xia was in decline, there were two divine dragons that stopped in the court of the Xia king and said to him: "We are the two lords of Bao." The king of Xia divined about whether to kill them, to drive them off, or to retain them, none of which was auspicious. He then divined about requesting their saliva and storing it, which was auspicious. Then he wrapped it in silks and announced it in writing. When the dragons died, the saliva remained; he put it in the cabinet and left it there. When Xia came to an end, they transmitted this box to the Shang, and when Shang came to an end, they again transmitted it to the Zhou. Through the three dynasties, no one dared to open it.

Late in the reign of King Li (857–828), the king opened it to look at it. The saliva flowed out into the court, and they couldn't get rid of it. King Li sent his consorts, naked, to shout at it. The saliva transformed into a black turtle and entered into the king's rear chamber, where one of the young concubines who was already mature encountered it and became pregnant. Giving birth without a father, she was afraid and cast out the baby.

At the time of King Xuan (r. 827–782), the young girls sang a ditty:

A rejected bow and bamboo quiver, Will really lose the state of Zhou.

With that, King Xuan heard that there was a husband and wife who had purchased this box. The king sent someone to arrest and execute them. They were escaping when they saw coming out into the road the weird baby that had been cast off by the girl from the king's rear chamber. Hearing its cry in the night, they felt sorry for it and took it up. The husband and wife then got away, fleeing to the state of Bao. Someone from Bao who was charged with a crime, offered the king the baby girl that had been cast off by way of paying their fine. That cast-off baby girl from Bao was Bao Si. In the third year of King You (779), the king saw her in the rear quarters and fell in love with her, and she gave birth to Bo Fu. The king deposed the Queen from Shen and her son, and made Bao Si his queen and Bo Fu the heir apparent. The Grand Secretary Bo Yang said: "The misfortune is complete indeed, there is nothing that can be done about it."[20]

It goes without saying that this story is entirely fictional. However, the story of Bao Si is repeated in texts of all sorts from ancient China, and so there must be a kernel of truth to it. The earliest such mention comes in one of the odes of the *Classic of Poetry*, from not too much later than the time of King You. One of the longest poems in the classic, "The First Month," recounts the troubles of the time in such detail and such passion that there can be no doubt that there was something seriously wrong. Here is just the beginning of the poem and the stanza that blames Bao Si for destroying the capital and the dynasty.

In the first month frost is heavy; My heart is worried and wounded. Lies and rumors of the people, Are brought forward ever more.

Thinking about my solitude, My worried heart pounding pounding.
Take pity on my trifling heart; Depression is making me sick.

When my parents gave birth to me, Why did they give me such
    torment?
It was not there before my time, It will not be there after me.
Beautiful words come from the mouth, Deceitful words come from
    the mouth.
My worried heart throbbing throbbing, Because of which I am
    accused.
. . .
Oh, the worries of the heart, Are as if it is tied in knots.
Now as for the governors here, Why are they so vicious like this!
When the flames are rising on high, How could anyone stamp them
    out.
Doubly majestic was Zongzhou, Bao Si has extinguished it.[21]

The fall of the Western Zhou was a long time in coming. It was surely not
the fault of Bao Si, nor even that of King You, though he doubtless did little
to mitigate the problems. The problems were institutional, and no single
man—and certainly no single woman—would have been able to change the
course of history.

CHAPTER 43
BIOGRAPHIES OF LI JI AND MU JIANG

Li Ji (d. 651) is perhaps the most famous femme fatale of the Springs and
Autumns period, and one of the most famous women of Chinese history.
Her story inevitably involves also the stories of many men. Li Ji was a
daughter of the ruler of the Li Warriors, a non-Chinese people living to the
north of the state of Jin in present-day Shaanxi province. In 672, Duke Xian
of Jin (r. 676–651) was determined to attack the Li Warriors. Before doing so,
he had a turtle-shell divination performed. The diviner told him that the
auspice indicated that it would be "Victorious and yet not auspicious," saying
that the oracle stated: "Clasped together with bit and bone: The teeth and
fangs are slippery, The Warriors and Xia (i.e., Chinese) in each other's
clutches." The diviner went on to explain that while the attack would be
successful, it would bring great trouble to the state of Jin. Duke Xian did not
listen to this prognostication, and attacked the Li Warriors as he had
intended. Having suffered a great defeat, the ruler of the Li Warriors
presented Duke Xian with Li Ji and her younger sister, Shao Ji. Smitten with
Li Ji's great beauty, he named her as his principal consort in the place of his
previous consort, who had died after giving birth to at least two children: a
son, Shensheng, who was the heir apparent, and a daughter, who would
become the wife of Duke Mu of Qin (r. 659–621). Duke Xian had two other
sons by secondary consorts, the famous Chong'er, who would eventually
become Duke Wen of Jin (r. 636–628) and the younger Yiwu, who would
rule Jin even sooner as Duke Hui (r. 650–637). Li Ji in her own turn gave
birth to two other sons, Xiqi and Zhuozi.

Li Ji wished to have her own son Xiqi named as heir apparent, so she
persuaded Duke Xian to send Prince Shensheng and his two younger half-
brothers, Chong'er and Yiwu, to oversee distant posts within the state, a sort
of internal exile. When the duke did so, Li Ji continued to plant suspicions
between the duke and Shensheng in particular. It is said that she caused
Shensheng to return to the capital, bringing with him sacrificial beer and

meats to be offered to his deceased mother, knowing that these offerings would be shared with Duke Xian at a banquet. After Shensheng arrived with his offerings, unbeknownst to either him or Duke Xian, Li Ji poisoned the foodstuffs. As they prepared to eat, Li Ji insisted that any food brought into the palace from outside should be tested. Giving it to a dog, the dog died; giving it to an attendant, he too died. At this, Li Ji pretended to be distraught, accusing Shensheng of attempting to murder his father. Urged by his own advisers to defend himself before Duke Xian, Shensheng committed suicide instead. Persuaded by Li Ji that this was part of an extended plot against him, Duke Xian then sent officers to kill his other sons Chong'er and Yiwu, both of whom escaped and went into exile outside of the state.

In 651, Duke Xian died. Without an heir apparent having been named, the state government fell into the hands of Duke Xian's two most important ministers, Li Ke and Xun Xi. Li Ji conspired with Xun Xi to have her elder son, Xiqi, named the ruler, but Li Ke immediately killed the boy. Li Ji and Xun Xi next turned to the second son, Zhuozi, but this time Li Ke killed Zhuozi as well. It would be another fifteen years before Jin finally recovered from this conspiracy. Li Ji never would. Li Ke had her publicly whipped and then executed. Her saga would prove the accuracy of the oracle: "Clasped together with bit and bone: The teeth and fangs are slippery, The Warriors and Xia in each other's clutches."[22]

Mu Jiang (d. 564) lived a century after Li Ji, and comes somewhat after her too in the annals of the most infamous women of the Springs and Autumns period. But she certainly ranks near the top of that unhappy list. Mu Jiang was a daughter of a lord of Qi (whence the surname Jiang), the wife of Duke Xuan of Lu (r. 608–591), and the mother of Duke Cheng (r. 590–573). Mu Jiang outlived Duke Xuan by several decades. During much of that time, she did not act the part of a grieving widow. It is not without reason that in the later *Biographies of Arrayed Women*, she is grouped among the "Scheming Lovers."

In Lu at this time, real power in the state was held by the heads of the three major lineages of the ruling house: Ji Wenzi (651–568), Shusun Xuanbo (better known by his name Shusun Qiaoru), and Meng Xianzi (624–554). After Duke Xuan died, his widow Mu Jiang began a quite public affair with Shusun Qiaoru. The two plotted to oust the other lineages and to confiscate their property. This plot finally came to a head in 575, at a time when the states of Jin and Chu and their respective allies, were about to engage in the major battle at Yanling. Lu was allied with Jin, but was delinquent in contributing troops to the battle because Lord Cheng was occupied defending his position against his mother and Shusun Qiaoru; this earned the enmity of Jin, which initially moved against Lord Cheng. However, the plot was exposed and Shusun Qiaoru fled in exile to Qi, and Mu Jiang was arrested and imprisoned in the palace of the heir apparent. When she was first imprisoned, she had a divination performed on her behalf to determine whether she would be set free.

The account of this divination, told as a flashback after her death in 564, is the most famous account of divination using the *Zhou Changes* or *Classic of Changes*, and Mu Jiang's interpretation of the result is often thought to portend the transformation of this book from a manual of divination to a classic of wisdom. The divination was apparently conducted with some divination text other than the *Zhou Changes*, resulting in one hexagram that would almost certainly have been inauspicious. However, the diviner, employing some sort of trick, suggested that if the *Zhou Changes* were used, the result would be the hexagram "Following," which he interpreted as auspicious: that Mu Jiang would certainly be released. Mu Jiang refuted his reasoning, quoting the text and providing a philosophical interpretation of it.

> Mu Jiang passed away in the Eastern Palace. When she first went there, she divined by milfoil about it, meeting the "eight" of *Gen* ☶ "Stilling." The scribe said: "This is called 'Stilling' ☶'s 'Following' ☶." 'Following' means getting out. Milady will certainly quickly get out." Jiang said: "Not so! In the *Zhou Changes* this says:
>
> > Following: Prime, Receipt, Benefit, Affirmed. Without trouble.
>
> 'Prime' is the leader of the body; 'Receipt' is the gathering of enjoyment; 'Benefit' is the harmony of propriety; and 'Affirmed' is the trunk of endeavors. Embodying humaneness suffices to lead people; enjoying virtue suffices to join the rites; benefiting others suffices to harmonize propriety; and affirming sturdiness suffices to strengthen endeavors. Thus, there can be no deception even if in this way it is 'Following. Without trouble.' Now I am a woman and have taken part in disorder. Solidly in a lowly position, I was also inhumane; this cannot be said to be 'Prime.' Not bringing peace to the state cannot said to be 'Receipt.' Acting and harming my person cannot be said to be 'Benefit.' And abandoning my position to indulge in licentiousness cannot be said to be 'Affirmed.' With these four virtues, one might 'Follow' and be 'without trouble.' But since I have none of them, how could I 'Follow'?

And since I have taken up evil, how could I be 'without trouble'? I will surely die here, and will not be able to get out."[23]

She did indeed die there, never having gotten out. However, her interpretation of this line of the *Classic of Changes* has allowed her name to live forever after.

CHAPTER 44
BIOGRAPHY OF DING JIANG

Ding Jiang was a woman of the state of Qi who became the wife of Lord Ding of Wei (r. 588–577). Unlike all too many women mentioned in early Chinese texts, and especially in the *Zuo Tradition* history of the Springs and Autumns period, who are portrayed as almost irredeemably evil, Ding Jiang was universally respected for her wise counsel, first to her husband, and then after his death to the various ministers of the state. She demonstrated great foresight in diplomacy, patience in the face of adversity, human tenderness in her relations with other women, and an uncanny ability to read the signs of divination. Her biography is contained in the later *Biographies of Arrayed Women* as an exemplary mother; she was this, and much more.

Although Wèi (not to be confused with the Warring States state of Wei, which was one of the three successor states of Jin) was one of the oldest states of the Zhou dynasty, first established shortly after the Zhou conquest of Shang and occupying what was then the strategic site of the former Shang capital, by the Springs and Autumns period it had ceased to have any influence on the inter-state stage. Surrounded by larger states, its survival depended on constantly changing alliances with those states. For instance, Lord Ding relied on the support of his wife's state of Qi, to its northeast, to fend off the growing power of Jin to its west. Wèi had been administered hereditarily by members of the Sun ("Grandson") lineage of the ducal family, descendants of Duke Wu of Wèi (r. 812–758), the longest reigning and greatest ruler of the state and the last one to have had real power. At the time of Lord Ding, the chief minister was Sun Linfu, better known by his posthumous name of Sun Wenzi. Sun Wenzi had the reputation of being arrogant and difficult, and was despised by Lord Ding, who forced him to flee into exile—in the state of Jin, which at that time was recognized as the premier of the states. It was just before Lord Ding's own death that his wife, Ding Jiang, first appears in the historical record, setting the tone for all of her subsequent activities.

In 577, during a diplomatic visit of Lord Ding to Jin, Duke Li of Jin (r. 580–573) attempted a reconciliation between Lord Ding and Sun Wenzi. Lord Ding refused to see him. After Lord Ding returned to Wèi, Duke Li of Jin again requested that Sun Wenzi be allowed to return to his home state. Lord Ding remained adamant that he would not receive him, but Ding Jiang interceded on behalf of Sun Wenzi, arguing that he was from an important family in the state and also had the support of an important patron in Jin, without which the state would surely perish. She concluded her remarks with wise advice to the lord: "Even though you hate him, wouldn't having him be better than losing the state. Milord should endure this. Isn't it acceptable to bring peace to the people and to pardon a great minister of the family line!"[24] Lord Ding accepted her advice, restoring Sun Wenzi to his position of chief minister; he would go on capably to lead Wèi through tumultuous events over the next two decades. Lord Ding, on the other hand, would die later in that same year.

Lord Ding and Ding Jiang's only son died before his father did. A story about his widow, and thus Ding Jiang's daughter-in-law, portrays Ding Jiang as accompanying her to the border of the state as she returned to her natal home. A later tradition says that Ding Jiang composed one of the poems included in the *Classic of Poetry* upon this occasion: "The Swallows." Its first stanza reads as follows:

Swallows, swallows going in flight, Up and then down flapping their wings.
Here is a girl who is returning, I go with her far in the wilds.
Gazing until I can't see her; Tears stream down as if it's raining.[25]

This is regarded as an indication of Ding Jiang's human kindness, but would also suggest her literary talents—at least as understood in the eyes of later people.

Since this son and widow were childless, when Lord Ding died, he was succeeded by a son of a secondary consort; this was Lord Xian of Wèi (r. 576–559, 546–544). As his dates of reign suggest, Lord Xian's reign was not smooth, a future that Ding Jiang is said to have predicted based on his failure properly to mourn his just deceased father: "As for this guy, not only will he bring the state of Wèi to ruin, but it will surely begin with this widow. Alas, heaven has sent down misfortune upon Wèi!" In fact, Lord Xian proved to be tyrannical in his rule of the state and contemptuous of Ding Jiang, who at least in terms of ritual ranked as his mother. After eighteen years in power, he was overthrown in a coup, and forced into exile. On his way out of the state, he commanded the chief priest to report his departure in the ancestral temple, and to state that he was without guilt. Ding Jiang refused to allow this, noting that he had mistreated the ancestors, the great ministers, and herself. She instructed the priest to report his departure, but not that he was without guilt, showing her resolute nature.

The last episode in the *Zuo Tradition* in which Ding Jiang is mentioned occurs in the year 563 when the small states Wei, Song and Zheng were caught up in a back-and-forth contest between the great powers Chu and Jin. At the time, Wei was allied with Jin, while Zheng was allied with Chu. When Chu invaded Song, Wèi came to its aid, causing the Zheng minister Huang'er to attack Wèi in turn. Uncertain about how to respond to this attack, and whether to counter-attack, Sun Wenzi, the chief minister of Wèi, had a turtle-shell divination performed. Apparently neither he nor the diviners were able to understand the auspices of the crack that appeared in the shell, which was in the shape of a mountain peak. Thus, he turned to Ding Jiang for her interpretation. She interpreted the crack to mean that a counter-attack would be successful, as indeed it turned out to be.

> Sun Wenzi divined by turtle-shell about pursuing them. He presented the crack to Ding Jiang. Madame Jiang asked about the oracle. He said:
>
> > The crack is like a mountain peak:
> > There's a man going on campaign,
> > And yet loses his leader.
>
> Madame Jiang said: "That the campaigner loses his leader is the benefit of driving off bandits; the great minister should plan on it." The men of Wèi pursued them, and Sun Peng captured Huang'er of Zheng at Quanqiu.[26]

Her ability to interpret the divination crack is meant to suggest, of course, that Ding Jiang had special mantic abilities. But more than this, that a chief counselor such as Sun Wenzi would turn to her to decide the course of a military campaign demonstrates the great prestige Ding Jiang had earned in her adopted state of Wèi. Throughout her life, she had shown herself to be a person of discernment, compassion, resolution, and intelligence, one of the great women of the age.

CHAPTER 45
BIOGRAPHY OF MAESTRO KUANG

Maestro Kuang, also known as Zi Ye, lived in the state of Jin in the middle of the sixth century. Blind from birth, he was famous as a musician, especially as a player of the zither. While he has gone down in history as the patron saint of musicians, his skills were by no means limited to just music. He parlayed his closeness to the Jin rulers into a position as a high-ranking officer, remonstrating about government and divination, in addition to comments about music. He is the subject of several stories in the *Zuo Tradition*, and also in later texts of the Warring States and Han periods.

He first came to the attention of the Jin court when Duke Ping of Jin (r. 557–532) cast a giant bronze bell, which all of the musicians at court pronounced perfectly in tune. Only Maestro Kuang disagreed, saying that it was out of tune. Subsequently, Maestro Juan from Qi arrived and demonstrated that it was indeed out of tune. Other examples of his uncanny ability to hear what others could not hear concern battles between Jin and its neighbors. On one occasion, in 555, when the Jin army was about to do battle with a much larger army from Qi, Maestro Kuang advised on the basis of what he said were the joyous sounds of the birds that the Qi army was actually in retreat; it turned out that this was in fact the case. Later in the same year, when an army from Chu was attacking Jin's neighbor Zheng, Maestro Kuang again correctly recognized that Chu would withdraw, saying that in his singing of the songs of the north and the songs of the south, he could tell that there were sounds of mourning in the southern songs; again, he was proven correct.

The latest episode in the *Zuo Tradition* in which Maestro Kuang figures suggests just how sharp his mind was, and what a firm command he had of history. In 543, a labor gang was working on a defense wall between Jin and Qi. An old man joined the gang, since he was childless and needed to work. When they broke for a meal, someone asked how old he was. The man said that he was ignorant of such things as dates, but knew that he had been born on a *jiazi* day (day one of the sixty-day cycle) of the first month, and that the sixty-day cycle had repeated 475 times, and was now a third of the way through the next cycle. The deputy in charge ran off to ask about this at court. Maestro Kuang immediately said: "It was the year that Shuzhong Huibo met with Que Chengzi at Chengkuang. In that year, the Di attacked Lu, and Shusun Zhuangshu thereupon defeated the Di at Xian, capturing Chang Di and Qiaoru, as well as Hui and Bao, for whom he named his sons. It was seventy-three years ago."[27] Thus, the old man was born in 616. This corresponds to the eleventh year of Lord Wen of Lu (r. 626–609), a year for which the *Springs and Autumns* does in fact record such a meeting: "In summer, Shu Pengsheng (i.e., Shuzhong Huibo) met with Xi Que of Jin at Chengkuang."[28] Thus, not only was Maestro Kuang's skill at multiplication accurate, but he named the exact year in the fashion of the time: by a great event that happened in it.

Probably the most famous story of Maestro Kuang's musical knowledge is recorded in several different books. It seems that one night while traveling from his home state to a diplomatic visit to Jin, Lord Ling of Wèi (r. 534–493) and his entourage was camped along the bank of the Pu River. During the night, the lord heard the sounds of a zither being played. Since no one knew what the song was, he asked his attendant Maestro Juan, the same musician who had correctly identified the Jin bells as being out of tune, to transcribe the song and to play it for him. When his entourage arrived in Jin and Duke Ping entertained them at a banquet, Lord Ling instructed Maestro Juan to play the song for Maestro Kuang. Before he had finished, Maestro Kuang stopped him, saying that it was "the sounds of a doomed country," composed by a Maestro Yan at the end of the Shang dynasty for the debauched King Zhòu of Shang (r. 1086–1045). He explained that after King Wu of Zhou (r. 1049/1045–1043) defeated the Shang at the battle of Shepherd's Wild (Muye), Maestro Yan fled to the east, committing suicide by throwing himself into the Pu River. He explained that the song that Lord Ling had heard must have been played by the ghost of Maestro Yan. Against Maestro Kuang's advice, Duke Ping of Jin insisted that Maestro Juan play the tune again. When he had finished Duke Ping asked if he had played it in the most intense scale. Maestro Kuang explained that Maestro Juan had played it in the clear *shang* scale, but that this was not as intense as the clear *zheng* scale. Duke Ping insisted that Maestro Kuang play it in that scale. Ordered to do so, before Maestro Kuang had played the opening melody, sixteen black cranes appeared from the south and perched on the top of the wall. As he continued, they began to sing along and even to dance. Duke Ping was delighted with this and ordered Maestro Kuang to play it again in a different scale. Maestro Kuang again objected, but was again overruled by the duke. When he began to play it in the clear *jue* scale, clouds began to rise in the west. As he continued, a storm began, the wind blowing the roof tiles off the palace. After this, Duke Ping became sick and the state of Jin suffered from three years of drought.

It is through these supernatural musical skills that Maestro Kuang is most famous, but he is also remembered for the sound political advice that he gave to Duke Ping. In 559, when the dictatorial Lord Xian of Wèi was overthrown in a coup and forced to flee his state, Duke Ping expressed concern that such conduct might spread to other states, including of course his own. Maestro Kuang's response is one of China's earliest disquisitions on the right of the people to determine their own fate. Eerily reminiscent of the American Declaration of Independence, it is worth quoting almost in its entirety.

> The Lord of Jin said, "In expelling their lord, have the people of Wèi not gone too far?" Maestro Kuang said: "Perhaps it is their lord who really went too far. A good ruler will reward skill and punish excess, will nurture the people like children, covering them like the heavens and containing them like the earth, and then the people will support their ruler, loving him like their father and mother, looking up to him like the sun and the moon, respecting him like spiritual brightness and being in awe of him like thunderbolts. Would it be possible to expel him?

> Now the ruler is the master of the spirits and the hope of the people. If he ties up the people's livelihood and diminishes the sacrifices to the spirits, and if the people lose hope and the spirits have no master, how would they use him? What could they do but expel him! Heaven gives birth to the people and established rulers for them, letting him oversee and shepherd them, and not letting them lose their nature. There being rulers, it makes assistants, having them teach and protect, but not letting them go beyond the bounds. This is why the Son of Heaven has dukes, why the many lords have chief ministers. . . . When they are skillful, they are rewarded; when they are mistaken, they are corrected; when they are troubled, they are rescued; when they are lost, they are overthrown. From kings on down, everyone has fathers and siblings to inspect their governance. Secretaries make the scriptures, blind music

masters make the poetry, craftsmen chant the admonitions, the great officers instruct, the intellectuals pass on the sayings, commoners complain, and merchants display their wares in the marketplace.... Given Heaven's love for the people's suffering, how could it let one man be placed above the people, to indulge his own excess and reject the nature of heaven and earth. It certainly would not be so.[29]

One final mention of the Maestro Kuang in the *Zuo Tradition* comes in 547, when the ministers at the Jin court were contending with each other— to the point of drawing swords against each other—over who should represent Jin on a diplomatic mission to Qin. When Lord Ping approved of this fighting among his ministers, Maestro Kuang simply but firmly contradicted him: "I fear that the ducal house will be brought down. Its ministers are not competing with their hearts but contending with their strength, are not striving for virtue but contending to be best. Since their private interests are already excessive, is it possible that the house will not be brought down!"[30]

While the state of Jin would survive for another century or more, six different ministerial houses would do far more than draw swords against each other; they would send armies against each other. Eventually, after a protracted civil war, the once great state of Jin would be divided into three smaller states. But Maestro Kuang's fame survives to the present day.

CHAPTER 46
BIOGRAPHY OF ZI CHAN

Gongsun Qiao, better known as Zi Chan (d. 522), was one of the greatest figures of the Springs and Autumns period. A nobleman of the state of Zheng, a small state in northern China (centered on present-day Zhengzhou, Henan), he was a grandson of Duke Mu of Zheng (r. 627–606), which explains his lineage name Gongsun ("Ducal Grandson"). Rising to be prime minister of the state, he is known for his governmental reforms, for his diplomatic skills, for his all-around common sense, and also for his good-humored humility, all of which made him much loved by the people of Zheng.

In the eighth century, at the beginning of the Eastern Zhou period, at a time when the many regional states had just become independent, Zheng, despite its small size, was an important power broker because of its relationship with the Zhou kings. However, as the large states of Qi, Jin and Chu began the process of absorbing smaller states, Zheng increasingly lost influence. Located at the crossroads of the north China plain (it is worth noting that Zhengzhou is where the main north-south and east-west rail lines of modern China intersect), it was constantly buffeted by its larger neighbors. Zi Chan is first mentioned in the historical record in 565, when his father was one of the generals leading the Zheng army to invade the small state of Cai, just to the south of Zheng. Although Zheng won a great victory, the young Zi Chan is said to have lamented that there was no greater harm for a small state than to be known for its military prowess, that this would surely lead to war with the larger states. The boy was admonished by his father not to talk about the business of adults, and certainly not about affairs of state. Nevertheless, before the year was out, the southern state of Chu did in fact attack Zheng. When Zheng then agreed to a treaty with Chu, in the very next year the western state of Jin also attacked it. Thereafter, Chu attacked again, and then Jin again, Zheng being forced to trade allegiance back and forth. This led to a decade of dictatorship in Zheng, during which time the people of the state grew increasingly restless. Finally, in 554, a popular uprising overthrew the government, which was replaced with a new government under the leadership of Gongsun Xia (d. 544), another nobleman; he appointed Zi Chan as his chief minister. From this time forward, Zi Chan would be intimately involved in all affairs of the state.

Five years later, he made his entrance on the stage of inter-state diplomacy, sending a letter to Fan Xuanzi (d. 548), the prime minister of Jin who was coercing all of Jin's allies to submit ever greater amounts of tribute. Surprisingly enough, Fan Xuanzi is said to have been pleased with Zichan's letter even though it was explicitly critical of Jin. Needless to say, Jin's other allies were pleased as well. Although it will not be possible in this brief biography to recount all of Zichan's exploits, this letter shows well his attitude toward government and includes even a final argument that resonates well with today's environmental notions.

> With you sir in charge of the state of Jin, the lords of the neighbors on all four sides hear nothing of your commanding virtue, but hear always of heavy taxation. As for me, I am perplexed by this. I have heard that when a noble man is head of state, he is not concerned with a lack of gifts, but only with the difficulty of not having a commanding reputation. By gathering the gifts of the many lords in your ducal house, the lords will be of two minds, and if you rely on them, then Jin will be of two minds. If the lords are of two minds, then Jin will be destroyed, and if Jin is of two minds, then your own house will be destroyed. Then what use will the gifts be. A commanding reputation is the wagon of virtue, and virtue is the foundation of the state. With a foundation, there will be no destruction. Shouldn't this be what you strive for! With virtue there is happiness, and with happiness then you can be long-lived. The *Poetry* says:
>
> > Happy is the noble person, The foundation of the country.
> > This is commanding virtue.
>
> > The God on high looks upon you, Let your heart not be of two minds.
>
> This is a commanding reputation. If you think of others using bright virtue, then it will carry a commanding reputation and move forward, and in this way the distant will be drawn near and be at peace. Wouldn't you rather have people say about you that "You really give us life" instead of "You mine us for your own life." That elephants lose their bodies for their tusks is because of gifts.[31]

After this time, Zi Chan proceeded to reform Zheng's government, establishing different policies for the city and for the countryside, redistributing the land, and simplifying the taxation system. He also instituted the first mutual responsibility system in China, a reform that would eventually be systematized two centuries later in the state of Qin. However, the promulgation of a written law code was probably Zi Chan's greatest governmental reform. In 536, he is said to have had the state's legal code cast onto bronze caldrons. This too led to an exchange of letters between the new prime minister of Jin, Shu Xiang (d. 528), and Zi Chan. These letters also deserve quotation in full. Shu Xiang sent the first letter, objecting that the good working of government depends solely on the virtue of the ruler; putting laws into writing as Zi Chan had done eliminates the role of the ruler, which would end up making the people litigious.

> Now, dear sir, as prime minister of the state of Zheng, you have created field-markers and ditches, established government reforms, regulated the three statutes, and cast the law code. Will it not be difficult to pacify the people in this way? The *Poetry* says:
>
> > It is proper to model the Cultured King's virtue, Daily pacifying the four quarters.
> >
> > It also says:
> >
> > A proper model was the Cultured King, The ten thousand states trust in him.
>
> In this way, what rule can there be! The people will know to compete over the fine points, rejecting ritual and fighting over the wording. With the tips of chisel and knife (i.e., sharpening their pencils), they will compete over everything. There will be more and more disorderly lawsuits, and bribes will be all about. By the end of your generation, will Zheng not be defeated! I have heard "When a state is about to be lost, there will certainly be many regulations." This is what it means.[32]

Zi Chan wrote back to him, sweetly but firmly disagreeing: "It is as you have said, sir. I am lacking in talent, and what I have done will not be able to reach to my sons and grandsons. I have done it just to rescue this generation. Although I cannot support your command, how would I dare to forget your great generosity!"[33] Despite Shu Xiang's prediction that Zi Chan's reforms would bring about the destruction of his state, in fact Zheng survived for another two centuries, outlasting even Shu Xiang's own great state of Jin.

There are many other events in the life of Zi Chan deserving of mention in even the briefest biography, but here I will note just two. In 535, the year after his exchange of letters with Shu Xiang, Zi Chan visited Jin on a diplomatic visit. While there, he was told that the ruler of Jin, Duke Ping (r. 557–532), had been suffering with a serious and prolonged illness. The local diviners identified the spirits causing the illness as Substance Submerging and Terrace Nag, but none of them knew who these spirits were. Zi Chan identified them as the heavenly constellations known in the west as Scorpio and Orion, and explained their history and significance. But he then went on to say that these spirits had nothing to do with Duke Ping's illness. Rather, he was suffering from an over-indulgence in sex.

> As for milord's body, this is a matter of his going out and in, drinking and eating, and his sorrows and pleasures; what do the spirits of the mountains and rivers, stars and constellations have to do with it! I have heard that a ruler has four time-periods: in the morning he hears court, in the afternoon he holds interviews, in the evening he polishes his commands, and at night he rests his body. In this, he regulates and distributes his breath, not allowing it to be blocked up or dissipated to harm his body, so that his heart is not sickened, throwing his hundred degrees into disorder. Now is it not that he focuses on just one of these? That is why he has become ill.[34]

In that same year, back in his home state, there was a rumor running rampant among the common people that someone had seen the ghost of Liang Xiao (d. 543), one of the dictators who had previously ruled Zheng but whose ministers put to death after he tried to re-enter the state after fleeing in exile. When predictions that two different men would be killed on particular days proved to be true, the people became hysterical, believing that it was the work of the ghost. Zi Chan, now in charge of the government, appointed Liang Xiao's son and the son of yet another dictator, Zi Kong (d. 554), who had also been executed, to calm the ghost; thereafter the sightings—and the hysteria—stopped. When asked why he had done this, he replied as the astute politician that he was:

> I did it to please them. As people, those two were without propriety and interested only in pleasure. But those in charge of government sometimes go against the rules just to curry favor with the people. If

we didn't curry favor with them, the people wouldn't have trust in us, and if they didn't have trust in us, they wouldn't follow us.[35]

Unusual among the political figures of ancient China, Zi Chan died a natural death, in the year 522. His parting advice to his successor in charge of government was:

Only someone of virtue is able to control the people with leniency. Next best is harshness. When the people see the flames of a fire they are afraid, and so few die from it. However, because water is soft and yielding, the people draw near to it and play around, and so many die in it. Thus, it is more difficult to be lenient.[36]

He was unusual too in having virtue. Perhaps that is still the case.

CHAPTER 47
BIOGRAPHY OF WU ZIXU

Wu Yun, better known as Wu Zixu (559–484), was born to a prominent family in the state of Chu. His biography, many details of which are recorded in the *Zuo Tradition* and in Sunzi's *Art of War*, and which were then elaborated in *Records of the Historian*, with its stories of rise and fall, loyalty and treachery, has been a favorite topic in later Chinese moral tales, making him one of the best known and most loved figures from ancient China. Still to this day, he is regarded as a sort of god throughout much of southern and eastern China.

Both Wu Zixu's grandfather Wu Ju and his father Wu She were important advisers to kings of Chu, Wu She being the Grand Tutor to the son of King Ping (r. 528–516), named Jian. In 522, King Ping dispatched Wu She's assistant Fei Wuji to Qin to procure a wife for the crown prince Jian. However, the woman that Fei Wuji brought back was so beautiful that he encouraged the king to take her as his own consort, which the king did in fact do. Fei Wuji then initiated a long campaign of intrigue against both the crown prince and his own superior Wu She, who remained loyal to the prince. Before long, Crown Prince Jian went into exile in states to the north of Chu, though Wu She remained in the capital and remonstrated against the king's treachery. On the advice of Fei Wuji, the king had Wu She arrested and condemned to death unless his two sons, Wu Shang and Wu Zixu, would come to the capital and be executed in his place. The elder son Wu Shang, who was noted for his filial piety, agreed to go to the capital, but Wu Zixu, who his father described as a cold-hearted realist, realized that the king would kill all three of them in any event, and so followed Crown Prince Jian into exile. When the elder brother Wu Shang arrived in the Chu capital, King Ping did in fact kill him, as well as his father, Wu She. Wu Zixu swore to do everything in his power to avenge their deaths.

While in exile in the north, Crown Prince Jian began to engage in his own intrigues. Although he had been granted exile in the state of Zheng and was well treated there, he plotted with the state of Jin to invade Zheng so that he might be rewarded with the rule of a local territory. When Duke Ding of Zheng (r. 529–514) and his wise minister Zi Chan (d. 522) discovered this plot, they had Jian executed. Recognizing that he too would be implicated in the plot, Wu Zixu left Zheng in the dead of night, headed for the far southern state of Wu. Up until this time, Wu, located at present-day Suzhou in Jiangsu province on the periphery of what could then be considered the Chinese world, had been a relatively unimportant player in the politics of the Springs and Autumns period. From the time that he arrived there, Wu Zixu became intimately involved in the internal politics of the state, befriending the Wu prince Guang, a son of the former King Yumei (r. 543–527) and nephew of the present king, King Liao (r. 526–515). The politics would soon involve other states as well, including once again the state of Chu.

In 516, King Ping of Chu died and was succeeded by a son by his consort from Qin. This son, who would be known as King Zhao (r. 515–489), could not have been more than six or seven years old at the time. Wu Zixu encouraged King Liao of Wu to take advantage of the succession in Chu to launch a surprise attack, though it is said that Wu Zixu knew that this attack would not succeed, hoping thereby to remove King Liao from power. When the attack in fact failed, King Liao's nephew, Guang, turned on the king and assassinated him. Guang then became king in turn, known as King Helü (r. 514–496), another of the most celebrated figures of the time. Helü made Wu Zixu his principal political adviser, while the commander-in-chief of the Wu army was none other than Sun Wu (544–496), better known as Sunzi, the author of the famous *Art of War*.

From the time that he took power, Helü determined to conquer the neighboring states, Chu to the northwest and Yue to the southeast. At first, Wu Zixu and Sunzi both advised caution, that the time was still not ripe to act. Finally, in 506, allying with the states of Dang and Cai, Wu attacked Chu, and over the course of several battles finally entered the Chu capital Ying. Wu Zixu, accompanying the army, sought for King Zhao of Chu, but he had already fled north to the state of Sui, a long-time ally of Chu now better known in the archaeological record as Zeng. Not finding the king, Wu Zixu dug up the grave of the former King Ping, who had executed his father and elder brother, and whipped the corpse three hundred times. King Helü for his part attempted to rape the queen mother; when she fought him off with a knife, he left the Chu capital in some shame. This was but the beginning of the tables turning for Helü.

Leaving the capital, Helü and the Wu army went in pursuit of King Zhao, besieging Zeng and demanding that it turn over the Chu king. When the ruler of Sui refused to do so, the people of the state divined about the matter; when the result was not auspicious, they held out and continued to give refuge to King Zhao. Meanwhile, Chu emissaries had reached the state of Qin requesting that it come to Chu's rescue. Qin, infuriated by news that King Helü had attempted to rape the queen mother of King Zhao, who was originally from Qin, sent an army of five hundred chariots to defeat the Wu army in the field. At the same time, the state of Yue, Wu's neighbor to the south, took advantage of the Wu army being away from home to attack Wu itself. Now defeated in Chu and with disorder at home in Wu, Helü had no option but to return home.

In 496, taking advantage of the death of King Yunchang of Yue (r. 537–497), who had ruled that southern neighbor of Wu for forty years, King Helü led the Wu army to attack Yue. However, King Helü was mortally wounded in the battle. He was succeeded by King Fuchai (r. 495–473), who in the second year of his reign once again attacked Yue, this time taking its King Goujian (r. 496–465) prisoner. Although Wu Zixu urged King Fuchai to kill Goujian, saying that he was capable of enduring much hardship and if allowed to live would eventually bring harm to Wu, King Fuchai did not listen. Instead, he allowed Goujian to live as his servant. Goujian served Fuchai well, and gained his trust, so much so that after three years he was allowed to return to Yue to be king again there.

Despite King Fuchai's trust in King Goujian, Wu Zixu continued to remonstrate, saying that Wu's relationship with Yue was like having an illness inside the body of the state. This advice too went unheeded. Instead, King Fuchai turned his attention to the north, to the state of Qi, which he hoped to conquer as well. He sent Wu Zixu there as his ambassador, hoping to gain intelligence about that distant state. After carrying out his embassy and before returning to Wu, Wu Zixu left his own son in Qi, telling him that there was no future for him in Wu. Upon returning to Wu, Wu Zixu once again found himself the victim of slander at court. King Fuchai was intent upon attacking Qi, which Wu Zixu advised against, still fearing that Wu's real enemy lay in its rear at Yue. But this advice was dismissed as self-serving. Even Wu Zixu's having left his son at Qi was regarded with suspicion. With that, King Fuchai presented him with a sword and instructed him to commit suicide. Although Wu Zixu protested his innocence and his service to the state, he obeyed the command. However, before doing so, he instructed his own retainers to cut out his eyes and post them on the gate of the city so that he would be able to see the Yue army when it came to invade Wu. With that, he did cut his throat.

That year, King Fuchai did in fact successfully attack Qi. Now the preeminent power in both southern and northern China, two years later Fuchai summoned the rulers of the northern states to an inter-state conference at Yellow Pool (Huangchi), in present-day Fengqiu county, Henan, where he competed with Jin to be named Premier of all the states. Although he was successful in this as well, his success was of very brief duration. Taking advantage of Fuchai's absence, King Goujian of Yue invaded Wu and killed its crown prince. Nine years later, he again attacked, this time when Fuchai was present in the state. Fuchai was forced to commit suicide in his own turn, and his state of Wu was brought to an end.

Thus did the eyes of Wu Zixu see his own vindication.

CHAPTER 48
BIOGRAPHY OF CONFUCIUS

Kong Qiu or simply Kongzi, Master Kong, usually referred to in the West as Confucius (551–479), is unquestionably the most famous person in all of Chinese history. Renowned as the Teacher for Ten Thousand Generations, he is credited with editing the three main ancient classics, the *Classic of Changes, Exalted Scriptures*, and the *Classic of Poetry*, as well as composing the *Springs and Autumns*, the early history of his native state of Lu, in present-day Shandong province. While these literary accomplishments are doubtless fictional, there is no question that he attracted a great number of disciples during his life and imparted to them a particular way of seeing the world that put mankind at its center, and argued that the cultivation of the individual person was the first step to world peace. This philosophy is perhaps best summed up in one of the quotations of Confucius included in the *Analects*, a text composed primarily of the Master's sayings:

> Yan Yuan asked about humaneness (*ren*). The Master said: "To overcome oneself and restore the rites is to be humane. If for a single day one could overcome oneself and restore the rites, all under heaven would return to humaneness through this. To be humane comes from the self; how could it come from others."[37]

There was nothing about Confucius's birth that would have predicted his greatness. His biography in *Records of the Historian* begins:

> Kongzi was born in Zou City in the Changping district of the state of Lu. His ancestor was a man of the state of Song named Kong Fangshu. Fangshu gave birth to Boxia. Boxia gave birth to Shuliang He, and He, together with a woman of the Yan clan, joined together in the wilds and gave birth to Kong Qiu.[38]

Biographies

Confucius's father, Shuliang He, is mentioned several times in the *Zuo Tradition*, twice commenting on his heroism in battle, but providing little other information about him other than saying that he was from Zou, the city where Confucius was born. Confucius's mother is said in other sources to have been named Yan Zhengzai, indicating that she was from the Yan family, which much later sources say also lived in Zou. The expression "joined together in the wilds" is a euphemism for an illicit sexual union. In the *Analects*, there is almost no mention of Confucius's family at all, though it should be noted that quite a number of his disciples were from his mother's Yan family. The *Records of the Historian* biography of Confucius says that his father Shuliang He was quite aged by the time that Confucius was conceived, and that he died shortly after Confucius was born. Indeed, when sometime later Confucius's mother too died, Confucius, wished to bury her with his father but did not know where he had been buried.

Despite Confucius's apparent illegitimate birth, given his father's heritage he was raised as a member of the *shi* or sire class. This provided him an entrée into the class of functionaries of the state of Lu, just below the ruling class. At this time most states in China were undergoing a social revolution in which the blood-based ruling elite was slowly being replaced—at least in terms of government positions—by people from the *shi* class chosen for their abilities. There is mention in the *Mencius* that during his youth, Confucius was a minor official in charge of sheep and cattle, perhaps as a sort of accountant. The earliest mention of him in the *Zuo Tradition* serving in any sort of official capacity comes in the year corresponding to 525, when he was twenty-six years old; it does not indicate what position Confucius held, so that it must have been quite insignificant. Sometime within the next few years, the Lu nobleman Meng Xizi (d. 518) is said to have sent his two sons to study ritual with Confucius. It is somewhat ironic that according to the *Analects*, Confucius, the man who barely knew his parents, emphasized to these two boys the importance of filial piety, the reverence for one's parents.

Sometime later, Confucius left Lu for the neighboring large state of Qi, where he is recorded as having had an interview with the ruler of the state, Duke Jing (r. 547–490). In the interview, Duke Jing asked his advice about government, prompting one of Confucius's most famous comments:

Confucius responded saying: "Let the lord be lord, the minister be minister, the father be father, and the son be son."[39]

This is usually understood to mean that people should satisfy to the best of their ability their social roles. However, those roles are not necessarily static; just as sons will someday grow up to be fathers, in some contexts ministers too will come into power. It was also in Qi that Confucius was introduced to some of the splendors of classical Chinese music. It is said that after having heard the *shao* music there, for three months he did not "know the taste of meat," and said "I never imagined that music could reach to this level."[40] Nevertheless, it would seem that he was not given a position there, and so departed hastily.

Back in Lu, sometime prior to 500 Confucius was finally given an official position of some importance: he was appointed Minister of Crime, essentially the police commissioner of the state. While serving in this capacity, Confucius is mentioned as taking part in two events, one quite minor, and one much more important. The minor event is that he participated in a ceremony marking a state visit by Duke Jing of Qi, his erstwhile sponsor in Qi. The more important event took place in 498, when he challenged the three houses of Huan, the preeminent authorities in the state of Lu. Unsuccessful in this challenge, Confucius left the state in the following year; he would be gone for thirteen years, traveling from state to state in north China seeking a ruler who would make use of his services. It is clear that he was accompanied in these travels by many of his disciples.

Confucius went first to Wèi, where he seems to have spent some eight years. There are a number of anecdotes about his time in Wèi including audiences with the head of state, Duke Ling (r. 534–493). While there he also visited Nanzi (d. 480), Duke Ling's beautiful but notorious wife (it was widely rumored that while the duchess of Wèi, she engaged in various sexual affairs in her home state of Song). This angered Confucius's oldest disciple, Zi Lu (542–480), who upbraided Confucius for the visit. Confucius defended himself saying: "If I have done anything wrong, let heaven punish me, let heaven punish me."[41] The last event during this sojourn came when Duke Ling asked him about military formations. Confucius responded "I have heard something about the affairs of ritual vessels, but I have never studied the affairs of armies";[42] it is said that he left the state the very next day.

From Wèi, Confucius traveled south, via Song and Kuang, to the states of Chen and Cai. In the course of this journey, Confucius and his band of disciples found themselves under attack, the place of the attack variously stated as Song, Kuang, and Chen. Some accounts suggest that they were attacked because of a case of mistaken identity; it is also possible that they were caught up in hostilities between Chen and the far southern state of Wu. In any event, it seems that they were on the verge of starvation. Many anecdotes show Confucius to have been stoic in the face of this crisis, even while the disciples were desperate to be saved. In one such anecdote, under siege in the state of Kuang, he is said to have exclaimed:

> The Cultured King (of Zhou) being dead, is it not the case that culture resides here with me? If Heaven intends to let this culture die, those who come after me will not be able to participate in this culture, but if Heaven has not let this culture die, what do the men of Kuang have to do with me.[43]

Confucius did make it as far as Cai, located near present-day Xincai in southeastern Henan province. There he met with Shen Zhuliang, the governor of She, and apparently stayed there for perhaps another five years. Like Duke Jing of Qi, this Governor of She also asked Confucius about government. Confucius's response proposed a modern translation of a line found in both the *Exalted Scriptures* and also the *Classic of Poetry*: "Let those near at hand be happy, and let those far away come."[44]

Despite Confucius's esteem for the Governor of She, he eventually tired of being away from his home state of Lu, and returned there no later than 484. Back home, he became something of a confidant to the new ruler, Duke Ai of Lu (r. 494–468) and also of Ji Kangzi (d. 468), the most powerful nobleman in the state. On separate occasions, both of these figures asked Confucius about the art government. Confucius's answers to both men were similar, though put in different words.

> Duke Ai asked: "How can I make the people obey?" Confucius responded saying: "If you raise up the straight and put them over the crooked, then the people will obey; if you raise up the crooked and put them over the straight, then the people will not obey."[45]

> Ji Kangzi asked Confucius about government. Confucius responded saying: "To govern is to be upright. If you lead by being upright, who would dare not to be upright!"[46]

Unfortunately, by then Confucius was already quite aged, especially for the time. He passed away in the fourth month of 479. There is a passage in the *Mencius* that the day after Confucius died, several of his surviving disciples wanted to elevate one other disciple, You Ruo, almost always referred to in the *Analects* as Youzi—Master You—to be their master, apparently because he looked like Confucius. One other disciple, Zengzi, refused to do so. In fact, Youzi seems quickly to have been forgotten by the others, while Zengzi would go on to have a decisive influence on the subsequent development of Confucianism.

CHAPTER 49
BIOGRAPHIES OF CONFUCIUS'S DISCIPLES

Confucius is renowned as the greatest teacher in all of Chinese history. In the biography of Confucius in *Records of the Historian*, it is said that his disciples numbered three thousand, while there were seventy-two of them that had mastered all of the six arts: the rites, music, archery, chariotry, writing and arithmetic. Although these numbers are probably exaggerated, earlier works already talk of Confucius having had seventy disciples. Of these disciples, only about twenty-five are mentioned in the *Analects*, the book that purports to record Confucius's conversations with his disciples, and of those disciples for whom there is evidence that they interacted with the Master, five are probably most important: Yan Yuan, better known as Yan Hui (521–481); Zhong You, better known as Zi Lu (542–480); Duanmu Ci, better known as Zi Gong (520–446); Bu Shang, better known as Zi Xia (b. 507)), and Zeng Shen, better known as Zengzi (505–432). Their stories are perhaps best recounted based on their appearances in the *Analects*.

Yan Hui was not Confucius's oldest disciple, but he was certainly his favorite. One passage in the *Analects* says that when Yan Hui died, Confucius cried so much that his other disciples criticized him for having gone overboard. To this Confucius responded: "Have I gone overboard? If I did not go overboard for one such as this man, then for whom?"[47] Elsewhere, Confucius is quoted as saying at the same time: "Ah, heaven has forsaken me, heaven has forsaken me!"[48] In the *Analects*, Yan Hui is simply portrayed as having come from a poor family. Confucius is again quoted as saying: "How worthy is Hui! A single bowl of food and a single ladle of drink, residing in a shabby lane; others couldn't bear the sorrow, but Hui's joy is unchanging. How worthy is Hui!"[49] In fact, Yan Hui's family background may explain much more about why he was so beloved by Confucius. In both the *Records of the Historian* biography of Confucius and also in the later book *Family Sayings of Confucius*, Confucius's mother is named as Yan Zhengzai, indicating that she was from the Yan family. Among the seventy-two disciples of Confucius named in traditional sources, fully eight of them are from this family, suggesting that Yan Hui and these other Yans were cousins of Confucius. Nevertheless, Confucius's esteem for Yan Hui could not have been based on only the family relationship, for his other disciples thought very highly of him as well.

> The Master asked Zi Gong: "Between you and Yan Hui, which is smarter?" Zi Gong responded: "How would I dare to gaze upon Hui! When he hears one thing, he understands ten. When I hear one thing, I understand only two." The Master said: "You're not as good as he is. Neither you nor I is as good as he is."[50]

Unlike some of the later disciples, Yan Hui is not quoted often in the *Analects*, but one quotation of his provides some indication of his personality and behavior. When asked by Confucius what his ambition was, Yan Hui responded simply: "I would wish not to boast of my goodness nor to task others."[51] In this response, he showed that he had taken to heart one of Confucius's most famous teachings about what it means to be humane (*ren*). It just happens to come from a chapter of the *Analects* named "Yan Yuan": "Do not impose on others what one does not wish for oneself."[52]

Zi Lu was Confucius's oldest disciple, certainly in terms of age, and doubtless also in terms of seniority in the time that he spent with Confucius. In the *Analects*, he appears beside Confucius more than any other disciple, and is the disciple most willing to criticize Confucius to his face. Still the two men more or less of the same age were obviously friends. Confucius admired Zi Lu's willingness to act, even at the same time wishing that he would think more before acting. Zi Lu is portrayed as a man of action rather than of education or introspection, a bravo who was willing to race into battle even without the proper preparation. He once asked Confucius: "If you were to set the Three Armies in motion, who would you take with you," to which Confucius responded "I wouldn't take someone who would wrestle with a tiger or ford the River and die without regret. If need be, it would be someone who would look at the situation with trepidation and would plan well what he could achieve."[53] Similarly, Confucius said to him: "To love firmness but not to love learning is the defect of rashness,"[54] and on another occasion said "Someone such as Zi Lu will not die a natural death."[55] In fact, Zi Lu did not die a natural death; he died fighting for the Lord of Wèi in 480, the year before Confucius died of old age.

According to *Records of the Historian*, Zi Gong was the most successful of Confucius's disciples, distinguishing himself both as a statesman and as a merchant. When Ji Kangzi, the most powerful man in Confucius's state of Lu asked Confucius whether Zi Gong could be entrusted with the government of the state, Confucius responded "With Zi Gong's accomplishments, how would he have any trouble administering the government!"[56] As for Zi Gong's wealth, Confucius contrasted him with Yan Hui, who as mentioned above was famous for his ability to endure poverty:

> The Master said: "Isn't Hui really peculiar! He's frequently broke. Zi Gong does not accept his fate, and in engaging in commerce he's frequently on the mark in his speculations."[57]

While Confucius did not hold Zi Gong's wealth against him, another anecdote suggests he thought he was overly concerned with saving money. When Zi Gong encouraged Confucius to eliminate the monthly sacrifice of a lamb to the new moon, Confucius refused to do so, saying "Zi Gong, you love the sheep, while I love the rite."[58] While one interpretation of this passage is that Zi Gong was concerned about the expenditure, a more charitable interpretation might be that he simply wished to spare the lamb. It may have been in this context that Zi Gong elicited from Confucius one of his most famous sayings about the single most important lesson in life, already encountered above in the biography of Yan Hui:

> Zi Gong asked: "Is there a single saying that can be practiced to the end of one's life?" The Master said: "Would it not be reciprocity! Do not impose on others what one does not wish for oneself.[59]

On the other hand, when Zi Gong once said that this was his motto, Confucius put him down, saying "Zi Gong, it's not something you're up to."[60]

If Zi Lu was the man of action and Zi Gong the man of accomplishment among Confucius's disciples, Zi Xia was the scholar. He is reputed to be the author of the earliest commentaries on both the *Classic of Changes* and *Classic of Poetry*, and his expertise on the latter of these two classics is on view in the *Analects*. When discussing a difficult passage in the text, Confucius was so moved by Zi Xia's explanation that he exclaimed "The one who inspires me is Zi Xia. Now I can begin to discuss the *Poetry* with him."[61] Many of the sayings attributed to Zi Xia concern the importance of education. These are collected together in the penultimate chapter of the

Analects, suggesting that he may have had some role in the appearance of this text as well.

> Zi Xia said: "A person who knows on a daily basis what he is lacking in, and on a monthly basis does not forget what he is capable of, can be said to be fond of learning."[62]

> Zi Xia said: "To study broadly and to be honest in ambition, to inquire deeply and to consider what is near at hand, humaneness lies in this."[63]

> Zi Xia said: "The hundred artisans reside in their shops to complete their business; gentlepeople study in order to extend their way."[64]

> Zi Xia said: "Petty people invariably cover over their faults."[65]

> Zi Xia said: "When one excels at work, then study; when one excels at study, then work."[66]

Another saying of his found at the very beginning of the *Analects* extends his view of education to all aspects of life:

> Zi Xia said: "Those who honor the worthy in the way that others enjoy the sexy, who exhaust themselves in serving their parents, who are able to exert themselves in the service of their lord, and who are sincere in speaking with their friends: even if you were to say that they are uneducated, I would certainly call them educated."[67]

It would certainly seem that Zi Xia was educated.

The youngest of Confucius's disciples was Zeng Shen, who is always referred to in the *Analects* as Zengzi, the suffix "zi" a sign of respect reserved only for teachers. As in the case of Zi Xia, he too is quoted at both the beginning and toward the very end of the *Analects*, suggesting again that he may have been involved in the editing of the text.

> Zengzi said: "I daily reflect on myself in three ways: When I think of others, am I disloyal? When I interact with friends, am I insincere? Have I passed on anything that I haven't practiced myself?"[68]

> Zengzi said: "I have heard it from the Master: 'People never exert themselves, except perhaps in the case of mourning for their parents.'"[69]

Zengzi said: "When superiors lose the way, the people will be dispersed for a long time. If you could gain their sympathy, then have pity on the unfortunate and don't feel too pleased with yourself."[70]

Zengzi was only twenty-six years old when Confucius died. After this he lived for another forty-two years, serving in turn as the teacher of Confucius's own grandson Zi Si (483–402). The two of them together could be said to be the architects of the developing Confucian tradition, and are especially credited with the psychological or inward turn to that tradition. In the case of Zengzi, this is particularly associated with his insistence on filial piety as the foremost of all human virtues. *The Great Learning*, which was later enshrined as one of the Four Books of Confucianism (the others are the *Analects*, the *Mencius*, and the *Doctrine of the Mean*) and the authorship of which is credited to Zengzi, spells out an eight-fold path leading in one direction to self-fulfillment and in the other direction to world peace.

Affairs have their roots and branches, situations have their ends and beginnings. To know what comes first and what comes after is to be near the Dao.

In ancient times, those who wished to make bright virtue brilliant in the world first ordered their states; those who wished to order their states first aligned their households; those who wished to align their households first refined their persons; those who wished to refine their persons first balanced their minds; those who wished to balance their minds first perfected the genuineness of their intentions; those who wished to perfect the genuineness of their intentions first extended their understanding; extending one's understanding lies in aligning affairs.

Only after affairs have been aligned may one's understanding be fully extended. Only after one's understanding is fully extended may one's intentions be perfectly genuine. Only after one's intentions are perfectly genuine may one's mind be balanced. Only after one's mind is balanced may one's person be refined. Only after one's person is refined may one's household be aligned. Only after one's household is aligned may one's state be ordered. Only after one's state is ordered may the world be set at peace.[71]

CHAPTER 50
BIOGRAPHIES OF MENCIUS AND XUNZI

Meng Ke, better known as Mengzi or, in the Western world, as Mencius (c. 385–303), is now generally reputed to be the most influential Confucian philosopher after only Confucius himself. He was born in the small state of Zou, in present-day Shandong province just south of Qufu where Confucius was born. He is said to have been descended from the lords of the state of Lu, the same country as Confucius. According to legends about him, Mencius's father died when he was young and he was raised by his mother, who is included in the Han-dynasty book *Biographies of Arrayed Women* as a paragon of motherhood. It is said that she moved their house three times, before finally relocating next to a school so that he could focus on his education. His teacher—or at least the teacher of his teacher—is supposed to have been Zi Si (483–402), the grandson of Confucius. Since no later than the time of Xunzi (c. 316–217), Zi Si and Mencius have been linked as one dominant lineage of Confucian teaching.

The dates of both Mencius's birth and death are uncertain, and nothing more is known of his life until the late 320s, when he presented himself at the court of King Huicheng of Wei (r. 369–334, 334–319), at the Wei capital Daliang, located near present-day Kaifeng, Henan. In the first of the five conversations between the two men recorded in the book *Mencius*, King Huicheng, nearly eighty years old himself at the time, refers to Mencius as "old man," a term of respect, and thanks him for coming "a thousand *li*" (about five hundred kilometers; in actuality, Zou is only about three hundred kilometers from Kaifeng, but this exaggeration was also a sign of respect). It is clear that King Huicheng had great respect for Mencius, but the king died shortly after Mencius's arrival at his court, and so was not able to put any of his policies into effect. King Huicheng died in 319, and was succeeded by his son King Xiang'ai (r. 318–296).

Unimpressed with this king's demeanor, Mencius moved to the northern state of Qi, where he remained at the court of King Xuan of Qi (r. 319–301) for at least six or seven years. King Xuan was famed for his patronage of scholars from the various states, having established what is generally referred to as the Jixia Academy to house them, and Mencius was clearly the senior-most of these scholars. The relationship between the two men seems to have frayed several years later in the aftermath of Qi's attack on the neighboring state of Yan. Some years earlier, King Kuai of Yan (r. 320–318, d. 314) had abdicated in favor of his chief minister Zi Zhi, deposing also his own son, the crown prince Ping. While philosophers of the time, including Mencius, had advocated for such abdication, seeing it as a return to the Golden Age of Yao and Shun, for the kings of the many states it posed an existential threat. When crown prince Ping of Yan revolted, King Xuan took advantage of the civil war in Yan to attack and annex the state, installing a puppet ruler. Mencius seems initially to have agreed with this intervention, but when the occupation turned disastrous, he became critical of King Xuan. With that, he left the state. It is unclear where or how he lived out his final years, or even how many years he lived. It is also unclear whether it was he himself who wrote the many conversations and thoughts contained in the book bearing his name, or if it was later disciples. However, for the most part the book preserves a consistent authorial perspective, even if the personality it reveals is multifaceted: Mencius could at times be brilliant, at times self-serving and self-righteous, and at times irritating (certainly so to those in power to whom he spoke truth). He was certainly human.

Mencius's philosophy is contained primarily in the book *Mencius*. The book is in seven chapters, each of which is divided into two parts. The first six chapters are mainly in the form of conversations with others, some of whom were—as noted above—rulers of states, and some of whom were other thinkers of his time. Mencius was probably most famous in his own day—and thereafter as well—for his dictum that human nature is inherently good. He argued this position with both logic and with parables. For instance, he suggested that anyone who saw a baby about to fall into a well would rush to save it. This response would be neither premeditated nor motivated by a reward, but rather would be spontaneous. From this, he drew the conclusion that "All people have a heart that cannot bear the suffering of others."[72] He extended this conclusion to argue too that all humans are equal, at least morally, stating that "all men can be a Yao or Shun."[73]

This moral philosophy almost necessarily entailed a political and economic philosophy. Mencius most emphatically did not argue that all men have equal political rights; he was a staunch defender of the divine right of kings to rule. However, he required that rulers deserve that right and continue to preserve it. Otherwise, Heaven would withdraw its mandate from them, and the people would be within their rights to revolt. This is the famous theory of the "Mandate of Heaven," usually associated with the Duke of Zhou at the beginning of the Western Zhou period; Mencius may have been even more important than the Duke of Zhou in ensuring that this theory would continue to influence Chinese political thought throughout the many dynasties that would follow the Zhou.

What he meant by deserving the divine right to rule was to be a true "king." In one of his conversations with King Huicheng of Wei, when the king claimed that he was ashamed that his kingdom was much smaller than that of Qin or Chu, Mencius responded:

> With a territory just a hundred *li* square, one can be a king. If Milord were to extend humane governance to the people, reducing punishments and fines, keeping taxes light, and ploughing deeply and weeding easily, then the able-bodied would have spare time to practice filial piety and deference towards elders, loyalty and faithfulness. At home, they would serve their parents and elder brothers, abroad they would serve their elders and superiors, and with nothing more than clubs they could beat the sturdy armor and sharp weapons of Qin and Chu.[74]

Mencius also espoused a consistent economic philosophy that is usually characterized as a "well-field system." This derives from the Chinese character for "well": 井. This character, originally a pictograph of a well, was taken to describe a nine-part division of a square plot of land, of which the eight parts around the perimeter were to be given to individual families. The families would jointly till the central square, the product of which would be their joint tax burden. According to Mencius, this was the rule of King Wen (r. 1099/1056–1050) even before the Zhou conquest of Shang. In addition to this well-field system, Mencius claimed that King Wen levied no taxes on trade, did not restrict the people from hunting and fishing, did not extend punishments for crimes to the relatives of criminals, and took care of widows and orphans and the elderly without children to care for them.[75]

As simple as this political and economic theory sounds, in the context of the *realpolitik* of the Warring States period Mencius did not persuade either King Huicheng of Wei or King Xuan of Qi, or any of the other rulers of the era, for that matter. Unfortunately, it has not been much more influential in other eras or in other states.

Criticism of Mencius began in the generation or two after his life, especially in the teaching of Xun Kuang, better known simply as Xunzi; he is generally regarded as the second of the great Confucian philosophers of the Warring States period after Mencius. Not much is known of his early life, though there are stories that he was alive during the time of King Kuai of Yan (i.e., 314) on the one hand, and that he lived to see the united empire (i.e., 221) on the other. Neither is there much known of where he was from, other than a tradition that he was born in the state of Zhao. By mid-life, there is somewhat more detail. He is said to have been in Qi at the time of King Xiang of Qi (r. 283–265), where for some period of time he was the director of the Jixia Academy, which attracted scholars from throughout the various states. During his time there, he is supposed to have been the teacher of both Han Feizi (*c.* 280–233) and Li Si (280–208), two thinkers who were the great proponents of Legalism and who made names for themselves in the state of Qin. Xunzi too is said to have spent a number of years in Qin, of which he had a positive opinion. Although there are, to be sure, Legalist tendencies in his teaching, Xunzi always regarded himself as a disciple of Confucius. Late in his life, he had the chance to put his teachings into practice, serving as the magistrate of Lanling, a town in the southern part of modern-day Shandong province. However, it is not clear how effective he was in this role. He lost the post two years after being appointed to it, when his patron, the lord of Chunshen (d. 238), the prime minister of Chu, was assassinated. Xunzi apparently remained in Lanling for the remainder of his lengthy life, though almost nothing further is known about those years.

The thought of Xunzi is known from the book bearing his name: *Xunzi*. It is a very substantial book of thirty-two chapters, most of which were probably written by Xunzi himself. Whereas earlier philosophical texts in China are often written in a disjointed manner, often making use of questions-and-answers or parables, the *Xunzi* is largely composed of essays that present a philosophical argument complete with a thesis, full supporting evidence, and a conclusion. Whereas Mencius had famously argued that human nature is inherently good, Xunzi argued the opposite: that human nature is evil. However, while these two positions seem to be diametrically opposed, in fact the two thinkers agreed that human nature is perfectible, and that education and ritual are the keys to this. Xunzi viewed ritual, which ought to be thought of broadly as correct behavior, rather than in the narrow sense of solely religious acts, as having been established by the sage kings of antiquity as a means of teaching the people to be good. He used the analogy of carpenters using steam to straighten warped lumber to illustrate the effect that ritual had on human behavior: left in their natural state, people would invariably behave badly; however, once straightened, they would remain on the straight and narrow thereafter, and would not revert to their original warped ways.

Xunzi conceived of education as the means of inculcating the ancient rituals. Indeed, the first chapter of the *Xunzi* is entitled "Encouraging Study." According to this chapter, it was the responsibility of scholars such as himself—followers of Confucius—to be the teachers. These scholars were to be broadly trained in the classics, especially the *Poetry* and *Scriptures*, and indeed many of the leading scholars of these texts during the subsequent Han dynasty traced their learning back to the teaching of Xunzi. He took a dim view of the utilitarian teachings designed for farmers, merchants or artisans, and he was especially critical of the many theories regarding the art of war, such as those by Sunzi (544–470) and Wu Qi (440–381). In the chapter of the *Xunzi* devoted to war, Xunzi argued that success in warfare depends not on generals or military strategies, but rather on the ruler gaining the trust of his people through virtuous rule.[76]

Xunzi argued that what sets humans apart from other forms of life is our sense of morality, which allows us to join together in social groups. A safe and stable society would be all the reward that people should expect. Xunzi emphatically denied any supernatural agency to heaven or to the gods, saying "the Way is not the way of heaven and is not way of earth, but is the way of directing people."[77] Heaven—by which we should probably understand the natural world—is constant, and does not change depending on the actions of mankind. Xunzi noted that good humans often die young, while people who behave badly sometimes live to an old age, or that the good are as likely to be poor and the evil rich. In line with this, Xunzi criticized the widespread belief of the time that one could see future events in the signs of nature, such as eclipses and extreme weather conditions. Droughts or floods can affect states ruled by good rulers just as well as those ruled by evil rulers; the difference is that good rulers devote themselves to the tasks of government, setting aside rainy-day stores in anticipation of droughts to come, and strengthening dikes before the inevitable rains come causing the rivers to rise. Evil rulers, on the other hand, concern themselves with such destructive tools as weaponry or, worse still, with their own enrichment.

There is much more in the *Xunzi* that would be—and has been—of interest to philosophers and statesmen alike that cannot be explored in a brief biography such as this. Xunzi was surely shaped by the events of his day, but his teachings often seem to speak to the modern condition.

CHAPTER 51
BIOGRAPHIES OF LAOZI
AND ZHUANGZI

Laozi is the putative author of a text known either by his own name, i.e., *Laozi*, or as *The Classic of the Way and Virtue*. This text in some five thousand characters has served in turn as the most important source for the ancient worldview known as Daoism, *dao* being a word the primary meanings of which are a "way" (in the sense of a road) or "being on the way." Daoism is typically considered as complementary to Confucianism among native Chinese ways of thought, or as one of the three religions of later times in China (Buddhism joining Confucianism and Daoism during the middle ages). It is said that the *Laozi* has been translated more than any text other than the Christian *Bible*. Part of the reason for the hundreds of translations is because the text is very enigmatic, such that different interpretations are often possible.

According to the biography provided in *Records of the Historian*, Laozi, the name meaning "old son," is supposed to have been born in a village called Quren in Li prefecture of the southern state of Chu. His surname was Li, and his given name was Er ("ear"); his posthumous temple name was Dan. The only substantive thing that Sima Qian said of Laozi's life is that he was a secretary in the archives in the Zhou capital, and that he was an elder contemporary of Confucius, so that he would have been born in the sixth century. The biography includes a story, much repeated in other texts of the period, that Confucius once went to the Zhou capital to ask Laozi about ritual. Laozi responded to him:

> Those you talk about are all already dead and their bones have rotted. Only their sayings remain. What is more, if a gentleman meets with the times then he rides in a chariot; if he doesn't he just covers himself up and walks off. I have heard that a good merchant stores away his wares as if his store was empty, and that a gentleman of full virtue appears as if a fool. Get rid of your haughty airs and your many desires, your insinuating manners and your lustful ambitions; these have nothing of benefit to your person. What I have to tell you is this and nothing more.[78]

Figure 51.1 Han Dynasty wall carving depicting Confucius meeting Laozi; from *Jin shi suo* (1821).

After taking his leave from Laozi, Confucius is supposed to have said to his own disciples: "I know that birds can fly, fishes can swim, and beasts can run. What runs can be trapped, what swims can be netted, and what flies can be shot down. But as for dragons, I don't know how they ride up into the heavens on the wind and clouds. Today I have seen Laozi, who is just the same as a dragon!"[79]

The only other story about Laozi's life is that he is supposed to have decided to leave China to depart for the western regions. When he arrived at the pass, the Keeper of the Pass (*Guanyinzi*) asked him to write down his philosophy before he would be allowed to exit. Laozi is supposed to have written his book in one night, and to have departed the next day. According to even later traditions, he underwent various metamorphoses, one of which was to become the Buddha. Needless to say, all of this is legend without any historical basis. In fact, many historians argue that there was no such person as Laozi, whether named Li Er, Lao Dan, or any other name, and that the book *Laozi* is just a collection of sayings that was compiled over the course of the Warring States period.

There was great excitement in 1993 when three separate manuscripts dating to about 300 BCE were discovered at Guodian, Hubei, each containing portions of the received text of the *Laozi*. In China, this was generally regarded as proof of the antiquity of the text, confirming the tradition that Laozi lived at the time of Confucius (even if Confucius died almost two hundred years earlier). On the other hand, in the West many scholars view these manuscripts as evidence that even as late as 300 there was still no complete text of the *Laozi*, and that it did not achieve its final shape until sometime in the next century. Any conclusion to this debate will doubtless have to await still further archaeological discoveries.

The received text of the *Laozi* begins with one of the most famous passages of Chinese literature. It is usually translated more or less as follows:

The Way that can be told is not the eternal Way.
The name that can be named is not the eternal name.
The nameless is the origin of heaven and earth.
The named is the mother of the ten thousand things.[80]

This translation (which is consistent with most Chinese understandings of the text) introduces a paradox: if the Dao or Way that can be told of is not the eternal Way, why then does the book go on for 5,000 characters trying to tell of it? This too is probably a question better left to future discoveries.

The second great philosopher of Daoism was Zhuang Zhou, better known as Zhuangzi (*c.* 369–286). Little more is known about his life than is the case for Laozi. According to his biography in *Records of the Historian*, Zhuangzi was a native of Meng (near Dongming county in southwestern Shandong province) in the state of Song, where he served at some point as an officer in charge of the Lacquer Garden. He is supposed to have lived at the time of kings Hui of Liang (r. 369/334–319) and Xuan of Qi (r. 319–301), so that he would have been a contemporary of the Confucian philosopher Mencius (*c.* 385–303). Other information about his life derives from the book that he is supposed to have written, usually referred to as the *Zhuangzi*. It is clear from numerous anecdotes in the book that Zhuangzi was a contemporary of Hui Shi (Huizi; *c.* 370–310), another philosopher of the time who was famous for his logical paradoxes; the two men were close friends, even if they were often antagonists. For instance, one anecdote in the "Autumn Floods" chapter of the *Zhuangzi* recounts that when Hui Shi was serving as prime minister of the state of Wei (sometime shortly after 312), Zhuangzi set off to visit him. Someone else told Hui Shi that this was because Zhuangzi wanted to replace him as prime minister, causing Hui Shi to be agitated. When the two men finally met, Zhuangzi used a parable to explain that he wasn't the least bit interested in taking Hui Shi's position in government.

> In the south there is a bird called Yuanchu; do you know of it? The Yuanchu starts off from the South Sea and flies to the North Sea, along the way stopping on nothing but a catalpa tree, eating nothing but white bamboo, and drinking nothing but sweet spring water. Once just as the Yuanchu was passing by, there was an owl that had gotten a rotten rat and looked up at it and yelled: "Scat." Is it that you are now scatting me on account of your state of Wei?[81]

On another occasion, a king of Chu is said to have sent two officers to invite Zhuangzi to become prime minister of that state. They found Zhuangzi fishing in the Pu River. Without looking at them, Zhuangzi said:

> I hear that Chu has a sacred turtle that has already been dead for three thousand years. The king stores it in the ancestral temple, wrapped in silk and placed in a rattan hamper. Would this turtle rather be dead and have its bones venerated, or would it rather be alive and dragging its tail in the mud?[82]

When the two officers allowed as to how the turtle would rather be alive, Zhuangzi told them: "Go away, I'll just drag my tail in the mud."

Of course, neither of these anecdotes is necessarily true. It would be entirely in character for Zhuangzi to have made up the stories. Indeed, the last chapter of the *Zhuangzi* provides brief characterizations of many of the thinkers of his time, including also Zhuangzi himself.

> Murky and without form; transforming constantly: dead or alive? together with heaven and earth? moving with spiritual brightness? empty, going where? forgetful, off to where? The ten thousand things all caught up, none worth returning to—of old these were some of the techniques of the Way. Zhuang Zhou heard their airs and delighted in them. Using faulty reasoning, outlandish phrasing, and unbridled words, he often let loose without care for others, and viewed things from no particular angle. He considered all under heaven to be so

mixed up that he couldn't use straight talk with it, so he used goblet words as analogies, *double entendre* as truth, and fables to expand upon it. Alone, he came and went with the spirit of heaven and earth, but did not look down upon the ten thousand things, did not insist upon right or wrong, but lived with the customs of the world. Although his writings are but linked baubles and beads, they don't do any harm; and although his wording is all mixed up, there's something to be seen in it, full of stuff that doesn't let off. Above he roamed with the creator, and below he joined with those beyond life and death, taking as friends those for whom there is no end or beginning. With respect to the root of things, he opened it wide and spelled it out deeply; with respect to the ancestor, he can be said to have been well attuned, following it on high. Nevertheless, in responding to transformations and cutting himself off from things, his reasoning was not thorough and his travels were not unbaggaged; murky and miry, he didn't get everything.[83]

This passage was almost certainly not written by Zhuangzi himself, but it is not a bad characterization of his book, one that has come to be viewed as one of China's great masterpieces of both literature and philosophy.

CHAPTER 52
BIOGRAPHIES OF SUN WU AND SUN BIN

Sun Wu, better known as Sunzi or Master Sun (544–496), is one of the best known names from ancient China, but one whose life is least known. He is the supposed author of *The Art of War*, the most famous of all Chinese treatises on warfare, one that has influenced generals and statesmen of all later periods not only in China, but more recently, also throughout the rest of the world. Nevertheless, he was never mentioned in texts from his own lifetime, or even shortly thereafter, and certainly not by name. Indeed, it is not even certain that Wu, which means "military" or "martial," was actually his name, or if it was a kind of title ascribed to him because of his fame as a general. It is not known either when he was born, or even where he was born. All sources agree that he served at the court of King Helü of Wu (r. 514–496), and was instrumental in making that ruler of what had previously been a minor state on the periphery of Chinese civilization the Premier of all the states of the time. Probably for this reason, the *Springs and Autumns of Wu and Yue* says that he was born in the southern state of Wu, and spent his entire career there. On the other hand, his biography in *Records of the Historian* says without any further elaboration that he was from the northern state of Qi.

The biographies of Sunzi in both of these sources consist almost entirely of a single anecdote, which most historians regard, however, as apocryphal. The account in *Records of the Historian* is somewhat shorter; it reads:

Sunzi was a militarist, a man of Qi. He showed his *Art of War* to Helü, King of Wu. Helü said: "I have glanced over all thirteen chapters; can we have a little test of your training of troops?" He responded saying: "OK." Helü said: "Can we test it with women?" He said: "OK." With that it was approved that the beautiful women of the harem were brought out, 180 in all. Sunzi divided them into two brigades, making the king's two favorite consorts the brigade leaders. He commanded them all to take hold of halberds, and commanded them saying: "Do you know your heart and your left and right hands and your back?" The women said:

"We know them." Sunzi said: "At 'Forward,' then look to your heart; at 'Left,' look to your left hand; at 'Right,' look to your right hand; and at 'Rear,' look to your back." The women said: "Alright." The instructions having been given, he then set up the battle-axe of authority, and then gave the command three times and explained it five times. With that, he drummed them to the right, and the women all burst out laughing. Sunzi said: "If the instructions are not understood, and the commands not well practiced, this is the fault of the general." Again commanding them three times and explaining five times, he drummed them to the left; the women again burst out laughing. Sunzi said: "If the instructions are not understood, and the commands not well practiced, this is the fault of the general. But if they are already understood and you do not do as you should, this is the fault of the troops." Then he was about to behead the left and right brigade leaders. When the king of Wu watching from the platform saw that his beloved consorts were about to be beheaded, he was greatly alarmed, and hastily sent a messenger to give an order saying: "I already know that the general is capable of using troops. Without these two consorts, my food would no longer have any taste; please do not behead them." Sunzi said: "I have already been commanded to be the general. When the general is with the army, he need not accept commands from the ruler." Thereupon he beheaded them accordingly, and made the next in line as the brigade leaders. With that, he again drummed them. All of the women went left and right, forward and back, knelt and stood exactly according to the rules, none daring to make a sound. With that, Sunzi sent a messenger to report to the king saying: "The troops have been trained. If the king would like to see them tested further, however the king would like to use them, they would brave even water or fire." The King of Wu said: "You can stop now, I have no desire to watch any further." Sunzi said: "Milord only likes the theory, but isn't able to make use of the reality." With that, Helü knew that Sunzi was capable of using troops, and in the end made him general. To the west, they destroyed the mighty Chu, entering the capital Ying; to the north, they put fear into Qi and Jin, and made their names manifest to all the lords, Sunzi taking part in the strength.[84]

We can let pass whether this demonstration took place or not. The account does seem to be consistent with the view of the general as portrayed in *The Art of War*. The statement to King Helü that "Milord only likes the theory, but isn't able to make use of the reality," intemperate though it seems, may allude to Chapter Six of the *Art of War:* "Emptiness and Solidity." One precept in this chapter combines well theory and practice.

> The shape of the army resembles water: the motion of water avoids the high and rushes to the low; the victory of the army avoids the solid and strikes the empty. Water controls its motion according to the terrain, and armies control their victories according to the enemy. Therefore, armies have no fixed dynamic and no constant shape; when they are able to change according to the enemy to take the victory, they are termed divine. Therefore, the Five Stages have no constant victory and the Four Seasons have no constant position; days are shorter and longer, and months wax and wane.[85]

The notion here of changing according to the circumstances is reminiscent of the philosophy seen in the *Laozi,* and for this reason *The Art of War* is often regarded as having Daoist influences.

The coda to Sunzi's biography in *Records of the Historian* alludes briefly to the great successes won by the Wu armies under the leadership of King Helü and Sunzi: defeating the great southern state of Chu and occupying its capital, which they did in 506. According to the *Springs and Autumns of Wu and Yue,* Sunzi commanded the Wu army at the decisive battle of Boju, when the Chu army was smashed, though a detailed account of the battle in the *Zuo Tradition,* the earliest and most authoritative history of the period, does not mention his name. As for "putting fear into Qi and and Jin," this would seem to allude to the success of King Fuchai of Wu (r. 495–473), the son of King Helü. It was Fuchai who turned Wu's attention to the northern states, succeeding in being recognized as Premier by all of the northern states at the conference of Huangchi in 482. Although some later sources suggest that Sunzi served King Fuchai, since he is not mentioned together with Fuchai in any of the standard historical sources, his date of death is routinely given as 496, the year in which King Helü died.

Of the many figures from ancient China credited with being great generals and especially with writing treatises on warfare, there is another Sun: Sun Bin (382–316), whose name "Bin" means "Kneecap." Whereas almost nothing is known about Sunzi's life, quite a bit is known about Sun Bin's life. Sun Bin was a native of the northern state of Qi and, according to *Records of the Historian,* he was a descendant of the great Sun Wu; this doubtless explains why that text says that Sunzi was also born in Qi. Sun Bin is supposed to have studied military strategy with the shadowy figure known as Guiguzi ("The Master of Ghost Valley"), the supposed author of a book by the same name that is one of the earliest Chinese writings on diplomacy. He is also said to have memorized Sunzi's *Art of War*. Among many notable students of Guiguzi, another figure who would become a general and whose life would be intertwined with that of Sun Bin was Pang Juan (385–342). Sun Bin and Pang Juan were close friends while they were classmates, but Pang Juan subsequently became jealous of Sun Bin's abilities. Later, when Pang Juan gained early success while serving under Lord Hui of Wei (r. 369/334–319), the greatest ruler of the time, he encouraged Sun Bin to come to Wei as well. However, after Sun Bin arrived, he was accused of treason, apparently instigated by none other than Pang Juan. The standard punishment for treason would have been execution, but in Sun Bin's case it was commuted to branding of the face and removal of the kneecap. After further travails in Wei, Sun Bin managed to escape and return to Qi, where he became a deputy to the general Tian Ji (fl. 354–333).

The fortunes of Sun Bin and Pang Juan would intersect twice in the middle of the fourth century. In both cases, Sun Bin would get much the better of his one-time classmate. In 354, a Wei army led by Pang Juan attacked the state of Zhao, besieging the Zhao capital of Handan (in present-day Hebei province). When Zhao sought relief from Qi, Sun Bin proposed a roundabout strategy of first attacking the Wei capital of Daliang (at present-day Kaifeng, Henan). Then, when the Wei army under Pang Juan broke off the siege of Handan to return to rescue Daliang, the Qi army ambushed them, winning a major victory at the battle of Guiling. Twelve years later, King Hui of Wei again sent Pang Juan on campaign, this time against the state of Han. Han too requested that Qi come to its aid, which it again did with an army under the combined leadership of Tian Ji and Sun Bin. Again employing a ruse, the Qi army feigned a direct attack against the Wei army, but then quickly withdrew behind a narrow valley. When the Wei army pursued, Qi fell upon them, inflicting a crushing defeat; Pang Juan committed suicide rather than be captured. This was the battle of Maling (in present-day Shenxian county, Henan), one of the most famous battles of the Warring States period; the state of Wei never really recovered from its defeat.

Despite winning a great victory, both Tian Ji and Sun Bin were apprehensive about returning to Qi, fearful that their enhanced reputations would bring about their downfall. Instead, they both went south, literally, to the state of Chu, where King Xuan of Chu (r. 369–340) installed Tian Ji as the lord of Jiangnan (the area to the south of the Yangzi River). Sun Bin, for his part, remained in Chu for more than twenty years, returning to Qi only in the last two or three years of his life, when he was hosted by King Xuan of Qi (r. 319–301). Despite having witnessed great violence during his lifetime, he seems to have died in peace.

Probably sometime after winning his great victory at the battle of Maling, Sun Bin wrote his own "art of war" book. *The Art of War of Sun Bin* is included in the Han-dynasty *History of Han* bibliography of the contents of the Han imperial library, described as being in eighty-nine chapters. The book was often quoted in medieval sources but was lost sometime before the beginning of the Tang dynasty (618–908 CE). This caused many historians to assume that the book never really existed, mentions of it mistakenly referring to Sunzi's *Art of War*. Then in April, 1972, archaeologists opened a Han-dynasty tomb at Yinqueshan, Linyi, Shandong, and in it found not only an almost complete text of *The Art of War* of Sunzi, but also fragments from sixteen different chapters of *The Art of War of Sun Bin*. It did exist after all.

丙
辰

CHAPTER 53
BIOGRAPHY OF SHANG YANG

Wei Yang or Gongsun Yang, better known as Shang Yang (*c.* 390–338), is often regarded as the architect of the traditional Chinese bureaucratic state. He was a nobleman of the small state of Wèi 衛 in the center of the north China plain, but made his name in the western state of Qin, where he served as the prime minister under Duke Xiao (r. 361–338). His reforms there touched on virtually every aspect of governance: land reform, the military, administration, law, taxation, and even weights and measures. Just before the end of his life, he personally led a Qin attack on the state of Wei 魏 (different from the state in which he was born, but where he had previously served), winning a great victory, for which Duke Xiao awarded him fifteen cities in Shang; it is for this reason that he came to be known as "the Lord of Shang" or simply "Lord Shang." He is credited with writing the book *The Book of Lord Shang*, which is usually regarded as one of the founding texts of the political philosophy known as Legalism. Despite his great accomplishments, Shang Yang made powerful enemies among the nobility of Qin, and did not long outlive his patron Duke Xiao.

As a native of Wèi, Shang Yang would have been familiar with the government and military reforms initiated there by Wu Qi (440–381) just decades earlier. As a young man still in his twenties, he came to the attention of Gongshu Cuo (d. 360), the prime minister of Wei, who induced him to move to that state. However, the ruler of the state, Lord Hui of Wei (r. 369/334–319), rejected repeated advice to give Shang Yang a position of responsibility, regarding him as too young. Gongshu Cuo is reported to have warned the lord—quite presciently—either to employ him or to kill him, that if he allowed him to serve another state it would certainly be to the detriment of Wei. During his short time in Wei, Shang Yang became aware of the thorough-going government reforms introduced there by Li Kui (455–395). When Duke Xiao of Qin succeeded in that western state and announced that he was seeking worthy advisers wherever they may be found, presumably as part of his desire to strengthen the position of the ruler vis-à-vis the nobility of the state, Shang Yang moved yet again, taking with him a copy of

Li Kui's *Classic of Law.*

Within just two years, Shang Yang began to implement his reforms, taking as his guiding principle that no single principle is always and everywhere effective; as the times change and new problems emerge, the policies used to address them need to evolve. In practical terms, he began with the first of what he called the two "handles" of government: agriculture (the other being the military). To strengthen agriculture, the entire population was registered, and no one was permitted to move off the land; people from other states were actively encouraged to migrate to Qin, so long as they were willing to work the land. Merchants were forbidden to sell grain, though they were employed as middlemen to handle the grain supplies for the army, for which purpose he standardized the size of carts carrying the grain. Most other mercantile enterprises were suppressed. Taxes on the goods that were permitted to be sold were raised dramatically. The nobility too saw their land taxes increased, and for the first time they were required to contribute labor to the state. Intellectuals were forbidden to engage in debates or otherwise to broadcast their views to the common people, who were likewise discouraged from attaining an education, on the grounds that it would distract them from their main responsibility. Nevertheless, he decreed that all people were equal under the law, including even the nobility, and the intellectuals.

Three years later, in 356, Shang Yang was appointed Assistant Head of the Multitudes, a part of a strict twenty-rank ranking system for all individuals that the state of Qin adopted at this time. Among the reforms that he instituted at this time was to systematize the former city and county structures, such that the populace was organized into affinity groups of five, ten, and fifty households. If any single individual committed a crime, the entire group was responsible for reporting the infraction; whoever reported such a crime would be rewarded by having his rank elevated. On the other hand, the property of the criminal would be confiscated and shared with the other members of the group. The military was organized in a similar fashion, first with units of five soldiers and then larger regiments of one hundred soldiers, all with shared responsibility. If any single soldier deserted, the other four members of the unit would be equally liable. On the other hand, the units and regiments would share in rewards for meritorious service: for instance, if any single soldier killed thirty-three enemy soldiers, the entire unit would have its rank raised by one grade. One of the responsibilities of the generals was to perform an after-battle investigation to evaluate the performance of each soldier, each unit, and each regiment, so as to determine rewards and punishments. Noble families without military accomplishments would be stripped of their noble perquisites; on the other hand, common soldiers could earn those sorts of perquisites on the battlefield. Soldiers who were killed in battle would have their rank passed on to their descendants.

Laws of inheritance also saw a general reform at this time, with important implications for the economy of the state. Families were recognized as independent units, but property was inherited equally by all male members. This was designed to break up the great extended families, whose power in the past rivaled that even of the state. Indeed, another reform was to outlaw all private militias and all fighting not specifically sanctioned by the state. These reforms initially met with resistance on the part of both the common people and especially of the nobility. However, public order was soon stabilized within the country as no one dared to break the law, while externally Qin grew stronger and stronger.

In 350, Shang Yang oversaw the building of a new capital for the state. Prior to this time, the capital of Qin had been at Yueyang, on the second-level plateau north of the Wei River near modern-day Baoji, Shaanxi. The new capital was located about one hundred kilometers to the east, on the north bank of the Wei River, just across the Wei River from the old Zhou capital. Designed according to the temple system in use in the old Zhou states of Lu and Wèi, this relocation of the capital simultaneously weakened the authority of the old nobility of the state, and also explicitly announced Qin's imperial intentions. In just one decade, through the reforms of Duke Xiao and Shang Yang, Qin had been rejuvenated, and King Xian of Zhou (r. 368–321) recognized Duke Xiao as Premier of the leaders of all the states.

In conjunction with the move to the new capital, Shang Yang promulgated a new series of reforms, which included the standardization of land parcels and taxes. Land was divided into separate rectangles 240 paces long. This was apparently the size of land that could be worked by a single adult male, which was consistent with the preceding change in inheritance laws encouraging small nuclear families. Also at this time, the previous system of counties was extended to the entire state, now with forty-one counties in all, each of which was administered by a governor and a general, all directly responsible to the central government. This would eventually be adapted by the First Emperor of Qin (r. 246/221–210), after his unification of all of the other states.

The lengthy reign of Duke Xiao of Qin came to an end in 338, when he died of illness. There is at least one report that before he died, Duke Xiao proposed that he be succeeded by none other than Shang Yang, but that Shang Yang declined this honor. Despite this, without his ruling patron,

Shang Yang's fortunes quickly changed dramatically. He knew that he had made many powerful enemies. Shortly after his first set of reforms was set in place, in 356, the state's crown prince Si, later to be known as Lord Huiwen (r. 337–324) and then as King Huiwen (r. 324–311), had broken one of the new laws. Since it was not possible to inflict corporal punishment on the crown prince, Shang Yang decided that his tutors should be held responsible for his conduct. He fined the ducal tutor Prince Qian and branded his teacher Gongsun Jia. Somewhat later, Prince Qian was again found guilty of yet another infraction, and was punished by having his nose amputated. Added to the personal enmity created by these decisions, Shang Yang's policies of breaking up the noble families had turned them against him. For that reason, after Duke Xiao's death, Shang Yang attempted to flee the country. According to one story, he was refused refuge at an inn because he did not have a proper registry identification, one of the laws that he had been responsible for establishing. Whatever the case, Lord Huiwen sent troops after him, and he was killed in battle. His corpse was returned to the capital Xianyang, where it was torn apart by five chariots, and his family was exterminated to the ninth degree.

Despite this unhappy end to his life, the legacy of Shang Yang has lived on in the bureaucratic state that has characterized China since his time. It still lives today.

CHAPTER 54
BIOGRAPHY OF SHAO TUO

Shao Tuo (d. 316), was an important court officer in the state of Chu, bearing the title Lieutenant. During his life he was responsible for economic and judicial affairs of the Chu capital area, creating quite a number of written records concerning the civil administration and court cases over which he presided. There are also records of divinations and prayers concerning his personal life. However, neither he nor any of these records were ever mentioned in any of ancient China's traditional literature. Were it not for the discovery of his tomb in the winter of 1986–1987, Shao Tuo would have remained totally unknown to history. The tomb was discovered in a cemetery at Baoshan, Jingmen, Hubei, just outside of the site of Ying, the capital of Chu. Fortunately, it was excavated by archaeologists prior to the great spate of tomb robbing that has cursed China since the 1990s. Thus, the tomb was preserved intact; in addition to a full inventory of grave goods, the tomb also included the first significant discovery of bamboo-strip documents dating to the Warring States period. It was these documents, taken to the grave with Shao Tuo, that documented his life.

Shao Tuo was a descendant of King Zhao of Chu (r. 515–489) and so was a nobleman of that state. His tomb was certainly fitting for someone of noble heritage. Situated in the middle of the Baoshan cemetery, it was flanked on either side by the tombs of his wife and certain male relatives. His body was wrapped in three layers of fine clothing, and then placed inside three nested coffins, ornamented with interlaced dragons and each draped in silks. These coffins were placed in turn inside two outer coffins, essentially a subterranean house. The tomb was divided into four compartments or chambers, one for each of the four cardinal directions. This outer coffin was covered in six layers of different-colored clay, while under the coffins was a pit with a sacrificed goat; this doubtless was intended to ensure good luck for the burial, the word for goat, *yang*, being close in sound with the word "auspicious" (*xiang*), and being part of the character used to write that word.

Even more impressive than the tomb itself were the lavish grave goods found inside it. There were different sorts of goods in each of the four compartments that surrounded the coffins. The eastern compartment, above where the head of Shao Tuo was located, was the Dining Room, holding sacrificial food offerings packed in baskets; although most of the foods had decomposed, an inventory written on bamboo strips that was placed in the tomb records at least the following foods: water chestnuts, chestnuts, dates, pears, persimmons, ginger, lotus root, onions, pepper seeds. There were also meats: chicken and pork, as well as a whole ox that had been cut into pieces. In addition to these foodstuffs, there were a great many bronze sacrificial vessels, including eighteen bronze caldrons, as well as actual musical instruments. Also found in this compartment were wooden figurines symbolizing servants and perhaps also the musicians to play the instruments. Moving clockwise around the tomb, the southern compartment was the armory, filled with numerous weapons and pieces of a chariot that had been dismantled. The western compartment had items for daily use, including furniture, clothing, tools, and blank bamboo strips. Finally, the northern compartment seems to have been intended to serve as Shao Tuo's office. It had all of the accouterments necessary for his professional life: a writing table, a writing brush, and a scholar's knife used to correct writing mistakes (by paring off the top layer of a strip of bamboo). There was also a bronze lamp, combs, and personal ornaments, as well as two wooden figurines, presumably representing his official servants. Most important for historians, it was in this chamber that 249 bamboo strips documenting Shao Tuo's life were found. 196 of these strips record official business over which he presided, including especially law cases, and thus provide rare information about the history of law in ancient China. However, there is also a considerable corpus, fifty-three strips, that record divinations that were performed and prayers that were offered on behalf of Shao Tuo during the last years of his life. Most of these divinations used turtle shells, though some of them used a method of milfoil divination more or less similar to that of the *Classic of Changes*. These are of particular interest to scholars of Chinese religion and philosophy.

The documents buried together with Shao Tuo provide the only information concerning his life. The documents concerning his official duties make up the bulk of the bamboo strips buried in the northern chamber of the tomb. These are divided into four different named categories: Collected Registries, Suits Based on Collected Registries, Assigned Dates, and Minutes of Court Cases; there are also a number of records without a named topic. The first two named categories concern the population records for which Shao Tuo, as a civil administrator, was responsible; all inhabitants of the region regardless of social rank were required to be registered, presumably for tax and corvee labor obligations. The Assigned Dates category provides detailed diary entries for where and when court cases were handled, and who was responsible for them; these mention in passing some aspects of these cases: police investigations, filings of reports, and records of fines paid.

Interesting as the first three categories of records are, it is the fourth category, Minutes of Court Cases, that provides the most information about Chu criminal justice and Shao Tuo's responsibilities in it. Some of these involve cases between two different parties of the populace, others complaints against the government (for unfair taxation, for instance). One of the simplest records reads:

> Jing De brought suit against Gong Qiu and Gong You, men of the southern district of Fan Mound, saying that they had killed his elder brother. On *jiachen* (day 21) of the ninth month, Yuan Xiu and Xin Yin, the minor detectives of Fan Mound returned the investigation, which said: The southern district of Fan Mound really did have a Gong You, but in the year that Gangu You became an officer in Xi, and now lives in ... district, except that Fanchang does not have a Gong Qiu. Secretary Qi recorded it, Dan Shang was witness.[86]

Although unusually for these official documents, this one does not begin with a formal date, it does include basic information: the name of the plaintive, the names and hometowns of the defendants, the report of the investigation, and the names of the officers who recorded and witnessed the report. Unfortunately, it does not tell us what role Shao Tuo played, but presumably he was in charge of adjudicating the case.

There is a smaller, but by no means insubstantial, number of strips that record divinations performed on behalf of Shao Tuo. These are of two types: more or less *pro forma* divinations praying for the success of his official service, and divinations, largely done over the last three years of his life, concerning his health. They begin with a date, noted as some great event in the history of the state (as if an American record were to say "In the year that Neil Armstrong walked on the moon" [i.e., 1969] or "In the year that President Nixon visited China" [i.e., 1972]). The dates show that the divinations about Shao Tuo's health became increasingly urgent in the last year of his life, when it was clear that he was dying. Almost all of these divinations involved two stages: an initial stage announcing the topic, the prognostication of which usually indicated some problem needing propitiation, and then a record of offerings to various spirits, and a further prognostication, suggesting that the propitiation had been successful. The following record is one such example.

> In the year that the Song emissary Sheng Gong Bian visited Chu (i.e., 318), on the *yiwei* day of the Jingyi month (first month of summer), Shi Beishang used the Instructing Turtle to affirm on behalf of Shao Yin Tuo: "From the Jingyi month until the next Jingyi month, throughout the entire year, would that his person have no trouble." Prognosticating it: "The long-term affirmation is auspicious, but there is a little external concern, and the intention and the affair will be obtained a little slowly." For this reason they exorcised it, praying to King Zhao with a specially-raised ox, and offering it; praying to Wenping Yejun, Wu Gongzi Chun, Marshall Ziyin, and Cai Gongzi Jia, each with a specially-raised piglet and wine and food; and praying to the wife with a specially-raised pig: "If the intention and the affair are quickly gotten, all will be quickly reciprocated." Prognosticating it: "Auspicious. Offering in the Xiayi month there will be joy."[87]

The divinations about Shao Tuo's health follow the same general format. The first of the following two examples was apparently performed using a sort of sortilege divination, of the kind known from the *Classic Changes* tradition. The result was announced as two sets of six numbers, akin to the hexagrams of the *Classic Changes*.

> In the year that the Great Marshall Dao Hua led the army of Chu to relieve Fu (i.e., 316), on the day *jimao* day of the Jingyi month (first month of summer), Chen Yi used Proffered Command to affirm on behalf of Commander of the Left Tuo: "Having had a sick stomach and heart, with breath rising and lack of appetite, would that it quickly improve and that there not be any hex." 1-6-6-1-1-1 1-6-6-6-6-1 Prognosticating it: "The long-term affirmation is auspicious, but the sickness has changed for the worse, there is a continuation and it will be slow to improve." For this reason they exorcised it, offering prayer to the Five Mountains: each one sheep; offering prayer to King Zhao: a specially-raised ox, presenting it; offering prayer to Wenping Xia Junzi Liang, to Wu Gongzi Chun, to Marshall Ziyin and to Caigong Zijia: each one specially-raised pig, presenting them. "May it attack and

dispel with respect to the ancestors and those who have died in battle."
Transferring Yan Ji's exorcism, making offering at the High Mound
and Lower Mound of the structure: each one whole pig. Chen Yi
prognosticated it, saying: "Auspicious."[88]

The final example seems to have come just before Shao Tuo's death. One
month later, no longer worrying about whether there was a hex or curse on
him, the initial divination simply prays that he not die. The curse is difficult
to understand, but it certainly required propitiation.

> In the year that the Great Marshall Dao Hua led the army of Chu to
> relieve Fu (i.e., 316), on the *jihai* day of the Xiayi month (the second
> month of summer), Guan Yi used Protect the Family (turtle-shell) to
> affirm on behalf of Commander of the Left Shao Tuo: "Given that he
> has ulcerous lesions and rising breath, would that he not die." Yi
> prognosticated it: "The long-term affirmation is auspicious, he will not
> die. There is a curse, visible in Continue Without Heirs and Gradual
> Tree Planting; for this reason dispel it." They offered to each of
> Continue Without Heirs a fattened pig, presenting them, and
> commanded to attack and dispel it with respect to Gradual Tree
> Planting; suppress the tail of its place and stop it; would that it be
> auspicious. Yi prognosticated it and said: "Auspicious. I do not know
> the name of its region."[89]

Even though the second-stage prognostication was optimistic, the lack of
any further divinations on his behalf suggests that Shao Tuo did in fact die
shortly after this day.

Although Shao Tuo has been unknown throughout China's long history,
it seems proper given both what he did in life and also based on what his
family provided for him in death that his biography, sketchy as it necessarily
is, be included in this brief history of ancient China. It tells us much about
the administration of justice in Chu and about the practice of divination,
and even something about notions of medicine at the time.

CHAPTER 55
BIOGRAPHY OF BIAN QUE

Qin Yueren, also known as the Physician from Lu, but best known as Bian Que (d. 310), was the most famous medical doctor of ancient China. It is likely that the name Bian Que referred to some medical technique (perhaps alluding to the scalpel used in surgery), and thus was a general term for excellent physicians; the "Biography of Bian Que" chapter of *Records of the Historian* recounts events from the seventh century through the early fourth century, and anecdotes in other sources would extend this to still earlier and still later times. In one story that would date to the seventh century, he is said to have been traveling through the state of Guo, near the great bend of the Yellow River at present-day Sanmenxia, Henan, when he saw the people mourning the death of the crown prince; he diagnosed the condition not as death, but as "corpse stumbling," a condition that he was able to reverse by rechanneling the yin and yang within the boy's body. This of course not only earned Bian Que the gratitude of the ruler of Guo, but also made him famous throughout all of the states. It is also unclear where he may have been from, suggesting that he was an itinerant doctor who traveled from state to state. During these travels, he was something of a shape-shifter, a specialist in gynecology in one state, in geriatrics in another, and pediatrics in yet another. Everywhere he went, he is said to have had an almost clairvoyant ability to detect illness, apparently through his ability to read a person's pulse. Indeed, the school of medicine that subsequently assumed his name was most associated with the diagnosis of pulse and the meridians or channels within the body, which has always been a fundamental skill of traditional Chinese medicine. He is credited with the authorship of the *Classic of Difficult Cases*, which is supposed to have been a direct precursor to the famous *Inner Classic of the Yellow Emperor*. All of this is but part of the legend of Bian Que. It seems likely that the historical figure most likely to have been given this name lived through most of the fourth century. In the latest account in which he figures, he cured King Wu of Qin (r. 310–307). However, in doing so, he angered the king's counsellors, and especially the court physician.

According to this account, Li Xi, that court physician, was jealous of Bian Que's skills and had him assassinated. This is probably as close to history as we are likely to get in the difficult case of Bian Que.

According to his biography in *Records of the Historian*, an elderly traveler named Lord Long Mulberry (Chang Sang jun), said elsewhere to have been a teacher of the famous Daoist writer Zhuangzi (*c.* 369–286), gave medicines to Bian Que and taught him how to use them, recognizing the potential in him to be an excellent doctor. The biography continues that after Bian Que prepared these medicines and ingested them for thirty days, he developed a sort of X-ray vision, able to see the condition of people's internal organs (and even able to see through a stone wall) just by looking at them. Most likely, this referred to his ability to understand people's health on the basis of their pulse. Another story about him also anticipates one of the miracles of modern medicine. The *Liezi*, traditionally regarded as the third of the great Daoist texts, but one that was surely written retrospectively in the early centuries of the common era, tells the story of a double heart transplant that Bian Que is supposed to have performed.

The two men Gong Hu of Lu and Qi Ying of Zhao were both ill, and both visited Bian Que to seek treatment. Bian Que treated them and they both got better. He said to Gong Hu and Qi Ying: "The illnesses that you suffered from before had entered from outside and were lodged in the internal organs and so could be treated with herbs and acupuncture. However, you now have congenital illnesses, that have increased as you have aged; how about if I cure you of them?" The two men said: "Could we first hear of the symptoms?" Bian Que said to Gong Hu: "Your will is strong but your *qi* is weak; it is enough to make plans but too little to finish them. Qi Ying's will is weak but his *qi* is strong; therefore he plans too little and harms himself in being too focused. If I switch your hearts then it will even out the strengths." Bian Que then gave the two men an anaesthetic liquor to drink, and both fell into a coma for three days. He opened their chests and took their hearts, switched them and replaced them. Giving them a spiritual drug, they awoke and were like new. The two men said their goodbyes. Gong Hu returned to Qi Ying's house and hugged his wife and children, but they did not recognize him. Qi Ying likewise returned to Gong Hu's house, hugged his wife and children, and they too did not recognize him. Because of this the two families sued each other, and sought testimony from Bian Que. Bian Que explained what had happened and the suit was brought to a close.[90]

This story probably says more about notions of psychology than of physiology. In fact, much of early Chinese medical theory is based on a correlation between psychological health and physical health. Much of this correlation is expressed in terms of *qi*, a term with a broad range of meanings. It originally referred to the steam that rises from cooked food (and, indeed, there has also long been a connection drawn between food and health) or to the vapor that is visible in the sky. However, within the body, it refers, on the one hand, to breath, and on the other to energy, both psychic and emotional. Keeping the *qi* harmonized was basic to maintaining health. For example, the *Pulling Scripture*, found in 1983 in an early Han-dynasty tomb at Zhangjiashan, Jiangling, Hubei, but certainly deriving from notions of medicine current during the time of Bian Que, states:

> The reason that noblemen become ill is that their joy and anger are not harmonized. When they are joyful, their yang *qi* is plentiful; when they are angry, their yin *qi* is plentiful. This is why those who cultivate themselves quickly inhale when they are pleased, and suddenly exhale when they are angry in order to harmonize them. By sucking in the essence and vapor of heaven and earth, they can solidify their yin, and therefore can be without illness.[91]

Similarly, the "Inner Patrimony" chapter of the *Guanzi*, a kind of meditation manual that dates to the Warring States period, also advises the need for the emotions and the *qi* to be "settled."

> Settle the heart within: the ears and eyes will be acute and perceptive, and the four limbs will be sturdy. They will be the abode of the seminal essence. Semen is the coagulation of *qi*.[92]

Probably the most famous story about Bian Que concerns his visitations with Duke Huan of Tian Qi (r. 374–357; not to be confused with the earlier Duke Huan of Jiang Qi [r. 685–643]). Employed as court physician, Bian Que told the duke that he had a disease just under the skin that, if not treated promptly, would surely become more serious; the duke dismissed this diagnosis, saying that he was perfectly healthy, and suspecting that Bian Que was inventing this illness as a way of earning profit from it. Five days later, Bian Que informed him that the disease had progressed to his circulatory system; again the duke rejected the diagnosis. Five days later, Bian Que said that the disease had reached the digestive tract, but again the duke rejected this. Five days later still, Bian Que examined the duke, but withdrew without a word. The duke sent someone to ask why he now had no diagnosis. Bian Que responded:

> When an illness resides just under the skin, it can be reached with warm presses; when it is in the blood system, acupuncture needles can reach it; when it is in the intestines, medicines can reach it; but when it is in the bone marrow, even the God of Fate can do nothing about it. Now, your illness is in the bone marrow; that is why I did not seek to treat it.[93]

As the story goes, five days later, Duke Huan became ill. He sent someone to summon Bian Que, but Bian Que had already left the state, and Duke Huan died. This is usually understood as speaking to the need for early treatment and preventive medicine. However, in another story, not included in his biography, Bian Que claims that it was his older brothers who were truly skilled in this art, not he. The book *Pheasant-Cap Master* recounts that Bian Que had audience with Lord Wen of Wei (r. 445–396), who asked him which of the three brothers in his family was the best doctor. Bian Que responded: "My oldest brother is the best, the middle brother next, while I am the least." When Lord Wen pressed him on this, Bian Que explained:

> My eldest brother can see the spirit; before an illness has formed, he gets rid of it. Thus, his fame has never gone beyond the family. My middle brother cures the illness when it is visible on the surface. Thus, his fame has not gone beyond the village. As for me, when it is in the blood system, I use medicines or cut beneath the skin, and for that I have become famous among the many lords.[94]

In fact, Bian Que did become famous among the many lords, his name now synonymous with medicine. Even today, the highest compliment that can be paid to a Chinese doctor is to call him a "living Bian Que."

CHAPTER 56
BIOGRAPHIES OF QU YUAN AND SONG YU

Qu Yuan, originally named Qu Ping, was the scion of a noble family of the state of Chu, and served at the court of King Huai of Chu (r. 328–299) as "Great Officer of the Three Wards," taking part in debates before the king and engaging in diplomacy with foreign visitors. However, according to his biography in *Records of the Historian*, Qu Yuan was the target of jealousy and slander at court, such that King Huai came to have suspicions about him. Sad that the king should so easily discount his talents and contributions, he composed the poem "Encountering Sorrow" to express his thoughts, and then afterward committed suicide by drowning himself in the Miluo River.

In 313, Chu was caught up in an inter-state intrigue involving most of the major states of the time. At that time, the western state of Qin was planning to attack the northeastern state of Qi, which was then allied with Chu. Prior to launching its attack, Qin feared that Chu would come to its ally's defense. Therefore, it sent the famous adviser and strategist Zhang Yi (d. 309) to go to Chu and promise King Huai that if Chu would not go to the aid of Qi, Qin would cede to it 600 *li* of territory. When Chu did in fact break its alliance with Qi and asked for the promised territory, Zhang Yi then claimed that he had said 6 *li* of territory, not 600. Double-crossed, King Huai sent an army to attack Qin, but the Chu army suffered a serious defeat at Danyang, in present-day northwestern Hubei province. King Huai then mobilized the entire state to invade Qin, reaching as far as Lantian, just to the east of modern Xi'an and the site where the First Emperor of Qin (r. 246/221–210) would eventually be buried together with the famous terracotta warriors. With the Chu army out of the country, the state of Wei took the opportunity to invade Chu, reaching as far as Deng in central Henan. The Chu attacking Qin had to withdraw to meet this threat, especially since its erstwhile ally Qi refused to come to its aid. Throughout these events, Qu Yuan was an outside observer, having been sent away from his home state to serve as a Chu ambassador in Qi.

Some ten years later, another inter-state intrigue took place again involving Chu and Qin, but this time as ostensible allies. King Zhao of Qin (r. 306–251) invited King Huai to a wedding ceremony in Qin. Qu Yuan, who had since returned to Chu, urged him not to go, arguing that Qin was never to be trusted, saying "Qin is a kingdom of tigers and wolves, and is untrustworthy." King Huai refused to accept his advice. When he arrived in Qin, he was detained there and asked to make territorial concessions to Qin. He refused and eventually died in captivity in Qin.

Regarding Qu Yuan himself, most of what can be said derives from his own writing—or at least from the author of the poem "Encountering Sorrow," which is included in the *Verses of Chu.* "Encountering Sorrow" opens with a sort of autobiographical statement, suggesting that Qu Yuan was not only high born, but also very satisfied with himself.

Descendant of Thearch Gao Yang, My august father was named Bo Yong.

The calendar pointed at the first month of the year, It was on *gengyin* that I descended.

The August Surveyor took my first measure, Awarding me a fine name.

Naming me Upright Model, Nicknaming me Numinous Balance.

Having bequeathed me this inner beauty, He added to it refinement and ability.[95]

The poem is far too long to quote in its entirety. The following two sections give some sense of the contents. The first speaks of Qu Yuan's situation at court, and his looking to the past for his moral norms. Peng and Xian were two famous ancient magicians—usually referred to as shamans. Because of this, "Encountering Sorrow" is often regarded as a poem about a shamanic spirit flight, perhaps even one taken under the influence of some hallucinogenic drug. While such drugs were certainly used in ancient China, it seems possible also to read the poem as a political metaphor.

Truly I have modeled myself on those in the past who were refined, Not what the vulgar of the world admire.

I am not at one with the people of today, Preferring to rely on the norms passed down by Peng and Xian.

Long do I sigh and brush away my tears, Sorry for the many troubles the people have in life.

Although I love to get made up I took on bit and bridle, Cursed by morning and replaced at night.

They replaced me for wrapping myself in orchids, Which I extended with angelica.

It being indeed the love of my heart, Even if I were to die nine times I'd have no regrets.

I resent the Numinous Refiner's excessiveness, In the end not taking account of the people's hearts.

The many women envy me my moth eyebrows, Singing satires that I am good at sex.

Certainly this is a trick of the times, Turning the straight and narrow on their head.

Turning their backs on the plumb-line to chase the crooked, Competing in beauty as their measure.

Bereft and in despair, I am alone and exhausted, bound to these times.

I would rather drown and float away, Unable am I to bear this attitude.

That raptors don't flock together, Has been a certainty since early times.

How can you fit a square peg into a round hole, How can you be content with those holding to a different path!

Bending one's heart and repressing one's ambition, Bearing the hurts and accepting the insults,

Bowing down to the clear and white to die for what is right, Is certainly what the ancient sages held dear.[96]

The second passage to consider, the very end of the poem, describes a little of his flight—certainly an imaginary flight on dragon-borne chariots— seeking a place where he might fit in, but concludes with his uncertainty about leaving home.

In the morning I set out for the Heavenly Ford, In the evening arriving at the Western Limit.

With phoenix wings the supporting flags, High we soared row upon row.

Suddenly I traveled over these Flowing Sands, Following the Red River and idled there.

Waving to the water dragons to bridge the ford, I summoned the Western August One to take me across.

The road being long with many difficulties, I roused the host of chariots and had them wait by the path:

Passing by Incomplete Mountain and turning left, I pointed out the Western Sea as where we would meet.

I massed my chariots a thousand teams, Jade axles racing forward in a line,

I hitched the eight dragons bobbing and weaving, Riding the sinews of the cloud flags.

Repressing my will to slow down, My spirit raced high into the distance.

Singing the *Nine Songs* and dancing the *Shao*, I approached the sun joyously.

Rising up to the climax of the performance, Suddenly I looked down upon my old hometown.

The driver was sad and my horses sensed it, Twisting their necks they would not go on.

The coda says: Enough already!

The state is without men yet no one recognizes me, So why should I feel for my former city!

Not enough here for a beautiful government, I'll go along to the home of Peng and Xian.[97]

With his one-time patron, and sometime critic, King Huai dying in Qin, Qu Yuan apparently had no road forward in his home state of Chu. According to at least one source, in the third year of King Huai's successor, King Qingxiang (r. 298–265; i.e., 296), Qu Yuan threw himself into the Miluo River, becoming in that act one of the most famous suicides in Chinese history.

Qu Yuan's most famous disciple, or perhaps just imitator, was Song Yu. His dates are unknown, but the biography of Qu Yuan in *Records of the Historian* places him after the death of Qu Yuan, and some sources show him as active during the reign of King Qingxiang; i.e., the first half of the third century. At least two of the poems included in the collection *Verses of Chu* are credited to Song Yu: the "Nine Discriminations" and "Summoning the Soul," and his name is often mentioned together with that of Qu Yuan as "Qu and Song." Several of the poems credited to him have some context attributed to their writing, showing that Song Yu, like Qu Yuan before him, was the victim of court intrigue. It seems that he was extremely handsome, making him the victim of considerable jealousy. One of the poems credited to him, "Criticism

Rhymeprose," has a colophon that states that Tang Le, another of the poets of the time often mentioned together with Song Yu as followers of Qu Yuan, accused him of seducing King Qingxiang's daughter: "Song Yu is handsome and clever with words, but while serving your majesty, he has been making love to your daughter. Your majesty must keep him at a distance."[98]

The most famous poem credited to Song Yu is entitled "The High Path Rhymeprose." It too begins with an introductory colophon setting the context. It describes one of the most famous daydreams of the Chinese literary tradition.

In the past, King Xiang of Chu and Song Yu were walking on Clouddream Terrace, looking off to the High Path Observatory, on top of which the vapor of a cloud was rising straight up. Suddenly it changed in appearance and in an instant transformed ceaselessly. The king asked Song Yu: "What kind of vapor is this?" Yu answered: "This is what is called 'Morning Cloud.'" The king said: "What's that?" Yu said: "Once upon a time in the past, when the former king walked the High Path, he was being lazy and took a nap during the day. He dreamt that he saw a girl, who said: 'I am the girl of Magic Mountain, the guest of the High Path. When I heard that milord was walking the High Path, I thought to offer him my pillow and mat.' With that, the king favored her. When he left, he made a verse saying: 'I was on the sunny side of Magic Mountain, the summit of High Mound. At dawn, I become Cloud Vapor; in the evening, I make it rain. Mornings and evenings beneath Sunny Terrace.' At dawn, he saw her as she had said, so he set up a temple called 'Morning Vapor.'"

The king asked: "When Cloud Vapor first comes out, what form does it take?" Yu replied: "When it first comes out, it's as luxuriant as a copse of pine trees. When you get a little closer, she shines like a beautiful girl who shields her face from the sun when gazing at her lover. Suddenly transformed, she's as swift as a chariot team of four horses, feather flags flying. Then she's as chilly as the wind, dreary as the rain. When the wind stops and the rain clears, the cloud is gone." The king asked: "Can I now go there?" Yu said: "OK." The king said: "What's it like?" Yu said: "High and open, it looks off into the distance; broad and expansive, it's the ancestor of the ten thousand things. Above, it belongs to the heavens; below, it plumbs the depths. So marvelous and strange that it cannot be told." The king said: "Try to sing of it for me." Yu said: "OK, OK."[99]

Another version of this colophon says that the girl's spirit attached itself to a divine mushroom, which when eaten worked as an aphrodisiac; whoever ate it, would meet her in a dream.

It is all but impossible here to give an indication of the verse Song Yu is supposed to have created for the occasion. Here is just a brief passage describing the birds of the Magic Mountain, how they sport and sing to each other—surely, we are meant also to hear the song of the poet in their songs.

Flocks of sparrows twitter-twitter, Hen and cock losing themselves in each other, Mournfully calling back and forth.

Osprey and oriole, "Just-at-dusk" and Chu dove, Cuckoo and "Long-for Wife," Long-tailed pheasants in a high nest.

Their calling is happy and gay, Sporting throughout the year. Singing back and forth in harmony, Melodies following the stream.[100]

CHAPTER 57
BIOGRAPHY OF XI

Xi, the name meaning "Happy," was born at Cockcrow on the day *jiawu* of the twelfth month of the forty-fifth year of King Zhao of Qin (r. 306–251; i.e., 262) at Anlu, in present-day Hubei province. This was originally part of the former state of Chu, but sixteen years earlier had been conquered by Qin; it was now the new South Commandery of Qin. In the first year of King Zheng of Qin (r. 246/221–210), at the age of sixteen he began his schooling. Two years later, he was drafted into the secretarial corps, and began a rapid climb up the ranks. In 243, he became the Secretary of Anlu, where he was born, and then two years later became Commandant Secretary, and then the following year Commandant Secretary of the larger area of Yan. In the twelfth year of King Zheng, 235, he was promoted to "govern lawsuits" there, apparently acting as a judicial magistrate. In 234, he joined the army, and in 232 was assigned to the Pingyang Army, just in advance of the many campaigns that Qin would undertake over the next decade to conquer all of the still independent states and to bring about the unification of the empire, which Xi certainly lived to see. It would seem that he died in 217, at the age of 45.

This degree of specificity about the details of someone's life in antiquity is very rare, especially one who passed his life more or less anonymously and who was never mentioned in any of China's later historical records. This biography is only possible because Xi's tomb was unearthed in 1975 at a place called Shuihudi, at Yunmeng, Hubei. In the tomb was found a great cache of documents written on bamboo strips, including an annalistic history of Qin named by the archaeologists who discovered the tomb as *Annalistic Record*. This history begins with the first year of the reign of King Zhao of Qin (306) and extends through the thirtieth year of the "current" king (i.e., the First Emperor of Qin; 217). Most of it consists of great events in the life of the state of Qin, especially military campaigns. Thus, it is recorded that in the twenty-eighth year of King Zhao, 279, Qin attacked, and presumably conquered Yan, the city that Xi would eventually administer, and then attacked Anlu the following year. These attacks took place before Xi was born, so it is clear that he inherited this portion of the annals.

Even after Xi became the Commandant Secretary in Yan, most of the records continue to concern events of state. For instance, the last year for which there is a record, 219, records simply that "The Current (King) passed through Anlu."[101] However, beginning with the record of Xi's birth in 262, there are also notes, written in a different hand, concerning his personal life. In 260, someone named Gan was born; it is likely that this was Xi's younger brother. In 254, his father was drafted into the Qin army, but he must have been at home sometime thereafter, for in 251 someone named Su was born; it is possible that this was a younger sister. Sometime later, in 236, there is the record of another birth, a child named Hu; it is likely that this was Xi's own son. In 231, his father died, followed by his mother in 227. Finally, in 220, "just at the hour of breakfast," Chuan Er (Pierced Ears) was born; this must have been a second child, born to Xi rather late in his life.[102] Needless to say, biographical details such as these are unprecedented for anyone from ancient China. We know that the Grand Councillor of Qin Li Si (*c.* 280–208), the most famous man of the time other than the First Emperor himself, had at least one son, but we know this only because there is a record that the son was executed the year before his father was.

Xi's tomb was relatively small, with just a single coffin, though it was well supplied with ritual implements, including some seventy bronze, lacquer, and pottery vessels. But for historians the most important grave goods were the 1,155 bamboo strips found inside the coffin. Although bamboo and silk manuscripts from the Han dynasty had been found before this, this was the first discovery from prior to the time of the Qin "burning of the books" (213), so it goes without saying that it excited great interest. What is more, there were ten different texts in the tomb. In addition to the *Annalistic Record*, there were five different manuscripts dealing with various topics of the law, which was fitting for Xi in his role as a judicial magistrate. Another document, given the title *Spoken Scripture* is dated to 227; it is the text of an address made by the governor of South Commandery, a man named Teng, to the administrators of all of the counties and marches within the commandery. Although at this time, South Commandery had already been under the control of Qin for over fifty years, the native inhabitants still identified with their former state of Chu and were not yet fully pacified. According to the *Annalistic Record*, just in the preceding year, 228, there was unrest in the area, and it is this unrest that Governor Teng warned the local administrators to be on guard against. His address begins:

Of old, the people all have their local customs, and what they regard as profitable and what they love and hate are all different; this is inconvenient for the people and harmful to the country. For this reason, our sainted king has promulgated the laws in order to settle the people's hearts, to dispel their perversions, and to get rid of their evil customs. When the laws and regulations are insufficient, the people are often sly and crafty, and that is why the edicts have been issued. In general, the laws and edicts are for the purpose of educating the people, to dispel their perversions, to get rid of their evil customs, and to cause them to act in the right way.[103]

Another document is called *How to Be an Official*, the contents of which are well described by the title. It would seem that it is a text that circulated widely throughout the Qin empire, other copies having since been unearthed from other tombs. Another type of manuscript found in the tomb has also been found widely throughout ancient Chinese tombs: these texts are known as "daybooks." They are a sort of almanac indicating what days are propitious for undertaking various activities. There were two such daybooks in the tomb of Xi, and they are still the most complete examples of this most popular of ancient texts.

Far and away the most numerous texts in the tomb are the legal texts, which the editors divide into five different types of texts. The first includes eighteen different statutes of the Qin state (each with multiple codicils): Fields, Stables and Parks, Granaries, Metal and Cloth (i.e., Money), Passes and Markets, Labor, Laborers, Equality of Labor, Statutory Labor, Supervisor of Labor, Appointment of Officials, Checking, Military Ranks, Food Rations, Forwarding of Documents, Ministry of Finance, Commandants, and Dependent States. These eighteen statutes certainly do not represent the entirety of the statutory code of the Qin state, but they do give some sense of just how detailed that code must have been. Each codicil is exceptionally detailed, and will be familiar to anyone who has ever worked in a government office or for a large company. This is followed by a separate text devoted to Checking, which essentially refers to Inventory Control. This text begins:

Concerning checking of general offices and prefectures: in case of a surplus or shortage, the value of the goods is to be determined and the responsible parties responsible for that of highest value, but not for the sum total. The office manager and those working there jointly repay shortages; surpluses are recorded.[104]

The text then continues to describe in great detail every contingency that might occur in taking the inventory of an office, the responsibilities of different workers, and the punishment for any infractions. There is also a text called by the editors *Miscellaneous Excerpts from Qin Statutes*, primarily concerned with personnel matters, many of which quote from numerous other named statutes (which, however, are not included in their entirety). These three texts all concern the general administration of a prefecture, such as the Anlu prefecture of which Xi was magistrate.

The magistrate was responsible not only for the general administration of the prefecture, but was also the chief legal officer. Xi's tomb also included two other manuscripts that concerned this aspect of his work. The first of these is a very lengthy text, containing 190 articles, called by the editors *Answers to Questions about Laws and Statutes*, while the second text is entitled *Models for Sealing and Investigating*; as the title indicates, it describes cases that required investigation, some of which read like early detective novels.

These manuscripts are too lengthy to describe in any detail here, but just the following examples of questions and answers included in *Answers to Questions about Laws and Statutes* will give some indication as to just how complex the job of a magistrate was under the Qin government.

A bandit enters the house of A and mortally wounds him. A calls out "Bandits," but his neighbors and the village chief and elders are absent and do not hear him. Question: Should they be sentenced or not? If investigation shows that the neighbors were absent, they are not to be sentenced. However, the village chief and elders are to be sentenced even if they were absent.[105]

A marries a woman who had been married to another man but left him, unbeknownst to A. They have children. She is caught. Question: Where do the children go, given back (to the woman's first husband) or confiscated by the government? Confiscation by the government is an exceptional matter.[106]

When children of the same mother but different fathers have sex with each other, how are they to be sentenced? Beheading.[107]

There is no way to know how many such cases Xi encountered in his work as magistrate of Anlu prefecture. However, that he took these texts to the grave with him, placed beside him inside his coffin, suggests that the information in them was an important part of his own self-identification. It is an identification that helps to put a human face on the complex bureaucracy of the Qin state.

CHAPTER 58
BIOGRAPHIES OF HAN FEI AND LI SI

Han Fei, better known as Han Feizi (*c.* 280–233), was a nobleman of the state of Han, one of the three states into which the great state of Jin divided in 403. Although his date of birth is unknown, it is known that he lived during the reigns of Kings Huanhui (r. 272–239) and An (r. 238–230) of Han, and it is usually thought that he was born about 280. Very little is known about his early life, other than that he spent some period of time studying with the Confucian philosopher Xunzi (*c.* 316–217). This may have been when Xunzi was in residence at the Jixia Academy in Qi, sometime during the reign of King Xiang of Qi (r. 283–265), or more likely from when Xunzi was magistrate of Lanling, a town in the southern part of modern-day Shandong province. One of his classmates at this time was Li Si (280–208), a person with whom he would reconnect at the end of his life, with very tragic consequences for himself.

Han Fei's native state was located all around the Zhou capital at Luoyang, extending from the southern part of modern Shanxi province through the central part of Henan. In his own day, the state was sandwiched between the larger and more powerful states of Qin and Wei. On the one hand, it was able to leverage these two states against each other to defend itself, but its survival was always precarious. As a nobleman of Han, Han Fei had a natural incentive to think about ways to administer the state such that it could survive.

One thing that is known about Han Fei is that he had a speech impediment, and so preferred to put his thoughts into writing that could speak for him. Some of these writings were apparently done when he was living in Han, since they use honorific language to refer to the rulers there. At least one other, called "Preserve Han," was certainly written in the last year of his life, from 234 to 233. In 234, Qin invaded Han and was on the verge of annihilating it. King An sent Han Fei to Qin as a sort of ambassador for his home state to persuade King Zheng of Qin, the future First Emperor (Qin Shi Huangdi; r. 246/221–210), to break off the invasion. Han Fei's writings had apparently already circulated as far as Qin, for King Zheng is said to have been a fan of them, and so was delighted finally to meet the writer. According to Han Fei's biography in *Records of the Historian*, after reading two of these writings, "Solitary Indignation" and "Five Vermin," King Zheng said: "Oh my, if I could get to see this man and have a walk with him, even death would not be detestable."[108] Unfortunately, death would come to Han Fei and not to King Zheng. At this time, Han Fei's erstwhile classmate Li Si was one of King Zheng's principal advisers. He convinced the king that Han Fei would naturally put the interests of Han before those of Qin, and so was a danger to Qin. With this, Han Fei was imprisoned. Li Si then supplied him with poison, ostensibly so that he could avoid any mutilating punishments. Han Fei drank the poison and died in 233.

In his relatively short life, Han Fei produced a great number of writings. The book known as the *Han Feizi* includes fifty-five chapters, and is one of the most extensive philosophical works of the pre-Qin period. Han Fei had studied with the Confucian philosopher Xunzi and had certainly adopted some of his views, especially the notions that the human condition was naturally warped, but also that it was possible to straighten it and to make people into productive citizens. However, whereas Xunzi had emphasized the role of ancient precedents—education and ritual, Han Fei espoused the role of governmental techniques, the main ides of which he adopted from earlier writings generally termed "Legalist": the *Book of the Lord Shang* attributed to Shang Yang (d. 338) of the state of Wei and the *Shenzi* of Shen Buhai (d. 337) of Han Fei's own state of Han. These books took as their central theme the exercise of government through explicit laws (*fa*) and techniques (*shu*), and advocated in particular that agriculture and the military were the main pillars of the state. The concept of *fa*, usually translated as "law" and thus giving this school of thought its name, "Legalism" (*Fa jia*), was based upon systematic policies set in writing and promulgated throughout the state. In theory, once set in place, these laws would be self-governing, with no further need for the intervention of the ruler; everyone would know what was expected of him or her, and would know the consequences—also made explicit– of not conforming to those expectations. As put into practice in the state of Qin—and then inherited by the Han dynasty (202 BCE–220 CE) and most subsequent Chinese governments, this entailed a massive bureaucracy, with a corps of functionaries copying and recopying government edicts, and ensuring that they were made available throughout the state—and later throughout the empire.

Although Han Fei and his *Han Feizi* are regarded as the most thorough exponents of Legalism, he was rather syncretic in his thinking. Not only did he absorb many of his ideas from Xunzi, such as the view that human nature is inherently evil, but he also adapted ideas from Daoism, especially that the ruler should be all-powerful but also invisible to both the government functionaries and also the people, not dirtying himself with the functioning of the government. The chapter of the book entitled "The Way of the Ruler" begins:

> The Way is the beginning of the ten thousand things, the main-line of right and wrong. This is why the enlightened lord holds to the beginning to know the origin of the ten thousand things and controls the main-line to know the ends of skill and defeat. Therefore, in empty and quiet he awaits edicts, their wording and action being clear and definite: empty, he knows the natural state of things; quiet, he knows the uprightness of movement. Those who speak set the terms, those who act set the forms, the forms and terms matching each other, the lord is then without any action and everything returns to its natural state. Thus, it is said: The lord does not make visible his own desires, for if he does, his ministers and generals will adapt to them; the lord does not make visible his ideas, for if he does, his ministers and generals will contort themselves. Thus, it is said: Get rid of love and hate, and the ministers will be pure; get rid of the old and wisdom, and the ministers will be complete of themselves. Therefore, being wise but uncalculating will cause the ten thousand things to know their places; acting but not through the worthy, you will see what those below the ministers rely upon; being courageous but not with anger, will cause the ministers to exert themselves in war. This is why by getting rid of wisdom there will be enlightenment; getting rid of worth, there will be success; getting rid of courage, there will be strength. The many ministers will hold to their jobs and the hundred officers will be constant, working on the basis of their abilities. This is what is called "practicing constancy." Thus it is said: Still, there is no place that he is located; limpid, no one can find his place. The enlightened lord is non-acting above, and the many ministers tremble with fear below. The way of the enlightened lord is to cause the wise to exhaust their calculations, on which the lord decides affairs; therefore, the lord never lacks wisdom. It is to cause the worthy to display their talents, which the lords takes advantage of; therefore, the lord never lacks ability. When successful, the lord has the worth; when mistaken, the ministers shoulder the guilt. Therefore, the lord never lacks fame. This is why those who take not being worthy as worth are the masters

and why those who take not being wise as wise are the governors. The ministers do all the work, and the lord gets the credit. This is the maxim of the worthy ruler.[109]

This may seem cynical, but it established the foundation of a political philosophy that would persist for at least two thousand years, and which may still exist today.

Whereas Han Fei was the political scientist responsible for the consolidation of Legalism, his one-time classmate Li Si was the consummate politician responsible for its implementation. Like Han Fei, he was probably born about 280, but unlike Han Fei, was not a nobleman; rather, he was born in a village in the southern state of Chu. Little is known of Li Si's early years, other than that he served as a petty clerk in his hometown and that he and Han Fei both studied under Xunzi. It becomes possible to trace his career development only beginning in 247, when he arrived in Qin to serve under Lü Buwei (291–235), Grand Chancellor under King Zhuangxiang of Qin (r. 250–247). King Zhuangxiang died in this year, and was succeeded by his son Zheng, with whom Li Si had an interview and was made a senior scribe. Ten years later, Lü Buwei was first forced into exile and then, in 235, forced to commit suicide; sometime thereafter Li Si became Minister of Justice. In 235 or 234, Han Fei had gone to Qin to save his native state of Han from being invaded. Li Si went in the opposite direction, from Qin to Han, trying to persuade King An of Han to go to Qin himself to sue for peace. When Li Si returned to Qin, he was responsible for Han Fei's imprisonment and suicide.

During the decade of the 220s, Qin undertook the annihilation of all of the other states, beginning with Han, in 230, and ending with the northeastern state of Qi in 221. With the unification complete, King Zheng gave himself the new title of First Emperor of Qin. His most important ministers recommended that he appoint his relatives to rule over the conquered lands, as had been done by the founders of the preceding Zhou dynasty. Li Si is said to have argued against this precedent, noting that this had eventually given rise to the independent states that Qin had just defeated. It would be better to subject all to rule from the central authority. The First Emperor agreed with Li Si, and ordered that the administrative structure of Qin be extended throughout the empire. Sometime after this, Li Si was promoted to the rank of Grand Chancellor, the highest rank in the government.

In 213, Li Si once again gave advice to the First Emperor, the advice for which he is best known—and most often castigated—in Chinese history. At a kind of conference attended by the many scholars at court and presided over by the emperor himself, Li Si urged the emperor not to look to the past for his model of government, a time that had devolved into constant warfare, but rather to bring about a unification of ideas, just as he had united the various states. He then went on to propose the burning of all books except those from the state of Qin itself and those technical manuals that could be useful, and the execution of all scholars who "use the past to negate the present." This proposal is quoted in the "Annals of the First Emperor" in *Records of the Historian*.

> In the past, all under heaven was in disorder, and no one was able to unite it. This is why the many lords acted in unison, all talking about the past to harm the present, decorating their empty sayings to disorder reality. People excelled at their private studies to negate what their superiors had established. Now, your majesty has united all under heaven, has differentiated white from black and settled a single order, and yet those private scholars join together to negate the teaching of the law. When people hear edicts, they all debate them on the basis of their own ideas, at court silently disagreeing, while in the streets they disagree openly, becoming famous for disagreeing with the ruler, getting promoted for weird notions, and leading the lower people to create slander. If this is not prohibited, then above the ruler's power will decline and below partisan groups will form. It is best that these be prohibited.
>
> I propose that everything in the secretarial office other than the Qin annals should be burned. Anyone in the world not employed in the Office of Broad Learning who possesses poetry, scriptures, or the sayings of the Hundred Schools should submit them all to confiscation, so that the deputies will burn them. Anyone who dares to talk about the poetry or the scriptures should be exposed in the marketplace, and those who use the past to negate the present should be put to death with all their family. Officials who see or know of these and do not report them should share the same crime. It should be decreed that if within thirty days the writings have not been burned, those with them should be branded and made into wall pounders. Those writings not to be gotten rid of are books of medicine, divination and agriculture. If there are those who wish to study, they should take the officials as their teachers.[110]

Ironically, at the same time that Li Si is infamous for the destruction of literature, he is also credited with the authorship of a book that contributed greatly to the unification of the Chinese script. This was called the *Fascicle of Cangjie*, Cangjie being the name of the legendary figure said to have invented writing after viewing the tracks left by birds and animals. The *Fascicle of Cangjie* was quite short, just seven chapters of sixty characters each, arranged as rhyming four-character phrases. This was designed to teach scribes how to write 420 of the most frequently appearing characters. By the Han dynasty, it had been expanded to include fifty-five paragraphs of sixty characters each, for a total of 3,300 different characters. Based on the numerous examples of the text that have been unearthed in recent decades, it does seem that it was a standard primer for scribes.

The last years of Li Si's life were not such to bring any further credit to his name. In 210, he was together with the First Emperor on a tour of the eastern territories when the emperor died. Together with the eunuch Zhao Gao (258–207), he forged a last will and testament of the First Emperor, naming Huhai (229–207), a younger son of the emperor, to succeed him, to be known as the Second Emperor of Qin (r. 209–207). This precipitated great unrest among the people at large, as well as intrigues at court, where Zhao Gao came to hold preeminent power, if only very briefly. Perhaps in an attempt to salvage something of Li Si's reputation, Sima Qian says in his biography that Li Si remonstrated against the excesses of the Second Emperor, for which reason Zhao Gao had him imprisoned and put to death in the grisliest of manners. In the seventh month of the second year of the Second Emperor (208), Li Si underwent the "five punishments" (branding, cutting off of the nose, cutting off one leg at the knee, castration, and execution), the latter of which was carried out by cutting him in two at the waist in the marketplace of the capital Xianyang. His family was then exterminated to the third degree.

CHAPTER 59
THE BIOGRAPHIES OF CHEN SHE
AND WU GUANG

Chen Sheng, better known as Chen She, and Wu Guang, also known as Wu Shu, both lived during the Qin dynasty. Chen She was a native of Yangcheng (near modern Nanyang in western Henan province), while Wu Guang was a native of Yangxia (in the eastern part of Henan). Both men began as common laborers, but Chen She had grandiose visions of himself. As the story goes, one day when working as part of a labor gang, he announced that if he were to become rich and famous he would not forget the others. This prompted ridicule from the others, but Chen She would soon become famous, even if he would not live long to enjoy it. Wu Guang, who played an important supporting role, would also meet an early end. However, the two men are credited with having precipitated the revolt that brought the Qin dynasty to its own early end.

In the summer after the death of the First Emperor of Qin (r. 246/221–210; i.e., 209), Chen She, Wu Guang and some nine hundred other men were called up for military garrison duty at the regional center of Yuyang, which was located far to the north near modern Beijing. The summer monsoon rains had made the roads impassable, and the squad of men soon realized that they would not arrive by the time of their appointment. According to Qin rules, late arrivals would be executed. Chen She and Wu Guang, who were both squad leaders, encouraged the others to desert, arguing that since the penalty for desertion was the same as that for arriving late, the men had nothing to lose. They also argued that the Second Emperor of Qin (r. 209–207) was not the rightful heir to the First Emperor.

In fact, the Second Emperor, Huhai (b. 230), was one of eighteen sons of the First Emperor. He had been traveling with the emperor when his father died. With the connivance of Commandant Zhao Gao (258–207) and Grand Councillor Li Si (284–208), Huhai forged an order in the name of the First Emperor naming himself successor and commanding that his brother Fusu (d. 210), the eldest son of the First Emperor and until then considered to be the heir apparent, be put to death. Putting Fusu to death, along with more than twenty other rivals, Huhai and Zhao Gao took over the government and are said to have introduced a reign even more terrible than that of the First Emperor. It was in this context that Chen She launched the revolt that would eventually bring down the dynasty.

To convince the labor gang to desert with them, Chen She and Wu Guang performed a divination proposing that Chen She be king. At the same time, they secretly inserted a bamboo slip with the words "Chen She will be king" in the belly of a fish that had just been caught. When the men prepared to cook the fish, they discovered the bamboo slip and believed that it was the answer to the divination. With this, as well as other ruses to gain the confidence of the men, Chen She, Wu Guang and their band determined that it would be better to attack the Qin army than to go quietly to an all but assured death.

Chen She and Wu Guang assumed command of their army, which they named the army of Great Chu. However, realizing that news traveled slowly, they pretended that Fusu, the erstwhile heir apparent, and Xiang Yan (d. 223), a popular general from the southern state of Chu who had died some years earlier, but about whom there was a popular notion that he had simply gone into hiding, were the leaders. They began by attacking small counties in the eastern part of the empire, in present-day Anhui province, attracting more and more followers with each victory. Turning north, they attacked Chen, the seat of one of the Qin commanderies located southeast of modern Kaifeng, Henan, which they also conquered. With the encouragement of the local leaders of Chen, Chen She declared himself king of the state of Zhang Chu: "Expanding Chu," named for the major ancient state of southern China.

This precipitated a general uprising in many commanderies and counties throughout the empire. Chen She appointed Wu Guang as Adjutant King and dispatched him to lead an army toward the west. The first major city that he encountered was Xingyang, near modern Zhengzhou, Henan, and the site of an important government granary. At this time, other local lords also rose up in rebellion against Qin. Other rebels sought to take advantage of the general unrest to strengthen their own local positions, with many of them fighting among themselves. One overly ambitious attack against the Qin capital region, led by one Zhou Wen, one of the leading figures from Chen, proved disastrous, with the Qin army under the command of the general Zhang Han (d. 207) crushing it; Zhou Wen ended by slitting his own throat.

After defeating Zhou Wen, the Qin imperial army continued eastward, eventually meeting the army of Wu Guang, which was still laying siege to the city of Xingyang. Sensing the hopelessness of their situation, Wu Guang's troops plotted to have him killed, forging an order from Chen She to this effect. They then killed Wu Guang. This did not save them from being defeated in turn by the Qin army. When the rebel troops retreated to Chen, Chen She had their leaders executed. When the Qin imperial army arrived, Chen She led his own forces out to meet it; the battle did not go well, and the Qin general Zhang Han soundly defeated Chen She's ragamuffin army. In the twelfth month of 208, Chen She fled south. However, upon reaching the area of present-day Anhui province his carriage driver turned on him and killed him. Chen She was buried near present-day Fuyang, given the posthumous title of Yin Wang, the Occluded King. Such was the unhappy end of the brief rebellion of Chen She and Wu Guang. It lasted all of six months.

Even though Chen She and Wu Guang's roles in the rebellion had come to an ignominious end, their revolt precipitated an empire-wide revolt. Two local leaders in particular came to prominence after the deaths of Chen She and Wu Guang: Xiang Yu (c. 232–202), like Chen She also from the ancient state of Chu, and Liu Bang (256–195), from the area where Chen She died, continued the fight. In the summer of 207, Xiang Yu met and defeated the Qin imperial army of Zhang Han at the battle of Julu, near the ancient city of Anyang, in present-day Henan province. When Zhang Han surrendered, Xiang Yu ordered that the 200,000-man Qin army be buried alive. About this time, he dispatched Liu Bang with a smaller force to attack the Qin capital at Xianyang, modern Xi'an, Shaanxi. By that winter, Liu Bang's army had entered Xianyang and forced the final Qin ruler, Ziying, to abdicate, bringing the short-lived Qin dynasty to an end.

The beginning of the succeeding Han dynasty, of which Liu Bang was the founder, is normally given as the next year: 206 BCE. However, this is fictional, driven by the notion in Chinese traditional political history that no year be without a government in power. In fact, Liu Bang and Xiang Yu engaged in an almost five-year long civil war, filled with battles and diplomacy, double-dealing and still more battles. The story of the final battle, at Gaixia, at which Xiang Yu was finally defeated and killed, has been read by Chinese schoolchildren of all ages, with most sympathizing with Xiang Yu's heroic last stand. By then, the Qin dynasty was already gone, if not forgotten.

CHAPTER 60
AUTHOR'S POSTFACE

"If you learn much and leave out what is doubtful, and are careful in what you say about the rest, then there will be few errors."

Confucius on the writing of history

This book has presented a history of ancient China in five "Basic Annals" surveying the first rulers and dynasties of the period, eight "Maps and Tables" that provide chronological information as well as maps of different sub-periods, ten "Essays" that explore in more detail some of the most important general topics, twelve "Regional Genealogies" that provide histories of regional powers that wielded much of the actual power for significant periods of time, and twenty-four "Biographies" of representative persons over the entire course of the historical period. These numbers correlate with the Five Phases (water, fire, metal, wood, and earth) that were thought in ancient China to be the fundamental constituents of matter and of its constant development; the Eight Trigrams of the *Classic of Changes* that map, for instance, the eight directions (the four cardinal directions as well as the four intermediate directions); the ten days of ancient China's ten-day week; the twelve months of the lunar year; and the twenty-four fortnightly periods of the solar year that describe the climatic variation throughout a single year. Adding this "Postface" makes a total of sixty chapters, corresponding to China's traditional repeating cycle of sixty days or years.

Readers with any familiarity at all with China's historical tradition will recognize the debt that this structure owes to that tradition. That structure was pioneered in *Records of the Historian* of Sima Qian (145–c. 89 BCE). Sima Qian ended his work with a personal chapter, which I will also imitate here, though without indulging in the sort of autobiographical reflections that he included. Aside from allowing the Western reader to experience, if only too briefly, the way that Chinese readers have long approached their own history, this structure offers at least a few advantages as opposed to the strict chronological approach favored by many Western historians. First, it avoids the most pernicious aspects of the teleology built into the narratives organized from early to late. Second, by approaching topics from different perspectives, the reader is invited to revisit—and reconsider—topics already introduced. Finally, by dividing the history into numerous independent items that do not necessarily follow any logical sequence, it can provide the reader with the opportunity to create her own order by reading back and forth among the various sections, creating a new history with each re-reading, almost as a kaleidoscope creates a new image with each twist of the tube.

I have not broken any new ground with this book; indeed, I have re-plowed fields that have been cultivated for two millennia, at least in China. Even in the West, this is an old story, already told by many fine historians. The earliest of these, beginning with *The Ancient History of China: To the End of the Chin Dynasty* by Friedrich Hirth (1845–1927),[1] followed in close succession by *La Chine Antique* (translated into English as *China in Antiquity*), of Henri Maspero (1883–1945) and *La Civilisation Chinoise: La vie publique et la vie privée* (translated into English as *Chinese Civilization*) of Marcel Granet (1884–1940), presented in-depth accounts by single individuals.[2] While Maspero's book was able to take some account of the first glimmerings of archaeology in China in the 1920s, these three books would be the last works primarily informed by China's traditional texts. In the same year that Granet's *La Civilisation Chinoise* was published, China's Academia Sinica, the national academy of science, began its archaeological exploration of Anyang, the last capital of the Shang dynasty. Over the course of the next several scholarly generations, archaeology became the driving force behind modern Chinese historiography; despite interruptions by foreign invasion and civil wars and domestic disturbances, China's archaeologists unearthed such a wealth of the material culture of antiquity, theretofore only faintly imagined from the traditional literature, that there have been repeated calls to "rewrite ancient Chinese history." In the West, at least, these discoveries induced a sort of scholarly paralysis among historians, who were unable to keep up with all of the new material becoming available and who were fearful that yet newer material would render obsolete any grand narrative before it was even published. It would be seventy years before the next attempt to describe that history: the *Cambridge History of Ancient China: From the Beginnings of Civilization to 221 B.C.* (New York: Cambridge University Press, 1999).[3] This massive volume (1,330 pages), written by fourteen leading scholars, attempted to synthesize both traditional accounts of ancient history and also all archaeological evidence. Despite what the subtitle of the book suggests, its coverage was generally restricted to the historical period (i.e., beginning with the first evidence of writing in the late Shang dynasty).

The turn of the millennium has seen an acceleration in the pace of archaeological exploration, as well as new methods of scientific analysis of the artifacts unearthed. These discoveries have prompted not only China's archaeologists, but also her historians to ask new questions of how civilization developed in China. Western scholars, too, have participated in the debates that have emerged in this context, publishing numerous volumes with different emphases. The first to appear was Maurizio Scarpari's *Ancient China: Chinese Civilization from Its Origins to the Tang Dynasty*;[4] first published in Italian, this volume boasts some four hundred exquisite photographs of recent archaeological discoveries. Five years later, Edward L. Shaughnessy published *Ancient China: Life, Myth and Art*, a similar illustrated history that explored in particular the lifeways and worldviews of ancient China.[5] In the last several years, several general histories have been written with different emphases. For instance, in 2014, Li Feng's *Early China: A Social and Cultural History* set out to update *The Cambridge History of Ancient China*, adopting its synthesis of traditional and archaeological evidence, but also introducing a sophisticated social dimension to his analysis; a particular interest of his is the development of literacy and its role in government administration.[6] In the very next year, Gideon Shelach-Lavi's *The Archaeology of Ancient China: From Prehistory to the Han Dynasty* explored the recent archaeological record, discussing in particular what it shows about the rise of agriculture during the prehistoric period, and then for the historical period the interactions among local cultures within the territory of China proper, and also that between them and neighbors to the north and west.[7] In the next year, Constance A. Cook and John Major published *Ancient China: A History*, a comprehensive traditional narrative history from the Neolithic period through the end of the Han dynasty and beyond.[8] Most recently, in 2020, Elizabeth Childs-Johnson has edited *The Oxford Handbook of Early China*, an 800-page overview of the entire period, beginning with the Neolithic period extending through the Warring States period.[9]

The present *Short History of Ancient China* now takes its place among these excellent studies. It cannot boast the beautiful illustrations seen in Scarpari's book, nor does it explore the archaeological record in detail in the way that Li Feng and Shelach-Lavi do in their books, nor does it provide the comprehensive narrative of the Cook/Major volume. Its main distinction lies in its format, which as noted above, replicates the traditional Chinese approach to history. That being said, I have attempted to integrate as many archaeological discoveries as possible, while at the same time not stinting the traditional history, and I have also tried to introduce the new perspectives one would expect in a twenty-first-century work. Of course, traditional Chinese histories did not have page limits, and so could explore their periods in much greater detail than most Western students will ever require. The size of this book has required decisions about what to include and what to leave out, and numerous compromises about topics of which a fuller account would certainly wish to reveal some of the complexity surrounding them. But the size is also an opportunity to focus on what is most critical to understand in the cultural history of ancient China, at least in the eyes of this one historian. Students intrigued by the choices I have made might wish to consult as well some of the other short histories mentioned in the preceding paragraph, or even *The Cambridge History of Ancient China*, or even to move to the hundreds of specialized studies of all the topics covered here—and also many topics not covered here. It is a period full of historical interest, becoming ever more fascinating with each new discovery.

NOTES

Notes to Basic Annals

1. *Mengzi*, 6B/2.

2. *Mengzi*, 3B/9.

3. Wu Zhenfeng ed., *Shang Zhou qingtongqi mingwen ji tuxiang jicheng* (Shanghai: Shanghai Guji chubanshe, 2012), #5677.

4. Ma Chengyuan ed., *Shanghai bowuguan cang Chu zhushu* (Shanghai: Shanghai Guji chubanshe, 2002), Vol. 2, *Rongchengshi*, ##18–20.

5. Zhongguo Shehui kexueyuan Lishi yanjiusuo ed., *Jiaguwen heji* (Beijing: Zhonghua shuju, 1982), #995.

6. Zhongguo Shehui kexueyuan Lishi yanjiusuo ed., *Jiaguwen heji*, #6484.

7. Zhongguo Shehui kexueyuan Lishi yanjiusuo ed., *Jiaguwen heji*, #36482.

8. Zhongguo Shehui kexueyuan Lishi yanjiusuo ed., *Jiaguwen heji*, #36567.

9. Zhongguo Shehui kexueyuan Lishi yanjiusuo ed., *Jiaguwen heji*, #36484.

10. Li Xueqin ed.-in-chief, Qinghua daxue Chutu wenxian yanjiu yu baohu zhongxin ed., *Qinghua daxue cang Zhanguo zhushu* (Shanghai: Zhong-Xi shuju, 2010), Vol. 1: *Cheng wu*, #1.

11. Zongguo Shehui kexueyuan Kaogu yanjiusuo ed., *Yin Zhou jinwen jicheng* (Beijing: Zhonghua shuju, 1984–1994), #6014.

12. Zhongdu Shehui kexueyuan Kaogu yanjiusuo ed., *Yin Zhou jinwen jicheng*, #9899.

13. Sima Qian, *Shi ji*, "Zhou benji."

14. Zhongguo Shehui kexueyuan Kaogu yanjiusuo ed., *Yin Zhou jinwen jicheng*, #2832.

15. Sima Qian, *Shi ji*, "Zhou benji."

16. Zhongguo Shehui kexueyuan Kaogu yanjiusuo ed., *Yin Zhou jinwen jicheng*, #2833.

17. Sima Qian, *Shi ji*, "Zhou benji."

18. Wu Zhenfeng ed., *Shang Zhou qingtongqi mingwen ji tuxiang jicheng*, 15298–15313.

19. *Mozi*, "Ming gui xia."

20. Li Xueqin ed.-in-chief, Qinghua daxue Chutu wenxian yanjiu yu baohu zhongxin ed., *Qinghua daxue cang Zhanguo zhushu* (Shanghai: Zhong-Xi shuju, 2011), Vol. 2, *Xinian*, ##5–9.

Notes

21. Zhongguo Shehui kexueyuan Kaogu yanjiusuo ed., *Yin Zhou jinwen jicheng*, ##262–263.

22. *Shi jing*, "Huang niao" (Mao 131).

Notes to Essays

1. For a photograph of the skeleton and the two animals made of cowries, see Michael Loewe and Edward L. Shaughnessy ed., *The Cambridge History of Ancient China: From the Origins of Civilization to 221 B.C.* (New York: Cambridge University Press, 1999), 51.

2. *Guanzi*, "Si shi."

3. For a line-drawing of this image, see Loewe and Shaughnessy ed., *The Cambridge History of Ancient China*, 834.

4. For a line-drawing of one such diviner's board, see Loewe and Shaughnessy ed., *The Cambridge History of Ancient China*, 840.

5. *Analects* of Confucius, 2/1.

6. *Zuo zhuan*, first year of Lord Zhao.

7. *Mengzi*, 6A/8.

8. *Mengzi*, 3B/9.

9. Zhongguo Shehui kexueyuan Lishi yanjiusuo ed., *Jiaguwen heji*, #10197.

10. *Xunzi*, "Li lun."

11. *Shi jing*, "Wei tian zhi ming" (Mao 267).

12. *Shi jing*, "Wo jiang" (Mao 272).

13. *Shi jing*, "Zai xian" (Mao 283).

14. Zhongguo Shehui kexueyuan Kaogu yanjiusuo ed., *Yin Zhou jinwen jicheng*, #4317.

15. *Analects* of Confucius, 2/7.

16. *Analects* of Confucius, 1/11.

17. *Xunzi*, "Li lun."

18. Zhongguo Shchui kcxucyuan Lishi yanjiusuo ed., *Jiaguwen heji*, #6057A.

19. Zhongguo Shehui kexueyuan Lishi yanjiusuo ed., *Jiaguwen heji*, #6412.

20. Zhongguo Shehui kexueyuan Lishi yanjiusuo ed., *Jiaguwen heji*, #811A.

21. Zhongguo Shehui kexueyuan Lishi yanjiusuo ed., *Jiaguwen heji*, #36481A.

22. *Shi jing*, "Da ming" (Mao 236).

23. Zhongguo Shehui kexueyuan Kaogu yanjiusuo ed., *Yin Zhou jinwen jicheng*, #2835.

24. *Sunzi Bingfa*, "Shi ji."

25. *Zuo zhuan*, twenty-second year of Lord Xi.

26. *Sunzi Bingfa*, "Shi ji."

27. *Chu ci*, "Guo shang."

28. Zhongguo Shehui kexueyuan Kaogu yanjiusuo ed., *Yin Zhou jinwen jicheng*, #2837.

29. Shuihudi Qin mu zhujian zhengli xiaozu ed., *Shuihudi Qin mu zhujian* (Beijing: Wenwu chubanshe, 1990), *Qin lü shiba zhong*, "Chuan shi lü," ##180–181.

30. *Shang shu*, "Kang gao."

31. Zhongguo Shehui kexueyuan Kaogu yanjiusuo ed., *Yin Zhou jinwen jicheng*, #10285.

32. *Shi jing*, "Wen wang" (Mao 235).

33. Shuihudi Qin mu zhujian zhengli xiaozu ed., *Shuihudi Qin mu zhujian, Qin lü shiba zhong*, "Xiao lü," ##164–166.

34. Shuihudi Qin mu zhujian zhengli xiaozu ed., *Shuihudi Qin mu zhujian, Fa lü dawen*, #6.

35. Shuihudi Qin mu zhujian zhengli xiaozu ed., *Shuihudi Qin mu zhujian, Feng zhen shi*, ##23–24.

36. Shuihudi Qin mu zhujian zhengli xiaozu ed., *Shuihudi Qin mu zhujian, Feng zhen shi*, ##42–45.

37. *Li ji*, "Yue ji."

38. *Shi jing*, "You gu" (Mao 280).

39. *Shi jing*, "Chu ci" (Mao 209).

40. *Chu ci*, "Zhao hun."

41. *Shi jing*, "Guan ju."

42. *Li ji*, "Yue ji."

43. *Xunzi*, "Yue lun."

44. *Analects* of Confucius, 13/23.

45. See, for instance, the remarkable basin from the tomb of Lord Yi of Zeng (d. 433) at Suixian, Hubei, pictured in Loewe and Shaughnessy ed., *The Cambridge History of Ancient China*, 678.

46. See, for instance, the tree-shaped lamp from tomb 1 at Zhongshan, pictured at Loewe and Shaughnessy ed., *The Cambridge History of Ancient China*, 690.

47. *Shuo wen jie zi*, "Xu."

Notes to Hereditary Houses

1. Zhongguo Shehui kexueyuan Kaogu yanjiusuo ed., *Yin Zhou jinwen jicheng*, #2739.

2. Zhongguo Shehui kexueyuan Kaogu yanjiusuo ed., *Yin Zhou jinwen jicheng*, #4041.

Notes

3. James Legge, *The Ch'un Ts'ew, with the Tso Chuen. The Chinese Classics* V (London: Trübner, 1872; rpt. Hong Kong: Hong Kong University Press, 1960), 709.

4. *Zuo zhuan*, seventh year of Lord Zhao.

5. Wu Zhenfeng ed., *Shang Zhou qingtongqi mingwen ji tuxiang jicheng*, #14789.

6. Zhongguo Shehui kexueyuan Kaogu yanjiusuo ed., *Yin Zhou jinwen jicheng*, #2628.

7. Zhongguo Shehui kexueyuan Kaogu yanjiusuo ed., *Yin Zhou jinwen jicheng*, #2840.

8. *Shi jing*, "Da ming" (Mao 236).

9. *Zuo zhuan*, twenty-second year of Lord Zhuang.

10. *Mengzi*, 1B/5.

11. Wu Zhenfeng ed., *Shang Zhou qingtongqi mingwen ji tuxiang jicheng*, #2419.

12. Wu Zhenfeng ed., *Shang Zhou qingtongqi mingwen ji tuxiang jicheng*, #4954.

13. *Mengzi*, 1A/3.

14. Sima Qian, *Shi ji*, "Wei shijia."

15. *Mu tianzi zhuan*, j. 4.

16. Shanxi sheng Wenwu gonzuo weiyuanjui ed., *Houma mengshu* (Beijing: Wenwu chubanshe, 1976), 35, 123: #156.1.

17. Sima Qian, *Shi ji*, "Zhao shijia."

18. Zhongguo Shehui kexueyuan Kaogu yanjiusuo ed., *Yin Zhou jinwen jicheng*, #157.

19. Ban Gu, *Han shu*, "Yiwen zhi."

20. *Taiping yulan*, j. 638.

21. *Ibid.*

22. *Chuxue ji*, j. 25.

23. Li Xueqin ed.-in-chief, Qinghua daxue Chutu wenxian yanjiu yu baohu zhongxin ed., *Qinghua daxue cang Zhanguo zhushu* (Shanghai: Zhong-Xi shuju, 2010), Vol. 1, *Chu ju*, ##1–2.

24. *Shi jing*, "Yin wu" (Mao 305).

25. Li Xueqin ed.-in-chief, Qinghua daxue Chutu wenxian yanjiu yu baohu zhongxin ed., *Qinghua daxue cang Zhanguo zhushu*, Vol. 1, *Chu ju*, ##2–4.

26. *Zuo zhuan*, fourth year of Lord Xi.

27. Guo Moruo, *Shi gu wen yanjiu / Zu Chu wen kaoshi* (Beijing: Kexue chubanshe, 1982), *Zu Chu wen*.

28. Zhongguo Shehui kexueyuan Kaogu yanjiusuo ed., *Yin Zhou jinwen jicheng*, #2751.

29. Zhongguo Shehui kexueyuan Kaogu yanjiusuo ed., *Yin Zhou jinwen jicheng*, #949.

30. Guo Changjiang, Fan Guodong, Chen Hu, and Li Xiaoyang, "*Zeng Hou Qiu bianzhong* mingwen chubu shidu," *Jiang Han kaogu*, 2020.1: 3–30.

31. Guo Changjiang, Li Xiaoyang, Fan Guodong, and Chen Hu, "*Mi Jia bianzhong* mingwen de chubu shidu," *Jiang Han kaogu*, 2019.3: 9–19.

32. Hubei sheng wenwu kaogu yanjiusuo and Suizhou shi bowuguan, "Hubei Suizhou Wenfengta M1 (Zeng hou Yu mu), M2 fajue jianbao," *Jiang Han kaogu*, 2014.4: 3–51.

33. Zhongguo Shehui kexueyuan Kaogu yanjiusuo ed., *Yin Zhou jinwen jicheng*, #5419.

34. Zhongguo Shehui kexueyuan Kaogu yanjiusuo ed., *Yin Zhou jinwen jicheng*, #4322.

35. Fan Ye, *Hou Han shu*, "Dong Yi liezhuan."

36. *Shi jing*, "Jiang Han" (Mao 262).

37. Zhongguo Shehui kexueyuan Kaogu yanjiusuo ed., *Yin Zhou jinwen jicheng*, #4464.

38. Terrien de Lacouperie, *Western Origin of the Early Chinese Civilization from 2,300 B.C. to 200 A.D. or, Chapters on the elements derived from the old civilisations of West Asia in the formation of the ancient Chinese culture* (1894; rpt. Osnabrück: Zeller, 1966).

39. For a photograph and several line-drawings of artifacts from this site, see Loewe and Shaughnessy ed., *The Cambridge History of Ancient China*, 214–216.

Notes to Biographies

1. Zhongguo Shehui kexueyuan Lishi yanjiusuo ed., *Jiaguwen heji*, #19998.

2. Zhongguo Shehui kexueyuan Lishi yanjiusuo ed., *Jiaguwen heji*, #6480.

3. Zhongguo Shehui kexueyuan Lishi yanjiusuo ed., *Jiaguwen heji*, #6412.

4. Zhongguo Shehui kexueyuan Lishi yanjiusuo ed., *Jiaguwen heji*, #17380.

5. Zhongguo Shehui kexueyuan Lishi yanjiusuo ed., *Jiaguwen heji*, #32757.

6. Zhongguo Shehui kexueyuan Lishi yanjiusuo ed., *Jiaguwen heji*, #3637.

7. Li Xueqin ed.-in-chief, Qinghua daxue Chutu wenxian yanjiu yu baohu zhongxin ed., *Qinghua daxue cang Zhanguo zhushu*, Vol. 2, *Xinian*, #13.

8. Zhongguo Shehui kexueyuan Kaogu yanjiusuo ed., *Yin Zhou jinwen jicheng*, #4140.

9. *Mu tianzi zhuan*, j. 6.

10. Quoted at Xiao Tong ed., *Wen xuan*, Li Shan's commentary to Zhang Heng's "Si xuan fu."

11. *Yi Zhou shu*, "Zhai gong xun."

12. Wu Zhenfeng ed., *Shang Zhou qingtongqi mingwen ji tuxiang jicheng*, #5362.

13. Zhongguo Shehui kexueyuan Kaogu yanjiusuo ed., *Yin Zhou jinwen jicheng*, #9455.

14. Zhongguo Shehui kexueyuan Kaogu yanjiusuo ed., *Yin Zhou jinwen jicheng*, #9456.

15. Zhongguo Shehui kexueyuan Kaogu yanjiusuo ed., *Yin Zhou jinwen jicheng*, #2836.

16. Zhongguo Shehui kexueyuan Kaogu yanjiusuo ed., *Yin Zhou jinwen jicheng*, #10174.

17. *Shi jing*, "Liu yue" (Mao 177).

18. *Shi jing*, "Zheng min" (Mao 260).

19. At https://baike.baidu.com/item/桀/67800?fromtitle=夏王桀&fromid=3145653, accessed January 6, 2022.

20. Sima Qian, *Shi ji*, "Zhou benji."

21. *Shi jing*, "Zheng yue" (Mao 192).

22. *Guo yu*, "Jin yu 1."

23. *Zuo zhuan*, ninth year of Lord Xiang.

24. *Zuo zhuan*, fourteenth year of Lord Cheng.

25. *Shi jing*, "Yanyan" (Mao 28).

26. *Zuo zhuan*, tenth year of Lord Xiang.

27. *Zuo zhuan*, thirtieth year of Lord Xiang.

28. *Chunqiu*, eleventh year of Lord Wen.

29. *Zuo zhuan*, fourteenth year of Lord Xiang.

30. *Zuo zhuan*, twenty-sixth year of Lord Xiang.

31. *Zuo zhuan*, twenty-fourth year of Lord Xiang.

32. *Zuo zhuan*, sixth year of Lord Zhao.

33. *Ibid.*

34. *Zuo zhuan*, seventh year of Lord Zhao.

35. *Ibid.*

36. *Zuo zhuan*, twentieth year of Lord Zhao.

37. *Analects* of Confucius, 12/1.

38. Sima Qian, *Shi ji*, "Kongzi shijia."

39. *Analects* of Confucius, 12/11.

40. *Analects* of Confucius, 7/14.

41. *Analects* of Confucius, 6/14.

42. *Analects* of Confucius, 15/1.

43. *Analects* of Confucius, 9/5.

44. *Analects* of Confucius, 13/16.

45. *Analects* of Confucius, 2/19.

46. *Analects* of Confucius, 12/17.

47. *Analects* of Confucius, 11/10.

48. *Analects* of Confucius, 11/9.

49. *Analects* of Confucius, 6/11.

50. *Analects* of Confucius, 5/9.

51. *Analects* of Confucius, 5/26.

52. *Analects* of Confucius, 12/2.

53. *Analects* of Confucius, 7/11.

54. *Analects* of Confucius, 17/7.

55. *Analects* of Confucius, 11/13.

56. *Analects* of Confucius, 6/8.

57. *Analects* of Confucius, 11/19.

58. *Analects* of Confucius, 3/17.

59. *Analects* of Confucius, 15/24.

60. *Analects* of Confucius, 5/12.

61. *Analects* of Confucius, 3/8.

62. *Analects* of Confucius, 19/5.

63. *Analects* of Confucius, 19/6.

64. *Analects* of Confucius, 19/7.

65. *Analects* of Confucius, 19/8.

66. *Analects* of Confucius, 19/13.

67. *Analects* of Confucius, 1/7.

68. *Analects* of Confucius, 1/4.

69. *Analects* of Confucius, 19/17.

70. *Analects* of Confucius, 19/19.

71. *Li ji*, "Da xue."

72. *Mengzi*, 2A/6.

73. *Mengzi*, 6B/22.

74. *Mengzi*, 1A/5.

75. *Mengzi*, 1B/5.

76. *Xunzi*, "Yi bing."

77. *Xunzi*, "Ru xiao."

78. Sima Qian, *Shi ji*, "Laozi Han Fei liezhuan."

79. *Ibid.*

80. *Laozi*, Ch. 1.

81. *Zhuangzi*, "Qiu shui."

82. *Ibid.*

83. *Zhuangzi*, "Tianxia."

84. Sima Qian, *Shi ji*, "Sunzi Wu Qi liezhuan."

85. *Sunzi Bingfa*, "Xu shi."

86. Hubei Jing-Sha tielu kaogudui ed., *Baoshan Chu jian* (Beijing: Wenwu chubanshe, 1991), #90.

87. Hubei Jing-Sha tielu kaogudui ed., *Baoshan Chu jian*, ##199–200.

88. Hubei Jing-Sha tielu kaogudui ed., *Baoshan Chu jian*, ##239–241.

89. Hubei Jing-Sha tielu kaogudui ed., *Baoshan Chu jian*, #249.

90. *Liezi*, "Tang wen."

91. Zhangjiashan 247 hao Han mu zhujian zhengli xiaozu ed., *Zhangjiashan Han mu zhujian (247 hao mu)* (Beijing: Wenwu chubanshe, 2001), *Yin shu*, ##107–108.

92. *Guanzi*, "Nei ye."

93. Sima Qian, *Shi ji*, "Bian Que liezhuan."

94. *Heguanzi*, "Shi xian."

95. *Chu ci*, "Li sao."

96. *Ibid.*

97. *Ibid.*

98. *Chu ci*, "Feng fu."

99. *Chu ci*, "Gao tang fu."

100. *Ibid.*

101. Shuihudi Qin mu zhujian zhengli xiaozu ed., *Shuihudi Qin mu zhujian, Biannian ji*, #35B.

102. Shuihudi Qin mu zhujian zhengli xiaozu ed., *Shuihudi Qin mu zhujian, Biannian ji*, #34B.

103. Shuihudi Qin mu zhujian zhengli xiaozu ed., *Shuihudi Qin mu zhujian, Yu shu*, ##1–2.

104. Shuihudi Qin mu zhujian zhengli xiaozu ed., *Shuihudi Qin mu zhujian, Xiao lü*, ##1–2.

105. Shuihudi Qin mu zhujian zhengli xiaozu ed., *Shuihudi Qin mu zhujian, Fa lü da wen*, #98.

106. Shuihudi Qin mu zhujian zhengli xiaozu ed., *Shuihudi Qin mu zhujian, Fa lü da wen*, #168.

107. Shuihudi Qin mu zhujian zhengli xiaozu ed., *Shuihudi Qin mu zhujian, Fa lü da wen*, #172.

108. Sima Qian, *Shi ji*, "Laozi Han Fei liezhuan."

109. *Han Feizi*, "Zhu dao."

110. Sima Qian, *Shi ji*, "Qin Shi huang Benji."

Notes to Author's Postface

1. Friedrich Hirth, *The Ancient History of China: To the End of the Chin Dynasty* (New York: Columbia University Press, 1908, 1911).

2. Henri Maspero, *La Chine Antique* (Paris, E. de Boccard, 1927); Frank A. Kierman, Jr. tr., *China in Antiquity* (Amherst, Mass.: University of Massachusetts Press, 1978); a Chinese translation has just been published: Xiao Qing tr. *Gudai Zhongguo: Zhonghua wenming de qiyuan* (Ancient China: The origin of Chinese civilization) (Beijing: Beijing Institute of Technology Press, 2020). Marcel Granet, *La Civilisation Chinoise* (Paris: Albin Michel, 1929).

3. Michael Loewe and Edward L. Shaughnessy ed., *The Cambridge History of Ancient China: From the Beginnings of Civilization to 221 B.C.* (New York: Cambridge University Press, 1999).

4. Maurizio Scarpari, *Antica Cina: la civiltà cinese dalle origini alla dinastia Tang* (Vercelli, Italy: White Star, 2000); *Ancient China: Chinese Civilization from Its Origins to the Tang Dynasty* (Vercelli, Italy: White Star, 2000).

5. Edward L. Shaughnessy, *Ancient China: Life, Myth and Art* (London: Duncan Baird Publishers, 2005).

6. Li Feng, *Early China: A Social and Cultural History* (Cambridge: Cambridge University Press, 2014).

7. Gideon Shelach-Lavi, *The Archaeology of Ancient China: From Prehistory to the Han Dynasty* (Cambridge: Cambridge University Press, 2015).

8. Constance A. Cook and John Major, *Ancient China: A History* (New York: Routledge, 2017).

9. Elizabeth Childs-Johnson ed., *The Oxford Handbook of Early China* (New York: Oxford University Press, 2000).

INDEX

The letter *f* following an entry indicates a page with a figure.
The letter *m* following an entry indicates a page with a map.

Index

Index

Index

Index

Index

Index

Index

Index